D0017187

The Reintegration of
American History

OTHER BOOKS BY WILLIAM W. FREEHLING

Prelude to Civil War
The Nullification Controversy in South Carolina, 1816–1836

The Nullification Era
A Documentary Record (Editor)

Willie Lee Rose
Slavery and Freedom
(Editor)

The Road to Disunion
Volume I
Secessionists at Bay, 1776–1854

Secession Debated
Georgia's Showdown in 1860
(Coeditor, with Craig M. Simpson)

The Road to Disunion
Volume II
Secessionists Triumphant, 1854–1861
(Forthcoming)

The Reintegration of American History

Slavery and the Civil War

WILLIAM W. FREEHLING

New York Oxford   OXFORD UNIVERSITY PRESS   1994

Oxford University Press

Oxford   New York   Toronto
Delhi   Bombay   Calcutta   Madras   Karachi
Kuala Lumpur   Singapore   Hong Kong   Tokyo
Nairobi   Dar es Salaam   Cape Town
Melbourne   Auckland   Madrid

and associated companies in
Berlin   Ibadan

Copyright © 1994 by William W. Freehling

Published by Oxford University Press, Inc.
200 Madison Avenue, New York, New York   10016

Oxford is a registered trademark of Oxford University Press

Library of Congress Cataloging-in-Publication Data
Freehling, William W., 1935–
The reintegration of American history: slavery and the Civil War / William W. Freehling.
p. cm.   Includes bibliographical references and indexes.
ISBN 0-19-508807-7
ISBN 0-19-508808-5 (pbk)
1. Slavery—United States—History.
2. Southern States—Race relations.
3. Southern States—History—1775–1865.
4. United States—History—Civil War, 1861–1865—Causes.
I. Title.
E441.F78   1994   975'.03—dc20   93-32698

9 8 7 6 5 4 3 2 1

Printed in the United States of America
on acid-free paper

For My Best History Teachers

Jack Ellison, Sonia Salk Heller,
at Chicago's Francis W. Parker High School

Bernard Bailyn, Arthur M. Schlesinger, Jr.,
at Harvard College

Adrienne Koch, Charles G. Sellers, Jr., Kenneth M. Stampp,
at the University of California, Berkeley, Graduate School

Lee Benson, David Brion Davis,
during my perpetual reeducation

Preface

Academics, for better or worse, become specialists. My specialty is the social and political history of the Old South and thus the history of slavery and of the southern side of the coming of the American Civil War. But as the following essays indicate, I've had to transcend specialized perspectives constantly in order to write my two-volume history of the southern *Road to Disunion*, the first volume of which appeared in 1990. To understand secession in 1860–61, I've had to go back to 1776 and forward to 1865. To understand the Old South's politics and ideology, I've had to analyze southern social and military history. To understand slaveholders' political revolution, I've had to study slaves' sociopolitical resistances to bondage, other Americans' quests for multicultural identity, and Latin America's lack of a civil war between whites over slavery. To understand Deep South cotton planters' apprehensions, I've had to comprehend the northern and Border South mentalities, to say nothing of competing mentalities within the Deep South. And to interest nonacademics in the story, I've had to reconsider academic literary forms.

The broadening of my work has led to a broader reconsideration of my profession. Academic historians' writing styles often attract only fellow academics. Their analytical explanations often intrigue only fellow specialists. We have a New Social History, which tends to exclude analysis of politics, a New Political History, which tends to exclude analysis of society, and a not-so-new military history, which tends to exclude nonbattlefield causes of battlefield triumph. We have a new theory of multicultural history, which emphasizes each American minority's separatist history, and a renewed theory of an American homogeneous history, which reemphasizes the melting of minorities into Anglo-American norms. We have women's history and African-American history and Native American history and western history and southern history and histories of this decade and that. But where is an *American* history, which synthesizes all aspects of all periods?

Historians increasingly worry about that long-unanswered question, not least because the profession has always had a splendid countervailing trend. It is no accident that in a book dedicated to my teachers and sometimes focused on relationships between mentors and students, my most influential guides have moved beyond narrow specialization. Thus Sonia Salk Heller wanted historical researchers to explore the philosophy of history; Jack Ellison used anthropological methods to enrich historical analysis; Bernard Bailyn argued that political history must be the widest sort of social history; Arthur Schlesinger, Jr., demonstrated that professional history can excite a nonprofessional audience; Adrienne Koch urged that petty political history often involved grand intellectual objectives; Kenneth Stampp clarified both the peculiar social history of a region and the general political history of a nation; Charles Sellers, Jr., portrayed the Southerner both as a provincial regionalist and as a cosmopolitan American; Lee Benson communicated widely with social scientists; and David Brion Davis placed the problem of U.S. slavery in the perspective of two thousand years of world history. These teachers' synthetic methods, however, have not swept up the profession. Never before have American historians paused so long before reintegrating our history. Never before have smaller studies of tinier communities so dominated historical discourse.

My quest for a reintegrated American history commences on an old-fashioned path. I enjoy history as story and political history as one way (not the only way) to pull American history together. I believe that all regions, classes, sexes, and ethnics eventually seek political power, whether to control the American mainstream or to separate from it. I further believe that these multicultural quests make for fine separate tales and for a rich story of highly imperfect national integration. But American history cannot be reintegrated as an exclusively political narrative of the white male elite. The American majority of nonwhites and nonmales have profoundly shaped, and been shaped by, the ruling minority's course. Without that newest of American historians' emphases, American political history becomes old-fashioned in the most chauvinistic and anachronistic way. Furthermore, unless politics are seen as the creation and creator of a social order, the analysis of white male political (or military) heroes verges on the antiquarian.

That position sounds like the currently fashionable "political correctness." I deplore the extremes of the viewpoint, which can impose an academic conformity dismally like McCarthyism. I also dislike the all-too-frequent opinions that only blacks can understand black history or that only women can write women's history or that only white Southerners can comprehend antebellum white Southerners. That antihistorical mentality surrenders the essence of the historical imagination: the capacity to empathize with very different people living in very different contexts. I furthermore regret current tendencies to minimize the study of white male elites, for power exerted from above profoundly conditions power exerted from below (and vice versa). The necessity is always to study a whole world.

But opponents of political correctness equally err when they condemn concentration on women and/or nonwhites as "present-minded." On the contrary, white male historians have long been too present-minded in their focus on past white males. Gentlemen forgot—and some important historians continue to forget—how widely past Americans, including white males, focused on non-whites and nonmales. Thus American Revolutionaries considered their revolution hypocritical unless black slaves were liberated. A half century later, nineteenth-century Whigs and Republicans considered Jacksonian Democracy undemocratic when Democrats used white men's republicanism to consolidate oppression over blacks and Native Americans. If it takes political correctness to see that such multicultural convictions helped define our past, or that the history of the peopling and transformation of the civilization must include all Americans, the excesses of current present-mindedness may be a terrible price worth paying.

The following essays, although written for separate occasions, share two reintegrating imperatives: that the history of one American group must be related to other groups, and that a fragment of American history must be related to the larger whole, chronologically and topically. Six of the eleven essays have not been previously published. All of the five previously published essays have been stylistically revised. The two most well known, on the Founding Fathers and on John C. Calhoun, have also been analytically reconceived, and two others, on Denmark Vesey and on James Henley Thornwell, have been analytically clarified. I thus hope that the book is fresher and more integrated than the customary collection of unrevised previously published essays. In keeping with that aspiration, the essays continually return to my central thoughts about my specialty, whatever the specific topic at hand: the problems with slaveholders' attempts to be paternalists; the nature and effect of slaves' resistance to that problematic paternalism; the divisions within the Old South; the need to observe U.S. slaveholders over a long time span and in comparison with other New World slaveholders; the reasons seemingly absurd political issues, especially the pivotal issue of whether blacks should be removed from the United States, were loaded with multicultural meaning; the causes of the Civil War and of the Confederates' defeat; the nonradicalism of the American Revolution and the tale of my evolution toward writing *The Road to Disunion.* The essays also keep returning to themes that transcend their specialized subject matter: the need to widen social history, to widen political history, to widen military history, to widen narrative style, to widen chronological perspectives, to widen the places studied, to widen multicultural history, to widen conceptions of what the best historians should publish, if we are to reintegrate American history.

Too many members of my generation of American historians, coming into the profession thirty years ago, lost the aspiration to synthesize the whole story, the most compelling aspiration for every previous generation of historians. Too many members of subsequent generations have followed our overly specialized course. After I publish the second volume of my *Road to Disunion,* thus finishing the mapping of my own cul-de-sac (which remains a cul-de-sac, no matter how much I widen it), I will spend full time on the lost aspiration. Thus, this collection of essays is both an old specialist's farewell survey of an ever-widening parochial spot and an aspiring generalist's first search for roads beyond all restricted locales.

April 1, 1993   William W. Freehling

Acknowledgments

This work draws on research financed by the Guggenheim Foundation, the National Humanities Foundation, and the American Antiquarian Society. More recently, The State University of New York, Buffalo's, Thomas B. Lockwood Chair in American History has paid for the work of my helpful editor, Cecile Rhinehart Watters, my wonderful secretary, Ellen Bennett, and my enterprising research assistant, Richard Newman. Unfortunately, my departure from The Johns Hopkins University has made conversations with Jack P. Greene rarer. But our talks over two decades still reverberate in these essays.

This is the first book in recent times that I have not dedicated to Alison. But she knows how much I owe my teachers—and how much more I owe to her.

W. W. F.

Contents

The Reintegration of
American History

1 / The Editorial Revolution, Virginia, and the Coming of the Civil War: A Review Essay

This piece, first published in Civil War History *in 1970,[1] reappears here with the permission of the Kent State University Press, with only stylistic revisions. I think the essay should remain analytically intact, as my first survey of the road to disunion. In this initial estimate, I already saw that the South of the Secession Crisis was divided against itself. But I was only beginning to understand that the history of the Age of Lincoln could not be divided from the history of the Age of Jefferson.*

Were I to revise this piece, I would update my comments on the twentieth-century editorial revolution no less than on the connections between 1776 and 1860. I would also applaud some editors for now publishing important politicians' papers more selectively and more promptly. I think particularly of Clyde Wilson's exemplary, almost completed edition of John C. Calhoun's papers, a project rather stalled in 1970. I would add that Ira Berlin and Leslie Rowland's magnificent edition of the Freedmen's Bureau Papers, a project unknown in 1970, ranks among the most important recent American history publications.[2]

That affirmation brings to mind a criticism made privately to me when this review essay first appeared. An older friend, one of America's best historians, declared me wrong in one essential. The best historians, he said, should not edit documents. The higher calling was to write history from the documents.

I long acted on that advice. But I recently coedited for publication, with Craig M. Simpson, one of the unpublished documents that twenty-four years ago I urged should be printed: the Georgia debate over secession in 1860.[3] The experience was a high point of my professional life. I relished making previously obscure documents widely available, documents that invite readers to be their own historians of disunion, documents that prove that the Old South had as classic a political debate as the antebellum North's Lincoln-Douglas Debates. As for the notion that only "lesser" historians should do this editorial work, "lesser" historians hadn't, for the very good reason that those writing the history can best identify the critical unpublished documents. Moreover, the historians who are writing the history can best place the best documents in the best perspective. May the editorial revolution continue, with all hands participating, for the best documents, no less than the best narratives, will further the reintegration of American history.

Some of the best-known American historical writers during the 1945–70 period are fading in importance. The so-called consensus historians, who discounted political conflict among Americans, already seem especially archaic. So too, practitioners of new historical techniques—literary criticism, status analysis, computers—have won their battle for respectability. But none of the victorious technicians has constructed a new synthesis of our history.

In the long run, historians' more lasting accomplishment since the Second World War may lie in another realm—historical editing. Led by Julian Boyd, editor of Thomas Jefferson's papers, innovative editors have made important source materials more available and more understandable. Some important analysts of history have also furthered the editorial revolution. Perhaps the most exciting reinterpretation of a major American event published in the 1960s—Bernard Bailyn's reexamination of the Revolution—was originally an introduction to Bailyn's massive edition of pre-Revolutionary pamphlets. Perhaps the most important mid-twentieth-century American historian, Perry Miller, made some of his greatest contributions as an editor of thick anthologies.[4]

The new documentary collections have transformed our understanding of the origins and aftermath of the American Revolution. But this editorial development has not yet revolutionized the study of the coming of the Civil War. Editors of the papers of some of the great antebellum politicians—John C. Calhoun, Jefferson Davis, Henry Clay, and so on—are bogged down in their subjects' early careers. No published source on America in the 1850s compares in importance to Bailyn's pamphlets on the Revolution or to Miller's anthology of the transcendentalists.

In view of such comparative poverty, the appearance of George Reese's four-volume edition of the Virginia Secession Convention proceedings and debates of 1861 is an important event.[5] Reese's volumes demonstrate that publication of major documents can change our understanding of the Age of Lincoln no less than of the Age of Jefferson. The Reese edition suggests an inquiry into why other editors of mid-nineteenth-century Americana, who work in Julian Boyd's spirit and have large funds at their disposal, have thus far failed to provide anything as significant as these Virginia secession debates. The newly published debates also invite a fresh look at Virginia's tortuous position during the southern Secession Crisis—and at why Southerners precipitated that crisis.

Reese's volumes partially exemplify the Boyd editorial tradition. Reese republishes the Virginia Secession Convention's complete proceedings and debates in an easy-to-read, accurate edition. Although the volumes are too expensive for most scholars, they are indispensable for most research libraries. Because of the inevitably low sales, such editorial editions must be subsidized—in this case, by the Virginia state government. This, in turn, meant that the state's financial constraints limited Reese's editorial apparatus. Reese provides little introduction, few explanatory footnotes, and no index. No attempt is made to recount what transpired in secret—particularly in the crucial Committee of Twenty-One which dominated the convention. In his only concession to new principles of editorial annotation, Reese begins each volume with a brief, day-by-day synopsis of the debates. This helpful material aside, an overall judgment must conclude that Reese's work, like Boyd's, presents a comprehensive collection of important sources but, unlike Boyd's, offers little editorial apparatus to make them more intelligible.

These editorial omissions make the debates much harder to use. The absence of an index, in particular, severely weakens Reese's volumes. Some might argue, then, that Reese made the wrong decision—that he should not have published the debates until he could do them editorial justice. I would respond that he made the right decision—and that the important contribution he makes with these volumes, even though they are deficient, indicates that better-funded editors should reappraise their lagging projects.

Reese obviously believes that editors must get crucial documents into print even if editorial apparatus must be sacrificed, for the importance of the sources counts most. In contrast, other editors of antebellum sources strive to set *all* documents into print, regardless of a manuscript's significance, accompanied by elaborate editorial annotation, no matter how long that process takes. Such procedures have crippled some Civil War projects. Every important antebellum politician's correspondence is loaded with patronage requests and administrative details. The attempt to publish, or even summarize, every bit of paper, accompanied by elaborate editorial explanations, leads to massive volumes of documentary trivia and editorial pedantry. Such compulsive editorial completeness also blocks the most important documents from reaching print any time soon.

Reese's documents rank among the most important pre–Civil War sources, for the Virginia secession debates illuminate the anxiety of the pivotal but declining Upper South state, obsessed with its lost greatness and weakened by the same internal contradictions that partially impelled the Lower South to secede. The Virginia Secession Convention convened on February 13, 1861, and voted for secession on April 17. During the intervening two months, delegates debated the nature of Virginia and the value of the Union, whether the federal government could legitimately coerce a seceding state and whether Lincoln's election would immediately menace slavery. These questions interest all pre–Civil War historians, and all will find rich answers in these volumes.

Hanging over Virginians' debates on these questions was a precarious tone of bravado—a prayer that Virginia could once again master its destiny and dominate the nation. Most speakers assumed the stance of starring actors in an epic. Their manner and words suggested that all eyes were on their convention, that decisions reached in Richmond would control policy in Washington and Montgomery. The assumption of domination came from memories of the nation's first decades when the Virginia Dynasty had governed the land. It was as if history had stood still and Jefferson's Virginia heirs still passed on the presidency to each other.

This tone soon became shrill, for decisions made elsewhere now controlled Virginia. Most delegates hoped that the seven seceded states of the Deep South would return to the old Union. But most leaders at Montgomery meant to preserve their new Confederacy. Again, a large majority in the Virginia convention favored the proposed federal Crittenden Compromise as a solution to the secession crisis. But they were uneasy about remaining in a Union

that retained only eight of fifteen slave states. That unease transferred the decision about their fate to Washington and to Montgomery. Unless Northern Republicans had surrendered opposition
to the Crittenden Compromise or the Lower South had surrendered
the Confederacy, Virginians were drifting toward a showdown with
Lincoln, even if the President had surrendered Fort Sumter.

Moreover, most convention delegates, from the beginning, favored secession if war came. They believed that after a state had
withdrawn its consent to be governed, federal coercion would violate a people's right peacefully to change their government. Given
this attitude, Virginia's future depended on Lincoln's position on
secession rather than on Virginians' rhetoric in Richmond. The
convention's 88–55 vote to secede on April 17 confessed that fact
and confirmed what many delegates had uneasily come to suspect—that Old Virginia was but a pawn in a game that nouveau
forces controlled.[6]

This reduction from queen to pawn led to an increasingly con-
scious sense of self-doubt—a sense that had secretly tormented Virginians for decades but that could be suppressed no longer. As the
convention proceeded, an implicit theme behind the explicit rhetoric became a search for cultural self-definition, a yearning to find
the lost soul of a great society. The speakers seemed to be asking,
ever more desperately asking, what is Virginia anyway?

What indeed? For as these debates indicate, the meaning of being a Virginian was hotly disputed. Some unwavering Unionists,
particularly from the largely nonslaveholding northwestern counties, thought of Virginia as akin to a northern yeoman state, with
the unfortunate, but probably necessary, side institution of slavery.
A surprisingly large group of compromisers, particularly from Virginia's central areas with only moderate numbers of slaves, considered their state neither northern nor southern. They hoped for a
third confederacy, composed of free-labor and slave-labor border
states. Finally, a fiery group of secessionists, particularly from the
eastern areas with a large population of slaves, considered Virginia
a classic slave community. They dared to dream of a quasi-
aristocratic southern Confederacy.

The debate over identity exploded most angrily over Waitman
T. Willey's proposal to raise the tax rate on Virginia slaves so that
it would equal the tax rate on white men's other properties. Willey
and his western Virginia supporters claimed they wanted equal taxation of whites, not abolition for blacks. Still, Willey bragged that
his tax reform movement would mobilize not just the western Vir-

ginians but also nonslaveholders statewide. Such provocative rhetoric raised visions of a white lower-class revolt against upper-class slaveholders. In addition to its division over secession, Virginia seemed, to secessionist leaders, divided over slavery itself.

The convention of 1861, in short, suffered both from increasing awareness of Virginia's lost power and from increasing consciousness of what had caused the decline. The Virginia Dynasty had lost its power, these debates indicate, not only because Jacksonian egalitarian democrats had replaced Jeffersonian aristocratic republicans and because the aristocrats had suffered financial decline. In addition, the rise of northern abolitionism and the concurrent rise of state internal divisions had forever undermined the Virginia slaveholders' serene confidence and self-identity.

This same concern about concurrent external and internal opposition to slavery, the debates show, helped impel Virginians toward disunion. The Reese volumes partially vindicate some traditional explanations of secession, such as a quest for southern honor and a fear of northern majorities. But secessionist speakers also called slavery too weak in Delaware, Maryland, Missouri, Kentucky, and even Virginia itself to withstand mild pressure from Abraham Lincoln. "Delaware," warned Professor James Holcombe of the University of Virginia, "is nominally only, a slave State. Maryland will soon be a free state; and so it is with Missouri and Kentucky." Lincoln would accelerate the incremental antislavery process and bring it home to Virginia, thereby driving slavery south, isolating the Gulf states, and drowning the Lower South in a torrent of black migrants. Slavery's precarious condition in the Upper South made Lincoln an *immediate* menace to slavery.[7]

Debaters particularly feared that Lincoln would menace areas where the black population had recently declined. Delegates from northwestern Virginia counties declared, in Leonard S. Hall's words, that "we have but few slaves—we cannot keep them—the emissaries of the underground railroad are always upon the alert, and the terminus of that road is at our very door."[8] Northwestern Virginia, added Alpheus F. Haymond, "has been almost entirely depopulated of its slaves, by the influence of Abolitionism."[9] While "almost entirely" exaggerated the phenomenon, statistics confirm that slavery had somewhat receded from Virginia's northernmost tier of counties during the 1850s. Secessionists such as George W. Richardson believed that Lincoln's election would quicken the trend. What, asked Richardson, is to stop border abolitionists "from pressing on still further and pushing it from the counties which come next in order, and so . . . sweep slavery away through Virginia . . . and into the far South?"[10] As former governor Henry Wise answered, "you talk about slavery in the territories; you talk about slavery in the District of Columbia—when its tenure in Virginia is doubtful."[11]

Lincoln could shorten slavery's Upper South tenure, Virginia secessionists argued, not only by stopping slaveholder expansion to new territories, not only by intensifying the fugitive slave problem, but also by using patronage to establish a *Southern* Republican Party. By enforcing free speech and a free press and by establishing Republican outposts within the Border South, Lincoln would provoke a southern internal debate over slavery. The President, predicted Jeremiah Morton, would shower patronage on all the border states and form a party in their midst, leaving "Black Republicans upon every stump, and organizing in every county; and that is the peace we shall have from this 'glorious Union.'"[12]

Open debate over slavery would become ever less peaceful, Virginia secessionists feared, as proportions of nonslaveholders became ever more dominant. Slave sales to the Lower South would stimulate nonslaveholder dreams of a Virginia without enslaved or free blacks. Yeomen would then no longer have to compete with planters for the best lands or with blacks for the best jobs. Despite Waitman Willey's disclaimers, his proposal to raise taxes on slaveholders at the very time slavery's fate was in the balance seemed to indicate that nonslaveholders already savored such visions. "As the white population . . . gain rapidly on the blacks," and as nonslaveholders' "interest in the institution of slavery sinks almost to zero," concluded George W. Randolph, "the odds against us in the struggle will be tremendous."[13]

The odds could be insurmountable, declared key secessionists, for Virginia slaveholders did not sufficiently relish proslavery dogmas. George Randolph worried that northern polemicists "are much more likely to make us wrong than we are to bring them right." Randolph called antislavery an old and powerful intellectual movement. The proslavery argument, in contrast, "is recent—it is comparatively a thing of yesterday—it has not been inculcated in early life, . . . it has hardly yet had time to be understood and appreciated by our own people. To dash it now against the ironbound fanaticism of the North," concluded Randolph, "would be the height of folly."[14]

Folly was the secessionists' word for allowing Lincoln to rule a divided Upper South. The fugitive slave danger on the border, the concentration of nonslaveholders in the more northern slave states, and the greater profitability of slave labor in virgin tropical lands were already nudging Border South masters to sell bondsmen to the Deep South. Who would now keep a fifteen-hundred-dollar slave in the border amidst open debate and provocative challenge from a Southern Republican Party? Soon slavery would be restricted to the eight cotton states, and the institution would be compelled, declared James Holcombe, "like a scorpion girdled with fire, to sting itself to death."[15]

Anxiety about border emancipation, widespread among the Virginia secessionist minority, also troubled Deep South disunionists, as Henry L. Benning demonstrated at the Virginia convention. Benning, an ex–Georgia Supreme Court justice and his state's commissioner to the Virginia convention, declared that Georgia seceded for one simple reason, "a deep conviction" that "separation from the North" alone "could prevent the abolition of her slavery." Benning warned that Republicans would halt the expansion of slavery and expand the number of free states. Meanwhile, "some of our own slave States are becoming free States." In some border states, the absolute number of slaves was dropping; in all of them, the percentage of slaves was declining.

"It is not wonderful that this should be so," declared Benning. Planters think slavery will not endure in the Upper South, and "self-interest impels them to get rid of a property which is doomed. The consequence is, that it will go down lower and lower, until it all gets to the Cotton States—until it gets to the bottom. There is the weight of a continent upon it forcing it down . . . and I fear that the day is not distant when the Cotton States, as they are called, will be the only slave States." Then "the North will have the power to amend the Constitution." With the Deep South a black sea, concluded Benning, whites "will be completely exterminated, and the land . . . will become another Africa or St. Domingo."[16]

The belief that Lincoln could drive slavery out of the Upper South, so omnipresent in Reese's volumes, pervades other sources on secession. Whether in private correspondence or in newspaper editorials or in the Georgia secession debates or in the massively distributed disunion pamphlets by John Townsend and his South Carolina compatriots, secessionists warned that border planters would sell their slaves out of the area, that border nonslaveholders would attack the institution if they had no free blacks to worry about, that the Cotton South and the Border South were different lands. These apprehensions had recurred throughout the 1850s. The fear of a geographically divided South had helped turn Southerners edgy and strident, ready to see danger in any abolitionist movement and able to spot concrete significance in what seems to us hopelessly abstract. This state of mind had helped produce southern demands for fugitive slave laws, particularly to deter border fugitives, and for territorial expansion, particularly to control areas adjacent to the South's vulnerable borders. Now, as the ultimate crisis drew near, uneasiness about Upper South weakness helped make Lincoln seem all too immediately an antislavery menace.

That climactic slaveholder concern about internal menace demands a fresh look at geographic and class divisions in the Old South—a subject that even our best Marxist historians have curiously neglected. Only such an analysis can explain those profound suspicions between Deep South and Border South, between eastern and western Virginians, and between planters and nonslaveholders that suffuse the Virginia Secession Convention debates. No other inquiry can so quickly dispel the misconception that blundering statesmen brought on a needless war in 1861. No other analysis can better explain why the confident Virginia of Thomas Jefferson gave way to the nervous land of Waitman Willey and George Randolph as the United States moved toward the Civil War.

George Reese's volumes, then, fulfill the most important reason to publish primary sources: to reopen historical issues that have too long been closed. Analysts of the pre–Civil War period need more such dividends from the editorial revolution. We need printed editions of the important manuscript letters of the Davises, the Clays, and the Calhouns. We also need modern editions of key Republican and secessionist pamphlets, of the congressional debates of 1836, 1850, 1854, 1858, and 1860–61, of the Georgia secession debates of 1860, of the Virginia antislavery debate of 1832, and of such magazines as *De Bow's Review*. One hopes that these future publications will include a more complete editorial apparatus than Reese could provide. And one hopes that in the future, more of the best antebellum historians, in the tradition of Perry Miller and Bernard Bailyn, will work as editors no less than as authors in one of the great historiographic movements of our time.

2 / The Founding Fathers, Conditional Antislavery, and the Nonradicalism of the American Revolution

By 1972, two years after publishing "The Editorial Revolution," I more clearly understood that the story of the events of 1860 must begin with the Founding Fathers. But I still hoped that my narrative of disunion could begin in 1850. I thus decided to publish my thoughts on the earlier history separately. The resulting first version of this essay, entitled "The Founding Fathers and Slavery," appeared in the American Historical Review in 1972.[1] "Founding Fathers" has been widely republished. I nevertheless regret its overemphasis on antislavery accomplishment. My changed title reflects my partial disenchantment. I am grateful to the American Historical Review for permission to republish some of the previous essay in this much-altered form.

When I wrote the original essay, historians were increasingly scoffing that the Founding Fathers ignored the Declaration of Independence's antislavery imperatives.[2] That denunciation has continued to swell despite my countervailing emphasis, indeed partly because of my overstated argument.[3] My original essay, as David Brion Davis pointed out, too much conflated Thomas Jefferson and the Founding Fathers.[4] The essay also erroneously portrayed the Founding Fathers as pragmatic reformers, eager to assault slavery whenever political realities permitted. They were in truth skittish abolitionists, chary of pouncing on antislavery opportunity. The Founding Fathers freed some slaves but erected obstacles against freeing others. They also sometimes moved past those obstacles for crass rather than ideological reasons. Thus historians who dismissed the Founding Fathers as antislavery reformers could easily dismiss my argument.

I have come to be more unhappy about the historians who appropriated "Founding Fathers." They have used my contention that the Founding Fathers chipped away at slavery to support their contention that the Declaration of Independence inspired a true American social revolution.[5] I find that argument unpersuasive, even about the white male minority. The notion is still less persuasive about African Americans and about other members of the nonwhite and nonmale majority, which means that the contention mischaracterizes American society writ large. Neither women nor African Americans nor Native Americans conceived that the American Revolution revolutionized their lives. Their position is relevant if we are to widen American history beyond Anglo-Saxon males, to write the story of a multicultural civilization.

Some historians answer that the majority's definition of a proper social revolution is irrelevant for judging the American Revolution, since only the white male minority had the power to define the event and the society. Such positions tend to narrow American history into solely a history of the white male power structure. But in the specific case of slavery, the elite's standard for judgment widens perspectives. Wealthy Revolutionaries' criterion, no less than poorer Americans' criterion and posterity's criterion, required a proper American Revolution to include the slaves. By that universal yardstick, the Founding Fathers achieved no social revolution.

The Founding Fathers instead set us on our nonrevolutionary social history. Despite their dismay at slavery, America's worst multicultural dislocation, they both timidly reformed and established towering bulwarks against reform, not least because many of them preferred a monoracial America. I have revised this essay to include more of the bulwarks against antislavery, in company with those who think the Founding Fathers did nothing to further abolition. But I hope the revision will yield more tolerance for my continued belief, and latter-day slaveholders' worried conviction, that the Founding Fathers also did a most nonrevolutionary something to weaken slaveholders' defenses. For without that ambivalent perspective on the nation's founders, we can understand neither the subsequent meandering road toward emancipation nor America's persistently nonradical road toward a radically new multicultural social order, based on the ethics of the Declaration of Independence.

The American Revolutionaries intended to achieve a political revolution. They brilliantly succeeded. They split the British Empire, mightiest of the world's powers. They destroyed monarchical government in what became the United States. They recast the nature of republican ideology and structure with the federal Constitution of 1787. Over the next generation, their revolution helped undermine their own aristocratic conception of republicanism, leading to Andrew Jackson's very different egalitarian republicanism.

With a single exception, the men of 1776 intended no parallel revolution in the culture's social institutions. The Founders had no desire to confiscate property from the rich and give it to the poor. They gave no thought to appropriating familial power from males and giving it to females, or seizing land from whites and returning it to Native Americans. They embraced the entire colonial white male system of social power—except for slaveholders' despotism over slaves. That they would abolish. To judge them by their standards, posterity must ask whether this, their sole desired social revolution, was secured.

The Founding Fathers partially lived up to their revolutionary imperative: They barred the African slave trade from American ports; they banned slavery from midwestern territories; they dissolved the institution in northern states; and they diluted slavery in the Border South. Yet the Founding Fathers also backed away from their revolutionary imperative: They delayed emancipation in the North; they left antislavery half accomplished in the Border South; they rejected abolition in the Middle South; and they expanded slaveholder power in the Lower South. These retreats both inhibited final emancipation where slavery had been damaged and augmented slaveholders' resources where slavery had been untouched. The advances and retreats set off both an antislavery process and a proslavery counteroffensive. Slavery would eventually be abolished, partly because the Founding Fathers shackled the slaveholders. But emancipation would be so long delayed—partly because the Founders rearmed the slavocracy—that the slavery issue would epitomize the social nonradicalism of the American Revolution.

1

Since every generation rewrites history, most historians achieve only fading influence. One twentieth-century American historical insight, however, seems unlikely to fade. In his multivolume history of slavery as a recognized problem, David Brion Davis demonstrated that throughout most of history, humankind failed to recognize any problem in slavery.[6] Then around the time of the American Revolution, Americans suddenly, almost universally, saw the institution as a distressing problem. Davis showed that throughout the Western world, a changed Enlightenment mentality and a changing industrial order helped revolutionize sensibility about slavery. The American political revolution quickened the pace of ideological revolution. Slavery, as the world's most antirepublican social system, seemed particularly hypocritical in the world's most republican nation. Most American Revolutionaries called King George's enslavement of colonists and whites' enslavement of blacks parallel tyrannies. "Let us either cease to enslave our fellow-men," wrote the New England cleric Nathaniel Niles, "or else let us cease to complain of those that would enslave us."[7]

Yet the Founding Fathers' awareness of slavery as a problem never deepened into the perception that slavery's foundations were a problem. A slaveholder's claim to slaves was first of all founded on property rights; and the men of 1776 never conceived of redistributing private property or private power to ensure that all men (or women!) were created equal. They believed that governments, to secure slaves' natural right to liberty, must pay slaveholders to surrender the natural right to property. That conviction put a forbidding price tag on emancipation.

The price escalated because these discoverers of slavery as a problem (and nondiscoverers of maldistributed property as a problem) also failed to see that other foundation of slavery, racism, as problematic.[8] Thomas Jefferson, like most of his countrymen, suspected that blacks were created different, inferior in intellectual talents and excessive in sexual ardency. Jefferson also worried that freed blacks would precipitate racial warfare. He shrank from abolition, as did most Americans who lived amidst significant concentrations of slaves, unless the freedmen could be resettled outside the republic.[9]

That race removal condition, like the condition that seized property required compensation, placed roadblocks before emancipation. To colonize blacks in foreign lands would have added 25 percent to the already heavy cost of compensated abolition. To coerce a million enslaved humans to leave a republic as a condition for ending coercive slavery could also seem to be a dubious step toward government by consent.

The Founding Fathers' conditional aspiration to free black slaves furthermore had to compete with their unconditional aspiration to build white republics. It was no contest. The American Revolutionaries appreciated all the problems in establishing free government; but that appreciation energized them, inspired them, led to sustained bursts of imaginative remedies. In contrast, these propertied racists exaggerated all the problems in freeing blacks; and that exaggeration paralyzed them, turned them into procrastinators, led to infrequent stabs at limited reforms.

The inhibitions built into the conditional antislavery mentality could be seen even in the Virginia abolitionist who scorned the supposedly necessary conditions. Edward Coles, James Madison's occasional secretary, intruded on Thomas Jefferson's mailbox with demands that the ex-President crusade for emancipation without waiting for slaveholder opposition to relent. Coles himself acted on antislavery imperatives without waiting for action on deportation imperatives. He migrated with his Virginia slaves to almost entirely free-soil Illinois, manumitted all of them, gave each family a 160-acre farm, and provided for the education of those who were underage. After that rare demonstration of how to turn conditional antislavery into unconditional freedom, Coles advised his ex-slaves to return to Africa! The black race, said Coles, might never prosper in the bigoted white republic. That message, coming from that messenger, well conveyed the national mentality that rendered an antislavery revolution impossible.[10]

2

In conditionally antislavery post-Revolutionary America, the more blacks in a local area, the less possibility of emancipation. Where blacks formed a high percentage of the labor force, as in the original Middle South states of North Carolina and Virginia (35 percent enslaved in 1790) and in the original Lower South states of Georgia and South Carolina (41 percent enslaved in 1790), whites' economic aspirations and race phobias overwhelmed conditional antislavery.[11] In contrast, where blacks were less dense and the slave-based economy was noncrucial, as in the original northern states (all under 5 percent enslaved in 1790) and in the original Border South states of Delaware and Maryland (25 percent enslaved in 1790), the inhibiting conditions for antislavery could be overcome—but only after revealing difficulties.

In northern states, the sparse numbers of blacks made slavery seem especially unimportant, both economically and racially, to the huge majority of nonslaveholders. The low percentage of blacks, however, made abolition equally unimportant, economically and racially, to most northern citizens. For the Founders to secure emancipation in the North, an unimportant set of economic/racial antislavery imperatives and a conditional strategy for solving the newly perceived slavery problem had to supplement each other, for neither tepid crass motives nor a compromised ideological awakening could, by itself, overwhelm a vigorous proslavery minority.[12]

That vigor will come as a shock to those who think slavery was peculiar to the South. Yet northern slaveholders fought long and hard to save the institution in temperate climes. Although neither slavery nor emancipation significantly influenced the northern economy, the ownership of humans vitally influenced northern slaveholders' cash flow. Slaveholders made money using slavery up North, and they could always sell slaves for several hundred dollars down South. These crass motives of a few could never have held back an ideological surge of the many had a disinterested majority passionately believed that illegitimate property in humans must be unconditionally seized. But since northern nonslaveholders conceded that this morally suspect property had legal sanction, the struggle for emancipation in the North was long a stalemate.

The only exception was far northward, in New Hampshire, Vermont, and Massachusetts. In those upper parts of New England, the extreme paucity of blacks, a few hundred in each state, led to the phenomenon conspicuously absent elsewhere: total abolition, achieved with revolutionary swiftness, soon after the Revolution. But in the more southerly New England states of Connecticut and Rhode Island, and in the mid-Atlantic states of Pennsylvania, New Jersey, and New York, where percentages of blacks were in the 1 to 5 percent range, emancipation came exceedingly gradually, with antirevolutionary evasions.

Blacks' creeping path to northern freedom commenced in Pennsylvania in 1780, where the Western Hemisphere's first so-called post-nati emancipation law was passed.[13] Post-nati abolition meant freedom for only those born after the law was enacted and only many years after their birth. The formula enabled liberty-loving property holders to split the difference between property rights and human rights. A post-nati law required that no then-held slave property be seized. Only a property not yet on earth was to be freed, and only on some distant day. Accordingly, under the Pennsylvania formula, emancipation would eventually arrive only for slaves thereafter born and only when they reached twenty-eight years of age. Slaveholders thus could keep their previously born slaves forever and their future-born slaves throughout the best years for physical labor. That compromised emancipation was the best a conditional abolition mentality could secure, even in a northern Quaker state where only 2.4 percent of the population was enslaved.

Connecticut and Rhode Island passed post-nati edicts soon after Pennsylvania set the precedent. New York and New Jersey, the northern states with the most slaves, delayed decades longer. New York slaveholders managed to stave off laws freeing the future-born until 1799, and New Jersey slaveholders, until 1804. So it took a quarter century after the revolution for these northern states to enact post-nati antislavery—in decrees that would free no one for another quarter century.

Slaves themselves injected a little revolutionary speed into this nonrevolutionary process. Everywhere in the Americas, slaves sensed when mastery was waning and shrewdly stepped up their resistance, especially by running away. An increase of fugitive slaves often led to informal bargains between northern masters and slaves. Many northern slaveholders promised their slaves liberty sooner than post-nati laws required if slaves provided good service in the interim. Thus did perpetual servitude sometimes shade gradually into fixed-time servitude and more gradually still into wage labor, with masters retaining years of forced labor and slaves gaining liberty at a snail's pace. In 1817, New York's legislature declared that the weakening system must end by 1827.[14] Although New Jersey and Pennsylvania never followed suit, by 1840 only a few slaves remained in the North. By 1860, thirteen New Jersey slaves were the last vestige of northern slavery.

For thousands of northern slaves, however, the incremental post-nati process led not to postponed freedom in the North but to perpetual servitude in the South. When New York and New Jersey masters faced state laws that would free slaves on a future date, they could beat the deadline. They could sell a victimized black to a state down south, which had no post-nati law. One historian estimates that as many as two-thirds of New York slaves may never have been freed.[15]

Despite this reactionary outcome for some northern slaves and the long delay in liberation of others, the post-nati tradition might still be seen as a quasi-revolutionary movement if it had spread to the South. But every southern state rejected post-nati conceptions, even Delaware, and even when President Abraham Lincoln offered extra federal inducements in 1861. Instead of state-imposed gradual reform, the two original Border South states, Delaware and Maryland, experimented with an even less revolutionary process: voluntary manumission by individual masters. Delaware, which contained 9,000 slaves and 4,000 free blacks in 1790, contained 1,800 slaves and 20,000 free blacks in 1860. Maryland, with 103,000 slaves and 8,000 free blacks in 1790, contained 87,000 slaves and 84,000 free blacks in 1860. The two states' proportions of black freedmen to black slaves came to exceed those of Brazil and Cuba, countries that supposedly had a monopoly on Western Hemisphere voluntary emancipation.

Just as fugitive slaves accelerated post-nati emancipation in Pennsylvania, New York, and New Jersey, so the threat of runaways sometimes speeded manumissions in Delaware and Maryland. Especially in border cities such as Baltimore and Wilmington, masters could profitably agree to liberate slaves at some future date if good labor was thereby secured before manumission. A hardworking slave for seven years was a bargain compared to a slave who might run away the next day, especially since the slavemaster as republican, upon offering a favorite bondsman future freedom, won himself a good conscience as well as a better short-term worker. This combination of altruism and greed, however, ultimately lost the slaveholder a long-term slave. That result, portending a day when no slaves would remain in northern Maryland, was deplored in southern Maryland tobacco belts, where manumission slowed and blacks usually remained enslaved.[16]

The Maryland-Delaware never-completed manumission movement failed to spread south of the Border South, just as the long-delayed northern post-nati movement never spread south of the mid-Atlantic. True, in Virginia, George Washington freed all his many slaves. But that uncharacteristically extensive Middle South manumission came at a characteristic time. President Washington profited from his slaves while living and then freed them in his last will and testament. President Thomas Jefferson freed a more characteristic proportion of his many Middle South slaves—10 percent. Meanwhile, Jefferson's luxurious life-style piled up huge debts, which prevented the rest of his slaves from being manumitted even after his death.

South of Virginia, Jefferson's 10 percent manumission rate exceeded the norm. A master who worked huge gangs of slaves in the pestilential Georgia and South Carolina lowlands rarely freed his bondsmen before or after he died. By 1830, only 2 percent of the South Carolina/Georgia blacks were free, compared to 8.5 percent of the Virginia/North Carolina blacks and 39 percent of the Maryland/Delaware blacks. The revolutionary U.S. sensibility about slavery had, with nonrevolutionary speed, emancipated the North over a half century and compromised slavery in the original two Border South states. But the institution remained stubbornly persistent in the Border South and largely intact in the Middle South; and Lower South states had been left unharmed, defiant, and determined to confine the Founding Fathers' only desired social revolution to the American locales with the lowest percentages of slaves.

3

National considerations of slavery in the Age of the Founding Fathers repeated the pattern of the various states' considerations. During national debates on slavery, many South Carolina and Georgia Revolutionary leaders denounced the new conception that slavery was a problem. Their arguments included every element of the later proslavery polemic: that the Bible sanctioned slavery, that blacks needed a master, that antislavery invited social chaos. They warned that they would not join or continue in an antislavery Union. They sought to retain the option of reopening the African slave trade. In the first Congress after the Constitution was ratified, they demanded that Congress never debate abolition, even if silence meant that representatives must gag their constituents' antislavery petitions.[17]

The Georgians and South Carolinians achieved congressional silence, even though other Southerners and all Northerners winced at such antirepublican intransigence. North of South Carolina, almost every Founding Father called slavery a deplorable problem, an evil necessary only until the conditions for abolition could be secured. The conditions included perpetuating the Union (and thus appeasing the Lower South), protecting property rights (and thus not seizing presently owned slave property), and removing freed blacks (and thus keeping blacks enslaved until they could be deported). The first step in removing blacks from the United States was to stop Africans from coming, and the last step was to deport those already in the nation. In between, conditional antislavery steps were more debatable, and the Upper South's position changed.

The change involved whether slavery should be allowed to spread from old states to new territories. In the eighteenth century, Virginians presumed, to the displeasure of South Carolinians and Georgians, that the evil should be barred from new territories. In 1784, Thomas Jefferson's proposed Southwest Ordinance would have banned slavery from Alabama and Mississippi Territories after 1800. The bill would theoretically have prevented much of the nineteenth-century Cotton Kingdom from importing slaves. The proposal lost in the Continental Congress by a single vote, that of a New Jerseyite who lay ill at home. "The fate of millions unborn," Jefferson later wrote, was "hanging on the tongue of one man, and heaven was silent in that awful moment."[18]

The bill, however, would not necessarily have been awful for future Mississippi and Alabama cotton planters. Jefferson's bill would have allowed planters in these areas to import slaves until 1800. The proposed delay in banning imports into Mississippi and Alabama stemmed from the same mentality, North and South, that delayed emancipation in Pennsylvania, New York, and New Jersey for decades. In Mississippi and Alabama, delay would have likely killed antislavery. Eli Whitney invented the cotton gin in 1793. By 1800, thousands of slaves would likely have been picking cotton in these southwestern areas. Then the property-respecting Founding Fathers probably would not have passed the administrative laws to confiscate Mississippi and Alabama slaves, since the conditional antislavery mentality always backed away from seizing slaves who were legally on the ground. Probabilities aside, the certainty about the proposed Southwestern Ordinance of 1784 remains. The Founding Fathers defeated its antislavery provisions. Nationally no less than locally, they preserved slavery in Lower South climes.

They also retained their perfect record, nationally no less than locally, in very gradually removing slavery from northern habitats. Just as state legislators abolished slavery in northern states, with nonrevolutionary slowness, so congressmen prevented the institution from spreading into the nation's Northwest Territories, with yet more nonradical caution. Although the Continental Congress removed Jefferson's antislavery provisions from the Southwest Ordinance of 1784, congressmen attached antislavery clauses to the Northwest Ordinance of 1787. Slavery was declared barred from the area of the future states of Illinois, Indiana, Michigan, Wisconsin, and Ohio. Antislavery consciousness helped inspire the ban, as did capitalistic consciousness. Upper South tobacco planters in the Continental Congress explicitly declared that they did not wish rival tobacco planters to develop the Northwest.[19]

The history of the Northwest Ordinance exemplified not only the usual combination of selfishness and selflessness, always present whenever the Founders passed an antislavery reform, but also the usual limited and slow antislavery action whenever conditional antislavery scored a triumph. Just as northern post-nati laws freed slaves born in the future, so the national Northwest Ordinance barred the *future* spread of slavery into the Midwest. But had the Northwest Ordinance emancipated the few slaves who presently lived in the area? Only if congressmen passed a supplemental law providing administrative mechanisms to seize present property. That a property-protecting Congress, led by James Madison, conspicuously failed to do, just as property-protecting northern legislatures usually freed only future-born slaves. Congressmen's failure to enforce seizure of the few midwestern slaves indicates again the probability that they would have shunned mechanisms to confiscate the many slaves in Alabama and Mississippi in 1800 had the Southwest Ordinance of 1784 passed.

The few midwestern slaveholders, their human property intact, proceeded to demonstrate, as did New York slaveholders, that slavery could be profitably used on northern farms. Slaveholding farmers soon found allies in midwestern land speculators, who thought more farmers would come to the prairies if more slaves could be brought along. These land speculators, led by the future president William Henry Harrison of Indiana, repeatedly petitioned Congress in the early nineteenth century to repeal the Northwest Ordinance's prohibition on slave imports. But though congressmen would not confiscate present slave property, they refused to remove the ban on future slaves.

Although frustrated, a few stubborn Illinois slaveholders imported black so-called indentured servants who were slaves in all but name. Once again, Congress did nothing to remove these de facto slaves, despite the de jure declaration of the Northwest Ordinance. So when Illinois entered the Union in 1818, Congress had massively discouraged slavery but had not totally ended it. The congressional discouragement kept the number of indentured black servants in Illinois to about nine hundred, compared to the over ten thousand slaves in neighboring Missouri Territory, where Congress had not barred slavery. But those nine hundred victims of the loopholes in the Northwest Ordinance kept the reality of slavery alive in the Midwest until Illinois was admitted to the Union and Congress no longer had jurisdiction over the midwestern labor system.

Then slaveholders sought to make Illinois an official slave state. In 1824, a historic battle occurred in the prairies over a statewide referendum on legalizing slavery. The leader of Illinois's antislavery forces was none other than now-Governor Edward Coles, that ex-Virginian who had moved northward to free his slaves. Coles emphasized that slavery was antithetical to republicanism, while some of his compatriots pointed out that enforced servitude was antithetical to free laborers' economic interests. Once again, as in the Baltimore masters' decisions to manumit slaves and in the congressional decision to ban slavery from the Midwest, economic and moral motives fused. The fusion of selfish and unselfish antislavery sentiments secured 58 percent of Illinois votes in the referendum, thus at last ending slavery in the Midwest. Yet the slaveholders still mustered 42 percent of the Illinois electorate. That too-close-for-comfort margin indicated how much conditional antislavery congressmen had risked when they failed to close those indentured servant loopholes. But in the Midwest as in the North, the new vision of slavery as a problem had finally helped secure abolition—half a century after the American Revolution.

4

While the Founding Fathers belatedly contained slavery from expanding into the Midwest, Thomas Jefferson and his fellow Virginians ultimately abandoned the principle of containment. In 1819–20, when Northerners sought to impose post-nati antislavery on the proposed new slave state of Missouri, Jefferson called the containment of slavery wrong. Slaves should not be restricted to old areas, he explained, for whites would never free thickly concentrated slaves. Only if slaves were thinly spread over new areas would racist whites free them.[20]

Given many Founding Fathers' conviction that emancipation must be conditional on the removal of concentrations of blacks, their latter-day argument that slaves should be diffusely scattered made more sense than their earlier argument that slaves must be prevented from diffusing. Still, the Upper South's retreat from containment of slavery illuminates the forbidding power of that race removal condition. If Upper South Founding Fathers had opted for diffusion of blacks rather than containment in 1787, as they did in 1819–20, even the diluted antislavery provision in the Northwest Ordinance probably would not have passed. Then the already almost-triumphant Illinois slaveholders probably would have prevailed, and slavery would have had a permanent toehold in the North. On the subject of the expansion of slavery into new areas, as in the matter of the abolition of slavery in old states, the Founding Fathers had suffered a total loss in the South, had scored a difficult victory in the North, and had everywhere displayed the tentativeness of so conditional a reform mentality.

5

To posterity, the Virginians' switch from containing slavery in old American areas to diffusing slavery over new American areas adds up to a sellout of antislavery. The Thomas Jeffersons, however, considered the question of whether slavery should be contained or diffused in America to be a relatively minor matter. The major issues were whether blacks should be prevented from coming to America and whether slaves should be deported from America. On these matters, conditional antislavery men never wavered.

In the letter Jefferson wrote at the time of the Missouri Controversy in which he first urged diffusion of blacks within America, he repeated that blacks should eventually be diffused outside the white republic. Four years later, in his final statement on antislavery, Jefferson stressed again his persistent conditional antislavery solution. His "reflections on the subject" of emancipation, Jefferson wrote a northern Federalist, had not changed for "five and forty years." He would emancipate the "afterborn" and deport them at "a proper age," with the federal government selling federal lands to pay for the deportations. Federal emancipation/colonization raises "some constitutional scruples," conceded this advocate of strict construction of the government's constitutional powers. "But a liberal construction of the Constitution," he affirmed, may go "the whole length."[21]

Jefferson's "whole length" required not only federal funding but also an organization that would resettle blacks outside the United States. That need found fruition in the Upper South's favorite conditional antislavery institution, the American Colonization

Society, founded in 1817.[22] William Lloyd Garrison would soon denounce the society as not antislavery at all. But to Jefferson's entire Virginia generation, and to most mainstream Americans in all parts of the country in the 1817–60 period, the American Colonization Society was the best hope to secure an altogether liberated (and lily-white) American populace.

The only significant southern opponent of the society concurred that colonization of blacks could undermine slavery. South Carolinians doubted that the American Colonization Society could remove millions of blacks to its Liberian colony. (The society, in fact, rarely resettled a thousand in one year and only ten thousand in forty-five years.) But South Carolina extremists conceded that an Upper South–North national majority coalition could be rallied for colonization. They also realized that once Congress voted for an emancipation plan, whatever the absurdity of the scheme, abolition might be near. Capitalists would never invest in the property. Slaves would sense that liberation was imminent. Only a suicidal slaveholding class, warned the Carolinians, would take such a chance. Carolinians threatened to secede if Congress so much as discussed the heresy. So congressional colonization discussion halted in the late 1820s, just as South Carolina's disunion threats had halted antislavery discussions in the First Congress.[23]

A few historians have pronounced these South Carolinians to be but bluffers, cynical blusterers who never meant to carry out their early disunion threats.[24] The charge, based solely on the opinion of the few Founding Fathers who wished to defy the Carolinians, does not ring true. Many South Carolina coastal planters lived among 8:1 concentrations of blacks to whites, a racial concentration unheard of elsewhere. The Carolinians farmed expensive miasmic swamplands, unlike the cheaper, healthier slaveholding areas everywhere else. Unless black slaves could be forced to endure the pestilential Carolina jungle, the lushest area for entrepreneurial profits in North America would become economically useless. So enormous a percentage of blacks might also be racially dangerous if freed. South Carolinians' special stake in slavery engendered understandable worry when Northerners and Southerners called slavery an evil that must be removed.

So South Carolinians threatened disunion. Posterity cannot say whether they would have had the nerve to secede if an early national Congress had enacted, for example, Jefferson's conditional antislavery plan of using federal land proceeds to deport slaves. South Carolinians might have early found, as they later discovered, that their nerves were not up to the requirements of bringing off a revolution against every other state. But though they might not have been able to carry out their threats, that hardly means they were bluffing. Their threats were credible because these sincere warriors intended to act, if the nation defied their non-bluff.

Still, the larger point is that so conditional an antislavery mentality was not equipped to test South Carolinians' capacity to carry out their threats, any more than that mentality's compromised worldview was equipped to seize presently owned property from recalcitrant slaveholders. The master spirit of the age was a passion to build white republics, not an inclination to deport black slaves; and South Carolinians threatened to splinter the Union unless congressmen ceased to talk of deporting blacks. The Founding Fathers' priorities prevailed. South Carolina's threats effectively shut off congressional speculation about removing slaves from America. That left only the other major conditional antislavery aspiration still viable: shutting off the flow of Africans to America.

6

South Carolinians long opposed closure of the African slave trade, too. But their opposition to stopping future slaves from traveling to America was mild compared to their opposition to deporting slaves from America. Like the northern slaveholders who could accept emancipation if they had fifty more years to use slaves, South Carolinians could accept the end of the African slave trade if they had twenty more years to import Africans.

Their potential interest in more African imports first surfaced at the beginning of the American national experience. When drafting the Declaration of Independence and cataloging King George's sins, Thomas Jefferson proposed condemning the tyrant for supposedly foisting Africans on his allegedly slavery-hating colonies. South Carolinians bridled at the language. Jefferson deleted the draft paragraph. Although Jefferson was not present at the 1787 Philadelphia Constitutional Convention, history repeated itself. When northern and Upper South delegates proposed that Congress be empowered to end the African slave trade immediately, South Carolinians warned that they would then refuse to join the Union. The issue was compromised. Congress was given authority to close the overseas trade only after 1807. South Carolinians had a guaranteed twenty-year-long opportunity to import African slaves.

In the early nineteenth century, with the emerging Cotton

Kingdom avid for more slaves, Carolinians seized their expiring opportunity. In 1803, the state officially opened its ports for the importation of Africans. Some 40,000 Africans landed in the next four years. Assuming the normal course of black natural increase in the Old South, these latest arrivals in the land of liberty multiplied to 150,000 slaves by 1860, or almost 4 percent of the southern total.

Jefferson was President at the moment when Congress could shutter South Carolina's twenty-year window of opportunity. "I congratulate you, fellow-citizens," Jefferson wrote in his annual message of December 2, 1806, "on the approach of the period when you may interpose your authority constitutionally" to stop Americans "from all further participation in those violations of human rights which have been so long continued on the unoffending inhabitants of Africa, and which the morality, the reputation, and the best interests of our country have long been eager to proscribe."[25] Closure of the African slave trade could not take effect until January 1, 1808, conceded Jefferson. Yet the reform, if passed in 1807, could ensure that no extra African could legally land in a U.S. port. In 1807 Congress enacted Jefferson's proposal.

Prompt enactment came in part because almost all Americans beyond South Carolina shared Jefferson's ideological distaste for slavery. The African slave trade seemed especially loathsome to most white republicans. But neither the loathing nor the enactment came wholly because of disinterested republican ideology. Jefferson and fellow racists hated the African slave trade partly because it brought more *blacks* to America. So too South Carolina planters were now willing to acquiesce in the prohibition partly because they considered their forty thousand imports to be enough so-called African barbarians. So too Upper South slave sellers could gain more dollars for their slaves if Cotton South purchasers could buy no more blacks from Africa. With the closure of the African slave trade—as with the Northwest Ordinance and as with the abolition of northern slavery and as with the manumission of Baltimore slaves—republican selflessness came entwined with racist selfishness; and no historian can say whether the beautiful or the ugly contributed the stronger strand.

The closure of the African slave trade emerges in the textbooks as a nonevent, worthy of no more than a sentence. Whole books have been written on the Founding Fathers and slavery without a word devoted to the reform.[26] Yet this law was the jewel of the Founding Fathers' antislavery effort, and no viable assessment of that effort can ignore this far-reaching accomplishment. The federal closure's impact reached as far as Africa. Brazil and Cuba imported over 1.5 million Africans between 1815 and 1860, largely to stock sugar and coffee plantations.[27] Slaveholders in the United States could have productively paid the then-prevailing price for at least that many black imports to stock southwestern sugar and cotton plantations.

The effect of the closure of the African slave trade also reached deep into the slaves' huts and the masters' Big Houses. If the South had contained a million newly landed "raw Africans," as Southerners called those human folk, southern slaveholders would have deployed more savage terror and less caring paternalism to control the strangers. The contrast between the United States, where the nineteenth-century overseas slave trade was closed, and Cuba and Brazil, where it was wide open, makes the point. Wherever Latin Americans imported cheap Africans, they drove down slave life expectancies. In the United States, alone among the large nineteenth-century slavocracies, slaves naturally increased in numbers, thanks to less fearful, more kindly masters and to more acculturated, more irreplaceable blacks.

The closure of the African trade also changed the demographical configuration of the South and the nation, to the detriment of slaveholders' political power. When white immigrants shunned the Slave South and voyaged to the free-labor North, the South could not import Africans to compensate. The North grew faster in population, faster in labor supply, faster in industrialization, faster in the ability to seize agricultural territories such as Kansas, and faster in the ability to control congressional majorities. Worse, after African slave trade closure, the Cotton South could race after the free-labor North only by draining slaves from the Border South. The combination of manumissions and African slave trade closure doubly hindered slavery in the most geographically northern slave states. In 1790 almost 20 percent of American slaves had lived in this Border South tier. By 1860 the figure was down to 11 percent. On the other hand, in 1790 the Lower South states had 21 percent of American slaves, but by 1860, the figure was up to 59 percent. From 1830 to 1860 the percentage of slaves in the total population declined in Delaware from 4 to 1 percent; in Maryland from 23 to 13 percent; in Kentucky from 24 to 19 percent; in Missouri from 18 to 10 percent; and in the counties that would become West Virginia from 10 to 5 percent. By 1860 Delaware, Maryland, Missouri, and the area that would become West Virginia had a lower percentage of slaves than New York had possessed at the time of the Revolution, and Kentucky did not have a much higher percentage. The goal of abolition had become almost as practicable in these border states as it had been in New York in 1776, twenty-five years before the state passed a post-nati law and fifty years before the last New York slave was freed. Had no Civil War occurred, fifty years after 1860 is a good estimate for when the last Border South slave might have been freed. Then slavery would have remained in only eleven of the fifteen slave states.

To sum up the antislavery accomplishments in the first American age that considered slavery a problem: When the Founding Fathers were growing up, slavery existed throughout Great Britain's North American colonies. The African slave trade was open. Even in the North, as John Jay of New York reported, "very few . . . doubted the propriety and rectitude" of slavery.[28] When the Founders left the national stage, slavery had been abolished in the North, kept out of the Midwest, and placed on the defensive in the South. A conditional antislavery mentality, looking for ways to ease slavery and blacks out of the country, prevailed everywhere except in the Lower South. If the Founders had done none of this—if slavery had continued in the North and expanded into the Northwest; if a million Africans had been imported to strengthen slavery in the Lower South, to retain it in New York and Illinois, to spread it to Kansas, and to preserve it in the Border South; if no free black population had developed in Delaware and Maryland; if no conditional antislavery ideology had left Southerners on shaky moral grounds; if, in short, Jefferson and his contemporaries had lifted not one antislavery finger—everything would have been different and far less worrisome for the Lower South slavocracy.

7

But the Founding Fathers also inadvertently empowered a worried Lower South to wage its coming struggle. "Inadvertent" is the word, for most American Revolutionaries did not wish to strengthen an intransigent slavocracy, any more than they wished to delay African slave trade closure or to silence congressional consideration of colonization. The problem, again, was that these architects of republicanism cared more about building white republics than about securing antislavery. So opportunities to consolidate a republican Union counted for much and the side effects on slavery counted for little—when side effects on slavery were even noticed.

Thus at the Constitutional Convention, Lower South slave-holders, by threatening not to join the Union unless their power was strengthened, secured another Union-saving compromise. Slaves were to be counted as three-fifths of a white man, when the national House of Representatives was apportioned. This constitutional clause gave Southerners around 20 percent more congress-men than their white numbers justified. Since the numbers of members in the president-electing electoral college were based on the numbers of congressmen, the South also gained 20 percent more power over the choice of chief executive. An unappetizing number illustrates the point. The South received one extra congressman and presidential elector throughout the antebellum years as a result of South Carolina's 1803–07 importation of Africans.

The Founding Fathers also augmented Lower South territory. In 1803, Thomas Jefferson's Louisiana Purchase from France added the areas of Louisiana, Arkansas, and Missouri to the Union. In 1819, James Monroe's treaty with Spain secured the areas of Florida, southern Alabama, and southern Mississippi. A desire to protect slavery was only marginally involved in the Florida purchase and not at all involved in the Louisiana Purchase. Presidents Jefferson and Monroe primarily sought to protect national frontiers. But they were so determined to bolster national power and gave so little thought to the consequences for slaveholder power that their calculations about blacks could not offset their diplomatic imperatives. Their successful diplomacy yielded territories already containing slaves. Then their antislavery mentality was too conditional to conceive of confiscating slave property. The net result: The Founding Fathers contributed four new slave states and parts of two others to the eventual fifteen slave states in the Union. That increased the South's power in the U.S. Senate 27 percent and the Lower South's economic power enormously.

If the Founding Fathers had done none of this—if they had not awarded the South the extra congressmen and presidential electors garnered from the three-fifths clause; if they had not allowed South Carolina to import forty thousand more Africans; if they had not acquired Florida, Louisiana, Arkansas, Missouri, southern Mississippi, and southern Alabama; if in short they had restricted the slavocracy to its pre-1787 power and possessions—the situation would have been far bleaker for the Cotton Kingdom. Indeed, without the Founding Fathers' bolstering of slaveholder power, their antislavery reforms, however guarded, might have been lethal. As it was, the American Revolutionaries made the slave system stronger in the South, where it was already strongest, and weaker in the

North, where it was weakest. That contradictory amalgam of increased slaveholder vulnerabilities and increased slaveholder armor established the pattern for everything that was to come.

8

In the 1820–60 period, and on the 1861–65 battlefields, the slaveholders fought their added vulnerabilities with their added power. By 1860, the slaveholders had fifteen states against the North's sixteen. But if the four Border South states fell away, the North's margin would widen to twenty against eleven. Then all sorts of dangers would loom for a once-national institution, which in the wake of the Founding Fathers was slowly becoming more defensively and peculiarly southern.

Southern proslavery campaigns, ideological and political, could be summed up as one long campaign to reverse the Founding Fathers' conditional antislavery drift. The conditional antislavery ideology, declaring emancipation desirable *if* blacks could be removed and *if* the Union could be preserved, persisted in the North and the Upper South throughout the antebellum period. That predominant national apologetic attitude toward slavery, Lower South zealots persistently feared, could inspire a national political movement aimed at removing blacks and slaves from the nation unless the Lower South deterred it.

Deterrence began with a determined proslavery campaign aimed at showing Southerners that slavery was no problem after all. In its extreme manifestations in the 1850s, proslavery visionaries, led by Virginia's George Fitzhugh, called wage slavery the unrecognized problem. The impolitic implication (although Fitzhugh disavowed it): Even white wage earners should be enslaved.[29] Proslavery polemicists more commonly called freedom for blacks the unrecognized problem. The common message: Black slaves should never be freed to starve as free workers in or out of America.

While proslavery intellectuals took aim at the Founding Fathers' revolutionary awareness that slavery was a problem, proslavery politicians sought to counter the waning of slavery in the Border South. With the Fugitive Slave Law of 1850, particularly aimed at stopping border slaves from fleeing to permanent liberty in the North, and the Kansas-Nebraska Act of 1854, originally urged by its southern advocates to protect slavery in Missouri, Southerners endeavored to fortify the border regime which the Fathers had somewhat weakened. So too the most dramatic (although unsuccessful) Lower South political movement of the 1850s, the campaign to reopen the African slave trade, sought to reverse the Fathers' greatest debilitation of the slavocracy.

The minority's persistent proslavery campaigns and frequent congressional victories eventually convinced most Northerners that appeasement of a slaveholding minority damaged rather than saved white men's highest priority: majority rule in a white men's republic. That determination to rescue majority rule from the Slavepower minority underrode Abraham Lincoln's election in 1860; and with Lincoln's election came the secession of the Lower South minority. Secessionists feared not least that the President-elect might build that long-feared North–Upper South movement to end slavery by deporting blacks, especially from the compromised Border South.

The ensuing Civil War would prove that latter-day Southerners had been right to worry about slavery's incremental erosion in the borderlands. The four Border South states would fight for the Union, tipping the balance of power against the Confederacy. Abraham Lincoln would allegedly say that though he hoped to have God on his side, he *had* to have Kentucky. He would retain his native Kentucky and all the borderlands, including his adopted Illinois, which the Founders had at long last emancipated.

He would also obtain, against his initial objections, black soldiers, who would again sense an opportunity to read themselves into the Declaration of Independence. Just as fugitive slaves had pushed reluctant Pennsylvania, New York, and Maryland slaveholders into faster manumissions, so fugitive blacks would push a reluctant Great Emancipator to let them in his army and thereby make his victory theirs. Black soldiers would help win the war, secure emancipation, and thus finally defeat the slaveholders' long attempt to reverse the Founding Fathers' conditional antislavery drift.

To omit the Fathers' guarded contributions to America's drift toward the Civil War and emancipation in the name of condemning them as hypocrites is to miss the tortuous way black freedom came to the United States. But to omit the Fathers' contributions to Lower South proslavery power in the name of calling them social revolutionaries is to deny the very meaning of the word *revolution*.

9

More broadly and more significantly, the American Revolutionaries' stance on blacks illuminated their ambivalent approach to the one truly radical social implication of the Revolution. As the historian Jack P. Greene has brilliantly shown, nothing was radical about the Declaration's affirmation of an American right to life, liberty, and the pursuit of happiness, so long as only white males' pursuits counted as American.[30] Whatever the poverty in urban slums and tenants' shacks, American colonials had long since developed a radically modern social order, dedicated to white males' pursuit of happiness and rooted in unprecedented capitalist opportunity. The Revolution, while expanding political opportunity and political mobility, only a little further widened an economic doorway already unprecedentedly open—but labeled "white males only."

For the others who peopled America—the women, the Native Americans, the blacks, in short, the majority—opportunity was closed. To include these dispossessed groups in the American Revolution—to open up a world where *all* men and women were at liberty to pursue their happiness—was the Declaration's truly radical social implication. No such color-blind, ethnically blind, gender-blind social order had ever existed, not on these shores, not anywhere else.

The Founding Fathers caught an uneasy glimpse of this potential social revolution. Despite their obsession with white republics and white property, they recognized that the Declaration applied to blacks, too. But their racism led them to take a step backward from the revolutionary promise of the Declaration of Independence. Most of them were no advocates of an egalitarian multicultural society *in* America. The Virginia Dynasty especially would extend equality to black Americans by moving them *out* of America. That reactionary black-removal foundation of antislavery statecraft, peculiar among all the New World slavocracies to these North Americans, did not a progressive social revolution portend.

Thomas Jefferson had captured the nonradicalism of the American Revolution in one of the great American phrases. "We have the wolf by the ears," he wrote at the time of the Missouri Controversy, "and we can neither hold him, nor safely let him go."[31] The Founding Fathers had more wolves by the ears than Jefferson had in mind: blacks, slaves, their own antislavery hopes, their implication that *all* people must be included in the Declaration of Independence. They propounded those ideals, but they quailed before their own creation. Someday, the ideals may prevail and Americans may cease to recoil from the Declaration's implications. But it would not happen to the Founders, not with revolutionary speed, not to men who equipped a nation to hang on to slavery's slippery ears for almost a century.

3 / Denmark Vesey's Antipaternalistic Reality

To obliterate the Founding Fathers' conditional antislavery position, slaveholders needed a convincing reconciliation of their political system, democracy, and their social system, slavery. A single concept, paternalism, best harmonized liberty for citizens who could take care of themselves with protection for noncitizens who would allegedly fail as freed people. Paternalism, so the slaveholders claimed, summed up the peculiar virtue of their special form of slavery, the essence of their superiority to employers of free laborers, and the critical reason slaves no less than citizens consented to be governed. The next four chapters discuss the development, character, usefulness, and faltering of this problematic attempt to synthesize democratic and authoritarian regimes.

The Denmark Vesey Slave Conspiracy, transpiring in Charleston, South Carolina, in 1822, was among the most famous U.S. black insurrection plots in the half century before the Civil War. Thomas Jefferson and many other Founding Fathers were still alive when this shockingly antipaternalistic episode occurred. But already the slaveholders' aspiration toward paternalism was the foundation of their post–Founding Father rationalizations. By undermining paternalism as the basis of the regime, Vesey undercut not least the paternalistic reconciliation of democracy and slavery. The slaveholders' quasi-despotic court, when seeking to try the alleged conspirators in a quasi-democratic way, threw further doubt on the compatibility of democratic and authoritarian realms. I first discussed these illuminating connections between the slaveholders' political and social histories in "Denmark Vesey's Peculiar Reality," published in 1986 in a festschrift hon-

oring Kenneth M. Stampp.[1] *I am grateful to the University of Kentucky Press for permission to republish material from the original essay, which has been thoroughly revised stylistically but only slightly altered analytically.*

Nineteenth-century southern slaveholders entitled their system for ruling blacks the "Peculiar Institution" and the "Domestic Institution." The titles contended that the Old South had developed a singular form of slavery, peculiarly based on familial models. Slaveholders in other places, said these patriarchs regretfully, had made the term *slavery* a title to be avoided. Slavery elsewhere was a vicious system to extract labor, akin to a coercive prison's forced toil. But in the South, claimed southern patriarchs, slavery deserved other names. Southern so-called slavery allegedly involved a mutually supportive agreement between patriarchs and wards, akin to a household's consenting relationships. Because these unusual slaveholders were putatively paternalists, their Peculiar Institution was supposedly a Domestic Institution.

1

The U.S. slaveholders more often claimed that they were paternalists and more often demanded that their slaves act out a charade of consent to that claim than did slaveholders elsewhere in the New World.[2] Why the special pleading and the special attempt to make the plea a reality? Of the several reasons for the peculiarity, one was most important. Nowhere else in the Americas was despotism over blacks enmeshed in an advanced republic for whites. The realm of the despot who ruled by coercion seemed antithetical to the realm of the democrat who ruled by consent. In part, the slaveholders used an impassable color line to reconcile apparently irreconcilable regimes. Paternalistic slavery, claimed these rulers, best enabled a superior race to govern a race incapable of governing itself. In contrast, egalitarian democracy best enabled equal whites to rule each other.

A worldview severed at the color line, however, did not quite make for a serene ruling class. Democrats could forget neither that even allegedly inferior blacks were people as well as property nor that people should consent to be ruled. The patriarchs' other alleged inferiors in the household *did* consent to be ruled. Both wives and children agreed that the benevolent Christian husband rightfully ruled the home. If slaves would also consent to being ruled by caring patriarchs—if slavery could be but an extension of the domestic circle and domestic consent could be but an extension of republican consent—a peculiarly democratic slaveholder could rule serenely over everyone, in the house and beyond the gates.

This prayerful hope divided regimes not at the color line but at the household's property line. Inside his domestic estate, the patriarch was absolute ruler over all consenting inferiors, whether the dependents were the supposedly inferior sex or the allegedly inferior child or the supposedly inferior race. Outside the private gates, those who were allegedly superior by right of sex and age and race, the adult white males, must never assume patriarchal airs with each other. They must shun governmental incursions inside each other's private domains. They must elect each other after egalitarian political campaigns, rule each other under an egalitarian constitution, and punish each other through an egalitarian judge and jury. The democratic slaveholders' split regime thus featured two sorts of rulers of two sorts of systems under one standard of legitimacy. Everywhere, those ruled consented to the system of rules appropriate to their respective innate abilities.

So comfortable a reconciliation of troubling contradictions could never be merely an abstract theory. Genuinely paternalistic slave treatment sealed the masters' sense of self-worth and secured their honorable reputation in the family and the neighborhood. These would-be paternalists were thus driven to rule "their people" and their "family friends," as they called their slaves, with a father's fairness and affection. Their system becomes unintelligible unless this paternalistic aspiration is credited.

2

Their system becomes equally unintelligible unless the hindrances to their paternalistic pretensions are noted. A major drawback, on the large plantations where over half the slaves resided, was the scale of operations. The white family was a small intimate enclave. The large plantation was an impersonal bureaucratic regime, where hired white overseers usually directed field hands and masters usually knew intimately only a few house servants.

The racist basis of the regime also hindered paternalistic feelings. Black adults were assumed not only to be innately childlike, as were white youngsters, but also to be innately animalistic, unlike white children in the family circle. The master could hardly feel for a supposed beast the same way he felt for a cherished offspring. The different purposes in governing further mocked the paternalistic analogy. Paternalists reared white male children to be ruling adults. They conditioned blacks to remain forever "boys," to use their other term for their "people" and their "family friends."

The economic purposes of slave labor, as opposed to the affectionate underpinning of white families, undermined the paternalistic analogy still more decisively. To support the white family, profits had to be made from slaves' brute labor. To avoid bankruptcy, blacks sometimes had to be sold, with the help of disreputable slave traders. The patriarch, in contrast, rarely thought of his white children as money-making laborers, and he certainly never thought of selling his sons for top dollar.

Proslavery polemicists conceded these many obstacles to the attainment of paternalism. Some theorists, especially George Fitzhugh, called racism a bar to paternalism. If masters considered blacks subhuman, Fitzhugh warned, humanistic paternalism was impossible. He would base patriarchy on a color-blind sympathy for dependents, not on a color line that encouraged unsympathetic scorn for beasts.[3] Other leading proslavery theorists, especially James Henley Thornwell, joined Fitzhugh in calling paternalism an ideal unachieved. They urged the state to require that treatment of slaves met paternalistic standards.[4] Leaders of southern public opinion also almost unanimously condemned slave traders and overseers for treating slaves like money-making objects rather than like "family friends."

More seriously still, the black "family friends" often failed to legitimate the master as paternalist. Supposedly independent masters ironically depended on supposedly dependent slaves to validate paternalism. Slaveholders could neither feel nor act like benevolent fathers unless blacks accepted the role of grateful "boy." Failure to secure slaves' consent to the familial regime led to terrorization. Undemocratic sprees of brutal lashing and branding were unlike any deterrence imposed on white families and all too like slavery everywhere else.

Many masters tried to avoid unfamilial viciousness. By blending kindness and punishment, they sought truly grateful wards—true "Samboes," to use posterity's term for the slave as docile cipher. Some slaves in fact became Samboes. They were treasured evidence, to their masters, that paternalism had been achieved. Other slaves self-consciously adopted the role of Sambo. Although secretly longing for freedom, they posed as Sambo in the paternalist's charade, to their master's slightly uneasy satisfaction. Still other blacks used paternalists' desire for a Sambo performance as a bargaining chip. They would consent to a truly paternalistic regime only so long as true paternalism involved compromised paternalistic authority. The slaves' definition of such a compromise included time to farm their garden plots during the workday and space to develop their own African-American culture after hours.

Many slaves, however, misplayed the Sambo role so badly that their consent to paternalism could not be credited. These bad actors lied, stole, feigned illness, misunderstood orders, set fires, and ran away. They turned many smiling masters into exasperated lashers. The system then more resembled a guerrilla war than a consenting home.[5] Warfare became particularly unfamilial on the southwestern frontier, where money-grubbing capitalists, with scarcely a pretense of paternalism, often lashed begrudging work out of resistant blacks, who displayed scarcely a pretense of Sambo.

Slaves best evidenced their dissent from any paternalistic compromise by trying to liberate themselves whenever possible. Alleged Samboes had a fine feel for any weakness in the system. Wherever space developed, they fled through it. Fugitive slaves hastened the pace of emancipation in the North, quickened the speed of manumissions in border cities such as Baltimore, and impelled the fugitive slave crises that helped produce the Civil War. When war came, slaves' rejection of paternalism reached its climax, as approximately 600,000 so-called Samboes fled from their so-called patriarchs.

The collision between paternalistic aspirations and antipaternalistic hindrances thus produced a variety of types on both sides of the paternalistic charade. On the white side, exalted paternalists flourished, as did befuddled paternalists, crass antipaternalists, money-grubbing overseers, and grasping slave traders. On the black side, true Samboes flourished, as did fake Samboes, guerrilla warriors, and fugitives from any paternalistic compromise. During the Civil War, the massive slave escapes revealed Sambo's consent to paternalism to be a widespread sham. Until the Civil War, a paternalist could almost believe that the charade of consent was a sincere act—until a slave conspiracy canceled the performance.

The United States had a thin tradition of slave conspiracies, compared to Latin America, and a still thinner tradition of conspiracies that produced revolts before being discovered. Still, the ultimate antidomestic act sometimes happened; and when supposed Samboes threw off the mask and sought to murder their alleged paternalists, the Domestic Institution had to become undomestic despotism. Since supposed boys had plotted patricide, serviles had to be tried and killed as men. Since patriarchal power had failed to provide public order, the domestic dictator had to abdicate. Democratic government, designed only for consenting whites, had to coerce unconsenting blacks. The resulting semidespotic judicial procedures mocked the word *democratic*.

With that newly strained mixture of democracy and despotism, the Peculiar Institution turned peculiarly distressing. Masters no longer mastered their people. Democratic government for whites placed despotic hands on blacks. Black was white; paternalism vanished. Oh, for the days when Sambo had supposedly consented to the patriarchs' script!

3

Denmark Vesey lived at a time and in a place where an especially permissive brand of an especially deep-rooted paternalism had made the Domestic Institution especially vulnerable.[6] The cult of domestic patriarchy flourished particularly in the oldest, seaboard South, where "nigger-drivers" were scarcer than on the southwestern frontier and ancestral estates more plentiful. Domestic pretenses also flourished particularly where slaves served their patriarchs in intimate domestic circles instead of working under overseers in far-off fields. Paternalistic management of slaves tended to be especially permissive when whites' parenting became most lenient.

Charleston in the early 1820s possessed these preconditions for permissive domesticity. The city's hinterlands, lush tidewater swamps full of malarial mosquitoes, long yielded the Old South's plushest profits and its unhealthiest inhabitants. Charleston, the relatively healthy center of this miasmic area, was wealthy planters' favorite spot during the especially sickly summer months. Coastal planters brought small armies of household slaves to town mansions, while large armies of field hands remained behind to work remote estates. Nowhere else were personal domestic servants so separated from impersonal agricultural gangs.

Charleston slaves, when not trusted house servants, tended to be trusted skilled laborers. Individual craftsmen provided preindustrial Charleston's mechanical services. The Carolina low country was too demographically black and too unhealthy to attract enough white laborers. So supposedly stupid slaves had special opportunities to become skilled artisans. Charleston's unusually high percentage of house servants and skilled slaves also came accompanied with a high percentage, for the Lower South, of free blacks. Nearly one of every eight Charleston blacks was free. Black slaves and freedmen together composed 57 percent of Charleston's population. No other southern city was so demographically black.

In the period immediately preceding Denmark Vesey's 1822 conspiracy, Charleston patriarchs tended to treat their especially large, especially talented, and especially domestic black population with special leniency. Although paternalism need not be permissive and fathers often ruled remorselessly, grim parental deterrence was waning in the 1820s. The cult of romanticism was softening attitudes toward inferiors throughout the Western world. Lenient child rearing struck an especially responsive chord in Americans, with their increasingly egalitarian attitudes toward white males and their increasingly sentimental attitudes about white ladies' moral superiority and white children's innate virtues. English visitors to Jacksonian America saw little strict English-style child rearing. American youths were often begged or bribed to be "papa's angel."[7]

In the 1818–22 period, Charlestonians, albeit with misgivings, sought to prove that the same permissive domesticity could control domestic slaves. "By far the greater number of our citizens," Charlestonians reported, "were rearing up" a "mild and generous" system, exulting "in what they termed the progress of liberal ideas." Slave mechanics were permitted to hire out their labor. Slave domestics were permitted to learn to read and write. Black worshipers were permitted to form religious congregations. Permissive gentlemen entertained "hope that as [slaves] were more indulged, they would become more satisfied with their condition and more attached to the whites." Instead of being brutalized into servility, slaves would consent to obey out of "affection and gratitude."[8]

Permissive slave government, by relying heavily on "affection and gratitude," was doubly dangerous, however. Too little coercion rendered too many slaves unafraid of their enslavers. Too many privileges left too many semiprivileged slaves plotting for the ultimate privilege, freedom. Charleston slaves in the pre-Vesey years had easily become the proverbial men with half a loaf who desire the other half; and the paternalists had not always intimidated the "boys" into thinking that adulthood was unattainable.

Leaders of the Vesey conspiracy exemplified expectations aroused and then thwarted. Denmark Vesey, a mulatto, was everything southern slaveholders were supposed to prevent. He was free;

blacks were supposed to be enslaved. He was a brilliant skilled laborer; blacks were supposed to be stupidly unskillful. He had many
enslaved wives and children; his bigamous family was no Christian
Domestic Institution. Enraged that his children would remain
slaves, he gambled everything he had achieved to destroy a system
that would deny his posterity their potential. Monday Gell, a hired-
out slave who had also achieved much, shared Vesey's rage. Gell
ran his own harness shop and gave his owner a percentage of his
profits. He would cut the Man's throat for taking a cent. He became a principal in Denmark Vesey's plot.

Thwarted slaves operating in a free atmosphere could use
whites' libertarian views to gather a black following. Vesey employed the Bible, the Declaration of Independence, and the Missouri Controversy congressional debates to teach blacks that all
people have a natural right to liberty. Vesey was thus a charismatic
persuader in the best tradition of the American Revolution. Yet he
also saw that persuasion was not enough. For the moment, a leader
of the underclass understood better than the master class that coercion must augment the soliciting of freely given consent.[9] Because
of the low level of slaveholders' physical deterrence, Vesey could
petrify those he could not persuade. Any black approached was
given a stark choice: kill or be killed. The slave Bacchus Hammett,
for example, initially found the conspirators' arguments uncon-
vincing. "Denmark then said," Bacchus recounted, that " 'any person who don't join us must be treated as an enemy and put to
death'; and I said, 'if that is the case, well I will join you.' "[10]

Vesey wished to extend Bacchus Hammett's "conversion" experience. The rebel chief would create a moment when the enslaved masses would have to choose between killing whites or being killed by blacks. Vesey planned a two-stage rebellion. First, a
few dozen blacks would raid Charleston's arsenals in a midnight
surprise attack. Then thousands of slaves would take up the captured guns. The few blacks siding with outnumbered whites would
be assassinated. Some of the conquering rebels might then sail off
for a black nation, perhaps Haiti, before white reinforcements
could arrive.

Vesey argued that a handful of crudely armed conspirators
could capture Charleston's firepower. Most governmental arms
were stored in the state arsenal. Whites usually left the mid-city
building unguarded at night. Two other structures in Charleston's
outskirts contained another seven hundred muskets. Bacchus
Hammett had a key to the larger storehouse, and no white man

guarded either structure at night. If a few conspirators' surprise attack on these vulnerable buildings succeeded, the rebels, armed initially with only clubs, hoes, and pikes, would command the whites' sophisticated weaponry. Then all Charleston blacks would face Bacchus Hammett's choice. The masses, predicted the chiefs, would prefer fighting for freedom to being slaughtered as Samboes.

But the black masses would face a moment of choice only if Vesey's few men remained confident and loyal enough to carry out the initial raid. To sustain morale, the chief again bolstered his democratic appeals by reversing slavery's customary balance of terror. To make black revolutionaries seem scarier than white masters, Vesey warned potential betrayers of vicious reprisals. Anonymous blacks, Vesey bragged, had pledged to murder any turncoat who informed the whites of the plot. To make white terror seem less menacing, Vesey's prime lieutenant, Gullah Jack, promised his listeners protection by the African gods. Jack, a conjurer back in Africa, was a wizened, bewhiskered little man, much given to violent gestures; he claimed that his charmed crab claws would keep their bearers safe.

Despite Vesey's rhetoric and Gullah Jack's African charms, black recruits remained nervous. Only several dozen attended Vesey's orations exhorting them to rise up. Would that be enough? To counter the question, Vesey claimed that he had recruited thousands. Plantation slaves, Vesey reminded city slaves, carried their masters' produce to city market on Saturday night. These marketeers, Vesey claimed, had agreed to take up guns from the initial raiders. Vesey boasted of long lists of black converts, as did Peter Poyas and Monday Gell.

Vesey knew that his opportunity also contained a drawback, that a revolution based on thwarted expectations was a two-edged sword. The semiprivileged might decide to guard the privileges they already had rather than seek more. Worse, some petted and pampered black might truly love his master. Worse still, a semiprivileged cynic might inform on the plotters, hoping that grateful whites would reward the betrayer.

Recruiters thus tried to avoid "waiting men who receive *presents of old coats, etc. from their masters.*"[11] But if they avoided semiprivileged Samboes altogether, the slave conspirators might miss the most likely rebels. Rolla and Ned Bennett, for example, were South Carolina Governor Thomas Bennett's most treasured "family friends." These supposed Samboes, when approached by Vesey recruiters, appeared ready to renounce their half-privileges, saying they wished to be fully free. They became revolutionary leaders.

In late May 1822, a month before the scheduled revolution, a recruiter approached the wrong "family friend." A trusted house servant proved trustworthy. He betrayed the rebels to his owner. Charleston authorities initially did not believe the informer. Ned Bennett, upon hearing his fidelity questioned, went voluntarily to the intendant (mayor) of Charleston. Ned scoffed at allegations that he meant to murder the governor, his own much-loved Massa Thomas. White paternalists, wishing to believe black "boys," relaxed.

Vesey, now uneasy, moved the revolt up two weeks. Several days before the rescheduled raid, however, another Sambo informed on the black liberators. Hysteria ensued among establishment and rebels alike. Governor Bennett called out hundreds of white troops and thousands of terrified whites lay wide awake through the night. Vesey, not sleeping either, frantically dispatched a city follower who was ignorant of the countryside to tell country recruits to march. The messenger, however, never had a chance to get lost in the jungle. Vesey apparently never bothered to ask if he had left. Patrols were out. A surprise attack was impossible. Denmark Vesey's little band now feared white retaliation more than the fearsome liberator.

4

As the patrols pounded the streets, the Domestic Institution seemed shattered. Not only the psychological comforts of the Sambo charade but also the prevailing conception of permissive control lay in ruins. Uncoerced Samboes, supposedly consenting to patriarchal direction out of affection and gratitude, were unmasked as anti-Samboes ready to brutalize white families. Time after horrifying time, those accused of the most murderous intentions had been the most trusted serviles. Some accused conspirators had slept in the family yard or in the master's bedroom. How could the masters guard against the servants, when the servants stood guard over the masters?

John Potter, a prominent Charleston merchant, co-owned one accused rebel. The slave had been loyal for "10 years. . . . When I left the City, I always directed him to sleep in the yard, which I thought safe under his charge." Potter cringed at the thought that if that supposed protector "had made his way into my bedroom, in the dead of the night." Well, the patriarch would not "own" up to such "unpleasant feelings . . . before my family, who have been more alarmed than I have ever seen."[12]

Families trembled throughout Charleston. Potter reported that John Drayton's cook, "who had hitherto behaved well," had plotted murder. A chef could easily poison the food. Another plotter had been Elias Horry's "favorite servant. . . . I believe his coachman!!" A driver could easily turn over the coach. "Good god," Potter exclaimed, "most of the coachmen and favorite servants in the City knew of it." Potter believed that if the initial raid had been "successful, even for a moment, all or nearly all" of his and everyone's favorite servants "would have joined!" Potter had discerned precisely Vesey's strategy: Only a few pretend-Samboes need capture unguarded arsenals to test all supposed Samboes' loyalty.[13]

Elias Horry, unlike John Potter, believed "his people's" loyalty would survive all tests. When constables came to arrest Horry's coachman, the master "assured them they were mistaken. He could answer for [the man's] innocence. He would as soon suspect himself." After hearing the evidence, Horry turned to his coachman. "Are you guilty?" he asked incredulously.

"Yes," muttered the black.

"What were your intentions?"

The coachman, with rage distorting a face where Horry had seen only smiles, whirled on the patriarch. He had meant "to kill you, rip open your belly, and throw your guts in your face."[14] As news of those horrifying words swirled around Charleston, alarmed directors of the Sambo charade began to debate whether servile professions of affection and gratitude had always camouflaged murderous ingratitude.

5

This panicky debate invites historians to speculate that the Vesey conspiracy was but an illusion of hysterical patriarchs. That speculation came to a climax in an influential article by the historian Richard Wade, published in 1964.[15] The key source on the conspiracy has always been the court record, as published by the judges who tried the Vesey conspirators. Wade charged that the court falsified the witnesses' verbal testimony. He also argued that the lack of corroborating physical evidence indicates that the supposed conspiracy involved little but "loose talk" among posturing slaves.

That analysis, a step backward in understanding Vesey's antipaternalistic *reality*, must be cleared away before contemporaries' debate over the conspiracy can be restored to center stage. As Wade saw it, a genuine conspiracy would have left behind lists of conspirators, caches of arms, at least a rifle or two. But Wade to the contrary, the very lack of such physical evidence speaks well for the conspirators' realism. Between the discovery of the plot and the first arrest, the Vesey leaders had ample time to destroy any lists of conspirators. Earlier, before their betrayals, conspirators would have been fools to stockpile weapons. They needed not one rifle to raid unguarded arsenals, which were loaded with rifles. They needed only to avoid detection before their surprise attack, and a weapons buildup would have invited detection.

If the lack of physical evidence hardly convicts these plotters of being mere loose talkers, their judges must be acquitted of falsifying the verbal evidence. Richard Wade thought the judges' published trial record fraudulent after he compared it to two slaves' unpublished manuscript depositions. Neither unpublished manuscript contained all the information in the court's published version of the two slaves' confessions. But Wade's two unpublished manuscripts turn out to be *pretrial* confessions, written down by the slaves' masters.[16] The published confessions at the trial supplement rather than contradict the two slaves' unpublished pretrial statements.

Wade not only unwittingly compared two unpublished pretrial manuscripts with the published trial record; he also did not realize that the entire unpublished manuscript trial record survives.[17] A comparison of the unpublished and published versions of the entire Vesey trial record exonerates the judges from ever falsifying a quote. The jurists claimed that they published language "as it was originally taken, without even changing the phraseology."[18] They did just that.

The manuscript version of the trial record remains more valuable than the published record. Although the judges never changed a quote, they did edit the trial manuscript. For the sake of clarity, they rearranged the evidence against convicted conspirators, and for the sake of simplicity, they omitted some trials of acquitted blacks. Most important of all, for the sake of public safety, the judges censored part of one accusation. They frankly admitted this solitary deliberate censorship by strewing stars across the published page.[19] We will return to this revealing censorship. But for the moment, the judges' candor about their only coverup climactically contradicts Wade's argument: The verbal evidence of conspiracy was not falsified in the slightest.

The question remains, does the unfalsified evidence demonstrate an undeniable conspiracy? No one who values democratic justice can be altogether sure. The Vesey conspirators did not receive a trial by jury or trial in public; they were not allowed to cross-examine all their accusers or to appeal their convictions. Moreover, by turning state's evidence, enslaved men could hope to escape the gallows. Betrayers of fellow blacks might even attain their own manumission.

But if posterity can credit only witnesses who had nothing to gain and only when they testified in altogether democratic courts, practically every supposed slave conspiracy must be automatically wiped off the historical record. Evidence of black conspiracies almost always came from blacks. The betrayers always had something to gain. They always testified in undemocratic courts. But instead of automatically dismissing such rich, albeit suspect, evidence, historians must suspiciously ask whether the conspiracy seems credible and whether the judges seem to have been scrupulous in weighing suspect testimony.

The Vesey conspiracy seems unusually credible and the Vesey judges unusually responsible. Vesey's essential plan, a surprise attack on unguarded arsenals, was surely credible. Vesey could have credibly expected blacks who outnumbered whites to wield captured guns. The first rebels could also have credibly expected to sail for Haiti before white reinforcements arrived. A period of permissive paternalism was just the credible opportunity that slaves often seized to escape their masters. Half-privileged slaves were usually the quickest to seize an opportunity. As for the judges who weighed the credibility of all this, we will see that they sought to avoid hysteria and to render judgment by semidemocratic standards.

Perhaps most important of all, the Vesey court had a brilliant critic in a high place, who knew the facts more intimately than any historian, who fought for democratic trial procedures as courageously as any libertarian, and who scrupulously took on Vesey's judges whenever he thought they transgressed. Yet he never thought that the plotters were but loose talkers.[20] It is time to forget unsubstantiated latter-day theories and to focus on the revealing controversy between the judges and their critic.

6

The judges' critic was the governor of the state and a wealthy Charleston merchant, Thomas Bennett. The critical issue concerned how many slaves would have joined the Vesey conspiracy if the initial raid had succeeded, and thus how much despotic procedure was necessary to deter the mass of slaves. Governor Bennett decided that Vesey's few would-be rebels must be merely childish plotters, for the mass of supposedly loyal, innately docile boys would never have taken up those captured guns. He therefore sought only a little pretrial despotism to uncover a limited conspiracy. The judges responded that Vesey was a mature plotter, that all slaves' familial loyalties were now suspect, and that pretend-Samboes might well have taken up seized arms. The jurists therefore meant to augment a little pretrial despotism with a little trial despotism in order to terrorize the many dissimulating slaves of softhearts such as Bennett.

Thomas Bennett had a particularly shattering experience with his own slaves' shams. Three of the first five rebels captured were his "family friends." Two of the six most important rebel leaders, Ned and Rolla Bennett, were his trusted "boys." Ned especially had thrown the government off stride by swearing his love for the governor after the first betrayal. Still, Bennett's greater embarrassment concerned Rolla, who blew the Sambo role into an impenetrable smokescreen after the second betrayal.

Before the conspiracy, Rolla Bennett, like John Potter's yardman, had been trusted to guard white women and children when the patriarch was gone. The governor had had no qualms about the guardian. Yet black witnesses accused Rolla of lusting after virginal whites. *"When we have done with the fellows,"* Rolla was reported to have said to a black,*"we know what to do with the wenches."*[21]

Wenches! Rolla raped with words. The black "boy" defiled white ladies with the degrading language that white chauvinists reserved for black "wenches." Still more debasing to Thomas Bennett, the "wench" Rolla had talked of deflowering was the governor's daughter! Rolla, when first hearing these reports of his words, displayed uncomprehending shock. His demeanor gave evidence of "utter ignorance of the intended insurrection."[22] His words evidenced adoration for his white family. Would he kill, rape, wreck his own household? He begged his patriarch for protection against "outsiders."

The protector did what he could for his slave. Bennett hired a superb Charleston lawyer, Jacob Axson. Axson hammered at Joe LaRoche, one of Rolla's prime accusers. The lawyer pointed out that Rolla was married to Joe's ex-wife. Axson insinuated that Rolla, not Thomas Bennett, was the intended victim of a domestic plot; Joe LaRoche, by seeking a court-sanctioned killing of Rolla, meant to retaliate for wife-stealing.

The shrewd defense could not save the clever domestic. Joe LaRoche, other witnesses reported, was glad to be free of a hated wife. Furthermore, Joe and Rolla were described as being closer to each other than either was to the woman. Accusers who had no reason to "get" Rolla kept appearing. They told of the supposed protector of the Bennett family who would savage the protected.[23] Rolla, expert at feeling for the appropriate pose, now saw that he had exhausted the wide-eyed innocent stance. He astounded his lawyer and his patriarch by confessing that he had joined Vesey's plot.

In his confession to being an anti-Sambo, Rolla portrayed a refined Sambo. Rolla conceded that Vesey "got me to join." But the slave claimed to have "said to myself, I cannot kill my master and mistress, for they use me more like a son than a slave—I then concluded, in my mind, that I would go into the country" before the conspirators "were to commence."[24]

Here was the Sambo puzzle at an exasperating level of difficulty and an excruciating level of danger. An actor, expert at fooling everyone, here showed that no one, black or white, could know what pretend-Samboes were really thinking. Nor can posterity know which if either Rolla was real. In his dangerous situation, Rolla might have bet his safety on deceiving blacks. His rape talk may have been designed to prove allegiance to the revolution. What a clever way to keep Denmark Vesey's hands off a dissimulator's throat!

Or perhaps Rolla deceived only whites. Rolla may have personified, on a particularly vicious level, that break between the Sambo pose before whites and the truer self before blacks that was a widespread African-American slave personality. Rolla's rape fantasy seems a thoroughly human way for the man who was forced to play "boy" to bring his manhood to the household's attention.

Rolla also might have been sheerly an accommodator. This genius at getting along may have thought, each step of the way, only of the most plausible pose. Sambo always ran the danger of being empty inside, like freer citizens who mindlessly conform. In Rolla

Bennett we come to the essence of latter-day academics' debate over U.S. slaves' personalities.

The mystery was not academic inside Rolla's home. In Thomas Bennett's family few illusions survived about Rolla's docility. "We, poor devils," reported Bennett's young niece, "were to have been reserved to fill their Harems—horrible." My "very beautiful cousin," Bennett's daughter, "was set apart for . . . one of their Chiefs."[25]

We do not know if the governor concurred that his daughter was reserved for his "boy's" harem. But we do know that whatever Thomas Bennett's disillusionment with Rolla, his illusions about Samboism survived. The Domestic Institution had escaped insurrection, Bennett thought, because the domestics had proved largely true. Black tyrants such as Vesey, the patriarch believed, had scared his "childish" blacks into a child's play of revolution. The black race had proved its "indolence," its "cowardice," its "total absence of . . . intelligence" by planning an abortive uprising. The revolt had not transpired because servants full of "Fidelity" for white patriarchs had betrayed black authority figures. Slaves' domestic "attachments," then, should not be "destroyed by unnecessary rigor."[26]

The court trying the conspirators scoffed at Bennett's faith in "Fidelity." Had the master learned nothing from a slave who panted after his daughter? Blacks, so most Charlestonians thought, had proved themselves not consenting boys but vicious men. True, two or three blacks full of fidelity had betrayed many more murderous blacks. But the betrayals had come barely soon enough. Displaying little cowardice, less indolence, and no fidelity, a few dozen slaves had almost raided the arsenals and thus had almost staged the ultimate test of a few thousand blacks' fidelity. White Charlestonians did not wish that examination rescheduled. Slaves must learn that no matter how many permissive private masters could be fooled, a remorseless public government would not be hoodwinked.[27]

Since Bennett conceded that some plotting had occurred, the issue between governor and court was whether the plot was dangerous. Bennett won part of the debate. The court claimed that even *after* white troops had been deployed, an uprising almost transpired.[28] But Vesey's panic, once the surprise attack lost the capacity to surprise, undermined that viewpoint. As Bennett pointed out, a plot is hardly "within a few hours of consummation" when a leader must send a city lad ignorant of the countryside twenty-two miles into a jungle to find the right plantation blacks and tell them to begin the rising. Nor was the plot still viable when the leader never bothered to find out if the messenger on the impossible mission had succeeded. The governor sought to comfort the terrified; and troops had kept the prospect of a razor across the jugular a couple of days rather than a couple of hours away—if Charlestonians found that fact comforting.[29]

The governor and the judges also clashed over the credibility of the raid *before* whites heard of the plot. To Bennett, the court's verbal evidence, though proving a conspiracy, did not demonstrate a viable conspiracy. Anticipating Richard Wade, Bennett argued that a viable plot would have left behind physical evidence. But no list of thousands of recruits was found, nor did so much as a rifle surface. Bennett concluded that "less than a hundred" blacks were involved, most only to the extent of "acquiescing" and all "unprovided with arms."[30]

The court answered, in the manner of Wade's critics, that Monday Gell, Peter Poyas, and Denmark Vesey had had plenty of time to burn incriminating lists and plenty of hatchets to break into unguarded arsenals.[31] The court's estimate of the number of slaves involved, however, was compatible with Bennett's. "Any opinion formed as to the numbers actually engaged," cautioned the judges, "must be altogether conjectural." Their conjecture, like Bennett's, was that Vesey "greatly exaggerated" his numbers, "and perhaps designedly so," in order to give his men the nerve to strike. Bennett could have written that sentence. He also might have accepted the court's hazy conclusion: "considerable numbers were concerned."[32] Bennett's "less than a hundred" conspirators, after all, were a "considerable number" to mass against unguarded arsenals. Nor were court and governor far apart on whether "considerable numbers" were armed. Where no rifles physically uncovered spoke to Bennett of a "crude" plot, inadequately provided with arms, verbal testimony about hoes and hatchets indicated to the judges a credible conspiracy, adequately armed for the initial surprise attack.[33]

Since governor and judges agreed that the plan involved several dozen plotters, none possessing a rifle, their disagreement centered on whether thousands would have joined if dozens had seized Charleston's firepower. The racist governor scoffed at the possibility that many potential killers were hiding camouflaged behind the slaves' consenting fidelity. Some urge, wrote Rolla's master, that "had the attempt been made by the small number who confederated, thousands would have joined." But that was "problematical." Conspirators had no wish to share their plans with the masses who would allegedly have joined them. When rebels "saw in thousands a Fidelity which they dared not tamper with," they could have had "no confidence in such a contingency" as loyal servants switching into disloyal killers.[34]

The court replied that the leaders distrusted the masses only *before* the raid, only *before* blacks rather than whites possessed guns, only *before* the question was whether to kill for freedom or be killed by black freedom fighters.[35] The court conceded that speculations about probabilities *after* a raid were "problematical." But then again, the judges thought, every plot of the few against the mighty is problematical. To avoid betrayal, conspiracies must be small. A few must create a confrontation situation that forces the many to take sides and gives them the nerve to strike for freedom.

This logic of conspiratorial politics suggests that whites or blacks who believed Denmark Vesey's bragging about recruiting thousands of slaves probably exaggerated the number of participants and misunderstood the strategy. As both court and governor realized, Vesey probably guarded his flanks by controlling his numbers and exaggerated his numbers so that the plotters would take heart. Vesey's was the nervy gamble that after a surprise attack by dozens, thousands who had faked fidelity would gain the nerve to fake no longer.

Bennett found that view problematic, for he did not believe that most Samboes faked fidelity. The judges found Vesey's strategy viable, for they no longer believed the Samboes' charade of fidelity. The issue was unresolvable because neither verbatim verbal evidence nor nonexistent physical evidence said a syllable about what thousands of black actors were really thinking. The terror of Denmark Vesey was that masters awoke one night to find that their households' safety rested on the invisible and unknowable.

7

The judges, believing that more plots were out there to be uncovered, had inquisitional power to ferret out secrets. South Carolina law guaranteed republican justice only to whites. When a slave was accused of a capital crime, any justice of the peace could select another justice of the peace and from three to five landowners to join with him in forming a so-called Court of Magistrates and Freeholders. The magistrates and freeholders were judge, jury, and court of last resort. As judge, they could use any procedure. As jury, they could convict by a simple majority. Nothing required them to give accused blacks any rights.[36]

Nothing except the conscience of a democracy, a conscience that the judges shared with Bennett. Before judicial procedures began, the governor privately demanded that the alleged conspirators trials be thoroughly democratic. But Bennett remained incensed that other masters' slaves had corrupted his "boys." Hopeful that dictatorial pretrial fact-gathering would trace corruption to its source, he privately urged Charleston authorities to form a "Court of Investigation." The preliminary despotic court, "untrammeled by the usual forms, could pursue fearlessly the mazes of the laby-rinth." Then regular courts, observing sacred democratic forms could give the accused a fair trial in open court.[37]

The judges brushed aside the governor's suggestion. Some blacks, they said, could be willing to testify in closed court, but be terrified of Vesey's threatened reprisals and remain silent in an open courtroom. Bennett's plan might despotically yield incrimi-nating evidence and then democratically permit frightened incrimi-nators not to testify at trials. No convictions would ensue. A liber-ator could remain the most credible terrorizer.[38]

The court meant to seize the balance of terror. The judges con-sidered Bennett the epitome of the no-longer-credible private co-ercer. The governor seemed too permissive on two fronts. As a pri-vate despot, he seemed to be a weak patriarch whose domestic regime had almost thrust his daughter into his slave's embrace. As a public ruler, he appeared to be a paralyzed democrat whose scru-ples might liberate murderous slaves. Some hard despotism must be forced on such soft democrats. Thus the court went ahead, try-ing three Bennett slaves and several other conspirators in secret session, limiting confrontations between accused and accuser, and disallowing any testing of justice in the open air.[39]

Fearing conflict-of-interest charges, Bennett waited until his slaves were tried before pressing his protest. Then he wrote Robert Y. Hayne, attorney general of the state, asking whether a republi-can court could try a man for his life within "closed doors" and without allowing the defendant to question his accusers. Hayne answered, correctly, that under South Carolina law, accused slaves had no legal rights. The trials proceeded. The governor silently suf-fered.[40]

In his special message to the legislature at the end of the year Bennett went public with his outrage. He "deeply lamented" that a criminal court should "close its doors upon the community," thereby shutting "out those accidental rays which occasionally illuminate . . . innocence and guilt." He deplored testimony "received under the pledge of inviolable secrecy," leaving the accused "convicted, and sentenced to death, without seeing the persons, or hearing the voices, of those who testified to their guilt." Bennett attacked the court's rationale: that several witnesses had been scared of open courtrooms. "The state," claimed the state's executive, "was competent to protect." Months after witnesses had testified, reported the governor, Charleston blacks "distinctly and generally" knew the identities of Vesey's betrayers. Yet the turncoats "pass unmolested."

Bennett also attacked court procedure in later phases of the trials, when Charles Drayton and Monday Gell, having already been convicted, turned state's evidence. Bennett accused Gell and Drayton of seeking their own survival by multiplying "the number of convictions" they "could make." Monday Gell's and Charles Drayton's chance to make convictions, continued Bennett, increased because they were once "closeted together" for hours. They could have collaborated to testify indiscriminately in hopes that a grateful court might spare them. Nothing could exceed such "chilling depravity."[41]

Bennett summed up his attack on chilling injustice when writing another South Carolina governor four years later. "I never could and cannot at this hour," declared Bennett, "separate myself from the conviction, that all the forms, proceedings, and solemnities of a trial affecting the life of a fellow being, should be the same whether *White* or *Black*."[42] With those words, Thomas Bennett earned a special place in the southern liberal tradition. But his liberalism must be kept in perspective. His was the noblesse oblige of the patriarch who believed that the superior race must be fair to the lesser. He saw no need for coercive court procedures because he considered blacks an innately childlike race, incapable of effective conspiracy and exuding consenting fidelity. The coercive court, though more offensive to latter-day jurists, was closer to the latter-day assumption that the black race, fully capable of resistance, had to be coerced into enslavement.

Nor was Thomas Bennett a modern advocate of liberal justice. He urged that pretrial investigators be invested with despotic power, trusting that truth would emerge in later trial procedures. He failed to comprehend that pretrial tyranny corrodes democratic trials. Even this heroic republican was democrat and despot too.

The judges, albeit less heroically, also struggled to live up to their democratic conscience. Their mix of democracy and dictatorship was far closer than Bennett's to despotic injustice. Yet like the governor, they revealed the mixed assumptions of this peculiar regime by striving to increase dictatorial coercion while still remaining honorable democrats. The judges totally rejected only Bennett's demand for public trials. The court was "certain that no colored witness would have ventured to incur the resentment of his comrades, by voluntarily disclosing his testimony in a public court."[43] Judges dismissed Bennett's argument that the state proved it could protect accusers *after* trials. Accusers had to accuse *before* the public state could establish its credibility as a coercive force, able to destroy Vesey's coercive power.

In every other way, the court sought a degree of democratic procedure. Defendants were guaranteed the right to have a lawyer and their master at the trial, to present their defense, and to cross-examine anyone except the early witnesses (a big exception). The judges, with another big exception noted below, followed the common law on conspiracy: For capital offenses, two witnesses must be credible.[44] Although they were judge and jury and could convict by majority vote, all convictions except two (two more big exceptions) followed the jury requirement of unanimity.

The court's handling of its despotic exceptions showed its democratic qualms. In both cases when a divided court decided to convict, the justices voted to expel rather than kill. They granted Prince Graham his request for transportation to Africa. The court sentenced Saby Gaillard to death, even though only one witness had testified against Gaillard. But the judges recommended that Governor Bennett commute the sentence to banishment from the United States.[45] Bennett instead commuted Gaillard's sentence to banishment from the state.[46] The court, perhaps secretly relieved about this outcome of a verdict repellent by its own standards, for once did not protest the governor's leniency.

The judges objected most to Bennett's charge that they had allowed Monday Gell and Charles Drayton to form a league to kill other blacks, in the later phases of the trials. A democratic court's obligation to ascertain witnesses' credibility is key to conspiracy convictions; and here the judges sought to be as scrupulous as if they had been trying whites.[47] Their results undermined Bennett's accusations. The court's manuscript trial record shows that Charles Drayton was called against forty defendants. He testified that twenty-eight were guilty. Monday Gell was called against forty-five defendants. He testified that thirty-two were guilty. These 70 percent rates of accusation hardly show indiscriminate determination to slaughter.[48]

Nor would a republican court have thrown out the Gell-Drayton testimony, as Bennett implied, because the two spent some time together and *might* have united on their stories. A key criterion of collaboration is whether stories in court are the same. Drayton and Gell testified against the same defendants thirty-one times. They agreed with each other seventeen times, disagreed fourteen times.[49] This supposedly united collaboration was disunited almost half the time. In the end, these uneasily despotic judges, in a time of extreme hysteria, acquitted almost half their defendants. Sixty-seven blacks were convicted and sixty-four set free. Of those convicted, thirty-five were hanged, including Vesey, and thirty-two were banished from the state or the United States.[50]

Both the governor and the court, although possessing different degrees of uneasiness about a democratic state's excursion into tyranny, wanted the semidespotic process ended quickly. The court wished to convict ringleaders and to terrorize slaves of permissive masters. Then the judges wanted out of the despotism business. In late July, "conceiving that enough had been done to serve as an example," the original court decided "to pursue the investigation no further." Bennett, relieved, ordered no more hangings of conspirators who had been previously convicted. "I conceived that I consulted the best feelings of my fellow citizens," he wrote, "in arresting these dreaded punishments, which were becoming but too familiar, ceased to produce a salutary terror, no longer served for example, and at which humanity wept."[51] Both a despotic court, struggling to provide somewhat democratic trials, and a democratic governor, eager for pretrial despotism, were delighted once again to divide public democracy from private despotism at masters' property line.

8

Governor Bennett's special message at the end of the year asked the state legislature to condemn the judges and to protect future black defendants. But 1822 was not Governor Bennett's year. The governor who had lost control over both his household and the court system had no control over the legislature. South Carolina legislators voted 80–35 to table Bennett's message without printing it. The court stood vindicated.[52]

The victory did not last. Eleven years later, South Carolina's governor urged reform of the slave codes. The reforming governor was none other than Robert Y. Hayne, the attorney general back in 1822 who had instructed Governor Bennett that black defendants had no legal rights. "While rigid discipline should be enforced," Hayne wrote to the legislature in 1833, "the law ought . . . to afford complete protection" against injustice. In response, the legislature authorized blacks to appeal in capital cases from a Court of Magistrates and Freeholders to the state's regular circuit court. That court could return the case to another freeholders court for retrial. Trial judges would never be regular judges. A jury would never be involved. But at least the circuit court, responsible for white justice, could check injustice to blacks.[53]

Still, Bennett's was but a partial victory. He wanted democratic trials, not yet more despotic trials. His semitriumph also came late. Why should eleven years have transpired before South Carolina insisted that despotic judges must be scrupulous or else new despotic judges must be appointed? After all, the Vesey court had agreed that scrupulous procedures must be part of the most despotic trial. The governor and judges had also agreed that massive hangings and a nightly deployment of armed horsemen would prevent another slave conspiracy. They were right. Nothing like the Vesey conspiracy recurred in antebellum Charleston. Why, then, did Charlestonians remain too nervous to nudge the democratic state away from dictatorial practices until a decade had passed?

That single instance when Vesey's judges censored their unpublished record provides the answer—and illuminates the slaves' most effective way of invalidating slaveholder paternalism. Here are the forbidden words in the court's manuscript record: Convicted conspirator Harry Haig told the court that Gullah Jack "was going to give me *a bottle with poison to put into my master's pump & into as many pumps he could about town & he said he would give other bottles to those he could trust to*" (words censored for publication are italicized).[54]

There it was, in thirty-three unpublishable words: the peculiar nightmare of a Domestic Institution. The court censored nothing about proposed *group* raids on arsenals. But testimony that an *individual* domestic might slip poison into a household's water was too terrifying to be published. Stealthful domestic poison was the unpublishable danger because it suggested Vesey's second and more ominous test of Sambo's credibility. Vesey's main conception, raiding arsenals and then seeing how deep fidelity ran, could easily be combated. A nightly mounted patrol could guard against the surprise attack of several dozen slaves armed only with pikes. The lesson of Denmark Vesey, not least to slaves, was that whites could slaughter a group of rebels as long as officials bothered to guard the rifles.

But the individual household assassin hiding behind an accommodationist's mask, like the individual runaway dashing toward freedom, did not risk Vesey's collective vulnerability. The solitary servile who sneaked poison into the drinking water need not worry about guns versus pikes. The man acting alone need not tremble that any of two dozen co-conspirators might betray him. The solitary rebel need have no concern about wide-awake troops outside the slumbering house. And when "his" white family started dying like flies, he could be all weepy solicitude, full of wonder about what strange sickness ailed master's house.

The sleeping household, unable to guard against a solitary "family friend," was even more vulnerable to a single fake Sambo's resistance when one other fake Sambo provided the means of murder. A conspiracy of two slaves was less vulnerable to betrayal than was a conspiracy of two dozen. Two slaves who murdered inside the house were also less vulnerable to white patrols than was a gang of slaves who massed outside the doors. A *Domestic* Institution was peculiarly vulnerable, physically and psychologically, to a pair of trusted household servants who would rather slay a would-be paternalist than validate his paternalism. The point is crucial: At this moment of one of the Old South's largest collective slave plots to seize control of the streets, a tiny domestic side plot was the unmentionable horror.

Given the unpublishable fright of the non-Sambo who would poison *his* (white) family, the democratic state had to hold despotic deterrence at the ready. Harry Haig's master could not alone protect the Haig household if Mr. Pritchard's uncontrolled Gullah Jack gave Harry vials of poison. The public state had to smash the slaves if a trusting paternalist such as Thomas Bennett allowed his neighbor's wells to be secretly polluted. As James Hamilton, Jr., intendant of Charleston, summed up the case against Thomas Bennett's liberalism, no scruple should block the state from teaching black would-be murderers that "there is nothing they are bad enough to do that we are not powerful enough to punish."[55]

Hamilton's was the quote of the year in South Carolina, the perfect answer to Denmark Vesey's antipaternalistic reality, the perfect response to Thomas Bennett's soft paternalism. All slaveholders elsewhere in the New World would have applauded it in this or any other year. But as the permanent basis of this peculiar U.S. regime, Hamilton's phrase was as repulsive as Rolla Bennett's Samboism. A white men's democratic state prostituted its essence by seizing the role of undemocratic terrorizer of blacks. The paternalist of a Domestic Institution abdicated his responsibility by allowing a government outside his gates to terrorize inside his house. To make any sense of this motley democratic/dictatorial system, the private familial absolutist, not the public democratic state, had to show *his* "boys" that *he* was powerful enough to punish anything they were childish enough to try. Not a democratic state over whites but a benevolent paternalist over blacks must coerce each slave into consenting to be Sambo.

Over many years, Charleston's Domestic Institution edged back toward that uneasy normality. Blacks' performances in the Sambo charade were said to be more credible than ever. Denmark Vesey's antipaternalistic reality, however, forever threw uncertain shadows over the credibility of the charade. An individual "family friend" as a rapist of daughters, as a poisoner of wells, as a slitter of master's guts—this flickered in the imagination, on dark and windswept nights, before echoes of Thomas Bennett's invincible faith and hoofbeats of the nightly patrol drove the specters back over the far edges of consciousness. That was the burden of paternalists who lost their way without each slave's consent—and who never again could altogether trust every Sambo's affirmation.

4 / Defective Paternalism: James Henley Thornwell's Mysterious Antislavery Moment

Thanks largely to an excellent critique by Eugene Genovese, I have slightly revised this analysis of the interconnections between southern slavery, Christianity, and politics, originally published as "James Henley Thornwell's Mysterious Antislavery Moment" in the Journal of Southern History *in 1991.[1] The essay focuses on another problem with supposedly paternalistic slavery, beyond the slaves' frequent refusal to validate their masters' paternalism. Assuming, went this additional question, masters' paternalism alone made slavery right, was the institution wrong—and should the state at least partially abolish it—if slaveholders deviated from paternalism? The Reverend James Henley Thornwell faced that question earlier and more creatively than any other slaveholding defender of paternalism. That prescience about defective paternalism—the precocious timing of Thornwell's antislavery moment and the precocious talent he showered on his early formulation— is the mystery about this greatest of proslavery clerics. To solve that mystery, one must turn to biographical data. No more fascinating a connection between biographical background and creative flowering can be found in American intellectual history.*

But nothing was peculiar to Thornwell, or mysterious, about his contention that the state must at least partially abolish slavery if many masters remained antipaternalistic and thus anti-Christ. That implication, commonplace in clergymen's defense of slavery, shows that proslavery was more a call to achieve Christian paternalism than a celebration of paternalism achieved. The resulting question tormented Thornwell sooner than any other

59

proslavery cleric: Was merely potential paternalism enough to ease Jehovah's wrath?

I discovered Thornwell's answer at the American Antiquarian Society, an underappreciated treasure house of antebellum slavery materials. I presented an early account of my discovery at a Tulane University history seminar, where Blake Touchstone, Bill McClay, Lawrence Powell, and Clarence Mohr were particularly constructive critics. I also benefited from a helpful correspondence with James Farmer and from fine conversations with Jack Maddex. I was fortunate that the Journal of Southern History first published the essay, for John Boles gave it especially scrupulous editorial care. I am grateful to the journal for permission to publish this revised version.

Although the mysterious episode concerned only one man's momentary speculation, his fleeting thought posed one of the Old South's most intriguing, revealing puzzles. How could the Reverend James Henley Thornwell, perhaps the slavocracy's most impressive proslavery intellectual and assuredly one of South Carolina's most prestigious Unionists, have chosen the moment of disunion to consider gradually abolishing masters' absolute power?[2]

The unusual timing stemmed from the Presbyterian theologian's unusual personal history. But timing aside, Thornwell's antislavery moment was a natural outcome of the conventional evangelical proslavery position. The tale of how and why the Slave South's gravest political crisis temporarily unnerved the regime's most important clerical defender reveals much about the skittish nature of South Carolina's opposition to disunion—and about the complicated nature of clergymen's argument for the South's supposedly paternalistic version of slavery.

The defense of slavery was no simplistic rationalization of a "positive good," not at least as written by the most sophisticated dialecticians. Rather, the best proslavery theorists, like most important American thinkers, devised fresh definitions and designs at a difficult level of abstraction.[3] Nor was the proslavery argument some celebration of what all Southerners already believed and practiced, not at least as written by the most worried moralists. Rather, abstract defenders of slaveholder paternalism feared that too many slaveholders failed to understand and/or practice the paternalistic creed. Particularly James Henley Thornwell, preacher to slaveholders, worried that his failure to win more converts raised questions about his audience's convictions and behavior—and thus about southern masters' Christian legitimacy.

Thornwell was the antebellum South's greatest theological abstractionist. But he was neither the original designer nor the supreme popularizer of evangelical proslavery dialectics. He instead took up slaveholders' key religious defense, analyzed its ambiguities with unprecedented depth, faced its antislavery possibilities with unusual honesty, and explained aspiring paternalists' unmet obligations with uncommon clarity.[4] His essays offer an intellectual adventure, for he explored clergymen's compunctions about secular absolute power to the edge of heresy and then finessed the danger. But for that brief moment in 1860, his logic could not relieve his qualms. The same uneasiness, three years into the Civil War, would impel widespread clerical demands for partial abolition of masters' power.

1

What enabled James Henley Thornwell to become the most prescient member of his intellectual school? The answer, as usual with such a question, involves in part a genius's innate talents—a genetic outcome that no mere historian can explain. But in addition to Thornwell's unrivaled gifts, a singular youthful trauma lent his proslavery essays their anxious precociousness. As a boy, Thornwell suddenly became an unusually vulnerable dependent, apparently adrift in a disordered world without paternal protection. He then became something seemingly more liberating but ultimately more suffocating: the perfect ward of the imperfect paternalist. To secure his Christian rights, the orphan had to teach his protector that paternalistic power must be abolished unless the paternalist observed Christian limits.

This eventual defender and moral teacher of the upper class was to the lower class born. His father, an impoverished South Carolina overseer, died in 1820 when Thornwell was eight. The hapless survivors included a mother trained only for the household, two sisters scarcely trained at all, an infant brother, and the eight-year-old patriarch, a frail and retiring youth. A witness reported that James Henley Thornwell, after standing over his father's corpse, wondered aloud, *"What will mother do? What will become of us?"*[5] The question pointed to a fearful imagined world, a realm of fierce competition between powerful white males, with weaker folk ground under in the chaos.

That would remain Thornwell's image of England and the North. But he found South Carolina to be something mercifully else: a society of hierarchy, of roles and responsibilities, of the strong aiding the weak. The family provided the first southern defense against savage competition. Thornwell's first protector, a middle-class cousin, epitomized the ideal by providing the bereaved clan with a nearby cabin. There the widow earned pennies by sewing and the eight-year-old attracted attention as a child prodigy. While husky lads played at rough sport, the diminutive Thornwell studied. While the less bookish slept, the pale scholar read deep into the night, despite the miserable light in the shabby dwelling.

The southern hierarchy for protecting orphans radiated out from the family to the school, and a teacher, proud of his prize pupil, soon replaced the cousin as the boy's provider. Then when Thornwell entered on his teenage years, his schoolboy reputation captured the attention of William H. Robbins, a Northerner come South to be a lawyer. Robbins unofficially adopted Thornwell, treated the adolescent as a younger brother, and eventually moved his ward's little bed to the foot of his commodious bedstead. Another wealthy gentleman, James Gillespie, equally endowed with a patriarch's sense of obligation for the unfortunate, helped Robbins finance Thornwell's preparatory and college education.

The white dependent regarded William Robbins with a troubled version of the untroubled gratitude that slaveholders hoped to receive from black dependents. Planters especially cherished the homecoming or departure scene, whereby weeping slaves supposedly demonstrated that the paternalist had been or would be sorely missed. The scene played best when dependents genuinely cherished the benefactor. Thornwell shrank from a parallel tableau one day, when Robbins temporarily left home. "You ask where I betook myself on the morning of your departure," Thornwell, then sixteen, wrote to Robbins, whom he habitually addressed as "my dear patron." The orphan explained that he could not publicly "shake hands" before Robbins stepped aboard the departing stagecoach, for Thornwell would have "broken forth there into childish lamentations" and become "an object of derision." Thornwell wished that "I could obtain a proper control of myself on such occasions. If I grieve at a temporary parting, what would be my feelings at a lasting separation?"[6]

A few months earlier, a grieving Thornwell, alarmed about the psychological peril in such dependency, had almost fled from Robbins. In the manner of the rebellious teenager, the orphan had bridled at the prospect of becoming the provider's abject puppet. Robbins wanted Thornwell to become a lawyer—to become just like him. Thornwell instead aspired to be a clergyman. The precocious seeker's aspiration surely involved a Christian's call to Christ. The calling may also have involved an ambitious dependent's way to become moral judge of the patriarch.

The showdown came in an excruciating scene. Thornwell, unable to confront his patron, wrote a letter. Robbins found it under his plate at tea. "I am incapable of speaking to you on the delicate subject without tears," the shocked paternalist read, for "the relation which has hitherto subsisted between us is now to be dissolved." Why must Thornwell "bid farewell, with great heaviness of heart, to a beloved patron, who kindly clothed me when naked, fed me when hungry, and, above all, has much labored to dispel ignorance from my mind"? Because the ward could not "reconcile my conscience to the practice of the Law." He must be a theologian, for "the glory of God and the good of men." He could not in conscience accept Robbins's largesse while defying him. So he must bid his defective paternalist farewell. "On the word, farewell, my heart lingers, with reluctance to leave you; and, oh! to think of parting pricks it to the core. But it must be; so farewell, my dear friend and respected patron."[7]

Robbins instantly repented. A true paternalist, he realized, must not annihilate a dependent's will or block a Christian's destiny. Robbins found Thornwell huddled on the porch, crying bitterly. Embracing the would-be cleric, the guardian assented to the theological venture.[8] Thornwell had reached the last stage of his journey from the disorder and dependency afflicting the vulnerable orphan toward the independence of the evangelist who aspired to teach a ruling class how—and when not to enslave.

South Carolina's institutions provided Thornwell's final ladder to the top. As an undergraduate at South Carolina College, his reputation as prodigy flared statewide. After three postgraduate years as teacher at Cheraw Preparatory Academy, he entered a year's training for the Presbyterian ministry. Remote South Carolina upcountry pastorates followed, then a call to teach at South Carolina College, then important pastorates in Columbia and Charleston, then the presidency of South Carolina College, and then his favorite post, a chair at the Columbia (South Carolina) Theological Seminary.

The world beyond the state's boundaries always disappointed

and often scandalized the theologian. Thornwell considered the atmosphere at Harvard godless, the capitalism in Liverpool pitiless.[9] When this former orphan called South Carolina, in the conventional phrase, his "Mother," the word was a prayer of thanks.

He was thankful most for theological opportunities, but not a little for earthly luxuries. Like many of those early deprived, Thornwell developed finicky, passionate tastes for the best clothes, the best wines, the best horses. The fastidious connoisseur could usually be seen through the smoky haze of the best cigars, persistently coughing, slight, frail, sallow, stoop-shouldered, with a long, grim face and an eerie drooping eyelid.[10]

His friends and family swore that the brooding theologian could be a merry fellow, even a practical joker. But nothing of the trickster invaded Thornwell's intellectual life. He loathed novels. He savored Presbyterian disputation. As a parish parson and teacher of undergraduates, he was slightly uncomfortable. As a theological scholar and director of graduate students, he was supremely confident. He dedicated his mind and life to Jesus Christ— and to the South Carolina social order, which, if it worked for slaves as it had worked for him, would join the church as the mother of salvation for dependents of all colors.

2

He never wrote a book on proslavery theology, just a few sermons, individually published. These gems commence at the Presbyterian starting place, with the precise words of the Bible. Just as John C. Calhoun insisted on a literal interpretation of the Constitution, so Thornwell seized onto every syllable of Scripture. "Beyond the Bible," warned Thornwell, the church "can never go." The only acceptable "argument is, *thus it is written.*"[11]

Slavery was written into the Bible, noted Thornwell. Old Testament heroes, such as Abraham, owned slaves. New Testament saints, critical of all earthly sin, never condemned the institution. Instead the Messiah and his disciples blessed servitude in Thornwell's favorite scriptural passage: "Masters give unto your servants that which is just and equal, knowing that ye also have a Master in Heaven."[12]

Abolitionists answered that "servants" did not need to be translated as "slaves." But linguistic parsing could not hide the literal facts. Many "servants" in biblical times were property for life, as were their offspring, and Christ never cried shame. Since

Thornwell and his fellow clerics thrived on this literal interpretation of Scripture, their opponents denied that linguistic technicalities should decide a moral debate. In the manner of nationalists who would interpret the Constitution broadly, antislavery clerics emphasized the spirit, not the picky words, of the inherited text. Slavery, Northerners declared, violated the spirit of Christianity, especially the spirit of the Golden Rule. Did slaveholders, having enslaved others, wish others to enslave them?

Proslavery writers responded with that treasured scriptural sentence: "Masters give unto your servants that which is just and equal." Christ here sanctioned a relationship between superiors and inferiors, even though he knew that masters did not wish to be servants. The Golden Rule thus hardly demanded that mastery must be abolished unless masters wished to be enslaved. The Golden Rule instead requires us, explained Thornwell, to "treat our slaves as we should feel that we had a right to be treated if we were slaves ourselves."[13]

This exegesis of the Golden Rule, common among southern clergymen, highlighted, for Thornwell, the issue between North and South. The South stood for superiors caring for inferiors, as the most able would wish to be cared for if they were the least able. The North stood for war on hierarchy, with the most powerful bearing no responsibility except for their selfish advancement. The South stood for the responsibility of the William Robbinses to provide benign order for fatherless orphans. The North stood for thrusting a terrified eight-year-old into the social disorder of all against all. As usual, remembered personal pain charged Thornwell's impersonal prose: At issue is "not simply whether we shall emancipate our negroes." The parties "are not merely abolitionists and slaveholders—they are atheists, socialists, communists, red republicans, jacobins on the one side, and the friends of order and regulated freedom on the other."[14]

But social order was not enough, Thornwell continued. Roles and responsibilities must be carried out in the Christian manner, as God directed in the Bible. That treasured scriptural line obligated masters to give slaves "that which is just and equal, knowing that ye also have a Master in Heaven." The Bible thus provided "the *true impregnable position of the Christian Slaveholder*," but "only when he obeys its directions as well as employs its sanctions. Our rights are there established, but it is always in connection with our duties; if we neglect the one, we cannot make good the other."[15]

James Henley Thornwell did not here win the biblical argument for the slaveholders. He defined the conditions under which the argument could be won. If slaveholders treated their slaves justly and equally, meaning as masters would wish to be treated if they were slaves, the regime's Christian position was invincible. But if slaves were treated as no potential Christian ought to be treated, God would scourge his slaveholders. The life-and-death question thus became, were masters Christian enough to earn scriptural—and Jehovah's—sanction?

3

James Henley Thornwell would have relished a sanguine answer. He believed that southern paternalists, infused with the ethic of organic society, lived up to Christian responsibility more than did northern employers, infatuated with the cult of selfish individualism. He also considered the slaveholders' physical brutality too exceptional to be relevant. He conceived, however, that psychological brutality was fearfully omnipresent. He loathed slaveholders for too often selling slave husband from wife, children from parents. Thornwell also despised masters who would not allow ministers to bring the Word to blacks. Nor could this Presbyterian sanction the more numerous masters who allowed preaching but would not permit their people to read the Bible. With no guarantee of Christian wedlock, no assurance that Christian salvation would be orally offered, massive hindrance to reading the Word, absolute secular power devastated too many slaves' Christian rights.[16]

Secular devastation at its most extreme, warned Thornwell, produced abject Sambo, denuded of will and spirit. Thornwell could bear to describe the appalling servile only in Latin: *"Obedientia fracti animi et abjecti, et arbitrio carentis suo"* ("The obedience of a broken and downcast mind, lacking even its own free will or judgment").[17] As an adolescent, Thornwell had rebelled against that potential obliteration of his own will. As a mature theologian and evangelical preacher, he the more squirmed at an anti-Christian travesty: willful men reduced to will-less robots. God's power to direct man's salvation already arguably mocked man's power to choose Christ. But heap on an abject Sambo, psychologically annihilated by his master's total power, and you have the will-less wafer, with no soul left for God or preacher to summon.

Thornwell here seemed to concede the abolitionists' main point: that absolute power crushed the Christian spirit. The South

Carolinian pushed his apparent concession perilously far. He acknowledged that slavery, as customarily defined, was illegitimate. Slavery supposedly meant ownership of body *and* soul, one man's absolute power over another's willpower. But "the absorption of the humanity of one individual into the will and power of another" was "an outrage upon humanity."[18]

At this hazardous juncture, Thornwell suddenly broke free from absolute power as outrage, free from Sambo, and free from his apparently suicidal concession to abolitionists. His mode of escape was a stunning definition of slavery. A master purchasing a slave, Thornwell claimed, purchased only the servile's labor, no less but absolutely no more. Slavery, he urged, could never legitimately go beyond "the obligation to labour for another."[19] This definition, giving masters only the right to a decent day's work, was not Thornwell's invention. He had picked up a definition fairly common among southern proslavery evangelicals, one they picked up from the early nineteenth-century English moralist, William Paley.[20] The Paley definition first reached the American center stage in the 1845 published debate between South Carolina/Maryland cleric Richard Fuller and Francis Wayland, president of Brown University in Rhode Island. When Fuller insisted on the Paley definition of slavery as limited to the workplace, Wayland retorted that absolute right to secure labor must include absolute power to overwhelm the will of recalcitrant laborers.[21]

Richard Fuller responded, and Thornwell agreed, that slaves would work as willingly as free laborers, assuming slaveholders avoided anti-Christian demands and bestowed Christian care. But Thornwell transcended Fuller and other clerics in making restricted slavery, Paley-style, the basis for routing abolitionists on the pivotal spirit-of-Christianity issue. Since masters, reasoned Thornwell, had bought a claim "not to the *man* but to his *labour*,"[22] they had purchased no power over Christian life after the laboring day. Slaveholders had not bought—no man could purchase with mammon's coin—the right to destroy Christian families, or the right to bar humans from learning to read the Holy Book, or the right to ban Christ's ministers from preaching to the heathen. In just the same way, the teenage Thornwell had denied William Robbins's right to interfere with a ward's theological training.

By limiting slaveholders' sway strictly to the workplace, Thornwell confined absolute authority to congenial terrain. Again in advance of other preachers, he placed unusual clerical emphasis on the Virginian George Fitzhugh's secular argument: that "free hirelings" were more miserably enslaved than were purchased bondsmen. Thornwell described a penniless "free laborer" as "a petitioner for a master." A would-be hireling had to seek a temporary employer, who might pay a pittance now, but nothing all too soon. Such a "wage slave's" family was in graver danger than that of an owned slave, for unemployment, poverty, and starvation broke up more marriages than did slave sellers.[23]

In one climactic sermon, Thornwell took Fitzhugh's class proslavery argument as far as it could go. Under southern slavery, declared Thornwell, "the master must always find work for his slave, as well as food and raiment." In a free-labor system, however, a "multiplication of laborers not only reduces wages to the lowest point, but leaves multitudes wholly unemployed." At some point, warned Thornwell, starving hirelings "will rise in desperation against a social order which dooms them to nakedness and famine." Southerners, not wishing to see such wild disorder, prefer that "organization of labor which Providence has given us in slavery."[24]

Still, for all his belief that slave owners surpassed employers in protecting the lower class, and for all this ex-orphan's dismay about unprotected dependents, Thornwell, like Fitzhugh, opposed slavery for American whites. Thornwell, ever the theorist of roles and responsibilities, conceived that God had not suited whites for a slave's role. "The free citizen of England and America," he explained, "could not endure the condition of African bondage—it would defeat his individual development." But "subjection to a master" is "the state in which the African is most effectually trained to the moral end of his being," assuming masters allowed slaves to be trained in Christianity.[25]

Having elsewhere made class relations a critical basis for enslaving an underclass, Thornwell here made race relations more critical and Christian training more critical still. If Southerners have "anything" to "fear," warned Thornwell, "it is the frown of Divine Providence for our neglecting the duty of soundly instructing our slaves in His truth." Let no man dare "hoist a black flag, an anti-Christian banner, against the improvement of this race." If we thus "array the Bible against our social economy, then our social economy must fall. Nothing ever yet stood up long against Christianity."[26]

In standing up for a Christian viewpoint, Thornwell scuttled the secular notion that slavery was "a good—a blessing." Rather, slavery sprang "from the nature of man as sinful, and the nature of society as disordered." Such a "natural evil" could be justified only as an effective "punishment" for Adam's "crime" and as "an effective, spiritual discipline." Considering "the diversities in moral position, which sin has been the means of entailing upon the [black] race," ran Thornwell's revealingly guarded conclusion, "we may be justified in affirming that, relatively to some persons and to some times, slavery may be a good, or to speak more accurately, a condition, though founded in a curse, from which the Providence of God extracts a blessing."[27] The question remained whether clergymen could reform the slavocracy so that the blessings of slave Christianity could be more broadly extracted.

4

When ruling Latin America, European authorities often empowered colonial clerics to jail anti-Christian masters. In the United States, republican codes repelled such a union of church and state. Preachers possessed only a citizen's democratic power: to persuade. Yet southern evangelical persuasion, because omnipresent, may have been more powerful than Latin American clerical coercion, because seldom used. In the mid-nineteenth-century United States, spoken words moved multitudes, as Christian revivalists' triumphs demonstrated. Between revivals, sometimes in opposition to proceedings under the revival tent, the established ministry pounded home Christian virtues, Sabbath after Sabbath, to congregants shuddering at eternal damnation.

Such wars against Satan transformed the slavery controversy. In the 1830s, northern revivalism inspired antislavery zealots; and from the mid-1840s onward, southern evangelicalism engendered proslavery answers. Southern clerics' proslavery tracts usually started as famous sermons, sometimes as renowned classroom lectures. Such publications usually stressed slaveholders' biblical duties. No sanctified patriarch could beat his people unmercifully, or break up slave marriages unconscionably, or bar blacks from Christ's Word.[28]

Ministers' sermons on masters' duties, although telling in print, possessed greater power in biracial churches. White preachers sometimes gathered blacks in segregated meetings to receive a message tailored exclusively for serviles. More often, evangelicals assembled whites and blacks together to hear a message aimed at both. The characteristic sermon stressed that slaves must serve truly Christian masters gratefully and that slaveholders must command truly Christian slaves paternalistically. The preacher, Christ's mediator, must ensure that paternalists and wards met their mutual obligations.

This sermon was partly about empowerment, the empowering of the minister to govern the paternalistic relationship. By calling slavery potentially a biblically sanctioned institution, proslavery preachers established their credentials as loyal Southerners. These patriots thus secured legitimacy to preach that antipaternalistic sins violated providential potentialities. In this ministerial role lies one answer to that recurring question, what did proslavery writers seek when defending the establishment? Clerics, who wrote the majority of proslavery tracts, were hardly lay intellectuals seeking secular notoriety or political power. Although they coveted earthly influence no less than did government leaders, their sacred circle was in another kingdom.[29] Their gospel was that slavery would become scripturally justified if slaveholders and slaves would act as preachers or, rather, as the Bible commanded.[30]

Historians cannot determine what percentage of antebellum slaveholders responded altogether as Christians should, by repudiating antipaternalistic sins. We know that an increasing number of masters allowed white ministers increasing access to the quarters.[31] But posterity again cannot know what percentage of slaves these preachers converted. True, many historians currently suppose that blacks always dozed while masters' favorite evangelicals preached on obedience and then eagerly responded when blacks preached African-American Christianity. That partially true image adds an important chapter to the history of American Christianity. A black theology did develop, with African religious traits incorporated. That development helps explain why ex-slaves poured out of white churches and into black ones, as soon as northern armies allowed widespread choice.[32]

Choice, however, was less widespread under slavery, which was a critical reason the Thornwells *did* convert an increasing number of slaves. Blacks lived mostly in scattered rural outposts. When serviles roamed to concentrated black gatherings, they were sometimes arrested. White patrolmen also sometimes broke up wholly black meetings. The resulting African-American services often had to be hushed affairs, the more passionate because illicit, but also the less pervasive.

Black participation in white churches, on the other hand, was increasingly easy—and could somewhat enrich black life. Black worshipers could effect that partial benefit, for they had some power over white preachers: precisely the power to sleep. If ministers droned on about "slaves, obey thy masters," blacks could and did yawn. Such spiritual inertia stung evangelical ministers.[33] Masters might wish mindless servility, but revivalists demanded impassioned conversion. The bottom line, in clerical proslavery, was that God brought supposedly heathenish Africans to America not to give abject service but to become aroused Christians.

Revivalists personally cared about those potential black converts. Bondsmen up in the balcony were intimately known parishioners, occasionally the preachers' own slaves, sometimes a favorite body servant. "I am greatly delighted to hear that things are going on so well in the church," Thornwell wrote his wife in 1860. "The work among the negroes is one in which I feel a special interest, and I do sincerely pray that Charles [Thornwell's body servant] may be led to the knowledge of true religion."[34]

In exhorting blacks to embrace true religion, ministers were hardly restricted to corpse-cold homilies on mindless obedience. Slaves' characteristic modes of day-to-day disobedience—thieving, lying, sabotaging, and so forth—all arguably involved Christian sins. The minister's most powerful message was that salvation, with blacks as with whites, involved renouncing such alleged sins, trading behavior that supposedly ought to shame any Christian for an ecstatic embrace of Christ.

Conversion offered the downtrodden more than religious exaltation, more than equality with masters in life after earth. Preachers also enticed slaves with talk of a better earthly condition. Before the northern antislavery assault of the 1830s, southern divines sometimes told masters and slaves that slavery should be abolished. Later, a more circumspect clergy offered slaves less than calls for freedom but more than justifications of subjection. Evangelical mediators urged that slave marriages and religion, cherished commodities in the quarters, should be protected.

Black members of white churches received a little more protection than ministers' words. In evangelical congregations, sinning parishioners, including masters, could be hauled before the membership, tried and censored, even excommunicated. Black members of the church could sometimes participate in these white interrogations. A very few even testified against masters. Nowhere else in southern life were slaves so empowered.

Let us neither exaggerate nor forget the limited power of the slave. Black members of white churches usually had to sit in the balcony. These second-class members exceedingly rarely secured their masters' conviction in church courts. But white churches offered slaves a little solace, a bit of power, a speck of color-blind religious brotherhood, and the sublime conversion experience. Converted nineteenth-century slaves thus understandably joined white congregations in increasing numbers, adding another important chapter to the history of American Christianity. That chapter clarifies why Thornwell honestly believed that slavery *was* becoming more Christian, that masters *were* becoming more paternalistic, and that evangelicals *were* bringing the Word to more blacks all the time.[35]

But some masters continued to block the Christian revival. Some slaveholders never came to church, or *they* slept through sermons. Some slaves were never permitted to hear a preacher; more were never allowed to read the Bible; and still more dreaded that their master might sell them away from their families. With sermons but a partial success, and with partial failure a Christian disaster, Thornwell and his fellow clerics turned, as Latin American priests had before them, to the coercive state. They could not become government bureaucrats, themselves coercive guarantors of slaves' Christian rights. In the United States, church and state had to be separated. But as private citizens, clergymen asked the state to accomplish what sermons could not—guarantee slaves the possibility of a Christian life.

In 1847, Thornwell's plea for state-guaranteed access to Christianity reached its climax. He chaired a committee of the South Carolina Presbyterian Synod, charged with writing a petition to the state legislature. "We shall probably recommend," he reported, "that a law may be enacted, to protect the family relations of the slave; and that the disgraceful statute, which prevents them from learning to read, may be repealed."[36]

Thornwell publicly championed these reforms in the late 1840s. Until "the real rights of the slave . . . are defined by law and enforced by penalties," he declared, "there is no adequate protection." Historically, "nothing in the relation itself" had been "inconsistent with this legal protection." Romans legalized slaves' "right to acquire knowledge." Spanish law "formally protected" the slave family. Southern laws guaranteed slaves adequate nourishment. Slaves' spiritual sustenance also required guarantees. "The injustice of denying to them food, . . . against which the law effectually guards, is nothing to the injustice of defrauding them of that bread which cometh down from Heaven."[37]

Thornwell's governmental antidote to slaveholders' injustice would legalize William Paley's definition of slavery. After the workday, no slaveholders would be allowed to subvert slave marriages or inhibit blacks' willful pursuit of Christ. Thornwell's horror creature, will-less Sambo, would no longer be seen in the quarters. "Legal protection" would counteract "servility and abjectness of mind. It would inspire a sense of personal responsibility—a certain degree of manliness and dignity of character. . . . The meanness, cunning, hypocrisy, lying and theft, which accompany a sense of degradation, would give" way to the Christian responsibility of the free agent who chose Christ.[38]

This wish that government would dilute masters' absolute power seemed to collide with another of Thornwell's verities: that government, being made up of sinning humans, must not tamper with God-given organic societies. But Thornwell saw nothing God-given about secular authority to obliterate Christ. "It is no part of the essence of slavery," he declared in an amazing sentence, "that the rights of the slave should be left to the caprice or to the interest of the master."[39] A Christian slave society must protect slaves' right to learn and practice Christianity. "Were it true," he went so far as to say, "that the religious instruction of this [slave] population is inconsistent with" slaveholders' secular power over the workplace, "there would still be no alternative for those who acknowledge Christ for their master."[40]

No Thornwell exclamation more impoliticly pitted the church against the slaveholders. Masters customarily called their sins "incidental" evils within a basically Christian system. But no candid theologian could minimize as "incidental" such Christian atrocities as depriving sinners of salvation or ripping apart slave families for slaveholder profit. Until 1863, few clerics dared enunciate a natural conclusion: that unless anti-Christian abominations could be excised, slaves ought to be at least partially emancipated. But the bolder Thornwell earlier went the whole distance: Crimes against Christian marriage and education must be outlawed, even assuming (and Thornwell denied the assumption) that the outlawing would necessarily lead to total abolition.

Most masters deplored that formulation. Their sins, they insisted, were incidental, not damning. William Paley, they were sure, misdefined slavery. The "essence of slavery," Thornwell to the contrary, was precisely dominion over the whole man, body *and* soul. *They* must decide when and whether to sell their slaves, even if that meant breaking up black families. *They* must decide whether teaching slaves to read was compatible with social order, even if Bible-parsing ministers objected. *They* must decide whether white clerics could safely preach to their slaves, even if preachers insisted that Christianity was benign. *They* must decide all things for the transcendent secular proslavery reason: because men who absolutely control human property will treat it selflessly, as all family patriarchs benignly treat all their kin and possessions.

Clerics could not be *that* euphoric about a purely secular solution to humanity's selfishness. Materialists who thought that the right arrangements between classes could altogether rout the consequences of Adam's fall, preachers scoffed, did not take Christianity seriously enough. Only Christ, operating through his clergymen, could transform selfish sinners into selfless saints. Although nothing could force sinning antipaternalists to hear the Word, the state could at least force unrepentant slaveholders to abdicate their power to bar Christ from the quarters.

Slaveholders scorned abdication, and their defiance exposed Thornwell's tactical dilemma. To achieve his only power over slaveholders, the ability to convince in evangelical sermons, a preacher had to be seen as a loyal Southerner, a believer in the system. But his persuasive powers might not sufficiently rout sin; and if he emphasized that slaveholders' spiritual crimes required state intervention, he might be seen as a disbeliever in the system. Then few slaveholders would listen sympathetically to his preaching.

The lay establishment's resistance to state reform thus forced clergymen to an unhappy choice. They could continue to insist on state intervention, thereby perhaps sacrificing the legitimacy to preach. Or they could drop political reform, thereby falling back on the perhaps inadequate power of the sermon. Proslavery evangelicals swiftly chose to stick to sermons. In addition to the very nature of their profession, the essential nature of their creed demanded that political reform be dropped if it led to convulsive controversy. At the center of Thornwell's personality, ever since his father's death, was a horror of a world without organic order. At the core of the clerical establishment, before and after Thornwell, was the desire to moralize an established hierarchy. If the establishment was going to dissolve into an angry war over proposed state-guaranteed Christianization, clerics would have to abort their proposal. They would have to rely on persuasive preaching to raise slaveholders' consciousness and thus to make slavery worth defending.

5

Ministers' surrender of state reform, without even a full-scale public debate, placed their salvation nervously on the line in every proslavery sermon. They were claiming God's support for a mortally flawed system. Now only their preachings—and God's mercy—could remove those damning flaws. Every slave converted thus became a sign that the system was scripturally justified—that God wished his ministers to defend an improving system. Every slaveholder who banned clerics from converting blacks was a sign that the system defied the Bible—and that God would curse the preacher who called the system Christian.

No clergyman scrutinized Jehovah's signs more uneasily than did James Henley Thornwell, for no proslavery theologian more obsessively believed that God visited the earth to punish him personally. In these visits, Thornwell believed, God tested him with afflictions, which only repentance could remove. On one occasion, for example, Thornwell reported that he "experienced a distressing [divine] visitation in the sudden illness of my wife. I feared that she was on the brink of the grave." Thus "deeply humbled under a heavy sense of my ingratitude to God for so sweet a gift," he knew "that I most richly deserved some decided manifestation of God's displeasure." By repenting his sins and relying on God's "grace, I trust I formed the resolution of living more faithfully for the glory of God." And so God "spared her, and restored her to me again."[41]

In 1850–51, a more widespread divine visitation, so Thornwell believed, demanded repentance from Americans everywhere. In the aftermath of the Compromise of 1850, South Carolina came closer than any other state to seceding. South Carolina opponents of secession often warned that disunion could yield frightful disorder. Thornwell, ex-orphan, found the possibility especially appalling. The "prospect of disunion," Thornwell wrote in the midst of the crisis, caused him "absolute horror." A "peaceful dissolution" was "utterly impossible." The ensuing civil war would "be the bloodiest, most ferocious, and cruel, in the annals of history." Worse, "the attempt to construct" new southern governments, "in this age of tumults, agitation, and excitement, when socialism, communism, and a rabid mobocracy seem everywhere to be in the ascendant, will lead to the most dangerous experiments, the most disastrous schemes." Worst of all, amidst "the upheaving of society from its very foundations," what would happen to "schemes of the different churches for the conversion of the world?"[42]

Thornwell, "hardly . . . able to sleep," could see only one hope. God's "chastisements" might "bring us to acknowledge Him." Only "repentance on our part, and wonderful mercy on the part of God, can save us from the just consequences of our national sins."[43] The sins were precisely national. Thornwell interpreted God's visitation as a condemnation of both sections' iniquities. Northerners, having too often attacked the ideal of paternalistic responsibility, now meddled irresponsibly with the southern hierarchy. Slaveholders, having sometimes not lived up to a master's responsibilities, now irresponsibly might place Christian order at the mercy of revolutionary chaos. Until Yankees renounced their theory of selfish individualism, and until Southerners better served their theory of hierarchical obligations, God would have no mercy on a dissolving nation.

At midcentury, God surprised Thornwell by taking mercy on Americans. South Carolina disunionism crumbled. Union endured. But in the fall of 1860, God apparently visited again. Thornwell, traveling in Europe, heard from home that Abraham Lincoln seemed sure to be elected and South Carolina sure to secede. Thornwell considered revolutionary chaos all too likely to erupt. He exclaimed on the "shame it will be to forfeit, by our follies and our sins, the noble inheritance to which Providence has called us!"[44]

The formula for coping with disaster had never varied. God signaled his anger. Humans then must repent in hopes that a merciful God would relent. An especially threatening visitation required an especially sweeping repentance. In 1861, Thornwell told his good friend and eventual biographer, the renowned Presbyterian minister Benjamin M. Palmer, that during the previous year "whilst in Europe he had made up his mind to move, immediately upon his return [to South Carolina], for the gradual emancipation of the negro, as the only measure that would give peace to the country."[45]

Did Thornwell in fact say this to Palmer? The evidence is only Palmer's reminiscence, based on a conversation that Palmer reported only in his biography of Thornwell, published fourteen years later. Still, the Reverend Mr. Palmer was devoted to truth and to telling Thornwell's story accurately. A fabrication would have been out of character; and as for an unintentional invention, a trick of the memory—well, the statement Palmer reported is so stunning that it was more likely based on some striking remembered utterance. James O. Farmer, Jr., author of the latest and best Thornwell

biography, rightly doubts that Palmer "would be in error on a matter so out of step with his own views."[46]
One would be more inclined to distrust Palmer's memory if Thornwell's utterance seemed out of character. But the cleric's ongoing opinions made his reported 1860 thought exceedingly plausible. The South Carolina theologian had long been mortified by God's visitations, terrified especially of disunion, and thoroughly of the belief that Jehovah's angry signs required slaveholders to repent—not for being slaveholders per se but for spreading slavery illegitimately beyond William Paley's legitimate limits. A "gradual emancipation" had thus long been mandatory, now more than ever, what with God forcing a final choice between catastrophe or repentance.

Palmer never explained in his Thornwell biography, and perhaps Thornwell never told him, what was meant by "gradual emancipation." Thornwell assuredly did mean "gradual." This Christian conservative could never have abided hasty abolition. But how did he think, back there in Europe, that emancipation should gradually commence?

His previous position indicates the probable answer. He likely meant to begin—and maybe end—with his long-standing reform program. If the legislature protected slave marriages, slave literacy, slaves' right to worship under white preachers, slaves would be liberated from the masters' sway, per the William Paley definition, everywhere except in the workplace, where Thornwell thought supposedly free laborers were more exploited. Thornwell may not have intended to move on to abolish workplace slavery for blacks, not at least unless the state protected a supposedly inferior race against the excesses of a supposedly more exploitative free-labor system.

Perhaps by "gradual emancipation" Thornwell meant also that blacks, after being gradually Christianized, could be gradually prepared for full freedom in Africa. Many proslavery preachers, especially in the Upper South, prayed for ultimate emancipation, accompanied by African colonization, at some remote future time. These divines hoped that converted African Americans would eventually convert the entire Dark Continent.[47]

James Henley Thornwell had never before shared this most grandiose of southern evangelical dreams. Like most Lower South Presbyterians, he had instead guessed that slavery, like sin, would persist until the millennium.[48] If, while still in Europe in 1860,

Thornwell for the first time toyed with long-run emancipation and removal to Africa, he likely remained more committed to the very short-run abolition that he had always cherished: dependents partially liberated to follow a Christian destiny, as William Robbins had liberated an orphan to become a clergyman. Perhaps this was God's appointed time to convince the slavocracy that it should abolish secular authority to block Christianity after the workday.

6

James Henley Thornwell found instead, upon returning to South Carolina, that the secession crisis was the wrong time to convince the slavocracy of anything. Disunionists, by demanding that Unionists conform, deployed an intimidation that, while largely verbal, was as proscriptive as if it had been physical. In this ugly atmosphere, continued resistance to disunion, much less a renewed movement partially to abolish masters' absolute authority, might bring on worse disorder than disunion itself.

Ever since 1850, Thornwell's Unionism, like most South Carolinians', had been premised on horror of just this revolutionary chaos. Now, calm and order seemed easier to restore by getting out of the way of inescapable revolution. So Thornwell's projected campaign for Christianization disappeared without a trace in 1860 as it had in the late 1840s, and for the same reason. Fright about social uproar was the wrong psychology for the reformer, when his cause would inevitably convulse his civilization.

Fear of mobocratic disorder was also a counterproductive psychology for South Carolina Unionists. Disunionists, by insisting that opposition to disunion caused chaos, silenced lay Unionists such as U.S. Senator James Henry Hammond no less than clerical Unionists such as Thornwell.[49] In unusually aristocratic, especially deferential South Carolina, no cause could win without the important figures, and most shuddered at the prospect of extensive demagoguery and electioneering. South Carolina Unionism, which started 1860 with such important names as Hammond and Thornwell giving it strength, ended up the year with no important Unionist daring to whip up the public. Reluctant Southerners elsewhere, observing the collapse of opposition to the first secession, felt in the grip of an irreversible revolution.

In yet another way Thornwell helped accelerate disunion. The gospel of divine visitation left mere mortals not always sure of

God's intentions. Perhaps in 1860–61, Jehovah's fury was directed solely at fanatical Yankees. Then his preachers should join the revolution and in the joining make severance from the North orderly, constructive. Thornwell, when over in Europe, had thought of that option.[50] Once on Carolina turf, surrender quickly seemed his only choice.

To Thornwell's relief, God apparently signaled that his clergyman had correctly interpreted his intentions. The revolution came off calmly, with no demagogic disorder. Thornwell gave thanks in one of his greatest sermons, which featured one long release of bated breath. Jehovah, rejoiced the theologian, had smiled on his imperfect slavocracy and on his relieved minister.[51]

Thornwell died in 1862. He thus did not live to suffer the putative divine visitation of 1863, when battlefield results would turn decisively against the slavocracy. Proslavery clerics, proclaiming the argument that Thornwell had likely considered in Europe in 1860, would then urge that God assuredly now demanded repentance and partial abolition of absolute power. Unless southern governments abolished the masters' power to destroy slave marriages and prevent slave salvation, Jehovah would continue to send those conquering Yankee armies.[52]

During the last stages of the Civil War, proslavery ministers, in addition to pressing Thornwell-style partial abolition, would face up to Thornwell's premise: that slavery's evils, far from incidental blemishes on a Christian system, were mortal sins that, unless corrected, would damn the system. "I do not think," the important Georgia Baptist N. M. Crawford would declare, that the state, by outlawing slaveholders' abuses, would subvert their authority. "But if it is so, it presents an unanswerable argument" that "slavery is in itself, and not in its abuse, irreconcilably opposed to God's law." In that spirit, Georgia's Methodist Bishop George Foster Pierce would bluntly tell the Georgia legislature that "if the institution of slavery cannot be maintained except at the expense of the black man's immortal interests, . . . I say—*let it perish.*"[53]

By demanding that the legislature force masters to let either anti-Christ or slavery perish, Bishop Pierce brought into sharp focus the big question about Thornwell-style proslavery. Did clergymen's defense of slavery, hinged as it was on reforming slaveholder behavior, reflect the slaveholders' mentality or only the clerics'?[54] By blocking partial abolition of their power in 1863–64, as in the late 1840s, absolutists again answered that their preachers exaggerated their iniquity. For this latest time in the history of evangelical Christianity, the respondents' confessions disappointed the revivalists.

Still, previous transactions between clerical accusers and slaveholding congregations, Sabbath after Sabbath, year after year, indicated some shared feelings of shame. Slaveholders were not famous for listening to critics gladly. Those weekly sessions before the anxious bench indicated some receptiveness on the part of the slaveholding audience, some admission that secular absolute power had its immoral potentialities—its unspeakable actualities. A raw nerve must have been delicately brushed, which helps explain why ruder outside critics provoked such ferocious defensiveness, while gentler inside reformers inspired some ameliorated behavior.

Still, a degree of slaveholder amelioration could leave a wary distance between masters and preachers. Increasingly paternalistic owners could become increasingly immune to revivalists' increasingly shrill demand for admission of guilt, repentance, reform. Proslavery religion, the farthest thing from a facile celebration of an unadulterated blessing, had its layers and layers of complicated communication and meaning, with worried ministers and troubled paternalists not always finding common ground.[55]

James Henley Thornwell, had he been alive in 1863, would surely have cheered the clerics' bold new insistence that the state force paternalists to the highest Christian terrain, for he would have suffered, so he would have believed, a frightful punishment for his previous timidity. In 1863, a Yankee bullet killed Thornwell's soldier son.[56] James Henley Thornwell had named that cherished offspring Gillespie Robbins Thornwell in honor of his benefactors, his first converts to patriarchal responsibility. After Gillespie Robbins Thornwell perished in a war fought to preserve yet another generation of insufficiently converted paternalists, the father could have had only one response, had he been there to mourn over yet another premature Thornwell corpse. What is to become Oh, Lord, James Henley Thornwell would have despaired, of your wayward slaveholders and their helpless dependents?

Clerical proslavery could generate such unhappy last words. But the argument could also climax in high hopes. The creed ever mixed towering pride about responsible slaveholders with nagging qualms about responsibilities unmet. The apparent divine visitation of 1860 had ended up reinforcing Thornwell's pride more than his unease; and southern military strength, three weeks before

Thornwell's death, seemed another sign that God most loathed the irresponsible Yankees.[57]

James Henley Thornwell, having suffered much uncertainty, thus expired in August 1862 with certitudes rather than questions on his lips. "You have stated your position," went one of the theologian's final statements. "Now prove it."[58] Those last words summed up preachers' proslavery lesson. The Thornwells could never prove the Christian case for slaveholders; they could only establish the requirements for proper slaveholder proofs. Should masters' proofs fail, clergymen must pronounce the regime short on scriptural credentials.

Thornwell died a year too soon to share with fellow proslavery clerics the radical consequences of that biblical necessity. But the ex-orphan's climactic bit of precociousness, that antislavery moment in 1860, would not come to seem very mysterious. He had flinched at his premonition that Abraham's purported heirs, having somewhat tarried in giving their servants "that which is free and equal," could no longer put off their "Master in Heaven."

5 / Beyond Racial Limits: Paternalism over Whites in the Thought of Calhoun and Fitzhugh

The South's secular proslavery extremists, when they defended paternalism over whites as well as blacks, faced a swollen version of James Henley Thornwell's clerical problem: How could supposedly paternalistic government be justified when the governors were not paternalists? These far-out secularists affirmed the usual tired orthodoxy: Supposedly inferior blacks needed benevolent masters. But they added a provocative contention: Poorer white males also needed paternalistic protection. Where South Carolina's John C. Calhoun urged elitist statesmen to rescue white commoners from corrupt demagogues, Virginia's George Fitzhugh seemed to summon paternalistic masters to salvage white employees from merciless employers. Fitzhugh, by seeming to imply that impoverished white laborers must be enslaved, and Calhoun, by insisting that gullible white citizens must be guided, raised the stakes in the search for disinterested paternalists. Since white men as well as blacks needed unselfish protection, how could still more numerous selfless guides be generated from sinning humanity— and in a republic that called faith in disinterested guides a dangerous illusion?

I first traced Calhoun's failed assault on this puzzle in "Spoilsmen and Interests in the Thought and Career of John C. Calhoun," published in the Journal of American History in 1965.[1] With the permission of the journal, I have here salvaged the piece's still-viable description of the contradictions in Calhoun's political theory. But the original essay, in the manner of political historians, focused too narrowly on the sheerly political roots of those contradictions. Because I ignored the materials of social history, I never noticed that Calhoun's supposedly paternalistic con-

trol over slaves fuelled his drive for paternalistic control over citizens. So too, Fitzhugh's analysts, in the manner of social historians, have focused too narrowly on the Virginian's comparisons of paternalistic control over slaves and nonpaternalistic control over free laborers. Because they ignore the materials of political history, they never notice that Fitzhugh sought political reforms to correct slaveholders' defective paternalistic slave management. By bringing Calhoun and Fitzhugh at last together, I would show that southern political and social historians must realize that they study the same slaveholder predicament: How could so antiegalitarian a concept as paternalistic guidance be secured, justified, and perpetuated inside the world's most egalitarian republican culture?

A purely racial argument for *black* slavery was U.S. slaveholders' natural response to their vulnerability in a white men's egalitarian republic. To perpetuate slavery, the slaveholding minority had to mobilize the nonslaveholding majority. Poor white men could never be rallied for color-blind enslavement—for their own enslavement—for they cherished their supposed equality to richer whites and supposed superiority to all blacks. Thus U.S. slaveholders' predominant proslavery argument called all white males too independently powerful to need a guide, much less a master. In contrast, all blacks were vulnerably dependent without a master's guidance and protection.

Unfortunately for racial proslavery theorists, that color-obsessed bifurcation of the South was an unnatural outcome of informed social analysis. Black belt southern communities contained some altogether independent free blacks, including a few rich black slaveholders. Dependent whites also shared slaveholders' neighborhoods. At the extreme of white dependency, so-called poor white trash ate mud to ease pellagra-caused stomach agony. Some more fortunate whites partially depended on rich men to sustain life. Wage-earning laborers supplied mechanical services for planters and towns. Other wage-earning whites, so-called overseers, supervised blacks on rich men's plantations. Many poor tenants rented a few acres from powerful landlords. Given these social dependencies and a slaveholder's paternalistic obligations, southern patriarchs arguably should have guided and protected all dependents, white as well as black.

Of the few proslavery extremists who drove that argument for color-blind paternalism to its logical (and politically suicidal) extreme, South Carolina's John C. Calhoun denied that all whites were politically independent, and Virginia's George Fitzhugh denied that all whites were economically independent. Where Calhoun sought safely patriarchal political rulers to guide dependent white voters, Fitzhugh seemed to seek safely patriarchal economic masters to own dependent white employees. Neither Calhoun's nor Fitzhugh's theories, however, could escape contradiction when explaining how color-blind paternalists could be secured and empowered. The two theorists' failure to ensure paternalism over whites illuminated the difficulty of ensuring paternalism over blacks—and of using paternalistic assumptions to reconcile slavery and democracy.

1

John C. Calhoun was no ivory tower theorist. Like the Founding Fathers whose paternalistic ideas he extended, Calhoun was an ambitious politician, determined to turn theoretical scenarios into historic events. Calhoun's favorite performance in his own script occurred in the Nullification Controversy of 1832–33. Then his state, acting out his philosophy, declared the national majority's federal taxes on imports null and void. If President Andrew Jackson enforced the nullified tariff law in their state, announced Calhoun and his fellow South Carolinians, they would secede from the Union. In defense of this defiance, Calhoun reasoned that the northern majority's taxes enslaved the southern minority; that to avoid reducing citizens to slaves, each minority must be able to veto any law; that each significant minority could control at least one state; and thus if any state could nullify any law, every minority would check and balance every majority.

President Jackson considered Calhoun's nullification doctrine not a legitimate extension of democratic checks and balances but an illegitimate paralysis of majoritarian government. The President announced that the majority would rule, that he would enforce the tariff, and that the United States might hang John C. Calhoun. Instead, the majority changed the law. In 1833, Congress passed a compromise tariff. The settlement averted armed showdown between minority veto and majority rule. South Carolina never again tried nullification. Calhoun played other roles in national politics for seventeen more years. But no part won his heart or inspired his creativity like that showdown with Jackson. In the late 1840s, as a dying leader, Calhoun wrote his ultimate theoretical defense of nullification. It was published posthumously in 1851, entitled *The Disquisition on Government.*

Calhoun began the *Disquisition* with the assumption that man "is so constituted, that his direct or individual affections are stronger than his sympathetic or social feelings." It follows that a group of men with similar concerns is more self-interested than disinterested. Therefore in a democracy, if one interest group contains a numerical majority, it will "pervert its powers to oppress, and plunder the others." If no pressure group can muster a majority, "a combination will be formed between those whose interests are most alike." In both cases, legislative edict will transfer minority riches into majority pockets. Neither a separation of powers between branches of the government nor a written constitution would protect the enslaved minority. The numerical majority would elect the president and the congress; the majority president would appoint majority judges; and the appointed judges would interpret the constitution, stripping away minority rights by judicial decree. Then nothing could check majority selfishness.[2]

Calhoun would replace the unchecked selfishness of the numerical majority with the checks and balances of the so-called concurrent majority. By *concurrent* majority, Calhoun meant that all minorities must unanimously concur before a *numerical* majority could pass laws. Calhoun's concurrent majority system would extend the superficial (and easily circumvented) checks and balances between governmental branches to in-depth (and thus unpassable) checks and balances between the major pressure groups in society.

Calhoun's critics, ever since Jackson, have retorted that this rigidly checked government would be stalemated and thus unable to govern. Then anarchy would ensue. Calhoun conceded that an impotent government would be intolerable, for anarchy would be disastrous. But he insisted that the concurrent majority would produce compromise rather than stalemate. Since anarchy was "the greatest of all evils," he explained, the various interests would selfishly seek selfless cooperation, whenever pending legislation became an "urgent necessity."[3] Furthermore, the necessity to compromise would force leading pressure groups to elect that rarity: disinterested statesmen. Calhoun assumed, in the manner of a slaveholder's patriarchal mentality, that masters, when directing slaves, escaped the human propensity toward malign self-centeredness, for selfless direction of their property was in their self-interest. In just the same way, the concurrent majority would ensure that selfish interests generated selfless rulers. "Each portion, in order to advance its own peculiar interests, would have to conciliate all others, by showing a disposition to advance theirs; and, for this purpose, each would select those to represent it, whose wisdom, patriotism, and weight of character, would command the confidence of the others."

With "representatives so well qualified to accomplish the object for which they were selected," continued Calhoun, "the prevailing desire would be, to promote the common interests of the whole." Here is "the feature, which distinguishes governments of the concurrent majority so strikingly from those of the numerical. In the latter, each faction, in the struggle to obtain the control of the government, elevates to power the designing, the artful, and unscrupulous, who, in their devotion to party,—instead of aiming at the good of the whole,—aim exclusively at securing the ascendancy of party."[4] Calhoun waxed lyrical about paternalism at the top: "instead of faction, strife, and struggle for party ascendance, there would be patriotism, nationality, harmony, and a struggle only for supremacy in promoting the common good of the whole."[5] Thus would the best men save minorities from enslavement, the republic from stalemate, and the culture from anarchy.

2

Calhoun's paternalistic answer to his critics—his reliance on disinterested patriarchs to rescue the concurrent majority from intolerable stalemate—is the mild surprise in the *Disquisition*. The major shock is an alien current of logic that courses through the polemic, sinking Calhoun's patriarchal solution in a sea of degraded politicos. I will call this seldom discussed theme the "theory of spoilsmen," to distinguish it from Calhoun's well-known theory of interests.

Where Calhoun's theory of interests assumed that societal pressure groups controlled politicians, the theory of spoilsmen assumed that politicians controlled everyone else. Spoilsmen, pursuing their own ambitions, determined political agendas. So too where the theory of interests assumed that the riches of minorities turned selfish majorities into plunderers, the theory of spoilsmen assumed that the spoils of office turned selfish politicos into demagogues. Since nations—like individuals and economic interests—were primarily selfish, governments had to maintain "vast establishments" to deter aggressive enemies. Since politicians—like almost all humankind—were self-interested, they would employ every effective method to control the spoils.[6]

Spoilsmen found demagoguery an especially effective means of control. Calhoun considered many voters to be susceptible to inflammatory appeals. To secure patronage, demagogues needed only to deploy "cunning, falsehood, deception, slander, fraud, and gross appeals to the appetites of the lowest and most worthless portions of the community." Soon the nation would be "thoroughly debased and corrupted." Demagogic spoilsmen would control gullible constituents. Meanwhile the party structure would be refined and extended. Patronage would control wayward legislators, and party bosses would discipline wandering subordinates. As Calhoun's prediction of democracy's dire future unfolds, perfected political parties will forget their constituents and obscenely struggle for patronage. Those "seeking office and patronage" will "become too numerous to be rewarded by the offices and patronage at the disposal of the government." Disappointed politicos will shift allegiances, causing governmental control to "vibrate" between the factions. Finally, "confusion, corruption, disorder, and anarchy" will force all social interests to replace their politicians with a military despot.[7]

A mortal two-party warfare would occur, warned Calhoun, even if a nation had no other social divisions. Were it "possible to find a community where the people were all of the same pursuits, placed in the same condition of life, and . . . without inequality of condition or diversity of interests," he declared, "the advantage of possessing the control of the powers of the government, and thereby, of its honors and emoluments, are, of themselves, exclusive of all other considerations, ample" to call forth "two great hostile parties."[8] How, then, could the remedy of the concurrent majority check the disease of political party as successfully as it checked the disease of social interests?

Calhoun hoped that minority veto would shrink majority-imposed taxes. Reduced taxes would diminish patronage, thereby lessening the clash between spoilsmen. In contrast, under a government of the numerical majority, minorities would continually pay higher taxes, thereby increasing patronage and stimulating spoilsmen.[9] Calhoun admitted, however, that minority veto reduced *national* patronage too little. Posterity remembers the South Carolinian more for his later years as a sectionalist than for his early career as a nationalist. Yet a fundamental premise of the early Calhoun, the assumption that military preparations alone would ensure lasting peace, devastated his later political theory. Although minorities would nullify unnecessary taxes, no interest would veto necessary expenses for national defense; and legitimate military appropriations would alone stimulate violent conflicts between spoilsmen. "For prompt and effective action," modern national states must stockpile "fortifications, fleets, armories, arsenals, magazines, arms of all descriptions, with well-trained forces." These "vast establishments must necessarily require a host of employees, agents, and officers." Thus "large sums must be collected" and "heavy taxes must be imposed." The government will control "an amount of honors and emoluments, sufficient to excite profoundly the ambition of the aspiring and the cupidity of the avaricious; and to lead to the formation of hostile parties, and violent party conflicts."[10]

Although Calhoun here conceded that minority veto would insufficiently reduce the fatal spoils, and although he thus admitted that demagogues' lethal selfishness would not have been negated, he still hoped that under the concurrent majority, selfless patriarchs would replace scheming politicos. Since minority veto would force pressure groups to cooperate, he reasoned, social interests would elect disinterested statesmen rather than aspiring spoilsmen. But this solution to the problem of spoilsmen rested on the premise of the theory of interests. It assumed that pressure groups controlled their politicians. In contrast, the theory of spoilsmen assumed that demagogues became uncontrollable. If, according to Calhoun's logic, the concurrent majority would indeed force selfish interests to seek selfless statesmen, the spoils of office would unfortunately continue to beckon corrupt spoilsmen. Since the "vast" military establishments would still offer rich patronage harvests, depraved politicians would continue their electioneering. Since the masses would remain dependently gullible, demagogues would still defeat statesmen in popular elections. The unsolvable problem was that whenever "party triumph and ascendancy" is placed "above the safety and prosperity of the community," the combined force of "falsehood, injustice, fraud, artifice, slander, and breach of faith" will "overpower all regard for truth, justice, sincerity, and moral obligation."[11]

The concurrent majority's failure to oust spoilsmen would be serious enough in itself. The race for patronage would yield revolution and dictatorship. Worse, invincible spoilsmen would destroy Calhoun's cure for the disease of interests. Calhoun's concurrent majority depended on selfless statesmen to find compromise between warring interests. But since irreducible military patronage would continue to attract spoilsmen, and since their demagoguery would continue to delude the masses, the foul and depraved, not the wise and virtuous, would continue to be elected. Thus governmental deadlock and social anarchy—Calhoun's designated intolerable evils—would ensue.

This theoretical impasse stemmed not so much from Calhoun's conception of irreducible military patronage as from his conception of irreducible mass gullibility. Patronage would be harmless if voters would choose fair over foul candidates. But "the wealthy and ambitious" could too easily delude "the more ignorant and dependent portions of the community." The "poor and ignorant," to make wise decisions, must have "leaders and protectors." Calhoun's political theory ultimately foundered on his inability to deliver paternalistic rescue of white dependents.[12]

3

The question remains, why did Calhoun think that white republics required paternalistic rescue? The Carolinian's conception of depraved party spoilsmen, his image of "vast" military establishments, his notion that whites as well as blacks needed "leaders and protectors"—all these foundations for color-blind paternalistic republicanism were heretical nonsense to most color-obsessed nineteenth-century slaveholders. Andrew Jackson, prime architect of the slaveholders' mainstream, racially exclusive, egalitarian republicanism, always found Calhoun's color-blind elitism unfathomable. How, Jackson wondered, could Calhoun conceive that the national military establishment was some monstrous menace? Jackson, America's supreme soldier, saw a paltry national army, with temporary local militia usually meeting national emergencies. Moreover, how could Calhoun presume that white men were dependent and needed protectors? The Carolinian, Jackson stormed, evidently could not distinguish between whites and "niggers." And how could Calhoun fear that party spoilsmen would delude "poor and ignorant" white males? Electioneering parties on the contrary helped innately sensible white commoners make wise public decisions. Why couldn't Calhoun see the essence of the Slave South: a regime where paternalism was limited to dependents, and where all white adult males were independent?[13]

Calhoun could not accept that racially constricted version of paternalism, first of all, because he was the Founding Fathers' disciple, not Andrew Jackson's protégé. The American eighteenth-century patriarchy, South no less than North, had never been racially selective about poor men's dependency. The vulnerable white masses, the Founding Fathers had feared, invited political corruption, particularly when selfish demagogues aroused the rabble. Here nineteenth-century slaveholder egalitarian republicanism, Andrew Jackson–style, broke decisively from eighteenth-century elitist republicanism. Where the Founding Fathers had thought that lower-class males of all races must have disinterested guides, the Jacksonian slaveholder thought that all white males could sagely decide public issues. Thus only lesser races and sexes needed paternalistic guidance.

Calhoun's old-fashioned retort to the new-found wisdom of white male commoners drew on both the fading and the precocious strains in the Founding Fathers' distrust of republican electorates. The Fathers' precocious line of thought, exemplified in James Madison's famous Tenth Federalist Essay of 1787, anticipated the modern conception that grasping social interests controlled voters and therefore the state.[14] Madison called larger republics sounder than smaller ones, for the more sweeping the geographic area, the more numerous were the selfish social interests, the less dominant was any one interest, and the greater was the likelihood that competing groups would cancel each other out. With selfish representatives neutralizing one another, selfless patriarchs—such as James Madison—would secure the vote and rule the state. To perpetuate Madisonian patriarchal republicanism, Calhoun had only to add a formal mechanism of minority veto to Madison's informal conception that selfish interests would block each other and elevate selfless rulers.

Where James Madison's Tenth Federalist Essay anticipated modern conceptions that self-centered social interests controlled voters and politicians, the Founding Fathers' alternative, premodern conception of defective electorates anticipated Calhoun's conception that malign spoilsmen dominated citizens and interests. Drawing on English eighteenth-century republican theory, the Founders warned that patronage-hungry politicos often formed their own social class. That class of governmental officials ruled in its own interest, not in the public interest or any pressure group's interest. The political class of corrupt patronage seekers especially destroyed republican virtue by making demagogical appeals to poor whites. The demagoguery became doubly dangerous when foul politicos organized political parties, devoted to collecting the spoils.

Leading American Revolutionaries always considered party conflict a great political danger. These upper-class republicans sought "to refine and enlarge the public view" by ensuring that a propertied elite would rule. If political parties developed, corrupt demagogues might "first obtain the suffrages, and then betray the interests, of the people."[15] As John Taylor of Caroline put it, "all parties, however loyal to principle at first, degenerate into aristocracies of interests at last; and unless a nation is capable of discerning the point where integrity ends and fraud begins, popular parties are among the surest modes of introducing an aristocracy."[16]

George Washington's Farewell Address of 1796 exemplified this antiparty viewpoint. Washington warned his countrymen "in the most solemn manner against the baneful effects of the spirit of party." Party agitation, he declared, "is seen in its greatest rank" in republican governments "and is truly their worst enemy." The spirit of party "serves always to distract the public councils and enfeeble the public administration. It agitates the community with ill-founded jealousies and false alarms; kindles the animosity of one part against another; foments occasionally riot and insurrection." Only "a uniform vigilance," said Washington, can "prevent its bursting into a flame."[17]

To Washington's vision of political parties setting a republic aflame, Calhoun had only to add combustible military patronage, just as the Carolinian had only to add formal mechanisms of minority veto to Madison's theory of neutralizing interests. Although the nineteenth-century U.S. armed forces were tiny by posterity's standards, the military, then as now, required the largest share of federal expenditures. From 1816 to 1824, Secretary of War Calhoun presided over this largest of federal departments. During these years, the Founding Fathers' primitive, distrusted first American party system was dissolving and the Jacksonian highly developed, cherished second American party system was emerging. Calhoun, eighteenth-century loather of party, spent eight years in the cabinet disgustedly sorting out nineteenth-century pleas for favors. His War Department tenure raised his doubts that patronage could be reduced to safe levels, given the invitation to corruption in the (necessary) military establishment.

Long before this practical experience, Calhoun had been conditioned to despise patronage and party. Educated at Connecticut's Yale College and Litchfield Law School at the beginning of the nineteenth century, the South Carolinian studied under Timothy Dwight, James Gould, and Tapping Reeve, three high priests of the

Federalist faith. Calhoun remained a Jeffersonian in spite of his mentors. But Jefferson himself prayed that "natural aristocrats" would govern, and the Federalists steeped the young Calhoun in the eighteenth-century conviction that enlightened elites must overcome corrupt parties.

Throughout his ensuing national career, Calhoun periodically fought to preserve the Founding Fathers' antiparty principles against the emerging political managers of the second American party system. As secretary of war under James Monroe, Calhoun opposed the presidential aspirations of William H. Crawford partly because the Georgian's party hoped "to attain power, not by placing itself on principles and policy . . . but by political dexterity and management."[18] Calhoun's growing concern with base political methods also partly motivated his crusade against John Quincy Adams's administration. Adams had risen to power, according to Calhoun, by striking a "corrupt bargain" with Henry Clay whereby Adams bought the presidency by paying Clay with appointment as secretary of state.[19] In late 1829, when President Jackson had chosen the politically crafty Martin Van Buren over Calhoun as the next leader of the Jackson movement, the South Carolinian wrote John McLean that "I deeply apprehend, that the choice of the chief magistrate will finally be placed at the disposition of the executive power itself, through a corrupt system to be founded on the abuse of the power and patronage of the government."[20]

Thwarted by Van Buren and isolated from Jackson in 1831, Calhoun became a leader of the South Carolina Nullifiers. He hoped that South Carolina's veto of the tariff would lower governmental revenues and thereby reduce executive patronage.[21] In 1835 Calhoun warned that Jackson's use of patronage to promote Van Buren's ascendancy was turning democracy into dictatorship. Arguing in his "Report on the Extent of the Executive Patronage" that the executive corps could perpetuate itself by patronage "alone, unconnected with any system or measure of policy," Calhoun urged Congress to outlaw "King Andrew's" manipulation of the spoils.[22] Thereafter, in every major policy decision, from distributing surplus revenue to enacting the Independent Treasury, from lowering the tariff to entering the Mexican War, Calhoun weighed the effect on executive patronage. For a time, in the late 1830s and early 1840s, Calhoun believed that patronage could be dried up. But by 1848 an embittered Calhoun had almost admitted defeat. He did not see "how any man who has the ability and the disposition to correct abuses and reform the government can in the present state of politics be elected. The governing, I might with truth say, the exclusive object of both parties, in electing the President, is to obtain the spoils. They are both equally ready to sacrifice any other consideration to it."[23] That was the ex-secretary of war whose theory of spoilsmen, derived from eighteenth-century elitist republicanism, would destroy his theory of interests, derived from James Madison.

4

No important American disliked contradiction more than Calhoun. So given this logician's taste for tight polemics, why didn't the loose ends in his eighteenth-century elitist speculations drive Calhoun toward nineteenth-century egalitarian assumptions? The ambitious South Carolinian, after all, hungered for the White House as much as for remorseless logic; and Andrew Jackson's up-to-date, racially selective paternalism followed a consistent polemical line straight to the presidency. Calhoun's color-blind paternalism instead wandered around eighteenth-century republican polemics, only to land on the hapless fringes of nineteenth-century political battles. Worse, Jackson's party secured national proslavery law and Jackson's statements on white men's independence won nonslaveholders' applause. In contrast, Calhoun's plea that dependent whites needed direction turned yeomen against condescending squires. How could the slaveholder minority hope to save slavery, in a nonslaveholder-dominated republic, by brushing white voters with the taint of dependency?

Calhoun answered, in effect, that saving an institution demanded affirming its essence. The essence of the paternalistic case for slavery was that superiors must rule inferiors. The essential Jacksonian notion, that dependent voters were as fit to rule as independent patriarchs, invited the rabble, or rather the demagogues, to control the masters' destiny. Lesser folks must instead follow those richer and wiser.

That increasingly rare eighteenth-century elitist insistence came straight out of South Carolina's nineteenth-century singularity. While slavery, of all American nineteenth-century social institutions, most invited the continued presumption that paternalists must rule inferiors, South Carolina's sociopolitical structure best enabled slaveholders to maintain the old color-blind elitism over whites as well as blacks. In no other southern state was the percentage of large plantations so high, the percentage of nonslaveholders so low, the slaveholders' control of every region so all-inclusive, or the commitment to perpetual servitude so ancient. Nineteenth-century South Carolinian elitists made only one concession to their egalitarian (for white men) era. They permitted all white commoners to vote earlier in the century than did other southern states. They then ensured that voters would decide only which of the betters would rule. As James Hamilton, Jr., put it, "The people expect that their leaders in whose . . . public spirit they have confidence will think for them—and that they will be prepared to *act* as their leaders *think.*"[24] Or as Daniel Huger answered in the state legislature when asked what his constituents would think of a proposed measure, "Think! They will think nothing about it—they expect me to think for them."[25]

The South Carolina Constitution institutionalized upper-class power to think for the masses. Any adult white male who had resided in South Carolina for two years could vote for state legislators. The legislators then elected other state officials, U.S. senators, and presidential electors. A high property qualification for the legislature kept lower-class opportunists outside the statehouse, and a skewed legislative apportionment gave low-country aristocrats extra power inside the legislature. The governor, elected by the legislature, served only two years and had no control over patronage. South Carolinians uniquely concentrated political power in a legislature of large property holders, which set state policy and selected the gentlemen to administer it.

The informal characteristics of South Carolina politics tightened upper-class control. Elections to the state legislature, the masses' only control over the government, were often uncontested and rarely allowed commoners a clear choice between parties or policies. Even in the state legislature, the Carolina gentry eschewed organized parties. Leaders of a well-disciplined legislative party might organize a statewide popular ticket and encourage the lower class to overreach itself by debating issues. Unscrupulous demagogues would subsequently oust disinterested patricians by deluding the rabble. Political parties would overwhelm the rich, well-born, and able, thus upsetting the squire-ruled republicanism that alone won South Carolina patricians' approbation.[26]

Calhoun gave classic expression to old-fashioned republicanism in 1838, when he denounced a proposed democratization of South Carolina. If his state allowed the people to elect the governor and the governor to appoint executive officials, Calhoun declared in the typical Carolina vein, "two violent parties would spring up." Neither party would defy federal tyranny, for the other would stand *"ready to become* the Union Party" and receive "federal aid and patronage." From being the one state still sustaining patriarchal republicanism, South Carolina would sink into the egalitarian muck. After being the last state with a "beautiful and well adjusted" aristocratic order, Carolina would foster "a wild, factious, and despotic democracy." All that because the people elected the governor![27]

Throughout the antebellum period, Calhoun and his fellow Carolina aristocrats successfully blocked popular election of the state's governors and other proposed dilutions of aristocratic republicanism in confined South Carolina. At the same time, Carolina gentlemen unsuccessfully opposed the spread of Jackson-style egalitarian republicanism over the sprawling Union. The irony of this differential success for Calhoun, in his role as James Madison's disciple, was that the right triumph occurred in the wrong place. Madison's Tenth Federalist Essay declared that elitist republicanism worked best in large republics, where social interests canceled each other out. Yet republicanism flourished according to Madisonian design in little South Carolina, while the unchecked war of slaveholding and nonslaveholding factions gutted the larger Union. Worse, at the national level, irreducible military patronage perpetuated spoilsmen, while South Carolina had little military buildup and its governor controlled no patronage.

South Carolina gentlemen's pride in state aristocratic republicanism and their dismay at national egalitarian mobocracy partially fueled their early preference for disunion. Calhoun, deploring premature disunionism, preferred instead to spread South Carolina's locally triumphant paternalistic governance to the nation. That objective helped lead to the Nullification Controversy. But in the great showdown with Jackson, numerical majorities overwhelmed the concurrent majority; and thereafter, even in the solitude of his study, Calhoun could not imagine how to reverse the triumph in militaristic national states. The unsolved problems in his climactic *Disquisition* left the national white voting body under the thumb not of disinterested paternalists but of greedy demagogues, whose search for patronage could destroy the concurrent majority, the dependent voters, and the independent slaveholders too.

5

While Calhoun struggled unsuccessfully to save dependent white voters from spoilsmen's exploitation, George Fitzhugh struggled still less successfully to save dependent white employees from capitalists' exploitation. These two exponents of paternalism over whites shared curiously little, except their mutual scorn for the assertion that no white men were dependent. Calhoun was from the newer cotton-growing section of up-country South Carolina; Fitzhugh, from the oldest tobacco-growing section of coastal Virginia. Fitzhugh was the descendant of a first family of Virginia; Calhoun, a second-generation aristocrat.[28] Calhoun had his house and study built on his booming new plantation; Fitzhugh possessed little, declared an unfriendly neighbor, except a "rickety old mansion, situated at the fag-end of a once noble estate."[29] Calhoun's spare prose served a controlled logician; Fitzhugh's extravagant verbiage announced a wild assaulter. Calhoun was a grim antagonist, given to righteous soliloquy; Fitzhugh, a cheerful insulter, eager to befriend Yankees whom he called "cannibals." Calhoun was a famous politician who hated patronage; Fitzhugh, an obscure journalist who sought petty political office. If the two ever conversed, it is not recorded; if they ever read each other's books, no influence can be discerned.

None of that mattered, for they shared an outlook. They were both of the oldest South, proud of its elderly ways and dismayed at the nouveau century. Both considered slaveholder paternalism a model for solving the universal problem of human dependency. They published their sustained pleas to extend protection and direction to whites almost simultaneously. Fitzhugh presented his *Sociology for the South; or The Failure of Free Society* in 1854, three years after Calhoun's *Disquisition* appeared. In 1857, Fitzhugh published his masterpiece, *Cannibals All! or, Slaves without Masters*. With his usual charming irreverence, Fitzhugh compared his books to the "swollen Mississippi," sweeping up indiscriminately "the flocks, the herds, the crops, the uprooted forest, and the residences of man."[30] His books were in fact chaotic compilations of previously published *De Bow's Review* and *Richmond Enquirer* essays. The essays themselves were on the chaotic side, full of booming verbal shots aimed helter-skelter at the Yankees.

Yet what devastating hits he scored on another of nineteenth-century America's then seldom criticized central institutions! Where Calhoun subjected American egalitarian republicanism to rare and withering criticism, Fitzhugh scrutinized American free-labor capitalism with unprecedented power and insight. Fitzhugh's title said it all: Capitalistic employers were cannibals all; supposedly free laborers were in factory owners' power; employers accepted no responsibility for their employees; and masters without responsibility feasted on dependents.

Fitzhugh had a merry time with that word *free* laborer. Wage slaves, Fitzhugh's preferred name for employed unfortunates, were indeed free—free to starve on their sub-subsistence wages. Employees were also free to be fired. The impoverished were furthermore free to desert their families out of economic desperation. The truth was that theoretical freedom meant actual enslavement unless an allegedly free laborer possessed independent power to protect himself and his own. Unfortunately, lamented Fitzhugh, the powerless white wage slave was as abjectly dependent on his all-powerful employer's mercy as the southern black was dependent on his master's paternalism.

Blacks were better off, for northern employers, unlike southern slaveholders, had no self-interest in being paternalistic. Like Calhoun, Fitzhugh assumed that humans will be selfish unless forced to be disinterested. Just as Calhoun's selfish numerical majority and equally selfish demagogic spoilsmen would exploit politically helpless voters, so Fitzhugh's selfish employers of wage slaves would squeeze economically helpless laborers. Where Calhoun countered political selfishness with the concurrent majority, for he hoped minority veto would force selfish interests to elect selfless patriarchs, Fitzhugh countered economic selfishness with enslavement to a familial patriarch, for he claimed that "within the family circle, the law of love prevails, not that of selfishness."

Governors of families, explained Fitzhugh, consider their family, hearth, and possessions an extension of themselves. They could best "promote their own well-being, by kindness to their inferiors." The squire must be lovingly kind "not only to his horses and his cattle, which are useful to him," but also to "his dog, which is of no use. He loves them because they are his." The domestic "affection which all men feel for what belongs to them and for what is dependent on them" thus becomes "Nature's magna charta, which shields, protects, and provides for wives, children and slaves."[31]

Since owners of laborers shielded and protected their property while employers of laborers exploited and fired their employees, Fitzhugh called the defense of "mere negro slavery" as a racially "exceptional institution . . . the most absurdly untenable proposition that ever was maintained by man." Indeed since racist contempt for blacks dampened sympathetic feelings for fellow humans, the defense of "mere negro slavery" was the most counterproductive proposition that ever justified paternalistic slavery. Few men, after all, could develop familial love for a subhuman beast. In one of his more astounding private letters, Fitzhugh complained to William Lloyd Garrison that slaveholders would be more paternalistic if only blacks "were white & straight haired, for then domestic affection would come into full play to correct those evils which difference of race . . . seem only to aggravate."

Still, whatever the cruelties of slaveholding racists, free-labor society was a crueler failure. "I am quite as intent on abolishing Free Society," Fitzhugh privately wrote northern opponents, "as you are on abolishing slavery." He affirmed, before Lincoln did, that a house divided against itself could not stand. "Slavery will everywhere be abolished, or everywhere be reinstituted." Just as Calhoun would abolish white men's egalitarian republicanism because aristocratic republicans must guide vulnerable voters, so Fitzhugh would abolish white men's supposedly free labor because a slaveholder's guidance, whether over "black or white, was right and necessary."[32]

6

Fitzhugh's economic paternalism here surpassed Calhoun's political paternalism as indiscreet provocation. True, Calhoun was gallingly asking egalitarian-worshiping voters to take political commands from above. Yet Fitzhugh more gallingly seemed to be asking white laborers to go find an owner. But the Virginian actually proposed no such outrageous thing as slavery for U.S. whites. His books feature as unexpected a countervailing theme as Calhoun's theory of spoilsmen in the *Disquisition*. Just as Calhoun's irredeemable spoilsmen will prevent a color-blind patriarchy from saving a national concurrent majority, so Fitzhugh's surprise argument surrenders his apparent proposal for enslaving American whites.

Fitzhugh paved his road away from white slavery in America with his consistent premise: that all independents should be free and all dependents enslaved. In crowded Europe, he argued, dependent factory workers had to accept starvation wages. But in America, with its underpopulated territories, factory laborers need never accept abject dependency. If exploited, the eastern lower class could "escape to the West and become proprietors."[33] Fitzhugh here anticipated Frederick Jackson Turner's famous "safety valve" position. Turner, the turn of the century frontier historian, argued that virgin western land emancipated eastern laborers from European-style exploitation.

Fitzhugh, in this respect Turner's precursor, declared that the poorest American white man, even if "out of employment or starving," could "immigrate to the Great West" and become a well-fed farmer. Given the frontier safety valve, exploitation of free laborers became "a potent agent for the advancement of human good." By making oppression intolerable, selfish capitalists would help "drive population westward, prevent its excessive accumulation on the Atlantic, . . . and open up the desert spots of the earth for the residences of man." In "very new and sparsely settled countries" such as America, wage slavery "is, on the whole, the greatest of human goods." It would "continue to be good and useful until the Northwest is peopled."[34]

That "until" was crucial. How long until the Northwest would be crowded and dependents in the Northeast thus enslaved? In his first book, Fitzhugh declared that "until" meant "soon." The flood of immigrants to the North, he wrote in *Sociology for the South*, was making "the situation for the laborer at the North as precarious as in Europe." He had not supposed that "the necessity of slavery . . . would be so soon felt in a new and sparsely-settled country." But in the later 1850s, Fitzhugh claimed instead that "many centuries may elapse" before America would need to abolish free labor. The more Fitzhugh thought about it, the more the centuries multiplied. "Thousands of years may elapse," he declared in *De Bow's Review*, before all lands "between the Atlantic and Pacific are settled and monopolized, and a refluent population is pouring back on the East." Why "anticipate evils that may never happen"? The North's situation, affirmed the North's severest critic, was "natural, healthful, and progressive."[35]

That stunning endorsement of northern free labor apparently made southern slavery indefensible. If no Negro should be enslaved "merely" because he was Negro and no dependent laborer should be enslaved when he could become an independent farmer, black laborers should apparently be freed to light out for the territories. In the vast unpeopled areas of Texas, Arkansas, Mississippi, blacks could apparently be free pioneers.

To escape that heresy, Fitzhugh reverted to other Southerners' orthodoxy. He said that blacks, unlike whites, were biologically incapable of independence. Fitzhugh's initial publication, at the beginning of the pre-secession decade, declared that "the negro's is not human freedom, but the wild and vicious license of the fox."

Five years later, in *Sociology for the South*, Fitzhugh argued that "negro slavery would be changed immediately to some form of peonage, serfdom, or villenage, if the negroes were sufficiently intelligent and provident to manage a farm." But the Negro is "a child, and must be governed as a child."[36]

Fitzhugh returned to his escape hatch of the "mere negro" in *Cannibals All*. "Until the lands of America are appropriated by a few," Fitzhugh wrote, "the personal liberties of all the whites will continue to be a blessing." For a black, however, "liberty is a curse to himself, and a greater curse to the society around him."[37] No "sane man in America," he added in 1856, "proposes to make slaves of white men." But "as well send monkeys to settle, reclaim and cultivate the far West, as free negroes. . . . Even in America, negroes should be slaves."[38] George Fitzhugh was color-blind paternalist no longer. Worse, by comparing blacks to degraded monkeys, Fitzhugh exhibited the very racism that he had told Garrison undermined paternalism.

Fitzhugh's surrender to racially exclusive U.S. paternalism underlined the staying power of Calhoun's drive for paternalism over all races in America. The South Carolinian, lifelong seeker of the national presidency, had more to gain by renouncing paternalism over whites than did the Virginian, seeker of notoriety among sectional extremists. Yet where Calhoun's political theory and career wandered in circles in an unending quest to revive the old-fashioned national patriarchal republic, Fitzhugh circled via the new western frontier away from American whites' need for patriarchal economic direction. Fitzhugh, ever the smiling polemicist, had always been provocatively playing with outrageous proposals to enslave white Americans, only to make the deadly serious point that dependents of all color needed paternalistic direction. But on the issue of paternalism over American white males, Fitzhugh ultimately stood with Jackson rather than with Calhoun: in mid-nineteenth-century America, the master sex of the master race could escape dependency.

7

Although he deserted Calhoun on American white male dependency, Fitzhugh continued to face Calhoun's essential problem: how to rout selfishness and secure selfless paternalists for those dependents who still needed guidance. Just as Calhoun knew that military patronage could beckon selfish spoilsmen, so Fitzhugh knew that domestic temptations could corrupt selfish masters. Fitzhugh had argued that the husband had nothing to gain by exploiting his kin and his property. But that was nonsense, as all feminists know and as Fitzhugh conceded in another surprise argument. "The head of the family," the Virginian warned in *De Bow's Review* in 1859, "possesses unlimited power. He is often deficient in temper, in wisdom, in morals, and in religion, for the despotism which he wields." His "tyrannical rule" "corrupts . . . and oppresses" his "family," and "yet there is neither law, nor point, nor censor to check or correct his misrule." While we have "discovered that kings may do wrong, and that popes are not infallible," we have only transferred "infallibility from the Vatican to the cottage." Thus "the want of some family supervision and control from without, is a crying defect in modern society."[39]

The most crying defect in males' uncontrolled domestic power, Fitzhugh thought, was the southwestern cotton entrepreneurs' unchecked exploitation of helpless blacks. Fitzhugh had an ancient Virginian's disdain for nouveau cotton capitalists. He thought that Old Virginia was home to caring paternalists and long-time black "family friends" and that the crude Southwest was mad for trade and profits. Because of slaveholder bonanzas out west, Fitzhugh lamented, Virginians often dispatched their familial servants to the booming frontiers. This selfish obsession with getting rich quick could fracture black families as well as black-white relationships.[40]

That dread of selfish slaveholders devastated Fitzhugh's reliance on familial selflessness to protect slaves, just as Calhoun's dread of military patronage undermined his reliance on disinterested patriarchs to save national government. Both theorists, however, had an escape hatch, although Calhoun deplored his. Despite his reputation as "the Father of Secession," the South Carolinian spent a lifetime seeking to escape the natural outcome of his ideology: that James Madison to the contrary, selfless patriarchy was unachievable in a sprawling, militaristic national Union and wonderfully achieved in confined South Carolina's nonmilitaristic government. Secession was Calhoun's logical but disliked route to color-blind paternalism.

Fitzhugh, in contrast, cherished his escape route from unachieved selflessness. He would have the public state check and balance the private power to be selfish. Fitzhugh, once again the old-fashioned Virginian, wished Virginia government to revive primogeniture and entail so that more ancestral estates would be inherited whole and fewer grasping nonpaternalists would sell familial slaves to the unseemly West.[41] Like James Henley Thornwell, Fitzhugh also wanted the state to impose paternalism on selfish masters. Fitzhugh only hinted at this heresy in a few sentences in his publications,[42] but in his private correspondence, he was bolder. "I differ widely with slaveholders generally as to the proper treatment of slaves," he asserted in one letter. He thought that slaves "should be educated, and that the law should compel masters to feed and clothe them well and to treat them humanely."[43] "I assure you Sir," he wrote in another letter, "I see great evils in slavery, but in a controversial work, I ought not to admit them."[44]

8

The public state must check the "great evils" of private paternalism unrealized! What a climactic surprise from George Fitzhugh, the theorist who advocated paternalism over white males, then surprisingly backed down from that heresy, denounced "mere negro" slavery, then returned to that orthodoxy, advocated familial governance as a guarantee of disinterested paternalism, and then backed away from that problematic notion. In the broader perspective of American history, Fitzhugh's argument for public regulation of private exploitation is even more surprising. The logic of paternalism, with its emphasis on mutual obligations and duties for all ranks in a social hierarchy, looked backward toward medieval feudalism, just as Calhoun's elitism looked backward to eighteenth-century republicanism. Yet the most advanced slaveholders' argument for public regulation of private power looked forward to the twentieth century. Up in the more progressive North, few reformers sought governmental control over manufacturers' power to exploit workers. Down in the more reactionary South, that modern American panacea, public power counterpoised against private power, swept up some of the strongest defenders of the ultimate private power, that of the slaveholder.[45]

That long-term irony, however, was not ironic at all in the face of the slaveholders' short-term problem. They above all had to reconcile a slaveholder's unlimited governance with a republic's limited government; and no reconciliation better suited a world infused with checks and balances than governmental checks on absolutists' power to be selfish. Laws would force dependents' protectors to become selfless paternalists. Here for a last time, Fitzhugh and Calhoun concurred on the essence of the human problem: the need to generate selfless leaders from selfish humanity. Where Calhoun would use minority veto to check spoilsmen, thus yielding selfless guides of white dependents, Fitzhugh would use governmental law to check domestic tyrants, thus yielding selfless protectors of all members of the household.

Fitzhugh's ultimate governmental solution, however, inherited the problems of Calhoun's failed political remedy. Where was the selfless government fit to check selfish masters? Except for aristocratic South Carolina, Calhoun could not even in theory design a selflessly patriarchal government, trustworthy enough to force paternalism on the slaveholders. Calhoun's practical failure matched his theoretical failure; not elitist republicanism but Andrew Jackson's egalitarian republicanism prevailed nationally and in the South itself, except in Fitzhugh's and Calhoun's ancient corner of the slavocracy. Even in Old Virginia, to South Carolina patriarchs' dismay, nonslaveholders gained ever more power over state government. Partly because slaveholders feared that demagogues would delude nonslaveholders, the minority of masters would not allow majoritarian government to regulate their plantations. In the end Fitzhugh's proposal for reformed paternalism in Virginia, like Calhoun's blueprint for a reformed republic in Washington, was unachieved and unachievable amidst the contradictions of slavery and egalitarian republicanism.

How ironic, then, that Calhoun and Fitzhugh have acquired the reputation of consistent reactionaries, men whose premises, once accepted, led remorselessly to inescapable conclusions. In fact, among Calhoun's and Fitzhugh's many polemical virtues, consistency was the most revealing missing attribute. Everywhere these defenders of color-blind paternalism argued in circles, whether the Carolinian was proposing a theory of interests and then contradicting it with a theory of spoilsmen, or the Virginian was proposing familial paternalism over white wage slaves and then denying that family patriarchs were necessarily paternalistic or that white wage earners necessarily needed a master. Such polemical gyrations, from such brilliant intellectuals, point to the only proper conclusion: They sought to make an unmakeable argument. Although paternalism over black dependents led perfectly logically to paternalism over white dependents, a white men's egalitarian republic was the wrong place to insist on that logical connection. As to whether would-be paternalists over blacks would find a logical and permanent place in a racist white republic, that more promising prospect would have to be worked out, to John C. Calhoun's horror, in Andrew Jackson's mobocratic, party-dominated arena. But that horror—that Calhounite rage over being cast aside for telling God's truth about dependent whites—forged a determination at the national political fringes that the mainstream Jacksons and Civil War historians could ignore only at their peril.

6 / Unlimited Paternalism's Problems: The Transforming Moment on My Road Toward Understanding Disunion

My first publication, which reappears in revised form in the previous chapter, argued that Calhoun sought patriarchal guidance of poorer white adult males no less than of white women, white children, and blacks. My first book, on the Nullification Controversy of 1832–33, portrayed the clash between Calhoun's paternalistic version of white men's republicanism and Andrew Jackson's egalitarian version. So I knew that slaveholders' aspiration to be paternalistic dominators sometimes had transcended Jackson's racial and sexist limits to include direction of nonslaveholders. But I long thought that in the postnullification period, Jackson-style egalitarianism for white males was so dominant, and Calhoun-style elitist republicanism was so fading, that I could recount the story of later southern politics without much mention of the 1832–33 confrontation.

Early in my writing career, I also described relationships between the Founding Fathers of the American nation and the founders of the southern Confederacy. But I long considered the 1776 and 1861 revolutions sufficiently discrete so that I could write about them under separate covers. Then at a moment of insight, I suddenly understood that to make sense of the road to disunion, I would have to recount all its elements in one sustained analysis.

The following previously unpublished essay tells the story of that transforming moment. In the manner of Norman Mailer's investigative reporting, I enter my narrative not just as the investigator uncovering a phenomenon but also as an actor experiencing a parallel phenomenon. This stylistic strategy, widespread in con-

temporary reporting, seldom informs historical reporting. But the medium seems promising for conveying historical messages. By making the reporter a persona in the report, I assume that the nature of the investigator, no less than the nature of the material investigated, conditions the nature and utility of the findings. With that assumption, most historians would agree. They usually warn that present-day subjective biases screen historians' perceptions of past objective evidence, just as the nature of the present influences the relevance of the past. Yet they will have none of writing themselves as subjective reporters and learners from the report into the history they strive objectively to describe. Here as everywhere, the profession curiously dislikes fresh literary devices more than creative analytical strategies. But I am persuaded that the interaction between the historian and the historical material, if presented as its own tale, can illuminate the process of writing history, the nature of the past, and the relevance of the past to the present.

I first tried out this stylistic experiment at the Commonwealth Center for the Study of American Culture at the College of William and Mary. My tolerant audience made many suggestions. When revising the piece, I especially utilized the comments of Robert Gross, Richard John, Thad Tate, and Fredricka Teute. I have since benefited from the criticisms of colleagues at SUNY and from suggestions of Kenneth Stampp, John d'Entremont, and Ron Formisano. I would also like to thank Margaret Cook, director of the college's Manuscript and Rare Book Department, who shared my delight when I discovered my transforming document, and Mary Carroll Johansen, who transcribed it for inclusion here.

Many Americans relish historical explanations, especially when colorful people and places enliven the analysis. But nonacademics dislike some academic historians' writing style, especially when abstruse models and arcane jargon encumber the interpretation. To foster wider communication, words must be memorable for nonacademics, central for academics, and critical for understanding a historical epic. Scholars who would intrigue nonscholars with the story of the slaveholders' road to disunion —and with academics' path toward becoming professors—possess such a universally evocative word: paternalism. An analysis of slaveholders' ever more limitless versions of paternalism illuminates the nature of slavery, the causes of the Civil War, the problems of graduate education, and the dilemmas of modern parents who would limit their own paternalistic domination.

1

Long before they rose up against Abraham Lincoln, slaveholders declared war on limited paternalism. A constricted version of paternalism erred, declared southern theorists, in supposing that paternalism should define only relationships between parents and offspring. The slaveholder claimed to control not only his children but also his wife and his slaves in the manner of a father: affectionately, altruistically, with determination to guide and protect his own.

This slaveholders' analogy between child rearing and slave managing was strained for many reasons. Thus interactions between masters and slaves rarely followed the slaveholders' paternalistic script. But even if the master could have treated his slave as benevolently as his son, and even if the slave could have been as grateful as was the heir, modern parents would find the slaveholders' second limitless extension of paternalism appalling. Modern parents' long-term purpose, in exercising short-term dominion over children, is to prepare those dominated to spring free from domination. Slaveholders, in contrast, considered parental abdication to allow young adults to make their own decisions a betrayal of paternalism.

The slaveholders' version of ceaseless child rearing sought antimodern results from paternalism. With white male children, slaveholders aimed for orthodox heirs who would perpetually think slaveholding the only right path. Modern parents, in contrast, seek free thinkers who will choose their own path. With females and blacks, slaveholders aimed for perpetual dependents who would always crave direction and protection. Modern parents, again in contrast, think all sexes and races must be raised to direct and protect themselves. Thus where slaveholding paternalists glorified lifelong paternalistic dominion over everyone except white adult males (and lifelong mental dominion even over male heirs), modern parents seek to raise children who will cast off paternalistic guidance.

How, then, slaveholders wished to know, could such a limited version of paternalism achieve parents' prime obligation to society: an ineradicable imposition of morality, standards, civilized discourse? The slaveholders here exposed the modern problem of parenting, for their question illuminated the tension between permissive and insistent parenting. Adults' power over children is awesome, especially when dominion comes coated with benevolence. How, then, can such an overwhelming power be truly ended so that an independent spirit can emerge? The modern answer, that parents must go light on the imposition and heavy on the encouragement, can inhibit the parental impulse to mold, form, direct. The modern parent has to calibrate the gradations of leniency and strictness just right.

That subtle mixture becomes especially elusive when children enter the teenage years. Then offspring, at once cherishing the benevolence above and yet trying to get out from under its power, meet parents, at once cherishing the fragile independence below and yet trying to stifle any wrong turnings. During this adolescent identity crisis, few children totally escape the parental shadow. Memories of parental commands perpetually inform consciousness (or, as Sigmund Freud thought, infect the subconscious). Despite the slaveholders' dismissal of modern paternalism as too limited, modern parenting has its limitless aspects. Precisely because paternalism can slip past all intended limits, the slaveholders' intentionally limitless version of familial authoritarianism remains eternally relevant, for all who would guide as teachers or as parents.

2

Anyone who has lived through an adolescent crisis of supposedly transitory paternalism (and who hasn't?) will empathize with academics' often difficult passage beyond a teacher's guidance. Teachers frequently exert a lifelong influence in the manner of a parent. The mentor of a Ph.D. recipient is particularly likely to cast lasting shadows. A senior professor, when directing graduate students' dissertations, possesses all the prerequisites for enduring paternalistic power. The mentor wields intellectual authority in the field and crasser authority over fellowships and early job opportunities. If to this transitory power is added a benevolent disposition and charismatic teaching, graduate students may become lifelong followers of their benefactor and inspirer.

Not every Ph.D. director fosters enduring paternalistic relationships. Especially at big universities and with busy and/or indifferent professors, the dissertation writer sometimes rarely sees the director, who becomes a remote and impersonal critic. That modern example of nonpaternalism parallels another problem with slaveholders' aspiration to be paternalists: often the plantation was too big and impersonal for master and far-off field hand to have close contact.

Intimate contact, however, was present in the Big House between the patriarch and domestic slaves; and intimacy also flourishes when senior professors and graduate students work closely together on each other's mutual interests. The charged interaction can even generate a new name. Aspiring Ph.D. candidates often become identified not in the pregraduate school way, as "Freehling's son," but in the rebaptized professional way, as "Stampp's student." The new name often captures not just a moment but a career. If Ph.D. recipients have written a dissertation on the professor's suggested topic in the professor's suggested manner, few can thereafter break free to create their own subjects and interpretations.

Ever since beginning work on my own Ph.D., I had known that Old South slaveholders wished to have an equivalent permanent control over their sons' ideas about slaveholding. I had also known that southern patriarchs demanded perpetual sway over white women and over blacks. But only much later, at the turning point in my quest to understand the Old South, did I suddenly understand why a minority of key southern disunionists pushed their paternalistic creed to a stunning extreme: They believed that white male nonslaveholders also needed paternalistic guidance. My moment of insight was doubly transforming, for I realized that to convey the boundlessness of these important secessionists' parental aspirations, I would have to break freer of my own mentors. Upon reading a single letter, penned in 1843, my projected book, sixteen years in the making, on the South's road to disunion, 1850–61, could no longer be written. I would have to write a still more time-consuming book—and a different book than my professors had written—to explain why an almost unlimited version of paternalism helped precipitate the southern revolution of 1860.

Historians' insights almost never strike so abruptly. Usually comprehension grows exasperatingly slowly, bit by elusive bit. Only after hundreds of days studying thousands of manuscripts does a dead epoch come alive to the researcher. Moreover, historians almost never find a previously unknown document that changes the shape of an important problem. Yet I say that a single unknown letter revolutionized my scholarly life and work?!

Well, it seemed that way at the time. Looking back at the transformation of my professional career, as at the southern revolution of 1860–61 which I seek to recount, I know that cataclysms are seldom as sudden as they seem. Indeed, that transforming manuscript affected my thinking especially powerfully because I had long pondered the paternalistic puzzles it clarified. The manuscript also shocked me into living up to a long-held, long-evaded proposition: that to explain a crisis, historians must analyze a forbiddingly long series of antecedent events. But that necessity did become inescapable instantly, as I read through Abel P. Upshur's extraordinary 1843 letter in the William and Mary College Rare Book Room. To make the event even odder, I was in the Williamsburg, Virginia, library that morning only because of a nearby dog show. More weirdly still, lining the walls of my scholarly reading area was one of the world's richest collections of scarce books on dogs.

3

I had expected no such ridiculous twist in a long journey—I had expected no long journey—when I started research on my second book. It was then 1967. I had just published a history of the first southern confrontation crisis with the Union, the South Carolina Nullification Controversy of 1832–33. That book was originally my doctoral dissertation, written under Kenneth M. Stampp at the University of California, Berkeley. The study begins in 1816, with South Carolina's John C. Calhoun among the premier American nationalists. The volume ends in 1836, with Calhoun and other South Carolina extremists well along the road to disunion. How natural, then, to write a sequel on the disunionists' culminating crisis of 1860–61.

My model was Professor Stampp's *And the War Came,* a history of the northern secession crisis. Stampp therein argued that "much can be learned about the general nature of the American sectional conflict from a study of . . . the five months between the election of Lincoln and the attack upon Fort Sumter," for "during this brief and dramatic period all the sharp issues which had divided the sections for a generation were telescoped and intensified."[1] Stampp's logic about the North, I assumed, would apply equally to the South. A book on the few months of the southern secession crisis, I further assumed, could be written in a few years—an enticing prospect for an ambitious young academic.

These assumptions violated two aspects of my initiation into the profession. First of all, in my book on nullification, I had focused on more than the few months of the Nullification Controversy. I had instead gone back sixteen years from the confrontation of 1832–33 and forward four years in order to place the showdown in perspective. Shouldn't a study of the southern secession crisis also require an extended temporal perspective, even if Kenneth Stampp had chosen a shorter time span for his study of the northern secession crisis?

Which brings me to my second violation of my principles. I had gone to work with Professor Stampp at Berkeley in 1958 after graduating from Harvard College precisely to avoid the teaching model of the paternalistic professor and the perpetual disciple. That model, I thought, often pervaded the Harvard Yard of the late 1950s. To Harvard undergraduates in American history, the most memorable father figure was Frederick Merk, the leading historian of the western frontier and of the Texas Annexation Controversy of the mid-1840s. The elderly "Mr. Merk," as everyone called him, lectured in the survey course in American history. For dense presentation of meticulously organized facts—and for insistence that every spoken detail be perpetuated in student notebooks and replicated in final exam blue books—Mr. Merk may still hold the all-time record. So too, for perpetuating a milieu where reputations could be made by dazzling classroom lectures, by quantities of graduate student disciples, and by biting repartee over lunch—instead of by publications addressed to a national community of scholars—nothing this side of England rivaled Harvard.

Or so I thought, probably erroneously, as a callow undergraduate. I hasten to add that Harvard may be different now, thirty-five years later, and that my history education there had many superb features, including teaching by Arthur Schlesinger, Jr., and Bernard Bailyn, two inspiring professors who demanded undergraduate creativity. But too often, I had to memorize Great Men's lectures (there were, in those bygone times, few women professors). I came to wonder whether memorization would lead to originality. I felt compelled to move westward for graduate work in order to develop my own historical vision.

This notion of escaping eastern models by moving from the Atlantic to the Pacific was naive, as I should have known from Mr. Merk's lectures on the frontier. Throughout our history, western institutions have replicated eastern prototypes, especially in institutions of higher education. The dominant aspects of history education—the lecture system for undergraduates and the mentor system for graduate students—pervades American universities, coast to coast. Everywhere creative scholars often seek, by lecturing to undergraduates, to maximize the spread of information, illumination, inspiration. Everywhere publishing scholars often endeavor, by guiding graduate students through similar scholarship, to multiply the production of useful monographs.

This nationwide system has several virtues and several antidotes to its drawbacks. A sophisticated lecturer can introduce unsophisticated undergraduates to the subtleties of historical analysis. An experienced mentor can also supply research topics and approaches to uneasy graduate students. Moreover, when the lecturer encourages undergraduates to think for themselves, whether in supplemental discussion sessions or in term papers or on final exams, an important scholar's lecture hardly blocks the path toward becoming a creative historian. So too, when mentors of graduate students demand criticisms of all ideas, especially their own, apprenticeship ends and creativity begins.

But lecturers and mentors risk a debilitating dependence among those, as the telling phrase goes, "sitting at their feet." The lecture system summons the copycat virtues, with undergraduates striving to transcribe every word. The mentor system equally invites replication, with graduate students seeking to research and write the way the professor does. Yet I could scarcely escape dependence by fleeing Harvard professors, not with the paternalistic system flourishing everywhere west of Cambridge, Massachusetts.

But though the lecture/mentor system dominated the Berkeley graduate school, Kenneth Stampp minimized its dependence-inducing tendencies. Professor Stampp had no interest in training graduate students to think as he did, indeed to think about the same matters as he did. He urged students to do their own projects their own way, emulating only his passion for exhaustive research and clear writing. He was the mentor as nonmentor. I cherished him for that. Yet there I was, several years after doing my Ph.D. dissertation under his direction my way, doing my second book his way.

The trouble was partly my own. I was ambivalent about paternal authority, as I revealed when fleeing from Harvard and settling in under Mr. Stampp. Where a heavy-handed mentor would have caused another flight, a supportive and noninsistent director was just the sort to influence my directions the most. The phenomenon illustrates another trouble with generalizing too broadly about slaveholder paternalism and slaves' response. Just as some planters (and some professors) labored in too impersonal a setting for paternalistic relationships, so when a paternalistic interaction did set in, many were the variations among slaveholders and slaves (and among professors and students).

Still, beyond individual variations lay the universal dynamics of the relationship itself. Paternalistic interactions can generate a result that neither party had intended. Only a long-term physical intimacy between adults is as intense as the transactions between paternal figures and dependents. Only a divorce or other such fracture of an adult relationship is as traumatic as daughters and sons breaking free from mothers and fathers. The finer the paternal guidance, the harder to break free; and Professor Stampp was a brilliant adviser of graduate students. His book on the *northern* side of the secession crisis was also exceptionally fine. The *southern* side of the secession crisis, however, was different, and I was a different person. That is why he insisted, in the modern paternalistic style, that his students must find their own techniques, indeed make their own mistakes. But whatever he said, his inspiring way was hard to avoid, as children of admirable parents always discover.

4

The sources on secession swiftly drove me back to studying the Old South my way. After reading manuscripts for a few months, I knew that to explain secession in 1860 no less than to explain nullification in 1832, I would have to explore at least the decade before the confrontation. The prospect was daunting. With nullification, I had felt compelled to study only South Carolina. That investigation of one state had taken many months. With secession, I felt obligated to study all fifteen slaveholding states and probably northern states, too. That inquiry would take many years. No quick book would be forthcoming from this aspiring academic.

But I could not write this second book unless I retreated to the 1850s. The sources on the secession crisis posed riddles instead of providing answers when I pressed an important question: Why did secessionists feel that President-elect Abraham Lincoln would immediately menace slavery? A generation before I commenced research, the dominant school of Civil War historians, the so-called Revisionists, had sought to revise away that question, as well as all questions implying that pre–Civil War politicians fought over practical menaces to slavery. The Revisionists ridiculed secession, as well as every attack on slavery or defense of it, as foolishly impractical. Their conclusion: A blundering generation of pre–Civil War demagogues whipped up a needless crisis over useless issues.[2]

The Revisionists especially derided the secessionists of 1860 for calling Abraham Lincoln and his Republican Party an instant threat to slavery. Republican voters had raised Lincoln to the presidency, Revisionists correctly pointed out, not to abolish slavery in the South but to stop slavery from spreading to new territories; and no massive numbers of slaveholders wished to spread to then-held federal territory. The Revisionists could have added that the Deep South expansionists who most wished the United States to seize new territories—southwestern imperialists centered in New Orleans—preferred to avoid secession. These Louisiana adventurers hoped to use the Union's power to capture Caribbean territory. Meanwhile the Deep South area that most wished to secede, low-country South Carolina, little desired Caribbean expansion. Carolina reactionaries preferred to consolidate their bounded Atlantic coast swamps rather than to seek the unbounded Caribbean. So why should exactly the Southerners who preferred a confined South consider Lincoln, who only insisted on containment, immediately menacing?

Lincoln sought to set to rest one obvious answer: that he might move beyond containment and impose abolition on southern states. In the Lincoln-Douglas Debates, Lincoln had segregated his program, banning slavery in new territories, from abolitionists' program, emancipating slaves in the old states. In his Inaugural Address, the President-elect endorsed a proposed Thirteenth Amendment, which would have forever barred the federal government from coercively abolishing slavery in a state. Because of Lincoln's arguably nonmenacing posture, most southern Unionists, meaning initially the huge majority of Southerners, called secession folly unless and until Lincoln violated his anti-interventionist pledge. No wonder, then, that Revisionist historians derided secession as a blundering generation's climactic blunder.

But neither the Revisionists nor subsequent historians had laid out the supposed blunderers' view of the matter. Why had rebels against Union considered Lincoln so immediately threatening that a potentially counterproductive civil war must be risked? As I researched the secessionists' answer, an unexpected viewpoint emerged. Instead of imposing antislavery as an outsider, secessionists warned, Lincoln would enlist insiders to corrode slavery. By using patronage appointments to recruit southern politicians, the President would form a heretical southern wing of the Republican Party. Especially in the Border South, where only one in eight voters owned slaves, the thin slaveholding minority could not stop

Southern Republicans' demagoguery from nurturing the thick non-slaveholding majority's nascent antislavery sentiments. Lincoln's Border South wing would thus eventually eliminate slavery from the upper third of the South, while Lincoln's northern majority would forbid the slavocracy from expanding into new territory. This process, if allowed to start, could never be aborted. After the number of free states sufficiently expanded and the number of slave states sufficiently contracted, the Republican Party could— and would—end slavery by constitutional amendment.

This secessionist prophecy undermined two classic interpretations of the Old South: the Great Reaction/Closed Society interpretation and the Herrenvolk interpretation. Almost all southern historians thought, and I had argued in my nullification book, that a southern Great Reaction in the mid-1830s had yielded a monolithic Closed Society. Supposedly, before 1832, Southerners openly debated slavery. Supposedly, after 1835, all Southerners rejected antislavery. Yet the secessionists of 1860–61 worried that Border South antislavery sentiments were still there to be nurtured. Thus a Southern Republican Party, agitating amidst largely nonslaveholders, could become all too menacing.

By worrying about democratic agitation addressed to poorer white men, secessionists violated the Herrenvolk no less than the Great Reaction/Closed Society interpretation of the Slave South.[3] The Herrenvolk label (meaning "master race" in German) is historians' shorthand description for an Old South society allegedly divided at the racial line. On the black side of the color line, Southerners supposedly believed that all members of the mastered race were irrevocably childish. But on the white side of the color line, Southerners supposedly believed that all male offspring of the master race would become equal adults. This supposed universal trust in white men underlay the slaveholders' supposedly universal faith in the foundation of southern antebellum politics: the national two-party system. Southerners cherished electoral contests between two national partisan machines, according to the Herrenvolk interpretation, because after politicians stirred up the voters, white commoners would choose sagely at the polls.

Andrew Jackson, large Tennessee slaveholder, epitomized the Herrenvolk South and its faith in two-party electioneering. Jackson assumed that Great White Fathers must forever guide childish blacks (and Native Americans). But whites must never patronize fellow citizens. Jackson feared that the best black man, if freed, would revert to savagery, as would the best Native American, if let loose from the reservation. The most ignorant white man, however, would vote as intelligently as the wisest scholar. Thus whichever electioneering leaders won the people's hearts deserved the people's offices.

This Herrenvolk map, by dividing the Old South at the color line, misplaces the border between Jackson's paternalism and his egalitarianism. Great White Fathers were precisely fathers, not mothers. Jackson exalted not the master race but the master sex of the master race. He wished white men to preserve perpetual paternalism not just over red men and black men but also over women of all races. As the historian Stephanie McCurry has recently brilliantly reminded us, this sexism gave lowly nonslaveholders a personal stake in lordly paternalism.[4] Although poorer white males did not own blacks, they loved to dominate their wives. But the Jackson-style male chauvinists, and especially the nonslaveholders, insisted that paternalistic dominance over white males must end when boys became men, no matter how poor the nonslaveholder or how grand the slaveholder.

Or so I thought late antebellum Southerners believed, until I encountered the extremists who first precipitated secession in 1860. These initial secessionists scorned white male egalitarianism, for trust in white males' decisions legitimated all national parties that presented options to (supposedly all-wise) commoners. Thus President Lincoln could legitimately use patronage to build a southern wing of a National Republican Party. Republican agitators could legitimately stir up Border South commoners, who could legitimately conclude that slavery was undemocratically anti-egalitarian. Southern extremists' fear of such a mainstream disaster looked very much like a distrust of white egalitarianism, a distaste for politicians and plebeians, and a dismay at patronage-fueled, two-national-party electoral campaigns.

Worse for the Herrenvolk interpretation, I found critical initial secessionists, in the very act of commencing their revolution, bypassing the color line that supposedly barred perpetual paternal governance of white males. Secessionists knew that in the whole South (including the Border South) immediately after Lincoln's election, most voters opposed secession. But the initial secessionists meant to guide this supposedly gullible antisecessionist majority. The eagerest southern secessionists maneuvered to have the first secessionist decision made not in some South-wide convention or referendum, where a southern majority would have trounced them, but in South Carolina, the state where they could most easily rally a majority for disunion. After the South Carolina fraction of the South seceded, the majority in other southern states would be forced to decide not whether secession was wise (most Southerners thought no) but whether Southerners should fire rifles at fellow Southerners (a *very* different matter). To ensure that the South Carolina majority forced the hand of the southern majority, the initial secessionists silenced South Carolina antisecession voices, especially that of the state's most powerful Unionist, U.S. Senator James Henry Hammond.[5] As the secessionist most responsible for silencing Hammond explained, "Whoever waited for the common people when a great movement was to be made? We must make the move & force them to follow."[6]

Slaveholding paternalists must force white majorities to follow, lest majoritarian demagogues incite plebeians to squelch first secession and then slavery too! What kind of disunion climax was this, from a culture that supposedly had used a Great Reaction to forge a Closed Society on the Herrenvolk basis of perpetual guidance for blacks, egalitarian majoritarianism for white males? If, as Professor Stampp had written, "during this brief and dramatic period, all the sharp issues which had divided the sections for a generation were telescoped and intensified," we did not understand the climactic generation of antebellum Southerners. I would have to investigate that generation's evolution, seeking to understand Southerners' distrust of each other—and especially of unguided white males. Despite the Great Reaction, had an underground southern antislavery consciousness survived? Despite Herrenvolkism, did class consciousness overwhelm racial and sexist consciousness in some slaveholders' view of the world? Did the most extreme Southerners wish to extend upper-class paternalism beyond wives and children and blacks and Native Americans so that the wealthy could guide middle- and lower-class white men too? Perhaps a history of the South, 1850–61, would illuminate the limitless paternalists' precipitation of disunion.

5

Ten years of research and tens of thousands of research dollars later, I knew that the 1850s could throw much—but not quite enough—perspective on these questions. With every crisis of the 1850s, I repeated my first question about the secessionists' view of President-elect Abraham Lincoln: Why did key actors find a particular issue a practical menace? Always my first key actor was the precipitator, the Southerner(s) who first thrust a provocative issue onto a reluctant national establishment's agenda. Lee Benson, an important American social scientific historian, introduced me to this research tactic. If crises arose from the spirit of an age, Benson argued, the general spirit must have motivated a particular person to precipitate a particular crisis. By asking *who* started a controversy and then asking what she/he/they sought to accomplish and why, the researcher grounded the frustratingly open-ended "what caused the Civil War" question in a closed and researchable specific inquiry. Especially in explaining the antebellum South, analysis of precipitators of issues paid huge dividends. Once a southern demand was made, a knee-jerk national interaction set in. Northerners called the minority dictation immoral, and Southerners called the northern moral presumption insufferable. The precipitator had started something that explosively spread, whatever subsequent actors thought about the practicality of the initial demand.

When analyzing the reaction to the initiation of an issue, Benson taught, the researcher should continue to ask *who* questions before *why* questions in order to make causal patterns concrete, irrefutable. Who among the Northerners called the precipitator an undemocratic agent of the dictatorial Slavepower, and why? Who among the Southerners called the northern anti-Slavepower critics unbearably holier-than-thou, and why? Who in the establishment carried the issue inside White House or congressional or party deliberations, and why? How did particular establishment figures react to the issue, and why? What particular voters reacted to which specific resolution of an issue, and why? If the researcher is fortunate, successive crises fall into a pattern on all these questions. The pattern becomes a generalization about Civil War causation. That generalization might become a more universal model, capable of explaining other human crises.

Lee Benson, though a social scientific historian, aimed, in the manner of a natural scientist, to generate a universal model from a defined and thus verifiable experiment. He sought to communicate with social scientists in other academic disciplines. While I also wished to ground airy generalizations in researchable specifics, I aimed to interest a wider nonacademic audience. Benson's social science strategies ironically served my non-Bensonian literary purposes. My most abstract academic model of Civil War causation, Greek to nonacademics, could be illustrated in colorful biographies of key precipitators. Better still, such biographies, unlike certain of my other literary strategies for bringing history alive to nonacademics, did not strike some academics as anti-academic. The past actors whom I sought to make compelling to nonscholars had helped generate my scholarly model in the first place. Such universally appealing biographical portraits, along with the use of such universally resonating words as *paternalism*, were as close as I came to reaching both my frustratingly different audiences at the same time.

My research into the crises of the 1850s revealed that secession in many ways brought repeating patterns to climax. Thus, just as the precipitators of revolution in 1860 feared Republican inroads in the Border South, so precipitators of the crises of the 1850s feared Yankee inroads across the South's northern borders. Whether U.S. Senator James Mason of Virginia was inaugurating the Fugitive Slave Controversy of 1850, particularly to protect slavery in western Virginia, or U.S. Senator David Atchison of Missouri was inaugurating the Kansas-Nebraska Controversy of 1854, particularly to consolidate slavery in western Missouri, the message was the same: Our Border South is no Closed Society. We must shutter all windows to the North. We cannot tolerate Yankee neighbors' open opportunities to incite enslaved blacks to flee and to provoke non-slaveholding whites to oppose slaveholders. Federal laws must close up our borders, or our most northern areas will be endangered.

My research further revealed that such rhetoric was hardly Revisionist-style irresponsible propaganda. Fugitive slaves *were* running away from Border South masters. Border heretics *were* proposing a racist (and therefore more seductive) form of antislavery: Get rid of slavery on the condition that you get rid of freed blacks too. Up North, Abraham Lincoln was suggesting that federal funds might be used to rid America of blacks. Within the Border South, white heretics and black fugitives were still too few to threaten the institution massively in the 1850s. Yet Lincoln in the 1860s could use the previously scarce dissenters to form the secessionists' bête noir, a native southern wing of a *National* Republican Party. That new party's agitations could yield more fugitive slaves, who could worry more border masters into selling more slaves to slaveholders located more safely in the deeper South.

But little in the 1850s threw perspective on why secessionists conceived that a national party's agitation in the South would yield more white dissenters. A southern shudder at national party agitation hardly pervaded the 1850s. Instead, the South's favorite national party, the Democratic Party, won such amazing slaveholder triumphs—the Fugitive Slave Law, the Kansas-Nebraska Act, the Dred Scott Decision—that Herrenvolk democracy and its national party institutions seemed the salvation of black slavery. Moreover, southern voters hardly seemed a potentially gullible menace. They usually voted for the Democracy and almost always against southern antislavery heretics. Even amidst South Carolina's soon-to-be secessionists, a National Democratic Party faction arose in the 1850s, and few Carolinians called it a demagogic danger. So whence came these extremists' 1860 notion that national parties were so dangerous, that southern antislavery heretics were so threatening, that white males were so gullible—in sum that white Herrenvolkism was such a precarious foundation for black slavery—that paternalists must force the first secession decision on white commoners, lest Lincoln's Herrenvolk party corrupt untrustworthy yeomen?

My problem was obvious to someone who had written about the 1830s: The 1850–61 period provided too short a perspective on secessionists' attitudes toward national parties. If southern fear of national parties was uncommon in the 1850s, when the Democratic Party brought slaveholders lush bounties, distrust of the national two-party establishment had been rampant among John C. Calhoun and the South Carolina Nullifiers in the 1830s, when the Democratic Party was less proslavery. In 1832, the Nullifiers had used minority veto to fight majoritarian democracy, in part because they feared that a national majoritarian party could corrupt morale and opinion in a not-yet-very-proslavery South. So too in 1835, South Carolina Nullifiers had precipitated the congressional Gag Rule Controversy, that attempt to silence national and southern debate on slavery. By demanding that Congress gag democratic discussion, as by insisting that majority law could be nullified, the Carolinians had denied the foundation of Jacksonian Herrenvolkism: that white majorities would make wise decisions after national party politicians presented the options. To make the value of the Gag Rule perspective even more obvious, South Carolina's James Henry Hammond, the Unionist who allowed secessionists to silence his antisecessionist dissent in 1860, had provoked the first Gag Rule Crisis to silence southern and national dissidence. So why not start my *Road to Disunion* in the 1830s instead of the 1850s?

Indeed, why not start earlier? South Carolina Nullifiers traced their antiparty heritage back to the Founding Fathers' anti-Herrenvolk, anti-egalitarian, color-blind paternalism. The patriarchs of 1776 affirmed that the best philosopher-statesmen must decide for the white masses—and that the worst spoilsmen must not be allowed to inflame white plebeians' passions. By tracing antebellum attitudes back to their beginnings in 1776, I could also follow the Border South's antislavery reformism (and its antiblack conservatism) back to Thomas Jefferson's conviction that slavery must be abolished, assuming blacks could be removed. Then by moving forward into the 1830s, I could investigate why Jefferson's conditional, racist form of antislavery had survived the putative Great Reaction, especially in the Border South.

Other Civil War historians' finest work, by going back much further than the presecession decade, also indicated that my 1850s straitjacket stifled my perspective. While I was studying exclusively the 1850s, Don Fehrenbacher, writing on the Dred Scott decision of 1857, and David Brion Davis, writing on antislavery, published superb books.[7] Fehrenbacher went back to the Founding Fathers; Davis, back to Greek and Roman times. Both authors' long time spans provided rich background. How, then, could I start as late as 1850? And especially, how could I begin in 1850? The territorial issues of 1850 stemmed from the American acquisition of Mexican territory (1848). The territorial acquisition stemmed from the United States–Mexican War (1846–48). The Mexican War stemmed from Texas Annexation (1845). Annexation stemmed from another important slavery controversy (1843–45). Could I ignore that stream of antecedents?

Intellectually, then, my 1850 starting point came to look indefensible. But in practical terms, an earlier starting point looked forbidding. At the beginning of the 1980s, practicality triumphed. Instead of taking years to extend my research into the pre-1850s, I spent a month writing a background chapter to my 1850–61 manuscript. My drafted chapter passed lightly over the Founding Fathers, Nullification, and the Gag Rule. It then ended with several pages on Texas Annexation.

In my Texas narrative, I recaptured my days as a Harvard undergraduate replicating notes from Mr. Merk. Frederick Merk had published little during his professorial years. Then he retired, shortly after I graduated, and swiftly poured out densely documented books on America's expansionist foreign policy in the 1840s.[8] Mr. Merk's books especially emphasized President John Tyler, Secretary of State Abel P. Upshur, and their 1844 treaty of annexation with Texas. According to Mr. Merk, these politically isolated Virginia Whigs, desperate for an issue to win a second term, "demagogically" spread the "propaganda" that if the proslavery United States did not annex the Republic of Texas with its relatively few slaves, antislavery England would sustain the struggling republic. Texans, in return, would supposedly emancipate their slaves. This Upshur-Tyler demagoguery, according to Mr. Merk, partially frightened Southerners, helped lead to annexation, and thereby increased sectional tensions in the most blundering way.

I uneasily knew that my Texas pages, by replicating Mr. Merk's Revisionist-like scoffing at demagogues and meaningless issues, contradicted my chapters on the 1850s, which sought the meaning behind supposedly absurd propaganda. I rather wished that Mr. Merk had explicitly considered whether Upshur and Tyler truly believed in their alleged demagoguery and/or whether an English menace really existed. But I recognized that the Texas Annexation Controversy especially lent itself to a Revisionist interpretation. Upshur and Tyler, as particularly isolated politicians, desperately sought a provocative issue. I also valued Mr. Merk's solution to the initial Lee Benson–style "who caused" question. Abel P. Upshur's diplomacy indeed first placed the incendiary annexation issue on President Tyler's and thus the nation's agenda. As to why Upshur precipitated an explosive stream of events, Mr. Merk's solution— to salvage a demagogue's power—came accompanied with voluminous documentation from Secretary Upshur's letters in the William and Mary College Library. Mr. Merk's dense footnotes resurrected his dense undergraduate lectures. *Mr. Merk* wrong about the *facts?* With that incredulous way of asking the question, I revealed that whatever my partial deviance from Mr. Stampp's time frames, I remained under another teacher's paternalistic sway.

6

Whenever I reread my affirmation of Mr. Merk's Revisionism, however, I nervously realized I should read Upshur's letters before I published my anti-Revisionist book. In late 1982, I started looking for a convenient way to spend a day in Williamsburg. The next fall, sixteen years into working on *The Road to Disunion*, I found a good occasion. On November 4, 1983, Puddin', my daughter's Dandie Dinmont terrier, would be competing at a dog show near Williamsburg!

I value the breeding and showing of Norwich and Dandie Dinmont terriers chiefly as a comic relief from academic pressures. But my hobby occasionally enriches my historical writing, too. At dog shows, I experience my closest personal contact with the nonacademic audience who I hope will read my books. The dog show world is rough, pushy, sensual. Dog show exhibiters love forceful striving, blunt conversation, vivid language. They have no patience with abstruse theorists, passive speculation, intellectual jargon. To interest these pragmatic activists in historical abstractions, a professor had better employ the vernacular tongue.

Some academics find everyday language embarrassing in a book of serious history. Their fastidious taste aside, these purists urge historians to use the vocabulary employed in the past, not the anachronistic words of our own era. Their books, however, sometimes bristle with an academic jargon unfathomable to most people now and to all folks in the past. Yet anachronistic academic words such as *Herrenvolk* seem to me perfectly appropriate. Historians write for their live audience, not for their deceased subjects; and many academics' hoped-for audience comprises only fellow academics. But since I write for nonscholars, too, I occasionally seek the common words that can convey scholars' uncommon abstractions.

My dog show friends prefer vivid words like *a tad* to pale words like *a little*. Some academics, however, wince at the supposed vulgarization. The Freehlings' only National Specialty Champion Norwich terrier happens to be named Ch. Justa Tad Tuff. We call the little hero Tad. Whenever I use the word *tad* and some professor blanches, I look down at Tad and smile.

Dog shows also yield perspective on some academics' less humorous rigidity. Judges govern the dog ring just as critics govern academia. A dog fancier judging which terrier is best can resemble a reviewer deciding which book is worthy. I especially see the resemblance when dog show judges award blue ribbons to dogs who repeat the look of their prized pets bred some ten years ago. These so-called kennel-blind arbiters are uncomfortably akin to the critics who like best the new volume that sustains their ten-year-old argument. But the best dog fanciers, like the best academics and the best parents, understand that progress sometimes occurs when their own work is superseded. One learns from their judgments.

My academic obligations, together with the travel expense, usually precluded my attendance at the widely dispersed show sites, where our professional handler paraded Puddin' before her latest judge. But the dog show near Williamsburg, the most important in Puddin' 's trot to her championship, could be reached inexpensively from Baltimore, where I was teaching at The Johns Hopkins University. In the morning, before Puddin' 's afternoon date with the judge, I could read the Upshur letters that had proved to Mr. Merk that the secretary of state was a cynical demagogue. The previous evening, I could meet another academic obligation. On my way to Williamsburg, I could consult with a graduate student who was working on a doctoral dissertation, ostensibly under my direction. My unease about that student, as much as my uninformed acceptance of Mr. Merk's thesis about Upshur's supposed propaganda, epitomized my continuing failure to see unlimited paternalism's full problems.

Just as children grow up to become parents and often unthinkingly repeat their parents' errors, so students grow up to become teachers and often instinctively replicate unlimited paternalism's drawbacks. As an undergraduate, I had seen the problem with passively listening to a dazzling lecturer. Yet as a fledgling lecturer, I enjoyed putting on performances, which was not all that surprising in a former student who was still dazzled by Mr. Merk. So too as a graduate student, I had chosen a mentor who did not wish to reproduce himself. But as a guiding professor, I enjoyed setting graduate students to work on my sort of project, done in my sort of fashion, which was not all that surprising in a former student who started out writing his second book Mr. Stampp's way.

A tragedy reawakened me to the drawbacks of limitlessly paternalistic teaching styles. In 1979, Willie Lee Rose, my wonderful colleague at Johns Hopkins, suffered a massive stroke. Since we shared the Civil War field, I inherited her graduate students. Since they were hers, no room existed for me to impose my ways. I could only encourage these students to finish up work foreign to me. I found that encouragement worked better than had impositions. Mrs. Rose's students were doing things very well, and not at all in my fashion.

One of Mrs. Rose's most interesting students, however, was taking a (to me) distressingly long time finishing a dissertation. So I stopped by that pre-dog-show evening to check on the supposed dilatory writer. I need not have bothered. The young scholar, progressing slowly but steadily, would eventually produce one of the finest American history dissertations at The Johns Hopkins University in the 1980s. I had my initial instruction, in that most instructive twenty-four-hour period of my life, that paternalists do not forever know what is best for those less powerful.

The supreme lesson came the next morning in the William and

Mary College's Rare Book Room. While waiting for Abel P. Upshur's letters to be delivered to my desk, I noticed that books on
dogs surrounded the reading room, on this day that a dog show had
brought me to Virginia. But practically the moment Upshur's letters arrived, I knew that I would not that afternoon witness a judge
scrutinize Puddin'. Almost immediately I came across *the* Abel P.
Upshur letter, one of the greatest of Old South documents. Upshur
dated the letter March 13, 1843. He was then President John
Tyler's secretary of the navy. Within weeks, he would become the
secretary of state who precipitated the Texas Annexation Controversy. Upshur was writing his intimate friend Nathaniel Beverley
Tucker, the William and Mary law professor and novelist. Upshur,
like Tucker, was a slaveholding conservative and intellectual from
the oldest part of Virginia. Beverley Tucker, owner of slaves in both
Virginia and Texas, prayed for disunion. Abel P. Upshur, an intense
admirer of John C. Calhoun's, preferred Calhoun's strategy: a
southern movement toward a southern convention. The conclave
could, so Calhoun and Upshur believed, probably save slavery in
the Union. If that Unionist strategy failed, the convention could
secure disunion.

Here, in its entirety, is Upshur's letter, never before published,
and I believe never cited before I saw it:[9]

Washington

March 13th 43

My dear Judge

I have this moment, received your letter of the 7th. I have long &
impatiently expected it, but did not intend to wait for it, before I
wrote to you. I have been promising myself that I would do this, for
many a long day past, but have never had a chance til now. And even
now, I do but make a *beginning*, not knowing how soon I may be
compelled to lay my pen aside. The truth is, I am *overworked*. Last
Wednesday, I fairly broke down, like an overtasked horse, & have ever
since, been confined to my house. No man who is determined to be
faithful in all things, can perform the task that is laid on me.

Deeply & sincerely do I sympathize with Mrs. T. & all of you, in
the loss you have sustained. [The death of Mrs. Tucker's brother, Reubin Smith.] Poor Reubin! most highly did I esteem him; an honest
hearted, true young man, worthy of all respect & confidence. I have
experienced too many bereavements of that kind, not to know how
vain are all the consolations which friends can offer. There is *no* consolation except what Time always brings, or that which Religion af-
firms, in a deep & abiding sense of the goodness of God, in all the

ways of his Providence. Parnell's Hermit presents the true philosophy of all such cases.

Why do you think that "our thoughts no longer run in the same channel"? Truly sorry am I, that they do, for I had hoped that my gloomy forebodings might be corrected by your cooler wisdom, & keener sagacity. But I find that the song which you have sung, is exactly my song; a melancholy strain which every true friend I meet, is destined to hear. *I have no hope for the country.* As to a reform in the government, it is impossible. The people do not wish it. I do not speak of the great mass of farmers & planters & property holders who have a real stake in the government. These are all right in their feelings, and would be right in their opinions, if they were not deceived. But it has been a long time since our country was governed by such men. They are too scattered in position & too quiet & contented in their circumstances, to enter into combinations or to be exposed to high excitements. Our public affairs are controlled by political managers in the cities, who regard the constitution as they do the charter of a private corporation; a thing out of which money is to be made. This is the universal feeling, north of Mason & Dixon; that is, it is the universal feeling among those who have the government in their hands. My own experience in my own department, proves to me that these people want no reforms. I have been struggling against them, ever since I have been in office, & the result is, that I only displace one rogue, to put in another. The radical defect is in the constituent body. How can a country be well governed, except by those who *own* it? The moment the right of suffrage ceased to belong to the *soil*, the axe was laid at the root of our institutions. Unfortunately there are no steps backward. When those who have no permanent stake in the country, are allowed to govern it, what can you expect, but the very riot of the largest liberty; the prostration of all law, the corruption of all morals, & the rapid overthrow of all free institutions, in anarchy at the beginning, & despotism at the end. This is our fate, beyond all possible doubt. I am surprised to see how general this opinion has become. That calm thinkers & well informed men should entertain it, does not surprise me; but almost every man who has any thing to lose, whether he be wise or foolish, is taught the same lesson by his *fears*. The prevailing sentiment now is, that *any* government, which will give security to life and property, is better than the ever changing & uncertain course of *free forms*, without the guidance either of wisdom or virtue. The last Congress has done more than all the events of the preceding twenty years, to disgust the people with free government, & to bring the very name of it, into derision & contempt. I look upon it with grief and dismay, but our course is onward, and no earthly power can check it. There are particular causes at work, to expedite the catastrophe. I give you three of them.

1   There is as systematic a conspiracy against the South & its institu-

tions, as ever Cataline formed in Rome. Domestic slavery must perish, or else, it must be fought for. I think exactly as you do, that the
end will be, consolidation, & the overthrow of the South. So long as
the Richmond Enquirer shall retain its influence, the South will not
be permitted to see its danger. That paper is generally right in its principles, and always wrong in its measures & its *men*. The South will
be deceived, and kept asleep until her hair will be shorn, & the Sam-
son will wake up, only to find himself powerless. As connected with
this subject, I anticipate an important movement in regard to Texas.
Poised as that country now is, it must look to Europe for aid, & it
must make the best bargain it can. England alone can save her, &
England will drive with her a Jew's bargain. The abolition of slavery,
if not throughout the whole territory, at least, in the western half of
it, will be one of the conditions; the free admission of British goods
for a given time, will be another. The consequence of this last, will
be that the whole of our Southern country will be filled with British
manufactures, smuggled across the border. This will be fatal to our
Northern manufacturers, & will render their tariff policy unavailing.
It will also, destroy our revenues, & render a resort to direct taxes
necessary for the support of government. How this will be borne, it
is easy to foresee. No direct tax can possibly be laid by Congress,
which will not produce an explosion. This is one view of the subject;
but there is also, an alternative. I very much suspect that Northern
politicians begin to see this thing in its true light, & as they are ever
ready to sacrifice both political & moral principle,—aye, & religion
too,—to their interest, they will take measures to forward such a result. I should not be at all surprised if a proposition to admit Texas
into the Union, should be made & carried, by northern men, during
the next winter. But it will be on condition that slavery shall not be
permitted there. Will the South endure this? Ought they to endure it?
This is one of the subjects upon which I have longed to converse with
you. Can slavery exist, surrounded on all sides, by free States? I fear
it cannot, & such, I doubt not, will be the view of the whole South.
But on the other hand, if it can be maintained, will it not be strengthened in its influence, by being concentrated? The more you diffuse,
the more you weaken it. If, on the other hand, you can confine it to
the States in which it now exists, the natural increase of the slaves
will enable every white man to be a slaveowner, & thus you have a
homogeneous population, bound together by a common interest; &
that interest, involving their personal safety, their property & their
political power. This might possibly be the result, & therefore I am
not certain that the South ought to oppose the admission of Texas as
a free state. But I do not believe that the South will take this view of
it, & the consequence will be, either revolution in support of slavery,
or a surrender of it, in despair. The latter I believe, will be the end
of it.

I wish you would weigh these things, not only as a politician, but as a question involving your own interest. I greatly fear that your slaves in Texas, will be lost to you, if you do not remove them.
2 The second point is this. Several of the States have refused to comply with the law for the election of members of Congress. They will send their members here, elected in the old way, & then, what will be done? Will they be admitted to their seats, or not? If Congress be Whig, it is certain that they will not be; if it be Van Buren, they will be admitted or not, precisely as they happen to be favorable or unfavorable to Van Buren. Is not the hazard great? If they be excluded, we have revolution at once, for these States will not submit to such treatment. I believe that the danger from this source, is imminent indeed, & this is one of the leading reasons with me, for desiring the defeat both of Clay & Van Buren. I do not believe that the government can last the full term of either of them.
3 There is yet another cloud overhanging us. [William] Cost Johnson's assumption scheme is likely to succeed. That will be consolidation, boiled down to an essence. Public virtue is utterly gone, & the people are ready to take any thing which will relieve them from debt, or put money in their pockets.

These are some of the thoughts which weigh upon my mind, like the nightmare. They are never absent from it, & every day's observation confirms me in the conviction that they are right. But although, as politicians, we may see and deplore these things, it will never do for us to fold our arms, & submit without an effort. I am pained, much pained, at the tone of your late letters. Why should such a man as you, look so gloomily even upon gloomy things. I see no reason why you should despond, for yourself or your children, even if you do for your country. You will leave them a good inheritance in property, & a better one in good education, good talents, good morals & a good name. I trust in god that many, many years, are yet reserved for yourself, in which you may make your talents useful to them & to your country. For myself, I will do what I can, to prevent mischief; & I will do positive good, if I can. I mean to leave public life with a clear conscience. I have never yet done one thing which I am unwilling that the world should see, both in the act & in the motive, & in that course, will I persevere to the end. If I can do good, I will not withhold myself from the work; if I cannot do good, I can at least avoid evil. With the blessing of god, my dying pillow shall have the consolation of a faithful discharge of every public trust, with which I have been, or shall be clothed.

[Henry] Wise was right in wishing to go to France. His health is broken down & his little fortune much injured. He would, as Pinckney did, employ his leisure in study, & return home to practice his profession. I think he was unjustly rejected. He has many noble qualities, rely on it.

I have written you a long, rambling letter, hardly worth your perusal except so much as relates to you personally. I will *try* to write to Mrs. T. but *how* to do it, is the difficulty. Give her every assurance of my high respect & warm regard, & be you assured that you are among the few men in the world whose friendship I value. God bless you and yours.

Truly yours,
A P Upshur

B Tucker Esq

I could no longer approvingly repeat Mr. Merk's Revisionist interpretation, not after reading this letter. Abel P. Upshur was no cynical demagogue who concocted some propagandistic nonsense about English abolition in Texas. Instead, the man who was about to become the secretary of state, certain that an unannexed Texas *would* abolish slavery, privately wrote his best friend that "your slaves in Texas, will be lost to you, if you do not remove them." I would later find almost as conclusive evidence, in equally candid private correspondence, that John C. Calhoun, John Tyler, and Andrew Jackson also considered an English-Texas antislavery understanding possible. I would additionally find evidence that important Texans and Englishmen tentatively explored the possibility of such an antislavery fusion until the annexation treaty aborted the overtures. With Texas Annexation, as with secession and all the events of the 1850s, one had to ask *why* Southerners believed menaces existed and whether such menaces in fact confronted them before concurring with the Revisionists that southern alarms were absurd and southern alarmists but office seekers.

Nor could I skim over pre-1850 events after reading Upshur's letter. The Texas Annexation Controversy led to the slavery controversies in 1850; we did not understand the Texas affair; and Upshur's attitudes toward annexation threw perspective on events thereafter. "Can slavery exist, surrounded on all sides, by free States?" Upshur asked Beverley Tucker; Southerners would hope to make Kansas a slave state in the mid-1850s, lest that deadly question face already-semi-surrounded Missouri. Upshur told Tucker that he would "enable every white man to be a slaveowner"; later southern extremists would seek to reopen the African slave trade in hopes that every nonslaveholder would become a slaveholder. They would also fear that President-elect Lincoln would constitute an immediate menace to the Border South, where too few Southerners were slaveholders. Especially national party politicians, Upshur wrote Tucker, could delude nonslaveholders;

that, I at last understood, was why southern secessionists feared a *National* Republican Party after Lincoln's election. No matter that national party politicians had usually routed southern antislavery leaders when heretics ran as independents. According to the Upshur view of mobocracy, which was a duplicate of Calhoun's viewpoint, harmless independents became dangerous demagogues when they entered a national party, determined to agitate the people in order to raid national coffers.

On this no longer obscure point as on so many others, Upshur's letter showered perspective on his and Calhoun's successors, the South Carolina extremists who precipitated disunion in 1860. Upshur's imminent Texas diplomacy would double Lower South territory. Yet the old-fashioned Virginian did not really want the South to expand, any more than South Carolina secessionists would much desire Caribbean expansion or John C. Calhoun would much desire territorial acquisitions from the Mexican War.[10] The oldest, most reactionary South, centered in South Carolina and extending a little into Upshur's eastern Virginia, instead usually preferred that slavery "be strengthened," as Upshur wrote Tucker, "by being concentrated." These aristocratic republicans' great fear was not a contained slavocracy but an antagonistic North and a Herrenvolk South. "The thoughts which weigh upon my mind, like the nightmare," wrote Upshur, centered around English antislavery capitalists who "will drive . . . a Jew's bargain," Yankees who will "sacrifice" every "moral principle," Southerners "deceived, and kept asleep" by national party "political managers" who consider politics "a thing out of which money is to be made"—in short, a national mobocracy "without the guidance either of wisdom or virtue." Under the management of Virginia spoilsmen, themselves managed by the Jacksonian managers of the *Richmond Enquirer,* the South would not be "permitted to see its danger," for demagogues would wish to keep their party, their Union, and their jobs intact. The end result of corrupt national party rule would likely be southern "surrender" of slavery "in despair."

Party managers could cause southern surrender, Upshur was certain, because propertyless voters could be deluded. "How can a country be well governed," went his crowning question, "except by those who *own* it?" When "the right of suffrage ceased to belong to the *soil*, . . . what can you expect, but the very riot of the largest liberty; the prostration of all law, the corruption of all morals, & the rapid overthrow of all free institutions."

This language will jolt anyone who adheres to the conventional wisdom about the Old South. Proslavery warriors were supposedly either Andrew Jackson–style advocates of racial slavery, who trusted the white masses and wished to enslave only blacks, or George Fitzhugh–style advocates of color-blind slavery, who supposedly wished to enslave lower-class whites, too. In fact, not even Fitzhugh wished to enslave American white employees; and his fellow Virginia extremists worried most about poor whites' political opinions, not about wage slaves' economic dependency. Abel P. Upshur did not desire to enslave impoverished whites. He instead wished to make propertyless voters into landowners and especially slaveholders. Where Andrew Jackson considered citizens trustworthy if they possessed nothing but a white skin, Upshur considered Jackson's Herrenvolk democracy untrustworthy unless all white males possessed a propertied stake in the system. So long as white males did not universally own property, and especially slave property, insisted Upshur, slaveholders must renounce Jacksonian Herrenvolkism, reject national parties, and return to the Founding Fathers' disinterested paternalistic rule.

Upshur would have concurred with Frederick Merk that irresponsible demagogues were deluding the masses and destroying the republic. But *he* was hardly the culprit, and irresponsible party propagandists were hardly arousing the slaveholders. Rather, villainous national party managers were anesthetizing the Southerners. Only the Calhouns and Upshurs—only the nonpartisan paternalists—would responsibly use such issues as Texas to rouse the people from their deluded state and protect them from their depraved politicians, from antislavery inroads, and from Andrew Jackson's mobocratic Democratic Party. Or to put Upshur's remedy the crucial way, paternalistic guidance must be extended not only over slaves and women and children but also over white nonslaveholders until they too acquired slaves.

No single letter, no matter how eye-opening, can reveal everything. I still did not know how Upshur hoped to rally white commoners to reject Jackson-style egalitarianism, with its flattering affectation that squires and yeomen were equal. Nor could I conceive how the Virginia aristocrat could expect the plebeians to embrace Upshur-style, Calhoun-style paternalism, with its insulting insistence that gullible whites needed guidance and protection. But Upshur had promised Tucker he would try for the almost unimaginable; he was a paternalist of unquestionable sincerity; and Texas figured to be at the center of his unlikely adventure. Imagine, in this anti-extremist American nation, a towering reactionary like this coming to power, determined to turn back the American clock a good half century! I was not going to any dog show until I found out how this incredible story unfolded.

7

Late that afternoon, long after the judge decided Puddin' 's fate, I finished William and Mary College's magnificent cache of Upshur letters. I found that Upshur, as secretary of state, decided to exploit the fear of an English antislavery menace in Texas that he knew Southerners would share the minute a paternalistic secretary of state pointed it out to a sleepy multitude. Upshur knew that he would differ from the southern masses' likely response: that an emancipated Texas would be an unambiguous menace. A disinterested patriarch, however, could responsibly use that oversimplification to elevate commoners beyond irresponsible party hacks' influence. By rousing Southerners to demand Texas "as indispensable to their security," Upshur wrote Calhoun, he would guide the section to see "a *Southern* question, and not one of Whiggism and Democracy."[11] Both parties would be routed, a purely southern party would emerge, and paternalists could guide plebeians and slavery to safety.

I now knew that in the nineteenth-century Old South, two versions of slaveholder republicanism persistently collided. The huge majority of white males cherished Andrew Jackson's racially and sexually selective version of egalitarian republicanism, one for white men only. The southern majority's Herrenvolk position somewhat belied yet another latter-day historical interpretation: that the nineteenth-century North wandered from eighteenth-century American republicanism, while the South preserved the old faith. In truth, Andrew Jackson, southern planter to his heels, led a national change in majoritarian sensibility that knew no North, no South.

Still, a small minority of crusty Southeasterners *did* cling to old-fashioned republicanism more successfully and with greater historical impact than did reactionary Northerners. The tiny elitist, anti-Herrenvolk contingent of slaveholder republicans triumphed with the Founding Fathers, faltered before Jackson's Herrenvolk version of white men's republicanism, regrouped with Calhoun's Nullifiers in the 1830s, almost disappeared during Jacksonian Democracy's proslavery victories in the 1850s, seized control of the beginning stages of the southern disunion movement in

1860, and yielded to the more popular white egalitarian republicans after the secession revolution spread beyond South Carolina. This waxing and waning of colliding traditions also dominated the history of southern attitudes toward slavery. No proslavery Great Reaction of the 1830s had annihilated the Founding Fathers' conditional and racist version of antislavery. Rather, holders of antithetical views of slavery's future continued to face off in the 1850s and in the secession crisis, with Southerners, particularly in the Upper South, periodically proposing that blacks be deported, at least from their area.

In all its aspects, the Slave South, never drably monolithic, was ever full of intriguing imagined options. To explain so complicated a world, historians seemed best advised to observe fancied options begin in 1776, continue, wax and wane, and finally drive most slaveholders to revolt against the Union—and many Southerners to war against the Confederacy. Upshur's letter compelled the road to disunion to be surveyed from its beginning—including the beginning of a paternalism that sometimes envisioned poor white men as dangerously dependent, too.

8

The sequel deepened my perspective on the more extreme slaveholders' unlimited version of paternalism. My ensuing investigations extended back to 1776. My swelling manuscript had to be divided in half. The first volume of *Road to Disunion*, covering slavery crises through 1854, appeared in 1990, seven years after that day in Williamsburg and twenty-three years after I first sought to emulate Kenneth Stampp's *And the War Came*. In retrospect, my several decisions to extend the study backward in time still seem wise. That strategy illuminated repetitive patterns in southern attitudes toward slavery, elitist republicanism, egalitarian republicanism, Northerners, and other Southerners, as well as the resulting repeating patterns of national slavery crises. Those repeating patterns forged a Lee Benson–like model of the causes of the Civil War, with a narrative of crises rather than a web of abstractions establishing the causal design.

Yet I hardly wrote the model history, if such a treasure exists. My widened chronological coverage, for example, obscured my widened substantive analysis. The eighteen new chapters on pre-1850 political crises overshadowed the six old chapters on southern social structure. Thus, only careful readers (the kind no author can count on) grasped one of my largest points: that political history flows from social history, and vice versa. The added length also lent the book a density unfriendly to nonacademics and a repetition of popular literary devices grating to some academics. Finally, I had to publish the lengthened *Road to Disunion* in two volumes, with the second volume to appear years after the first. All the uncontrollable southern divisions in 1860–61, which I went back to 1776 to explain, were still under control in 1854, when Volume I ended. I thus invited the preliminary conclusion that my divided South was not divided at all!

I could have avoided these problems, even after Upshur's letter captured my attention. My most important subsequent research findings, those concerning the Gag Rule and Texas Annexation, filled nine of my eighteen new chapters. If I had published separate monographs on Texas Annexation and on the Gag Rule, my *Road to Disunion* could have skimmed over those two stopping places. But by segregating these two most illuminating, I think, of slavery crises, I would have lost the perspective that recurring controversies throw on each other. Whichever publishing path I chose to convey such massive and subtle material, I would have incurred assets and liabilities. Which is to say that even at scholars' most legitimate moments of arrogance, when they discover that rarity, a critical unknown document, they must humbly realize that a right way to convey their new truth—and perhaps even the truthfulness of the truth—may be a chimera.

9

Arrogance combined with humility: what a difficult synthesis. Yet the reconciliation is mandatory for all who would spend a lifetime advancing historical understanding. Without an almost arrogant confidence, one cannot publish the big book, pontificating on how to interpret fragmentary historical remains. But modesty must accompany rectitude, for all writers make mistakes; they must salute their correctors, and they must themselves drive corrections to higher levels of insight.

Some think that teaching and publishing require antithetical virtues. But that same combination of confidence and humility underlies the best modern teaching, as it underlies the best modern parenting. Whoever would direct others, whether by writing or teaching or child rearing, must think they see a path more clearly than those directed. Yet guides triumph most when those guided move on to better paths still. The crucial part, for the self-confident but bounded leader, is the self-effacing part; the hardest part, for the admiring follower, is the breaking free to total independence.

The slaveholders throw fine perspective on the process, for they denied all the hard, crucial parts of guiding while simultaneously abdicating as guide. They had no need to be humble, for they were not bounded, and in their minds, dependents must never break free. Slaveholding paternalists fought for a world where lessers would always be lessers, where the childish would never grow up, where father would always know best, for himself, for all non-fathers, and even for most other fathers. That worldview fed on itself, swelled according to the imperious essence of a slaveholder's absolute power, until among extreme ideologues such as Upshur, perpetual paternalism demanded paternalistic direction of supposedly lesser white men too. That unbounded pride ultimately hastened the slaveholders' extinction—for father, being human, did not always know best, not for those under him, not even for himself. And paternalists would not listen to anyone supposedly lesser.

Thus Abel P. Upshur conceived that a Texas treaty would oust the deluding politicians and elevate the disinterested paternalists, who would rescue the deluded commoners. He especially wished to destroy the Democratic Party and the *Richmond Enquirer*'s managers. Instead the Democratic Party and the *Richmond Enquirer* rallied to the Texas treaty and secured annexation. That triumph set off a stream of slavery-enhancing national laws that made Southern Democrats—including the managers of the *Richmond Enquirer*—dominant in the South. Then Upshur-style anti-party paternalists had to seek temporary cover.

The secessionists in 1860, like Upshur in 1843, thought they saw the peril more clearly than did the southern multitude. Indeed, they thought that a potentially deluded multitude constituted the worst peril. This secessionist "nightmare," to appropriate Upshur's word, was not as ridiculous as Revisionist historians think. If the southern Unionist majority had routed secessionists in 1860, more fugitive slaves might have run away, Lincoln might have developed a southern wing of his party, and Lincoln's proposed policy of removing blacks from America might have gained more adherents among Upper South voters. In the face of that uncertain climate for investment in human property, Border South capitalists might have cashed in their slaves at Lower South auctions. Such sales southward were always the most realistic of the Upper South's black removal scenarios. Eventually, likely well into the twentieth century, some Border South–North fusion might have abolished Lower South slavery, probably by the difficult constitutional amendment process.

Southern Unionists in 1860 denounced this speculation as an irresponsible basis for statecraft. They thought they saw a swifter, more savage, more unspeculative menace, to nonslaveholders and slaveholders alike, in a civil war. And as the Civil War would demonstrate, the supposedly gullible masses indeed saw more clearly than did the latter-day Abel P. Upshurs. Secession yielded abolition at the earliest possible date and at the bloodiest possible cost. But the secessionists' blunder seemed to them hardly "needless," to use the Revisionists' hindsight word. To the South Carolina patriarchs who first made the southern revolution, disunion seemed absolutely needful in order to perpetuate paternalistic governance. They had to destroy Lincoln's Union, lest Republican demagogues destroy their power to guide lesser white men and thus lesser blacks, too.

That climactic paternalistic imperative, immensely swollen and thereby more swiftly punctured, will always offer perspective to those who struggle toward a more limited version of parental guidance. However difficult is the modern task of leading while instructing the led to lead themselves, the slaveholders' antimodern ideal of perpetual guidance depends dangerously on finite human beings' capacity to be all-seeing, all-benevolent. The denouement of the slaveholders' limitless paternalism exemplifies the new history of private life at its most important: as a source of insight into the most intimate aspects of modern existence, including the conundrums of how to be teacher or parent.

So too the coming of the Civil War exemplifies the continued significance of the old history of public life. Twentieth-century Americans have been tempted to think that peaceful decision at the ballot box could everywhere succeed. Yet the democratic method failed its greatest American test. That failure ought to generate a saving humility about spreading our way elsewhere, just as parents and teachers need a saving humility about perpetuating their way forever. These two examples illuminate a pivotal truth about sophisticated history—that it is too illuminating to instruct only academics. That is why professors should seek an audience beyond the academy if they can find the common touch without sacrificing the subtle analysis.

Amid all the uncertainties surrounding my day in Williamsburg—whether academic and nonacademic readers could simultaneously be reached, whether my new strategy for *The Road to Disunion* was right, how Upshur could have conceived that boundless elitism could rout Jacksonian egalitarianism, whether a bounded version of paternalism could simultaneously guide and prepare for an end to guidance—at least one thing came out, so I thought, comically right. That is a hilarious aspect of dog shows: the antic certainty. Someone wins, for the moment irrevocably. Everyone else loses, for that day absolutely. To round out the story, I suppose I should report that while I was finishing my most memorable day in a library, Puddin' won the maximum 5-point major toward her 15-point championship. Although I cannot give eyewitness testimony, I can offer a historical proof that is almost as rare as an unknown critical document. I have Puddin' 's victory photograph. The picture may even be more conclusive—and it is assuredly lovelier—than the aged, almost indecipherable letter on limitless paternalism that led me, so I hoped, at last to see the boundless road to disunion.

7 / "Absurd" Issues and the Causes of the Civil War: Colonization as a Test Case

Just as the Revisionist historians ridiculed the alleged absurdities that free-labor Kansas or fugitive slaves or Abraham Lincoln or English influence in Texas could have menaced the slaveholders, so almost all current American historians dismiss the alleged absurdity that colonizing blacks outside the United States could have been considered a viable way to achieve antislavery. Yet many antebellum Americans cherished the colonization route to emancipation. How could such a preposterous (to us) idea and all those other preposterous (to us) ideas have become credible enough to cause one of history's worst civil wars?

The answer demands historians' most important and rarest talent: the ability to transcend their own perceptual frameworks and see the world as past actors saw it. The key to crediting proposals to deport blacks is to realize that controversial new migrations into and out of a multicultural social world everywhere conditioned antebellum Americans' angles of vision. In this new essay, I argue that the supposed absurdity of colonization is not absurd at all, once a movement-obsessed multicultural America is seen through nineteenth-century rather than latter-day lenses. Or to put the analytical strategy another way, to understand a baffling political issue, the political historian must become a social historian in the widest sense.

I first tried out this theory at the Yale Law School's Legal Theory Workshop. I am grateful to Owen Fiss for arranging the enlightening session, to David Brion Davis for especially brilliant criticism, and to Davis's students, Rob Forbes and Erik Ledbetter, for demonstrating that different generations of historians can be

*allies rather than antagonists in our mutual task of reintegrating
an American multicultural history.*

Why does a new historical explanation replace an old conventional-
ity? Sometimes newly found evidence vindicates a fresh conception. Thus, Abel P. Upshur's 1843 letter to Beverley Tucker, written just before Upshur became the secretary of state who
precipitated the annexation of Texas, clarifies the roots of that
transforming event.[1] When historical editors bring such unknown
or underappreciated sources into the public domain, they can be
among the most important historians.[2]

More often, not newly uncovered evidence but newly reasoned
theory makes an altered explanation viable. To construct a plausible theory, the theorist must line up the right people in the right
place. An explanation of why poor people precipitated a revolution,
for example, falls apart if rich people precipitated the revolution.
To be credible, a theory must also be based on a plausible view of
human nature. Rich people cannot plausibly be explained as rising
in revolt to secure better jelly beans, for example, if the pursuit of
improved jelly beans seems too absurd a cause of revolution.

The so-called Revisionists of the 1930s, in their endeavor to
revise away slavery as the cause of the Civil War, wielded these
two analytical weapons so brilliantly that the field of inquiry has
never been the same.[3] The right people were not in the right place,
the Revisionists claimed, for the Civil War to have been a showdown between slaveholders and abolitionists over emancipation.
On the southern side, most Southerners were not slaveholders.
Moreover, neither most slaveholders nor most nonslaveholders
wished to secede immediately after Abraham Lincoln's election or
then considered Lincoln an immediate menace to slavery.

On the northern side, continued the Revisionists, most Northerners were too racist and too apprehensive of disunion to be abolitionists. Abraham Lincoln, the canny mainstream Yankee, thus po-
sitioned himself to the right of William Lloyd Garrison. While
calling slavery wrong and hoping for its ultimate extinction, Lincoln pledged never to force antislavery on the South. He also endorsed a constitutional amendment that would have forever
banned federal coercive abolition.

Since Lincoln supported a constitutional amendment to forbid
federally imposed abolition, reasoned the Revisionists, and since
most Southerners considered the President-elect no immediate

menace, the Civil War hardly began as a showdown over emancipation. Instead, issues tangential to immediate abolition led to the battlefields. Controversy swelled over fugitive slaves, when maybe a thousand out of 4 million slaves successfully escaped to the North in an average year. Sectional strife also mounted over slavery in Kansas, when perhaps only a hundred slaves a year lived in that area. For contention so slight in immediate practical consequence to swell into an internal catastrophe, something more must have made the implausible seem plausible.

The Revisionists' conception of the something more—blundering demagogues who needlessly aroused popular passions—no longer seems very plausible, however. To several generations of historians since the Revisionists, pre–Civil War American politicians have seemed no more blundering than most leaders of most American generations. So subsequent historians have sought other reasons why supposedly absurd issues produced the Civil War. The most plausible recent explanation of the North's movement toward the battlefield, the so-called republican theory, holds that Northerners cared less about abolishing black slavery than about saving white republicanism. No matter, runs the theory, how absurd were such matters as a few slaves in Kansas and a few slave runaways from Maryland. The point is that the southern minority tried to dictate to the northern majority on these issues, and the dictation assaulted sacrosanct majoritarian procedures. In response, Northerners felt compelled to defend American republicanism and thus America's contribution to world civilization.[4]

This republican theory lines up the right people in the right place. In 1860, not only Lincoln's Northern Republicans but also Stephen A. Douglas's Northern Democrats emphasized that the minority South must not force law on the majoritarian republic. Douglas's party-shattering ultimatum was that the local majority of settlers in a national territory, not the southern minority of delegates to the Democratic Party convention, must decide whether slavery should enter a new national area. Lincoln's election-winning message was that the congressional majority must end the Slavepower's minority dominion over the national territories and government, not that the North must abolish slavery in the South. The republican theory of northern motivation is also plausible. If a racist, conservative North would seem unlikely to have gone to war to free blacks, a section infatuated with the Union as democratic experiment would seem credibly capable of risking life and limb for a majoritarian government of the (white) people, by the (white) people, and for the (white) people.

Still, if the southern minority's aggressive domination of a majoritarian republic impelled the northern mainstream to antisouthernism, why did the South aggressively demand the fugitive slave and Kansas laws, and why should elements of the slavocracy have aggressively risked war rather than be governed by Abraham Lincoln? To answer those questions, post-Revisionist southern historians have proposed several explanations, all helpful in explaining some episodes but each lining up the wrong people in the wrong place in other critical crises. According to one Marxist theory, southern planters needed to expand, even to expand over an area so implausible for slavery as chilly Kansas, since slavery was an anachronistic institution incapable of generating profits without virgin lands. That theory helps explain impoverished southern agriculturalists' drive for Texas in the depression-racked 1840s. But it cannot explain increasing crises over expansion in the 1850s, when most planters were extremely prosperous and booming slaveholding entrepreneurs sought more slaves to develop a large excess of virgin land. To make expand-or-perish economic thought even more implausible as a cause of secession, the only agrarians who were still severely economically depressed in the 1850s, the highly disunionist South Carolina rice planters, usually *opposed* the most plausible slaveholder territorial expansion, that into the Caribbean tropics. Meanwhile the most fervent Caribbean expansionists, the highly Unionist New Orleans merchants, were not agrarians.[5]

In another post-Revisionist attempt to explain why supposedly absurd issues such as Kansas became psychologically plausible, some southern historians have emphasized that slaveholders and nonslaveholders cherished *their* equality. Yankees who called the South depraved thus had to be opposed, no matter how trivial the ostensible issue, lest Southerners plead guilty to being morally unequal to Northerners. In a competing version of such psychological logic, some historians claim that Southerners *did* privately think they were morally wrong to own slaves in a land of liberty. Thus Yankee criticism, again however impractical the issue, inspired righteous defensiveness, in the typical angry manner of a man publicly defending what he secretly considers indefensible. In yet another version of psychological logic, some historians urge that Southerners suffered from the growing pains of an increasingly modernistic economy. Yankee critics became scapegoats for the psychic unrest of economic change, once again no matter how absurd the ostensible issues.[6]

These psychological explanations help explain why many Southerners hated Yankee insulters enough to die for the slavocracy, whatever the practicality of slavery issues. But other Southerners, always the precipitators of slavery controversies, consistently considered crusades to save slavery exceedingly practical. Moreover, at the key moment of decision, the secession crisis, the wrong people lined up in the wrong place for psychological theories to explain everything about disunion. The Border South did not secede; and borderites cared as much about their honor and their equality as did inhabitants of the Lower South. Moreover, border Southerners, compared to Deep South planters, were demonstrably more dubious about the morality of slavery and more involved in allegedly psychologically upsetting industrial, commercial, and transportation revolutions.

Since neither anxiety about modernizing economic revolutions nor unease about slavery's morality can explain why the less economically modern, less morally distressed Lower South most wished to secede, or why the more economically modern, more morally distressed Border South wished to cling to Union, the secessionists' own explanation of disunionist behavior is worth considering. Lower South disunionists called Lincoln an immediate menace to slavery because the new President would collaborate with Border South lovers of Union to put slavery on the fast road toward ultimate extinction. Disunionists knew that Lincoln's antislavery methods were not Garrison's. They acknowledged that the President-elect sought slow emancipation by incremental advances in public opinion, perhaps taking a hundred years. They saw that Lincoln sought to persuade Southerners to consent to abolition, not to impose emancipation on a recalcitrant South. They further saw that the President-elect speculated that freedmen could be resettled outside the United States. Is it then plausible that the secessionists would precipitate a killing war over something that might happen to them in a hundred years, only with Southerners' own consent and with the hope (a plausible hope?) that 4 million blacks would be removed from the nation?

Just here, the secessionists bring us closer to answering the absurdity puzzle, for they claimed that Lincoln's incremental antislavery methods could work, and in more like twenty-five than a hundred years. The secessionists' reasoning: Border South residents, owning relatively few slaves and harboring great devotion to Union, might consent to Lincoln's antislavery (and antiblack) overtures, might even vote for Lincoln's party in the next election. Most borderites, the secessionists rightly saw, preferred to rid their region of slaves if they could rid their region of blacks; and Lincoln's program included national help to remove blacks from America. Lincoln's party might also help border fugitive slaves to escape. Such turmoil would lead insecure Border South masters to sell their slaves to the more secure Lower South. Because of that same fear for the security of slavery at the edges of the South, southern precipitators of the Texas, Kansas, and Fugitive Slave Controversies had considered these issues not at all absurd—had called these issues precisely the ones that must be raised. Despite the difficulties of safeguarding the border between slavery and freedom, protection of southern outposts was crucial, or slavery would sink down to the tropical fraction of the nation. Or to use the modern metaphor, the top tier of slave states would fall like a row of dominoes.

A domino theory of the cause of the Civil War has the right people lined up in the right places. The secessionist Lower South, with its heavy and ever-increasing slave population, emerges as worried about the Unionist Border South, with its sparser and ever-decreasing slave population, and about the racist North, with its suspicion that the removal of blacks might best save white men's republicanism. A Lower South fear of a North–Border South collaboration to rid America of blacks seems plausible. But was the hope for black deportation itself plausible? Could Lincoln, the North, and the Border South have actually believed that 4 million blacks could be colonized outside the United States? In the name of transcending all the Revisionists' supposed absurdities, we have come full circle to what would seem the most ridiculous cause of the Civil War yet suggested.

1

But the conception that blacks could be removed was not at all ridiculous in the antebellum Border South, where blacks had slowly been removing themselves and where proposals to speed the departures abounded. Blacks had for decades been furthering an incremental fugitive slave process, and it showed signs of quickening. Fugitive blacks always fled most successfully from southern areas closest to the North. Border runaways not only freed themselves but also helped forge a temporary form of slavery, quite common in the Border South. Many masters in effect bribed slaves not to gamble on flight. These pragmatic slaveholders promised their slaves manumission in a few years in exchange for hard work in the interim. Such semiprivileged slaves and their semipermissive masters placed the institution of slavery on a knife's edge. On the one hand, let the balance of power in the area tilt a little toward freedom and more temporary slaves might gamble on removing themselves permanently from the South. On the other hand, let the balance of power tilt toward slaveholders and potential runaways would be less likely to risk losing future freedom. Those delicate dynamics help explain why a little pressure from the northern side of the border could lead to slaveholder fears that a few more blacks—and then a few more—might try to remove themselves.

Such fears could bring off the most plausible scenario for black removal: Border slaveholders would cash in their investment at Lower South slave auctions. Why, after all, risk a $1,500 slave close to the North when the money could be invested in banks, which did not run away? Interregional slave sales had already helped cut the percentage of slaves in the Border South's total population in half between 1790 and 1860. Only one in eight borderites was enslaved on the eve of the Civil War, compared to two in five inhabitants of the Lower South. A little acceleration of the pace of border fugitive slaves might impel border masters to get off the knife's edge, place more slaves in the interregional trade, and turn to safer investments.

White politics no less than black runaways could lead capitalists to resettle blacks elsewhere. A small minority of border antislavery (and antiblack) politicians, led by gubernatorial candidate Cassius Clay of Kentucky and Congressman Frank Blair, Jr., of Missouri, proposed that state legislatures declare blacks free on a future date. Then slaveholders would dispatch blacks southward before the deadline. Such proposals never rallied more than 10 percent of borderites in the 1850s. But 10 percent of voters was a beginning, and a 50 percent majority did not have to be secured. Let border slaveholders see that the Clay-Blair movement was growing, and they would likely pursue that most plausible of black removal contingencies—the safe sale of an unsafe investment.

In this context, an added possibility of national colonization of blacks could be the proverbial straw that broke the camel's back— or to put it more prosaically, finally caused uneasy capitalists to cash in their slaves. Let a presidential administration be lax in enforcing the fugitive slave laws, and/or friendly to Border South anti-

slavery politicians, and/or disposed to offer federal bounties to remove blacks from America. Then slaves might flow faster from the
Border South to the Lower South. A latter-day observer might even
compare the scene to the toppling of a pile of dominoes.[7]

2

Still, even assuming that a Lincoln proposal to remove blacks from
America was hardly absurd in the Border South context, could colonization as an antislavery idea have been equally plausible anywhere else? Historians have usually finessed the question by denying that the colonization conception was even entertained for long
elsewhere. The idea of ending slavery by removing blacks was supposedly discarded many times. The American Colonization Society
itself allegedly destroyed colonization's plausibility by removing
only 0.2 percent of American blacks. Jefferson supposedly repudiated the deportation panacea at the time of the Missouri Controversy; Virginians supposedly abandoned it again after Nat Turner's
insurrection; William Lloyd Garrison supposedly killed it everywhere in the mid-1830s. In fact, however, the hope of dispatching
slaves elsewhere never died in the Upper South. Nor did Garrison's
contempt for the idea prevail in the North, except among the most
extreme abolitionists.

Jefferson, for example, became if anything more committed to
deporting blacks after his personal "Firebell in the Night," the Missouri Controversy, awakened him with the terror that the slavery
issue would destroy the white republic. He urged correspondents
to seek constitutional amendments authorizing emancipation
through colonization. Nor did Jefferson's Virginia successors repudiate colonization after their Firebell in the Night: the Nat Turner
slave uprising of 1831, followed by the Virginia legislative debate
over abolition in 1832. Although that charged state discussion
brought forth a paler experiment in colonization than even the
American Colonization Society's weak effort, leading Virginians
still hoped to deport blacks eventually. Continued Virginia proponents of future removal of blacks included prominent preachers
who defended temporary bondage (William A. Smith and Thornton
Stringfellow), the state's leading early secular proslavery writer
(Thomas R. Dew), Virginia's most persistent disunionist (Beverley
Tucker), and the Old Dominion's most embattled Caribbean expansionist (Admiral M. F. Maury).[8]

Because the hope for colonization persisted, Edmund Ruffin,

the Virginia secessionist who fired the Civil War's first shot, published his *African Colonization Unveiled.* The publication date: not 1819, not 1832, but 1859. Ruffin, whose eve-of-the-war obsession with putting down southern colonizationists also permeates his private diary, continued to rail at an idea that he knew had outlasted Thomas Jefferson not only in Virginia but everywhere in the South and in America. Latter-day proponents of an eventual black exodus included Mississippi's U.S. senator Robert Walker, that most prominent of Texas annexationists, who prayed that the Lone Star State would be the "safety valve" through which those "evils," slaves and free blacks, would be colonized in Mexico; Kentucky's Henry Clay, whose ideal American System included federal appropriations to dispatch blacks to Africa; some Northern Republicans, on the rare occasions when they explained how America could secure the ultimate extinction of slavery; the Blair family of Maryland and Missouri, Lincoln's men in those states, who favored Caribbean expansion to secure a receptacle for U.S. blacks; Lincoln himself, who called colonization a practical form of antislavery; and Harriet Beecher Stowe, who ended her massive best-seller, *Uncle Tom's Cabin,* with a black's dream of freedom in Africa.

Stowe's literary climax was appropriate, for in the climactic 1850s the colonization dream spread beyond the moderate white establishment, North and South, to become many leading black intellectuals' fondest hope. Indeed, the first colonizer of blacks had himself been a black. Paul Cuffe, a Boston ship owner, in 1815 transported thirty-eight African Americans to Africa. Cuffe, an evangelical capitalist, hoped to spread Christianity to Africa and to engage in trade between his African beachhead and the world.[9]

Cuffe died a year later and his black nationalist example, while influencing the whites who formed the American Colonization Society in 1817, almost dropped out of black Americans' consciousness. Throughout the 1820–50 period, most black leaders repudiated the white Jeffersonians' premise—that racist whites would always make America forbidden ground for blacks—and demanded instead that America become a color-blind nation. That black dream, however, waned in the 1850s as white racism waxed strong. Many northern black leaders had been successful fugitive slaves. Their most pressing problem, after the Fugitive Slave Law of 1850 was passed, became not further liberating the North but avoiding their own capture and reenslavement in the South. That danger helped turn some important black foes of colonization into proponents of migration to Haiti, Canada, or Africa. The roll call of black converts to colonization includes the Reverend James Theodore Holly, Presbyterian leader of black nationality in Haiti; the novelist and physician Martin R. Delany, sometime proponent of black nationalism in Canada and leader of the Niger Valley Exploring Party in Africa; and the New York editor Henry Highland Garnet, a founding father of the African Civilization Society.[10]

The leading black opponent of colonization was the African Americans' most famous crusader. Frederick Douglass, brilliant orator, newspaper editor, and autobiographer, continued to call America a redeemable home for African Americans. But Douglass was the exception who proved the rule, for even he, for one auspicious moment, toyed with colonization. In January 1861, while President-elect Lincoln was preparing to take office (and preparing to brandish that slavery-perpetuating constitutional amendment), Douglass publicly lamented "that inducements offered to the colored man to remain here are few, feeble, and very uncertain." He could "no longer throw" his "little influence against a measure which may prove highly advantageous to many families." This long-time opponent of colonization then accepted James Holly's invitation to visit Haiti. Douglass canceled the trip when war broke out. But Frederick Douglass, of all people, had illuminated the lure of voluntary exodus from the "Great White Republic," home of slavery, segregation, the Fugitive Slave Law, and crushed black hopes.[11]

3

The conception of colonization as a practical strategy, having transcended Jeffersonian planters and seized important antebellum imaginations North and South, white and black, persisted during the Civil War and beyond. Lincoln as president beseeched free blacks to quit America. He also urged Congress to pay for the exodus. In March 1863, Congress authorized $10 million to $20 million in federal bonds to implement Lincoln's plan in Missouri, but the House and Senate versions of the bill differed. The congressional session ended before the bills could be reconciled. Thereafter, northern military victories changed the very nature of the issue.[12]

After the war, the American Colonization Society continued to attract members, and the dream of black nationalism in Haiti continued to spark controversy. A showdown between President Ulysses S. Grant and Senate Foreign Relations Committee Chairman Charles Sumner occurred over the annexation of Santo Domingo in 1870. The issue, in part, concerned whether some blacks might benefit from leaving an unremittingly racist America, as President Grant suspected, or whether the existing American nation must be made color-blind for blacks, as Senator Sumner demanded. A decade after Santo Domingo annexation failed, six thousand blacks migrated to Kansas, hoping to move out from under white men's exploitation. In the same spirit, though with different followers and proposed colonies, Henry McNeal Turner in the early twentieth century, Marcus Garvey in the 1920s, and W. E. B. Du Bois and Stokely Carmichael in the 1960s revived black dreams of exodus to Africa.[13]

4

Although the colonization idea remained rooted in the American mentality a century after the antebellum period, pre–Civil War antislavery and proslavery extremists anticipated posterity's judgment that the conception was preposterous. Anticolonizationists pointed out that colonizationists split on the practical details. Northerners wished to remove largely slaves. Southerners wished to expel free blacks first. In another clash, Northerners such as Lincoln were loath to force slaves to go. Southerners (with some notable exceptions such as James Madison) thought that slaveholders could coerce slaves to go anywhere. Finally, and most important, the deportation of 4 million souls to Africa would likely cost $400 million. Where were all those dollars (and all those ships) to come from in a capital-starved America that preferred to spend scarce dollars on white enterprise?

In 1860, colonizationists answered that the black population should never have swollen to 4 million people. The colonization movement had caught its stride in the 1830s, when 2 million slaves inhabited the South. Colonizers had hoped to deport high proportions of women of childbearing age, thereby slicing the natural rate of increase. Moreover, colonizers continually denied that the most expensive black destination, Africa, was the only option. Black nationalists often preferred the cheaper route to the Caribbean, as did Jefferson and Lincoln. Some thirty thousand antebellum U.S. blacks migrated to a yet cheaper destination, Canada. These new Canadians constituted three times more migrants than the American Colonization Society sent to its Liberian colony. The first important white advocate of emancipation via colonization,

Benjamin Lundy, had hoped for a still less inexpensive black migration: to preannexation Texas.[14]

Furthermore, Lincoln again and Clay wished to spread the hoped-for black exodus over a hundred years, hardly straining an annual federal budget that never before (or again) was so unstrained. With the federal debt at an unprecedented zero from the mid-1830s to the late 1850s, Clay wished to distribute millions in annual surpluses to the states, in part to finance colonization. With public lands also massively available, Jefferson wished to employ the billion-dollar national treasure to solve the nation's greatest problem.

These federal resources would more than suffice, colonization advocates believed, because government need pay only for the first tickets and secure the first colony. Then blacks themselves would prefer to move toward freedom in a flourishing black nation than to remain mired in exploitation in a racist white republic. Black colonists not only would voluntarily migrate but would send money back so that their relatives could journey toward opportunity. In just the same way, Irish and German immigrants sent money to the Old World so friends and kin could join them in the land of liberty. As for the notion that not enough blacks could afford to transport themselves, slaves could be required to work months or years after being quasi-freed, to finance their fully liberating journey.

Hearing those sensible-sounding arguments, and knowing that pragmatic conservatives thought that colonization was the painless way to save (and whiten) the republic, southern extremists dared not allow Congress to debate the issue. Yet the black migration idea lingered, especially because it seemed *so* plausible if only southern fire-eaters would allow the plausibility to be tested. So why did so many cling so long to this vision?

5

In part, because they wanted to believe. We all cling hardest to our most comfortable solutions to our most uncomfortable problems. The institution of slavery conflicted uncomfortably with the two most cherished texts in antebellum America, the Bible and the Declaration of Independence. To reconcile slavery and scripture, proslavery polemicists declared that Christ brought the heathen to American plantations to be converted. Even proslavery preachers, however, called the reconciliation underachieved in practice, particularly because some slaves lacked full access to evangelical Christianity. Colonization allegedly offered blacks a fuller participation in the American revivalistic dream. After Africans were brought to America and raised to Christ, they would be returned to Africa to Christianize the Dark Continent. With that vision, any slaveholders who remained uneasy about perhaps living in the backwaters of American Christendom marched to the forefront of the mission to redeem the world.

Colonizationists also marched to the rhythms of a national Manifest Destiny to democratize mankind. If *all* men should be included in the Declaration of Independence, as the Jeffersons and Clays and Lincolns thought, and if white men would never make voters or jurors of blacks, as Lincoln conceded, to mire emancipated blacks in America was to perpetuate slaveholders' violence against the Declaration. But to send the freedmen to Africa, there to be utterly free, and to encourage these products of American democracy to democratize the Dark Continent was truly to make America a City Upon A Hill.

Colonization also seemed the safe way for republican America to redeem itself. The most threatening obstacle to perpetual Union was agitation for emancipation and for disunion. The greatest reason Southerners preferred disunion to emancipation was fear of freed blacks. But emancipation need not be feared if the freedmen would be deported. Everything would be improved, in the minds of racists who cherished the Declaration of Independence, if slavery could be excised and only whites would remain in a perfected American republic.

Colonization was finally a psychologically soothing reason to forget the psychological burdens of slavery. Slaveholders who called slavery wrong could blithely go on exploiting slave labor so long as abolition required removal of blacks and removal had not yet been arranged. So too, Northerners who cherished Union but disliked both slavery and free blacks need not shatter the Union with demands for abolition if the eventual colonization of blacks could someday peacefully yield an all-white, nonsectionalized nation. Nothing could be more glorious than a serene future route toward national and world redemption—which for the moment sanctioned doing nothing about slavery except enjoying its profits.

6

Many historians, after approving that peroration, will say that analysis of why the colonization dream persisted need go no further.

They forget that antebellum Americans believed in colonization because belief was easy no less than pleasant. To solve problems by moving away from the site of exploitation was simply the common sense of the matter in antebellum America. Those who would move out to be free included the immigrants who moved out from Europe and the eastern laborers who moved out to the West and the fugitive slaves who moved out from the South and the northern blacks who moved out to Canada and the secessionists who moved out from Washington, D.C., and the Mormons who moved out to Utah—and the feminists who moved out from the household. The pre-Civil War era was the first American age when such women as Angelina Grimké, the South Carolina heiress turned Yankee abolitionist agitator, and Margaret Fuller, the northern transcendentalist editor of the *Dial,* entered previously all-male pursuits. Both Grimké and Fuller, significantly, migrated outside physically in order to move outside domestically. Grimké quit her South Carolina home to flourish on northern lecture podiums. Fuller left her American home for Europe, ultimately marrying an Italian count. Their great opponent, Catharine Beecher, urged women instead to stay in the household and uplift the men therein. Beecher, however, thrived outside her own home. She traversed the North to preach domestic virtues on Grimké-style public podiums.[15]

For all antebellum Americans, as for the women who moved out from the house, a new migration toward freedom was the master theme of antebellum history, an exhilarating, controversial movement of an unprecedented variety and number of peoples. Before 1815, the United States was a constricted, largely Atlantic seaboard nation. Its territory ended on largely uninhabited midwestern plains. Its white population overwhelmingly claimed British Protestant forebears. Its nonwhite people, mostly Native Americans and African Americans, usually lived inside white settlements, especially in the South.

By 1860, American territory sprawled to the Pacific, as did its white people's settlements. An Atlantic seaboard nation of nineteen states and 10 million people had become a continental nation of thirty-one states and 32 million people. America's center of population had shifted from Baltimore to Cleveland. Its center of political power had moved from Washington's and Jefferson's Virginia to Lincoln's and Douglas's Illinois. Its Native Americans, especially in the South, had been moved beyond the Mississippi. Almost 5 million European whites had moved toward freedom in America, only 15 percent of them British Protestants, fully 39 percent of them Irish Catholics, and another 31 percent German and heavily Catholic. These oppressed Europeans set sail for America's eastern cities; and the oppressed eastern urbanites lit out for the sprawling Midwest and on to the Pacific.[16]

These fresh movements toward liberty lent hope to the disadvantaged, opportunities to the enterprising, and alarm to the traditionalists. While those starving in famine-ridden Ireland or unemployed in slum-infested New York saw new hope in migration to the prairies, middle-class Protestants in elderly New England towns feared a barbarization of folk once confined in Christian communities. Armed with new public schools, fresh Bibles, and growing temperance societies, Whiggish bluebloods sought to tame the expanded West, to Americanize the European newcomers, and to wean the new Catholic citizens from their supposed allegiance to the pope. Swiftly despairing of this latter project, Whiggish Protestants embarked on their so-called nativist campaigns, seeking to move immigrants out of the voting booths.[17] Sometimes the same nativists sought to resettle blacks outside America.

Jacksonian Democrats wanted white ethnics to move *inside* the polling places, in part because non-British newcomers usually voted Democratic. But the Democratic Party had its own target for expulsion. The Jacksonians wished to remove Native Americans from the white republic. In the 1830s, some 46,000 Native Americans were force-marched on their Trail of Tears to lands beyond white settlements, beyond the Mississippi, with federal guns and dollars forcing the out-migration. The federal government spent close to $100 million on the expulsion, including $68 million to buy eastern land from Native Americans and $20 million to win the Seminole Wars of 1835–42, thereby ousting 2,833 Seminoles (and losing 1,500 white soldiers).[18]

Here, as everywhere, governmental involvement with the new migrations was another master theme of the age. Posterity thinks of pre–Civil War government as quaint, small, and devoted to laissez-faire, partly because Andrew Jackson, symbol of the age, spoke against big government and for individual enterprise. But just as Jackson's government moved Native Americans beyond the white man's frontier, so governments, state and national, aided the dispersal of the whites and the homogenization of the dispersed. The explosion of Americans across the continent required a Transportation Revolution and government helped provide it, building roads, financing canals, and enriching railroads with gigantic blocks of public land. The knitting of spread-out communities into a national culture required a Communications Revolution and government again helped provide it, commencing a telegraph line, establishing a far-flung postal network, giving printing bounties to national newspapers, and distributing congressmen's national speeches. Here, the political and social merged. The politics of moving blacks beyond the republic, the politics of moving Native Americans beyond the Mississippi, the politics of moving immigrants outside the voting booths, the politics of promoting and/ or civilizing the westward movement—all this political history is important social history.

Antebellum ethnic groups, when faced with white Anglo-Saxon males' political drives to remove them and/or Americanize them, always debated the same two countervailing strategies. Southerners debated coming out from Washington, D.C., or staying inside the capital city and seeking to dominate it. Women debated coming out from the home, as Grimké advocated, or staying inside the household and seeking to moralize the men, as Beecher advocated. Denigrated groups in the North debated between staying inside Wasp communities and fighting for their distinctive identity or leaving and establishing their own communities. Of those who voluntarily moved away to be free, the Mormons are the most obvious. But the antebellum landscape was dotted with the self-exiled and their ethnically pure communities: the transcendentalists' Brook Farm, the Owenites' New Harmony, the Shakers' twenty colonies in eight states, John Humphrey Noyes's Oneida, the midwestern Irish, Norwegian, and German towns.

Of those who remained in their communities and fought for power and respect, having already migrated to America, the Boston, New York, and Philadelphia immigrants are the most obvious. But even the new immigrants had advocates of another exodus. The critical foreign-born proponent of mass departure from America was Thomas d'Arcy McGee, an embattled ex-Irishman and one of antebellum America's most irrepressible characters. McGee, distressed by the squalor and misery in New York slums, envisioned an Irish utopia in the Canadian wilderness, just as Martin R. Delany sometimes prayed for a black utopia in western Canada. In 1856, McGee was the moving spirit behind the Buffalo Irish Immigrant Aid Convention. That conclave of ninety-five Irish colonizationists, however, like the American Colonization Society could produce only a faint shadow of its grand design: the Reverend Jeremiah F. Tracy's Nebraska Colony of six hundred Irish families. Unfortunately for Tracy's and McGee's strategy, too many Irish Americans, led by such Catholic heroes as Bishop John Hughes, preferred to stay in America and fight discrimination.[19]

The battle between advocates of departure and advocates of defiance was closer and bloodier among the Cherokees. When Supreme Court Justice John Marshall's pro-Cherokee decisions proved no match for President Jackson's anti-Cherokee thrusts, a group of Cherokees led by Elias Boudinot determined to cut the best deal and leave. Their situation was hopeless, Boudinot declared. To save their character and integrity, they must move away from the murderous whites. Boudinot's Removal Party, although not the Cherokees' legal government, signed Jackson's Treaty of New Echota in December 1835. The Cherokees' official rulers, led by Chief John Ross, denounced the treaty. The chiefs favored not removal to an isolated frontier but survival within the white nation. Ross won inside his tribe. Only two thousand of eighteen thousand Cherokees followed Boudinot into voluntary exile. Ross, however, lost among whites. In May 1838, Gen. Winfield Scott, under orders to enforce the Treaty of New Echota, expelled the Cherokees down the killing Trail of Tears. Twenty-five percent of the marchers died on the trail to Boudinot's favored destination. After they arrived, Boudinot was brutally assassinated.[20]

In the contexts of these chilling events and of the wide-ranging forces of migration, ethnic pluralism, and Waspish homogenization which the battle over Cherokee removal epitomized, the long contest over black colonization acquired, for antebellum Americans, a patina of realism. Martin Delany versus Frederick Douglass as well as Abraham Lincoln versus William Lloyd Garrison on the expediency of black departure from America resembled Angelina Grimké versus Catharine Beecher on the wisdom of female departure from the home, Edmund Ruffin versus Henry Clay on the expediency of southern departure from Washington, D.C., Thomas McGee versus Bishop John Hughes on the glory of another Irish exodus, and Elias Boudinot versus Chief John Ross on the necessity for final Cherokee departure. Lincoln, advocating the departure of 4 million blacks in a hundred years, sounded reasonable in an age that witnessed the arrival of 2 million Irishmen in thirty years. Henry Clay, advocating several million federal dollars annually for African colonization, and Thomas Jefferson, urging that federal land revenues be used to finance black departure, sounded feasible in an era when Washington authorities were spending millions of dollars to deport Native Americans and bestowing millions of acres on railroads to expedite white dispersals. In an age of forced exoduses, forced Americanization, and massive movements of peoples, a purifying federal migration experiment with blacks looked as pragmatically American as a Trail of Tears.

7

Black exodus looked even more practical in global perspective. Antebellum Americans knew that Africans in chains were still being sailed to enslavement in the New World. Between 1830 and 1850, Brazilian and Cuban slaveholders annually imported some forty thousand new African slaves, at an annual cost of some $4 million. The worldwide maritime fleet clearly could remove forty thousand American blacks yearly; and equally clearly, the American government could finance the $4 million annual cost. The average annual cost of removal of Native Americans in the 1830s had been $10 million, and the federal surplus in the 1850s ran as high as $15 million a year.[21]

The relevance of continued mass African migrations to Brazil and Cuba was clearer in the perspective of the fastest-rising Deep South dream of the 1850s, the movement to reopen the African slave trade to U.S. ports. The Revisionists and almost all historians since have derided the supposed absurdity of that idea, too. But once again, derision, however right by present-day moral standards, blocks an analysis of why the supposedly preposterous seemed plausible by past people's standards. The dream of reopening the African slave trade seemed to its Lower South proponents the most plausible way of solving every southern problem. If the Lower South could buy slaves from Africa, the Border South might keep its slaves, nonslaveholders might become slaveholders, virgin southern lands might be cultivated, and the South might have the population to compete with the North in Congress and in national territories such as Kansas.[22]

In the fiery controversy within the South over this proposal, no one doubted that forty thousand more Africans *could* be brought to America annually. But was the migration of more Africans to America wise or right? The overwhelming answer, especially in the Upper South, was that too many Africans already peopled America. Then why not send the forty thousand annually the other way?

8

That had been Jefferson's question, then Clay's, then Lincoln's; and the question summed up one reason the secessionist South considered President-elect Lincoln an immediate menace to slavery. The perceived danger was not federal coercive intervention to force

Southerners to abolish slavery. Lincoln repudiated this involuntary imposition and, so secessionists argued, the part of the South with the fewest slaves might voluntarily accept the Black Republican President's noncoercive lures. By offering patronage positions to Border South politicians and by offering colonization bounties to Border South masters, so the disunionists' nightmare went, the President might build a Black Republican Party, assuredly in the most vulnerable Border South and maybe even in the Deep South. The most numerous of Lincoln's southern appointments, hundreds of postmasters in the remotest southern outposts, would be administering the post office, that key institution in the federal government's Communications Revolution. Lincoln's postmasters could open the South to antislavery communications—could crack open a partially closed society to an open debate over black removal. Then even hardline Border South slaveholders might panic about their property and sell blacks to the Deep South. With that vision of how slavery might contract if hostilely encircled, disunionists brought to a climax three decades of (so they thought) highly practical concerns about the migration of slavery out of the southern outposts—and perhaps out of America.

9

In the climactic secession crisis, as in the preliminary Texas and Kansas and fugitive slave crises, many southern moderates doubted that extremist methods of fighting folk migrations made pragmatic sense. Anticipating the Revisionists, they scoffed that governmental edicts would not deter black fugitive slaves from fleeing toward freedom or impel canny slaveholders to move toward such a remote, chilly, and dangerous an outpost as Kansas. Instead, impractical proslavery proposals would impel Northerners toward the abolitionists and propel Southerners out of the Union.

Southern moderates, however, always had trouble opposing southern extremists, for the hotheads defended southern rectitude, Yankees desecrated southern virtue, and southern patriots were loath to side with northern insulters. That welling up of anti-Yankee hatred probably rallied more southern folk than did practical calculations about dangers to slavery, which is why the post-Revisionist search for psychological causes of supposedly absurd issues is helpful. The countervailing strategy suggested here, to ask whether the issues *were* absurd in the nineteenth-century context, is intended to complement, not to replace psychological strategies.

The two post-Revisionist strategies, taken together, make that aggressively defensive slavocracy altogether understandable. Precisely because Southerners tended to spring to the defense of the colors whenever a Southron raised a flag, especially when a Yankee ridiculed the emblem, precipitators of southern crusades were extremely important. The precipitators always acted on their image of danger to slavery, and almost always their eyes fastened on the edges of the South. Always they feared that fugitive blacks would remove themselves or that nonslaveholders would succumb to black removal schemes or that slaveholders would sell slaves out of the hinterlands. Never did they doubt that the wrong President and Congress could quicken the wrong movements of people. In the end, they seceded not just from the Union but from the way that the South's and the Union's folks were migrating. They may have been absurd to think they could alter the migratory trends. But they were not absurd to see the trends—and to see that a President who suggested that blacks move out of a migration-obsessed America was not the most reliable man to keep the top tier of slavery from falling.

8 / The Complex Career of Slaveholder Expansionism

The importance of the colonization issue suggests a slogan to sum up the roots of secession: Demography is Destiny. Assuredly ante-bellum Southerners did agree that the movement of population would decide the destiny of slavery. But that agreement aside, dis-putes between Southerners abounded about how and where the black population should move as well as about whether slavery should be preserved or removed. Witness another issue wherein Southerners felt Demography to be Destiny: the controversy over whether slavery should be expanded to new American territories. Just as the wider perspective of antebellum multicultural history illuminates the perceived reality of the colonization issue, so the wider perspective of slaveholder expansionism throughout the nineteenth century clears up the puzzling complexity of southern climactic attitudes toward the territories. The following new ex-ploration of this most important of pre–Civil War slavery issues is appearing more or less simultaneously, although in a slightly dif-ferent form, in the Encyclopedia of the Confederacy, *ed. Richard N. Current (New York, 1993). I am grateful to Michael Morrison, to Jeannette Hopkins, and to the editors of the* Encyclopedia *for their helpful comments on the piece.*

The myth of a monolithic, unchanging Slave South everywhere dis-torts the history of the slavocracy. Thus the Civil War supposedly matched the South against the North. But, in fact, the four Border South states never left the Union, West Virginia seceded from Vir-ginia, and over 100,000 white Confederate residents joined Lin-coln's army. So too, before the Civil War, the South supposedly massed unanimously behind the "positive good" of perpetual slavery. But in fact, most Upper South residents prayed that slavery would be a "temporary evil." They hoped blacks and slaves could be eventually removed from their northerly half of the South. Meanwhile important Lower South clergymen considered slavery short on Christian blessings. They urged state legislatures to bar the breaking up of slaves' families through sales and to protect slaves' access to Christianity. In response, most masters derided state intervention as meddling interference, not proslavery Christianity.

These divergent viewpoints within the South, involving the pivotal matter of whether slaveholders' absolute power should be perpetuated or limited or removed to other locales, helped generate another key southern intramural clash, over whether slaveholders should seek new territories. According to the standard account, Southerners combated only Northerners in pre–Civil War controversies over whether slavery should expand into national territories, with "expand or perish" the southern entrepreneurs' persistent motto. So when Abraham Lincoln won the presidency in 1860, pledging no expansion of slavery, Southerners supposedly concluded that the Union, not slavery, must perish.

The expand-or-perish interpretation, while apparently distilling the essence of secession into three catchy words, actually reduces a complex phenomenon to a muddle. The oversimplification is useful only to warn all who study southern slaveholders that fluctuations from one era to another and from one place to another must be noticed. Southern beliefs about the *economic* necessity for more slaveholding terrain especially fluctuated. Slaveholders' convictions about their *political* need for territorial expansion flourished more consistently—with some important exceptions. The exceptions predominated in the climactic 1850s, when especially erratic expand-or-perish thinking hardly paved a straight road to disunion. As the Civil War approached, South Carolina's planters, who feared they might perish without disunion, tended to oppose southern territorial expansion. These most ardent of secessionists feared that slavery might fade from their decaying old state if Southerners expanded to fresh Caribbean horizons. In contrast, New Orleans' merchants, who thought they might perish without Caribbean expansion, tended to oppose disunion. Those most ardent of expansionists feared that their best chance to reinvigorate their urban, mercantile economy might evaporate if secession interfered with the acquisition of Caribbean trade routes and terrain. Meanwhile, the Border South's residents often supported territorial expansion as a way not to save slavery but to remove the "temporary evil" from their area. Yet they sometimes opposed expansion southward lest a worse evil than slavery, disunion, might result.

Just as southern attitudes about territorial expansion changed from one place to another, especially in the 1850s, so the expansion issue changed from one era to another. Southern drives for more territory accelerated from 1793 to the mid-1830s, swerved in the 1840s, and veered yet another way in the 1850s, as the southern economy fluctuated from half recession to unrelieved depression to almost universal prosperity. A paradox illuminates the point: That myth of a climactic universal southern insistence on territorial expansion, while distorting the essence of the climactic 1844–60 period, fits the facts perfectly for the half century before 1844. As for the period before 1793, then southern zeal for expansion could scarcely be found.

1

From 1793 to 1843, southern expansionists were making up for earlier southern generations' characteristic lack of desire for new territorial acquisitions, while displaying little of later southern fears that exotic territorial adventures would destroy old cultural stabilities. During the eighteenth century, the Slave South had been predominately an Atlantic seaboard civilization. Residents had been usually (although not always) uninterested in spreading west of the coastal colonies. Instead, Native Americans, whether Creeks or Choctaws or Seminoles or Cherokees, had cultivated some of what became upland South Carolina and Georgia, northern Mississippi and Alabama, and western Tennessee. Non-English peoples had also controlled the rim of the Anglo Lower South, including the French-owned areas of what became Louisiana and Arkansas, and the Spanish-owned areas of what became Texas, Florida, and southern Alabama and Mississippi.[1]

Eighteenth-century entrepreneurs did not yet covet what became the southernmost tier of the United States because they could not yet conceive of a lucrative crop suitable for the Lower South's westward, noncoastal tropics. They considered Lower South latitudes too tropical for the Upper South's staple crop, tobacco, and not tropical enough for South America's staple crops, sugar and coffee. Only the South Carolina and Georgia coastal malarial swamps could support the colonial Lower South's most coveted crop, rice; and only the Sea Islands along the coast could support the secondary staple, silky Sea Island cotton. West of the coast, some colonial South Carolinians grew indigo for a limited market, which was lost after the American Revolution. Other Carolinians produced the cheaper grades of cotton, also commercially limited without a then-uninvented gin to separate seeds from fibers.[2] So while black slaves outnumbered white citizens more than eight to one in some Georgia and especially South Carolina coastal areas, almost four out of five North American slaves toiled north of the future Cotton Kingdom. Slaves especially peopled the Upper South tobacco belts, although whites still outnumbered blacks in these Chesapeake Bay locations.

Eli Whitney's invention of the cotton gin in 1793 at last sent Lower South entrepreneurs swarming to southwestern frontiers, now densely populated by slaves. Two virtually simultaneous developments accelerated the population surge from the oldest South to the new cotton frontier. Almost at the moment when the Cotton Kingdom required more slaves, Congress abolished the African slave trade (1807). And almost at the moment when the newer South's economy ascended, the older South's economy declined. In Upper South tobacco belts, debilitated soil and poor prices produced chronic stagnation. In South Carolina's coastal rice swamps, the land was more worn and profits less fabulous than in colonial times; and in that state's up-country area, the first cotton spree yielded the first cotton-exhausted soil. Throughout these old eastern locales, struggling planters needed to shrink their operation or lose their property. Out in the new southwestern Cotton Kingdom, buoyant developers, now legally barred from buying slaves from Africa, competed for contracting slaveholders' unneeded bondsmen. As a result, some 750,000 blacks were relocated from 1790 to 1860. The Lower South's share of U.S. slaves leapt from 21 percent to 59 percent over these years.

In the wake of slavery's spread over previously uncultivated tropical regions, contracting slave sellers in older tobacco areas had the cash to finance a modest postboom survival economy. Meanwhile, expanding slave buyers in new cotton areas had the laborers to produce a post-eighteenth-century bonanza. The process of paying leaner Peter to fatten hungry Paul served more than economic desires. Among eager entrepreneurs who wanted to preserve slavery, slave buying was the key to consolidating slavery's Lower South empire. Among tired aristocrats who wanted to remove slavery *and* blacks from their area, slave selling was the key to producing an all-white Upper South.

Even some southern opponents of slavery, who had earlier opposed slaveholder expansionism, now exulted that the expansion of slavery could rid some areas of slaves. In the eighteenth century, before the cotton expansion, Thomas Jefferson of Virginia had considered slavery's expansion wrong because slavery was wrong. But by 1820, after the Cotton Kingdom was well established, Jefferson called expansionism right, even though slavery was as wrong as ever. If slavery were to be bottled up in old areas, he explained, fearful whites would never free the densely concentrated blacks. If slavery were to be "diffused" into new areas, on the other hand, whites would more readily emancipate the scattered slaves.[3] "Diffusion" was the key word. It united Southerners who hoped to remove all slaves from their declining area and Southerners who wanted more slaves to proceed toward their advancing area.

That unanimity imperiled both Native American landowners inside the Lower South's domain and foreign landowners just outside. Newly expansive cotton magnates, while wishing the Lower South swept of all alien whites and Native Americans, especially sought to remove neighbors who encouraged slave resistance. The most menacing servile resistance came not from the few groups of slave insurrectionists, who were always quickly put down, but from the more numerous individual runaways, who ultimately helped defeat Confederate armies. During the Civil War, runaways increased when slaveholders' enemies massed close by; and in the early nineteenth century, Lower South slaveholders sometimes considered foreigners and Native Americans uncomfortably close to potential fugitives.

In Spanish Florida, for example, some Spaniards, Seminoles, and an occasional Englishman encouraged Georgia and South Carolina slaves to flee. In the face of this unrest, slaveholders in afflicted U.S. areas argued that either the government must protect property or property holders must protect themselves. Farther north, on the Tennessee frontier, Andrew Jackson had become a symbol of the armed protector. In 1818, President James Monroe ordered General Jackson to chastise some Seminoles who were troubling whites on the U.S. side of the Spanish Florida border. Jackson did more. He chased the Seminoles over the Spanish border, seized their fort, killed several of their chieftains, hanged two Englishmen said to be their accomplices, and expelled a Spanish garrison from Pensacola.[4]

Southern statesmen, in a pattern that would become crucial in the 1850s, divided along geographic lines on the wisdom of such adventuring as Jackson's. Southwestern frontiersmen cheered Jackson's raid. But South Carolina's John C. Calhoun (privately) and Kentucky's Henry Clay (publicly) deplored private raids that arguably exceeded governmental authorization. Nevertheless, Southwesterners, South Carolinians, and border Southerners alike urged the government to oust aliens and make private assaults unnecessary. After the Missouri Controversy of 1819–21, slaveholders sought territorial expansion for increasingly political as well as economic reasons. More Lower South land would mean more southern states and thus more congressional defenders of slavery.

Safer southern frontiers would also mean safer American frontiers. Because of that nationalistic reason for expansion southward, Southerners easily rallied a national consensus to evict foreigners and Native Americans from the entire Lower South during the first four decades of the nineteenth century. In 1803, President Thomas Jefferson, as part of the Louisiana Purchase, bought the future slave states of Louisiana, Arkansas, and Missouri from the French. In 1819, another Virginian, President James Monroe, taking advantage of the Spanish weakness that Jackson's raid had revealed, purchased the future state of Florida and southern areas of Mississippi and Alabama from Spain. In the 1830s, yet another southern president, Jackson himself, deported Native Americans to reservations across the Mississippi River. And in 1844, the last antebellum president from Virginia, John Tyler, brought four decades of unanimous southern zeal for expansion to a climax—and to an end—with his insistence that the Union annex Texas. That republic had secured its independence from Mexico in 1835, which had secured its independence from Spain in 1819.

President Tyler sought a national consensus to make the United States the latest nation with sovereignty over the vast Texas acreage. He thus did not emphasize one aim of fellow southern territorial expansionists: increasing the South's power in Congress. He did, however, reemphasize the slaveholders' problems with neighbors perceived as hostile. If neighboring enemies incited fugitive slaves, Jackson had said and Tyler now repeated, slaveholders must be able to control the contiguous land. Jackson had worried about allegedly slave-inciting Spaniards, Englishmen, and Seminoles in Spanish Florida, which abutted Georgia. Tyler thought that English antislavery influence might eventually prevail in the Texas Republic, which abutted Louisiana and Arkansas. Better to annex another area contiguous to the Lower South, Tyler declared with the aging Jackson's support, than to expose potential fugitive slaves to antislavery neighbors.

Tyler reiterated not only Jackson's determination to seize contiguous areas but also Jefferson's desire to acquire outlets for deportation of slaves. A new economic slump throughout the South lent urgency to Jefferson's old argument for diffusing slaves. In the 1840s the adolescent southwestern Cotton Kingdom, no less than the aging seaboard South, suffered an economic crisis. Cotton prices, which had averaged 16.4¢/pound in 1835–36, plunged in the 1840s, after the devastating Panic of 1837, to an average of 7.9¢/pound. Only an exorbitant yield could compensate for these 50 percent lower prices, and only virgin lands could spawn 50 percent higher yields. Not even the relatively undeveloped Southwest now seemed sufficiently unscarred. An unspoiled Texas would provide an economic safety valve, said Tyler, to drain redundant slaves from decaying slaveholding areas.

This newest safety valve argument continued to promise racial as well as economic relief. If no Texas outlet was secured, annexationists warned, the black population would swell in states suffering economic decline. If economic depression then persisted, whites would flee from their excess blacks. Were Texas to be annexed, on the other hand, slaveholders would sell unneeded slaves through that outlet. Here, in pristine form, was slaveholding agrarians' expand-or-perish argument. Unless slavery could spread into new areas, the slaveholders' depressed economy would collapse and the South's racial order would dissolve. Add to this formula for disaster the possibility that English abolitionists in Texas, right across the Louisiana-Arkansas border, would incite blacks to flee or to pillage or worse. This logic then yielded a clear choice: increase the number of southern congressional seats and double the Lower South's land by adding Texas to the Union or expect a racial inferno. That southern reason for national expansion, however, made Northerners increasingly resistant to American Manifest Destiny, slaveholder-style.[5]

2

If the southern expand-or-perish argument had remained unchallenged in the mid-1840s and had pervaded the 1850s, no historian would deny that a monolithic South massed behind slave diffusion. But in Texas Annexation times, the expansionists' diffusion argument inspired, in dialectical fashion, the first nineteenth-century southern breach over the question of slavery's expansion. In 1844, Southern Democrats, with rare Border South exceptions, united be-

hind the expand-or-die thesis. When Southern Democrats thus almost unanimously insisted, reluctant Northern Democrats almost
had to appease their party brethren, for the Democratic Party was
always stronger in the South than in the North. In contrast, when
Northern Whigs insisted, Southern Whigs could hardly defy their
party allies, for Whiggery was always stronger in the North than in
the South. In 1844, after Southern Democrats relentlessly demanded Texas and after Northern Democrats reluctantly acquiesced and Northern Whigs contemptuously disapproved, Southern
Whigs were driven to ask whether slavery would in fact perish unless the institution could diffuse into Texas.[6]

That query undermined Lower South unanimity on the
expand-or-perish dogma. How, after all, would Texas save slavery,
in or out of Congress, if the institution would drain from eight
Upper South states and South Carolina into a single annexed state?
Furthermore, how could new cotton production in virgin Texas rescue the older Cotton South from a depression caused by cotton
overproduction? Annexation, warned Whig South Carolina Congressman Waddy Thompson, would "very soon" remove slavery
from "Maryland, Virginia, North Carolina, Tennessee, and Kentucky." Even in aging South Carolina, he feared, slavery would become "an incumbrance which we shall be glad to get rid of; and
. . . it will afford me very little consolation in riding over my
fields, grown up in broomsedge and washed into gullies, to be told
that . . . slavery still exists and is prosperous" in Texas.[7]

The Border South's Henry Clay, Whig nominee for president in
1844, reversed Waddy Thompson's Lower South logic. Although a
large Kentucky slaveholder himself, Clay looked for the day when
his South, then the deeper South, could rid itself of slaves and of
free blacks. He declared Texas Annexation desirable in the abstract, because more slaves would then be diffused from the Upper
South. But he considered diffusion worth neither a foreign war nor
a sectional controversy. A statesman's "paramount duty," he declared, was "preserving the Union," not saving slavery, a "temporary institution."[8]

Slavery a "temporary institution"! Preserving the Union the
"paramount duty"! With those four words, Henry Clay under-
scored, as if in Civil War blood, the difference between the Border
and Lower Souths in their priorities about slavery, expansionism,
and Unionism. But if the Lower South's Waddy Thompson, hoping
to keep slaves in South Carolina, and the Border South's Henry
Clay, hoping to keep Americans in the Union, rejected annexation

for contrary Whig reasons, the Whigs' alliance against Texas almost killed expansionism. Three months after the Democrats' ultra-expansionist James K. Polk defeated Clay in the November 1844 presidential election, the U.S. Senate nearly rejected the admission of Texas into the Union. The margin for Texas was slim, 27–25, because only three of fifteen Southern Whigs joined with the unanimously pro-Texas Democratic senators. Subsequently, despite continued Whig opposition, the Democratic Party–led administration and Congress annexed Mexican territories from Texas to the Pacific, including California, in the Mexican Cession of 1848.

3

In the half-century after the invention of the cotton gin, U.S. land in Lower South latitudes had swept across the continent. That omnivorous territorial expansion, achieved in the 1840s despite increasing southern opposition and greater northern opposition, bid fair to override all obstacles once again in the 1850s. During that pre-secession decade, southern attempts to control Kansas, California, New Mexico, Arizona, Cuba, Nicaragua, and Mexico divided the nation, helped provoke the election of Abraham Lincoln in 1860, and helped lead to the formation of the Confederacy. Yet all latter-day southern expansion efforts failed, in part because Northerners massed powerfully against them, in part because Southerners failed to mass unanimously for them.[9]

The lack of unanimous southern zeal for expansion in the 1850s stemmed first of all from expansionism's very success. During the pre-secession decade, slaveholders could never cultivate all the Texas and Arkansas acres previously acquired. Nor could most Southerners still think that the Slave South would perish economically. As the 1840s ended, so did the post-1837 depression for all Southerners except South Carolina rice growers. During the 1850s, other Southerners' prosperity exceeded pre-1837 levels. Cotton prices, which had averaged under 8¢/pound in the 1840s, averaged 11¢/pound in the 1850s. The Lower South now needed more slaves to exploit unused land, not more outlets for unneeded slaves. Meanwhile, the Upper South, also enjoying better times, no longer needed to sell slaves to survive. So Lower South demand for slaves exceeded the supply, and the price of slaves soared 70 percent between 1850 and 1860.

One shocking proposed solution demonstrated how completely

times had changed. In the 1840s, many declining Southerners, growing too much of their cotton on too many tired acres, had sought fresh lands as a way to export excess blacks. In the 1850s, some booming Southerners, possessing too few laborers to grow enough cotton, sought to import Africans as a way to develop excess land. A Lower South movement to reopen the African slave trade grew with stunning rapidity in the mid-1850s. By buying slaves from Africa, ran one rationale for the proposed panacea, the Lower South could expand its Cotton Kingdom continually without contracting the Upper South's number of slaves counterproductively. With the Upper South keeping its slaves while the Lower South consolidated a hemispherewide empire, went the dream, southern states, ever more numerous in Congress, would transcend the debilitating divisiveness of Texas Annexation.

The proposal, however, caused a worse divisiveness. In the Upper South, angry slave sellers noted that by seeking to reopen the African slave trade, slave buyers in the Lower South sought to slice prices, even to cut U.S. sellers out of the market. Reopening the trade, opponents warned, would also defy federal laws, enrage the North, and lead to disunion. After this Upper South outcry, the Lower South proposal sank almost as fast as it had arisen. But by urging that the South had overly abundant territory and insufficient slaves, the reopeners finished off the diametrically opposite Texas-outlet logic.[10]

In yet another indication that the economic side of the planters' expand-or-perish rationale had become past history, the sole remaining group of economically pushed planters tended now to oppose territorial expansion. South Carolina coastal rice aristocrats suffered through a crippling economic slide in the 1850s, with the value of the rice crop sinking 25 percent below 1840s levels.[11] South Carolina up-country cotton producers fared better, but their economic recovery was less spectacular than that of Southwesterners. Some seven thousand whites and seventy thousand blacks departed from South Carolina for the cotton frontier in the 1850s, preserving that stagnating state's distinction as the only slave-exporting Lower South state. The state also retained its distinction as the only declining eighteenth-century locale of slavery that crusaded to keep slavery forever.

That singular determination to retain departing slaves turned many South Carolinians against tropical meccas. Waddy Thompson had put it well in Texas times: Who would stay in depleted Carolina if they could go to virgin El Dorados? John C. Calhoun came around to a similar attitude in 1846, opposing a southwestern drive to acquire all of Mexico. Some leading South Carolinians continued to harbor distaste for proposed Caribbean expansion in the 1850s. Mexico seemed full of non-American peons, Cuba full of free blacks, and the Southwest full of coarse frontiersmen. "It is not by bread alone that man liveth," intoned South Carolina's revered Francis Sumter in 1859. "We want some stability in our institutions."[12] South Carolina reactionaries wanted to stabilize their people—in South Carolina.

Many South Carolinians opposed a supposedly destabilizing Caribbean empire because they favored a supposedly stabilizing disunion revolution. These disunionists hoped that outside the Union and beyond unsettling northern attacks, a settled South could flourish. They feared that if the Union did acquire vast tropical lands, grateful Southwesterners would never secede and declining Carolinians would never stay east.[13] Still, a taste for staying home and distaste for expansionism swept up the powerful South Carolina Unionist U.S. Senator James Henry Hammond, just as it did the secessionists. "I do not wish," said Hammond, "to remove from my native state and carry a family into the semi-barbarous West."[14]

While South Carolinians, the most avid disunionists, often considered slaveholder expansion into raw land the semibarbarous road toward their own extinction, New Orleans businessmen, the most important proponents of Caribbean expansion, also cared little about acquiring new agricultural land. Instead, these avid imperialists longed for new urban markets. New York City and other northeastern urban centers were routing New Orleans in the competition for midwestern trade. In response, New Orleans merchants dreamed of commanding South American trade from U.S. ports in the Caribbean. Not contracting planters but the South's most expansive merchants feared they might perish unless the North American republic spread farther south.[15]

New Orleans merchants, as capitalist as any Northerners, and South Carolina planters, more anticapitalist than any other Americans, clashed not only over whether capitalistic hustle was salutary but also over the most effective means of southern survival. Most South Carolinians favored disunion as a way to escape the materialistic North. Most New Orleans capitalists favored the Union as a means to acquire a materialistic empire. If we exert enough pressure on Northern Democrats, New Orleans newspapers editorialized, the party will use the Union's power to acquire Cuba's har-

bors and then other lucrative Caribbean ports. If we fail to leave
the Democratic Party and the Union, responded many South Carolinians, we will be left hopelessly behind in a dangerously expansive nation.[16]

That climactic southern intramural war undercuts an important latter-day explanation for slaveholder expansionism. The
southern slave-labor system, runs some historians' argument, generated less efficient laborers and less entrepreneurial owners than
the northern free-labor system; and hence without constant expansion to fresh lands, Southerners supposedly feared that their allegedly anachronistic system would perish.[17] The best evidence for
that interpretation derives from the Texas Annexation struggle in
the 1840s, when the Cotton South was staggering economically.
But during the climactic struggle over Caribbean expansion in the
1850s, when cotton growers were booming, New Orleans up-to-
date capitalists became the avid southern territorial expansionists,
South Carolina's not-very-capitalistic planters often became anti-
expansionists, and southwestern slaveholders, whatever they
thought of Cuba, sought more slaves so they could pile up higher
profits than northern employers of free laborers could muster.

With economic expand-or-perish imperatives now impelling
only nonagrarian merchants, the political taproot of southern agriculturalists' expansion became preeminent. Throughout the eras
when Southerners sought more land, then less slaves and more
safety valves, then more markets and more slaves, defensive defiance was these slaveholders' political style. Slaveholders' aggressive defensiveness usually took the form of drives for more congressional seats and especially for more secure borderlands, lest
Northerners overwhelm slaveholders from without and corrode
hinterlands from within. The old concern about slaveholders' vulnerable outposts, however, shifted in the 1850s from Lower South
to Border South latitudes. True, near the Mexican border, Lower
South expansionists continued to complain about Mexican seduc-
tion of fugitive slaves, just as Spanish Florida's neighbors had complained about disturbances of their slaves. That recurring border
complaint helped impel abortive southern efforts to acquire Mexico in the 1850s. Near the Gulf of Mexico, other Lower South expansionists focused on Cuba. They claimed that English abolitionists wished to emancipate (or, as the word went, "Africanize")
Cuba, just as Englishmen had wished to emancipate Texas.[18] An
"Africanized" island commanding the Gulf, ninety miles from
Florida, could not be tolerated. But Southerners farther from the

Gulf considered English-inspired "Africanization" less credible than in Texas times.

With a Lower South reaching from the Atlantic to the Pacific now acquired, the greater border menace seemed to be northward, where more Northerners seemed to be helping slaves escape from the Border South. This shift in the direction of greatest southern concern created a revealing phenomenon: Southern congressmen cared less about acquiring California and Cuba, on the one hand, than about securing the Fugitive Slave Law and Kansas, on the other. During the crisis of 1850, some Southerners demanded the opportunity to make California a slave state. Southern California's lush terrain, they correctly urged, could produce fabulous cotton yields. Yet southern congressmen surrendered California to the North in exchange for a new Fugitive Slave Law, especially designed to protect the Border South where less plantation slavery was possible than in California. Four years later, southern drives to acquire Cuba and to open up Kansas to slavery came to climax at practically the same moment. Cuba, already a slave island and more tropical than the most tropical Lower South, possessed even more fertile land for slaveholders than did California. In contrast, Kansas, difficult to win for slavery and located northward in the Border South temperate zone, could never sustain cotton and offered less potential for other plantation crops as well. Yet in 1854, southern congressmen fought harder for the Kansas-Nebraska Act than for Cuba. Subsequently, southern congressmen more insistently demanded that the Union admit Kansas than that the nation acquire Cuba.

These southern priorities exasperated William Marcy, a New York Democrat and Franklin Pierce's secretary of state (1853–57). The South's demand for Kansas, wrote Marcy, "has sadly shattered our party in all the free states," depriving "it of that strength which . . . could have been more profitably used for the acquisition of Cuba."[19] Marcy could have also applied his irony to 1850, when the South's insistence on a dubiously enforceable Fugitive Slave Law ruptured southern sympathy in the North and deflected southern energies from southern California, which was highly adaptable to slaveholding.

Such priorities were less bizarre than Marcy thought. A now land-rich South understandably put lower priority on the acquisition of California and Cuba, both lush but neither located on a slaveholder's porous border. The higher priority involved consolidation of the vulnerable Border South. Inside that embattled mid-

dle ground between the free-labor North and the heavily slaveholding South, many inhabitants often hoped that their relatively few
slaves would drain southward. Meanwhile, some northern neighbors hoped to entice border fugitive slaves northward. The border
slave state of Missouri, already surrounded on two sides by free-
labor Illinois and Iowa, could not retain slavery, so Missouri slaveholders said, if a free-labor Kansas beckoned fugitive slaves from
a third border. With this critical initial argument for the Kansas-
Nebraska Act, Missourians reemphasized the revealing constant in
the changing story of southern expansionism. Whether in Louisiana in 1803 or Florida in 1819 or Texas in 1844 or Kansas in 1854,
Southerners feared slaves would flee from borderlands unless land
could be seized from enemies over the border.

But if most Southerners put high priority on controlling the
Kansas borderlands, southwestern congressmen continued to sup-
port the lesser priority of Cuba. As U.S. Senator Albert Gallatin
Brown of Mississippi put it, "I want Cuba, and I know that sooner
or later we must have it, . . . for the planting or spreading of slavery" and to expand slaveholders' congressional power.[20] Presidents
Franklin Pierce (1853–57) and James Buchanan (1857–61), both
Northern Democrats, tried to meet this demand by buying Cuba
from Spain. When Spain would not sell, Pierce's ministers to Spain,
England, and France issued the famous Ostend Manifesto (1854),
warning that if Spanish possession of Cuba endangered America,
"by every law, human and divine, we shall be justified in wrest-
ing it."

Spain would not be bullied, whereupon Caribbean expansionists embraced so-called filibustering. Antebellum Americans used
that term (linguistically derived from *freebooter*) to connote private
armies that hoped to sail from a U.S. port, land in a Caribbean
nation, lead an allegedly popular revolution, and annex the supposedly liberated nation to the United States. Such private invasions,
which culminated in John F. Kennedy's quasi-similar Bay of Pigs
fiasco in Cuba in the 1960s, bore a resemblance to Andrew Jackson's incursion into Florida in 1818. A disproportionate percentage
of 1850s filibusterers came from Jackson's Tennessee frontier. The
most successful filibusterer, Tennessee's William Walker, briefly
captured Nicaragua in the mid-1850s. The Jackson-Walker raiding
spirit found its perfect financial complement in the New Orleans
mercantile community's worried imperialism.

The combination of New Orleans cash and Tennessee adven-
turism might have been lethal to Caribbean nations—if the U.S.

government had failed to enforce the Neutrality Law of 1818, which forbade U.S. citizens from invading foreign nations. But Northerners would have condemned any president who allowed lawless Southerners to capture a slaveholder's empire (and hence gain more congressional votes). Northern Democrats always preferred to appease the South a good deal while standing firm against southern demands a little, thus keeping the party electable in the North and overwhelming in the South. In pursuit of that politic goal, northern presidents sought legal purchase of Cuba while imprisoning illegal filibusterers. Only a resolutely unified South might have budged Presidents Pierce and Buchanan from that seemingly balanced statecraft.

Southerners could not muster unanimous support for illicit private raids on Caribbean nations any more than they could for reopening the African slave trade or for Jackson's 1818 strike on Florida. Just as John C. Calhoun had considered Jackson an enemy of hierarchy and order, so South Carolinians often considered the filibusterers to be disorderly pirates who were seeking to seize disorderly nations. Just as Henry Clay had feared that Jackson's raid (and, later, Texas Annexation) would disrupt the Union, so many Upper South Democrats declared piracy in Cuba not worth disunion in America. With Southerners fighting Southerners, Northern Democratic presidents could follow northern constituents' desires. Thus federal judges and naval officers blocked critical filibuster expeditions before invasions reached the targeted nations, aborting especially former Mississippi governor John Quitman's plot to capture Cuba in 1855 and William Walker's assault on Nicaragua in 1857.

Although Southerners divided as badly on filibustering as on reopening the African slave trade, they were more united in seeking Kansas. Yet irresolution plagued even this main southern expansionist effort of the 1850s. By securing the Kansas-Nebraska Act in 1854, Southerners acquired the right to race northern settlers to Kansas. Instead of speeding to chilly Kansas, however, most migrants to the Southwest headed for tropical Texas and Arkansas. With more Northerners peopling Kansas, not even determined southern congressmen could pressure enough Northern Democrats to admit Kansas as a slave state in defiance of most Kansans' wishes.

Not enough Northerners appeased the South because too many Southerners deserted. In 1858, the House of Representatives rejected Kansas as a slave state by a vote of 120–112. If the six Upper

South ex-Whigs who voted "no" had voted "yes," the South would have had its prize. Instead, southern opposition, having almost defeated the annexation of Texas as the fifteenth slave state, had blocked the acquisition of Kansas as the sixteenth. The only southward expansion to triumph in the 1850s was the Gadsden Purchase (1853) of a strip of lower California—an acquisition aimed at building railroads, not planting cotton.

4

The frenetic southern expansion efforts of the 1850s, which upset most Northerners and yet acquired not one slave state, contrasted dismally with the sustained expansion efforts of 1793–1843, which had distressed few Northerners and had secured a Lower South empire. But back in the heady pre-Texas days, all Southerners had cherished expansionist objectives, even if some had winced at Jackson's methods. With southern unanimity over expansionist goals dissolving and northern protest rising, Southerners were fortunate that Texas squeaked through; and no luck could thereafter win further expansion of the slavocracy. Even in Kansas, despite the Kansas-Nebraska Act, late antebellum slave society's demands eventually outran its power. Disunited Southerners could not forever successfully defy the more numerous, and in the end, equally resolute Northerners.

In the 1850s, Northern Republicans would have denied that southern division hindered southern expansion. During that decade, it seemed to them that everywhere they looked, whether toward Cuba or Nicaragua or Kansas or Mexico, Southerners were seeking to take over the Union, indeed, the hemisphere. Moreover, whenever Republicans called slavery too morally disgusting to be allowed to spread, Southerners retorted that Republicans must silence their hateful slander.

Republicans were right that *some* Southerners wanted every inch of New World space in the 1850s and that *no* Southerner could abide northern insult. By calling slavery too barbarous to spread, Republicans took the expansion issue beyond pragmatic considerations, such as whether Caribbean acquisitions would depopulate South Carolina, to patriotic considerations, especially whether Southerners were a barbaric people. Republican righteous slurs generated a charged southern vocabulary: Would Southerners "submit" or "resist"? In this white man's egalitarian nation, white males could not "submit" to charges of moral inferiority without surrendering self-respect and honor. Indeed, a failure to "resist" moral condemnation itself had practical consequences in a southern world still divided on the morality of permanent slavery. If Border Southerners submitted to Republican insult, these disbelievers in slavery's permanence might be lost to the slavocracy. Instead, waverers must be rallied to resent the Republicans. If clergymen who criticized slaveholders' Christian imperfections saluted Republicans' antislavery morality, no Southerner would listen to them. Instead, internal reformers must be mobilized to castigate outside agitators. Proslavery warriors against the Republicans had a pragmatic stake in pressuring all Southerners to condemn northern critics, just as they had a pragmatic stake in pressuring Northerners to consolidate southern outposts.

This climactic aggressiveness once again illuminated the most constant aspect of southern expansionism, whatever the changing economic motives: slaveholders' propensity to defend by attacking, whether by pressuring southern waverers or by trading insults with northern detractors or by seeking additional congressional seats or by fortifying vulnerable hinterlands. As Republicans sought to contain these aggressive defenders, Southerners retaliated not only with scorn for the insulters but with expansionist proposals, each more provocative than the last and each Union-shattering initiative originating in futile endeavors to secure precisely the phenomenon Northerners thought they already observed: a consolidated Slavepower, united in its border outposts no less than in its Lower South core.

But if Southerners almost universally resented Republican condescension, they endlessly clashed over filibusterers and reopening the African slave trade and moving to Kansas—and over whether slavery was a permanent positive good. So, too, in the secession crisis, while Southerners almost universally acknowledged that Abraham Lincoln's antislavery criticism must be resisted, they hotly disputed the necessity of resisting only outside the Union. After anti-expansionist South Carolinians precipitated disunion, pro-expansionist Louisianians felt compelled to follow their Lower South brethren. But not-very-proslavery Border Southerners felt a countervailing compulsion: to save the Union. Here again, the southern politics of the 1850s, so often aimed at making border areas more southern than northern, had failed.

The resulting southern disunity would prove to be even more fatal to Confederate armies than it had been to Caribbean filibusterers and to the reopening of the African slave trade and to the securing of Kansas. In war even more than in peace, the infuriated Southerner would be an awesome force. But not even the South's fabled courage could ultimately defeat the more numerous Northerners, plus the Border South third of southern white folk, plus the runaway southern black folk. And fugitive slaves, by fleeing toward Northerners during the Civil War, would prove that prewar southern expansionists' fears of nearby "aliens" had been all too prescient.

9 / The Divided South, Democracy's Limitations, and the Causes of the Peculiarly North American Civil War

I at first intended that this essay would sum up solely the southern side of the coming of the Civil War for Gabor Boritt's symposium at Gettysburg College in June 1992. I tried out the initial draft at the University of California, San Diego, where Michael Johnson, David Rankin, Julie Saville, Stephanie McCurry, Steve Hahn, and Rachel Klein supplied especially helpful criticism. Craig Simpson, Seymour Drescher, Catherine Clinton, Gabor Boritt, and Jeannette Hopkins usefully criticized a later version.

But a memorable encounter with David Brion Davis, when I presented another chapter in this volume to a Yale University symposium, changed the very nature of the essay. Davis asked me if and how the William Lloyd Garrison campaign for immediate abolitionism had helped cause the Civil War. I had never concentrated on that question, for the northern pre–Civil War mainstream persistently rejected intervention in the South to abolish slavery. In 1860, Abraham Lincoln did not win a mandate to impose emancipation on the southern states. Rather, the President-elect rallied the North to contain an aggressively defensive slaveholder minority's dominion to the South. I have accordingly focused on the causes of the South's aggressive defensiveness and the transforming impact of that aggressiveness on northern public opinion. But Davis's question remains apt. To rephrase his query in a way I find illuminating: Should the abolitionists be major players in my story of the way provocative slaveholders aroused Northerners to seek containment of the so-called Slavepower?

Professor Davis also mentioned his intriguing discovery that

Latin Americans usually shunned Garrison's righteous antislavery posture, with its contempt for "sinning slaveholders" and for gradualist reform. A less strident antislavery tone fit the very different Latin American situation, for individual accommodations between masters and slaves slowly led to more manumissions than in the United States, and almost all Latin nations (but no southern state) enacted gradualist antislavery measures. The one Latin American experience with quasi-Garrisonian intransigence is the exception that proves the rule. At the tail end of the Brazilian story of emancipation, abolitionists insisted on converting already-enacted gradualist antislavery into immediate emancipation. But even this triumphant 1880–88 Brazilian immediatist campaign lacked Garrison's contemptuous tone, which castigated U.S. slaveholders as Satan's minions. Why the difference in the dialogue over slavery and action on antislavery? The question demonstrated that a perspective broadened to include the antebellum North as well as the antebellum South would still focus too narrowly on the United States.

Professor Davis thus set me to thinking about how to widen my story of the Old South's road to disunion and emancipation. This resulting venture into the comparative history of abolition in the Americas has not had the benefit of his as yet unpublished Slavery in the Age of Emancipation, *the most eagerly awaited book in the field of pre–Civil War history. But I hope this essay extends the spirit of his previously published volumes on slavery, which teach by example that a reintegration of American history requires the transcendence, in both subject matter and chronology, of specialists' work on tiny pieces of Americana.*

This essay is being published, more or less simultaneously, in Why the Civil War Came, *ed. Gabor Boritt (New York, 1994).*

Democracy has become the most coveted American export. The cold war has been won; the democratic way vindicated. Throughout yesterday's totalitarian half of the globe, long-repressed voices demand freedom of speech, free elections, and majority rule. As the twenty-first century approaches, Americans have seemingly lived up to their seventeenth-century forebears' ambition: to become a City Upon A Hill for all the world to emulate.

Such ideological imperialism, however, has sometimes ill-served this nation. In striving to spread their supposedly ideal political system, Americans on occasion have generated foreign policy disasters, especially in Vietnam. So now more than ever, historians must remind their fellow citizens that democracy, like all things human, is no universal panacea. American democracy indeed could not peacefully resolve our own gravest social problem, slavery. It is a telling historical irony that of all the New World slavocracies, only slaveholders in the United States lived in an advanced republic, and only the United States required a civil war between whites to abolish slavery for blacks.

Despite that singularity of the American Civil War, violence sometimes accompanied emancipation in less republican New World regimes. Abolition in Haiti evolved out of an equally singular civil war, in that case between slaves and slaveholders. Agitation over emancipation also led to some bloodshed in Cuba. So too, slaveholders' rage at not receiving recompense for their slaves helped inspire a revolution in Brazil after emancipation. But nowhere else in the Americas did slaveholders rise in revolution before emancipation, accepting the risks of a military showdown with nonslaveholders.[1]

The southern slaveholders' unique acceptance of trial by warfare demanded unique self-confidence. Secession required both nerve and the perception of power. The Brazilian and Cuban slavocracies could have no such nerve in the 1870s and 1880s, after watching U.S. slaveholders go down in flames in the 1860s. Nor did their nondominant position in their respective political power structures embolden Cuban or Brazilian slaveholders with the illusion that they could win a civil war.

Latin American slaveholders also lacked illusions about their worldwide economic power. No Caribbean or South American planter imagined that his European customers would intervene on his side in a New World civil war. Fantasies that European customers would bolster King Cotton's army, however, rarely dominated the secessionists' thinking. Rather, U.S. slaveholders' unique political power inside a peculiarly advanced republic above all else instilled in them the illusion—and for a long while the reality—that they could control slavery's fate.

Or to be more accurate, the minority of slaveholders inside the U.S. majoritarian republic swung between feelings of infuriating powerlessness and perceptions of imperial powerfulness, as they exerted their unusual leverage over slavery's destiny. On the one hand, some ideological and institutional aspects of U.S. republicanism empowered nonslaveholding majorities to assault the slaveholding minority. Because of the possibility of majority control,

U.S. slaveholders were potentially as much at the mercy of outside forces as were Latin American slaveholders, who could only postpone their less democratic governments' emancipation decrees. On the other hand, some aspects of the U.S. republican system, as embedded in the Constitution, empowered the slaveholder minority to resist emancipation in a manner impossible elsewhere in the Americas. The southern minority's power over the northern majority inspired a new northern word, the most charged in the antebellum political vocabulary: *Slavepower*. The term connoted the driving force of the U.S. sectional controversy: the slaveholders' arguably undemocratic power over northern white citizens no less than over southern black slaves.

All of the resulting thrusts for power—the northern majority's disavowal of the Slavepower's dominion over whites, the southern minority's secession from the Union after the northern majority rejected Slavepower rule, fugitive slaves' escape from their masters, the Border South's defiance of Deep South disunionism, the North's reversal of slaveholders' secession from the Union—all this unraveling of a republic and coercive reconsolidation stemmed from the foundations of American democratic practice and belief. But America had become an ugly City Upon A Hill, demonstrating that the world's most advanced republic could end slavery only by one of the bloodiest fratricides in human history.

1

The divergent U.S. and Latin American roads toward emancipation began with dissimilar colonial settlements. During the seventeenth century, England, the most republican of the European colonizing nations, sent to the North American mainland by far the largest percentage of nonslaveholding settlers to be found in any New World area containing large numbers of slaves.[2] Because of that comparatively huge white republican population, the thirteen colonies had special leverage to resist English metropolitan impositions on colonial republicanism; and out of that resistance came the American Revolution and the first New World liberation from Old World control. With the establishment of the federal Union, the Revolutionaries encased one of the most extensive slaveholder regimes in the Americas inside the most republican nation in the New World.

Within the republican Union, advanced Anglo-American antislavery ideas could especially flourish—if abolitionists could mobilize the majority of nonslaveholders. Yet within the Union, the minority of slaveholders had a special New World power to protect themselves—if they could mobilize the masses. Nowhere else in the New World did slavery's fate hang on popular mobilization.

A second peculiarity in colonial settlement of the future United States ultimately threatened slaveholder mobilization of southern public opinion. Just as a higher proportion of nonslaveholding whites peopled the original thirteen colonies than could be found in other New World locales with large numbers of slaves, so only North American colonists planted slavery primarily in nontropical areas. Anglo-American economists have always echoed the Latin American colonials' conventional wisdom that tropical climates spawned the largest plantation profits. Seventeenth-and eighteenth-century English settlers, however, considered the climate of the most tropical part of North America, the Lower South, too cool for sugar and coffee, Latin America's profitable plantation products. North American colonists turned to other tropical crops for the Georgian and South Carolinian swamplands and Sea Islands on the Atlantic coast. In these Lower South tropics, huge slave gangs grew rice, indigo, and Sea Island cotton.

Nowhere west of the Lower South's coastal swamps, however, could these crops be lucratively extended. The most far-flung North American eighteenth-century slaveholder enterprises instead thrived northward, still farther from the sugar- and coffee-producing tropics. North of South Carolina—in Middle South latitudes—North Carolina and especially Virginia planters raised primarily tobacco. North of the Middle South—in Border South latitudes—Delaware and especially Maryland planters raised less tobacco and more grains. Farther yet from the tropics—in the most southern part of the eventually free-labor North—Pennsylvania, New Jersey, and New York grain farmers used some slaves; and in New England, a few Puritans utilized house slaves. In late eighteenth-century North America, the coolest locale of New World slaveholders, almost four slaves out of five lived north of the more tropical Lower South.

As the eighteenth century gave way to the nineteenth, an invention and a law pressed U.S. slavery toward tropical habitats. Eli Whitney's invention of the cotton gin in 1793 impelled the movement of slaveholders toward Lower South frontiers. Fourteen years later, in 1807, the federal government's closure of the African slave trade contracted the Cotton Kingdom's source of slaves. Unlike mid-nineteenth-century tropical developers in Cuba and Brazil, the two other large New World slavocracies, cotton planters could not legally buy slaves from Africa. But only U.S. slaveholders could purchase slaves from their own northerly, relatively nontropical areas, which had concurrently fallen into chronic economic recession. A slave drain ensued, especially from the more northern South to the more southern South. Between 1790 and 1860, some 750,000 Middle and Border South slaves traveled downriver to the Cotton Kingdom. The Lower South, which had had 21 percent of U.S. slaves in 1790, had 59 percent in 1860. Maryland and Virginia, with 60 percent in 1790, had 18 percent in 1860. Thirty-seven percent of Lower South white families owned slaves in 1860, compared to only 12 percent in the Border South, down from 20 percent in 1790.[3]

At the same time that the more southerly U.S. slaveholders expanded toward Latin American–style tropical locations, the more northerly U.S. slavocracy contracted toward Latin American–style antislavery ideas. The Latin American slavocracies lacked the power to defy worldwide antislavery currents in the manner of Lower South slaveholders. Latin slaveholders instead gave ground grudgingly, stalling for more time to reap profits, mostly through the passage of so-called free-womb laws. These edicts freed only slaves born after a given law's enactment and only after they reached a distant target age, usually eighteen or twenty-one. These laws set a clock ticking toward the end of slavery.

The clock ran slowly, satisfyingly so from Latin American slaveholders' perspective. A slave born even a day before a law was passed would never be freed, which meant that slavery could profitably persist for at least fifty years. As for lucky slaves born at the right time, they were lucklessly doomed to involuntary servitude throughout their youth; and by the time they were twelve years old, black children toiled hard in the fields. A series of Latin American regimes with relatively few slaves, including Chile, Peru, and Venezuela, first tried delaying emancipation through free-womb laws. Then in the two Latin American countries with large slave populations, Cuba's Moret Law (1870) and Brazil's Rio Branco Law (1871) brought the free-womb tradition to climax.

Nowhere did free-womb emancipation work as slowly as entrepreneurs had hoped. Abolitionists and slaves pressed for a faster end to the system. Slaves born only a short time before passage of a free-womb law deployed especially angry resistance. In response, slaveholders often bargained individually with their slaves, scheduling freedom for each before the law freed any. Slaves, in return, promised to labor willingly during the interim.

These bargains drew on older Latin American manumission traditions. Latins had long liberated favorite slaves under certain conditions: when a master and a cherished black woman had a sexual relationship; or when beloved mulatto offspring had resulted from such a union; or when a slave had given especially valued economic service. The combination of free-womb laws, expanded manumissions, intensified abolitionist attacks, and more widespread slave resistance finally toppled the regimes in Cuba in 1886 and Brazil in 1888—or before these slavocracies' respective free-womb laws had freed any slave.

These Latin American patterns, shunned in U.S. tropical areas where slavery was concentrating, had originated in U.S. temperate areas where the institution was dwindling. Free-womb emancipation bore a different title in the United States—post-nati emancipation—but only the name was different. In 1780, Pennsylvania enacted the hemisphere's first post-nati law. In 1799, New York followed suit, as did New Jersey in 1804. In 1817, New York followed up its preliminary post-nati law in the later Cuba/Brazil manner, declaring an end to the institution ten years hence.[4]

South of these belatedly emancipated Middle Atlantic states, slaveholding states never passed a post-nati law. The Border South, however, emulated another aspect of Latin American gradualism: individual manumissions. Different nations took censuses of their populations in different years, which makes comparisons imprecise. Still, a similar pattern of manumission is clear enough. In 1830, 19.5 percent of black residents of the Border South were free, compared to 23 percent in Brazil (in 1817–18) and 46 percent in Cuba (in 1846).[5] Two Border South states manumitted their slaves at rates faster than the Latin American norm. By 1830 in Maryland, 34 percent of the resident blacks were free, as were 83 percent of Delaware's blacks.

But just as post-nati laws penetrated no farther south than the Middle Atlantic states, so manumissions flourished no farther south than the Border South. While 21 percent of Border South blacks were free in 1860, the percentage sank to 7 percent in the Middle South and 1.5 percent in the Lower South. The Border South manumission story was a subplot of the larger tale: that U.S. slavery was incrementally waning in northern nontropical habitats but rapidly strengthening in southwestern tropical locales.

With slavery swiftly concentrating southward and slowly fading northward, different social attitudes and political priorities developed. Lower South slaveholders came to call slavery a probably perpetual blessing, while Border South masters persistently called the institution a hopefully temporary evil. So too Lower South political warriors cared more about perpetuating slavery than the Union, while Border South leaders would compromise on slavery in order to save the Union. Still, even in Delaware, where over fifteen thousand slaves in 1790 had shrunk to under two thousand in 1860, slaveholders resisted final emancipation. In Maryland, where manumissions plus slave sales to the Lower South had halved the percentage of white slaveholding families, the increasingly outnumbered slavocracy counterattacked desperately in the mid-1850s, futilely seeking to reenslave the freed blacks. Concurrently, in Missouri, the state's even faster declining fraction of slaveholders counterattacked still more desperately, unsuccessfully seeking to establish slavery in neighboring Kansas.

In the mid-nineteenth century, then, slaveholders overwhelmingly controlled the Lower South, which had been belatedly but massively developed. The slavocracy somewhat less solidly controlled the Middle and Border South, where percentages of slave owners were slowly dropping. But even in the Border South, vestiges (and sometimes defiant concentrations) of the old relatively nontropical slavocracy occasionally fought to salvage a fading system. The mature Slave South had a tropical base of states, containing large slave populations, and several layers of buffer zones to the north, with less tropical conditions and less proslavery commitments and fewer slaves in each successive tier above.

Yet despite this degree of geographic disunity, no other New World slavocracy could muster as united a front against worldwide antislavery currents. The difference between slaveholders' unity, albeit incomplete, in the United States and their utter disarray in Brazil is especially revealing, for similar experiences yielded dissimilar outcomes. In both countries, a once-flourishing northerly slaveholding region fell into decline and sold many of its slaves to a newly flourishing southerly region. In the United States, the Upper South Tobacco Kingdom sold hundreds of thousands of slaves to the Lower South Cotton Kingdom. In Brazil, the Northeastern Sugar Kingdom, which in 1822 had held almost 70 percent of the country's slaves, transferred equally huge numbers of blacks to the South Central Coffee Kingdom, which by the early 1880s owned 65 percent of Brazil's slaves.[6]

There the similarity ended. In Brazil, the old sugar provinces, despite a population still 15 percent enslaved, led the movement for free-womb abolition, with the Ceará region in the vanguard. When the national Chamber of Delegates voted on the Rio Branco free-womb bill in 1871, the Northeastern sugar provinces favored gradual emancipation, 39–6, thus canceling out the South Central coffee provinces' 30–12 vote against.[7] The Border South, in contrast, usually voted with the Lower South on slavery propositions in Congress and never enacted a post-nati law.

A more intense racism fueled the U.S. slaveholders' greater capacity to mobilize a united front. Because Latin American racial attitudes toward blacks were less hidebound than in the United States, greater tolerance for free-womb emancipation, for mulattoes, and for individual manumissions—and less willingness to fight a civil war over the issue—pervaded Latin American slavocracies. Because U.S. racism was so extreme, a more unified slaveholding class and more support from white nonslaveholders—and thus a greater capacity to fight a civil war—infused the Slave South.

Behind the more severe U.S. racism lay in part a different heterosexual situation, itself another result of the largest white migration to an important New World slavocracy. English colonists to the future United States migrated far more often in family groups and/or with equal numbers of unmarried males and females in the entourage than did colonists headed farther south, who more often sought their fortunes as unattached males, with only slaves available for sexual liaisons. More frequent and less taboo interracial sexual intimacies resulted south of British North America, which led to more mulattoes and less insistence that the world be rigidly separated into black and white.

Politically no less than biologically, U.S. slaveholders preferred nothing between black and white. The very basis of black slavery, in so republican a regime for whites, had to be a rigid color line. The Old South had to cleave advanced republicanism for whites totally from abject slavery for blacks. That black and white separation mystified Brazilian quasi-republicans, to say nothing of Latin American nonrepublicans. Only U.S. slaveholders, in short, considered *free black* an oxymoron.

Some historians doubt that racism was more culturally deep-seated in the United States than south of the border. That position founders before the greater U.S. taboo surrounding miscegenation and the far greater desire to deport blacks from antebellum America than from any other New World slavocracy. But the comparative power of cultural racism *before* slaveholders politically mobilized is unimportant to the comparative history of emancipation, for uniquely in the United States, slaveholders had to mobilize nonslaveholders, and racism was their most potent weapon. After southern slaveholders had used the distinction between equality for all whites and inequality for all blacks to rally the nonslaveholders, southern racism inarguably had become an especially powerful idea.

The racial foundation of Southwide unity, however, was a two-edged sword. For racism to unite nonslaveholders and slaveholders, the black race had to be significantly present. With the slave drain to the Lower South and the movement of European whites to such northerly slave states as Maryland and Missouri, Border South blacks became steadily less visible. As for that highly visible group of blacks in northern Maryland and Delaware, the free blacks, their energetic labor and law-abiding deportment demonstrated that racial control hardly required slavery.

That conclusion had proved fatal to slavery in northern states where percentages of blacks had declined. In the colonial period, New York had had slave proportions in the 1860 Border South's range, about 15 percent of the total population. As New York's slave percentage had dwindled toward 5 percent, sentiment for post-nati emancipation had grown. Mid-nineteenth-century Border South states were in no immediate danger of becoming a New York, much less a Brazilian Ceará. But given the Border South's waning percentage of blacks, its Latin American–style manumissions, its propensity for thinking of slavery as a temporary evil, and its commitment to Union-saving compromises on the institution, could the Lower South rely on its northern hinterlands' future loyalty?

On the answer hung the Slave South's capacity to be that unique New World slave regime: the one that could defy an emancipating century rather than settle for a few more decades of slaveholder profits. Latin American slavocracies lacked not only the South's intensely racist reasons to stonewall antislavery but also its political basis for confidence that emancipation could be routed. The Latin American slavocracies were either too vulnerable to black insurrection (as in Haiti) or too much under the power of European empires (as in the French and British West Indies and in Spanish-owned Cuba) or too small a minority (as in Venezuela and Peru) to command their fate inside a government that could abolish slavery. True, the Latin American regime closest in type to the southern slaveholders, the Brazilian slavocracy, also possessed a powerful minority in a partly parliament-ruled (and partly monarchical) nation. But Brazilian slaveholders, compared to their more intransigent U.S. counterparts, were too divided against each other over slavery's future, too lacking in a rigid racism that might control the nonslaveholders, and too fond of a *regime des notables* to risk enfranchising and mobilizing the "nonnotables." Unable to mount a united front, in or out of parliament, the Brazilian slavocracy could only postpone emancipation with Rio Branco laws. The Old South, in contrast, had various powers to command a majoritarian democracy despite its minority status—*if* all fifteen slave states hung together and the Border South did not go the way of New York, or worse, Ceará.

Numbers indicate how much was at stake in that *if*. The seven Lower South states of 1860 (South Carolina, Florida, Georgia, Alabama, Mississippi, Louisiana, and Texas, with 47 percent of their population enslaved) could not fight off the sixteen northern states (containing 61 percent of the American population) without the enthusiastic support of the four Middle South states (Virginia, North Carolina, Tennessee, and Arkansas, with 32 percent of their population enslaved) and the four Border South states (Maryland, Delaware, Kentucky, and Missouri, with 13 percent of their population enslaved). Those buffer areas above the Lower South could come under siege—the siege of democratic public opinion. Would the Border South remain foursquare behind slavery and the Lower South, even if the slavocracy's northern hinterlands came to possess scantier and scantier percentages of blacks?

That question transcended the Border South. The slaveholders' worst internal problem involved not a single localized place but a regionwide lopsided distribution of blacks. While the Border South was the most widespread locale with a relatively low percentage of slaves, some areas farther south also contained few blacks; and everywhere a paucity of slaves allowed more nonslaveholder hostility toward slaveholders. Wherever blacks were concentrated, whites drew together, however much the poor resented the rich, for lowly whites despised lowlier blacks even more than they resented lordly masters. But whenever blacks were scarce, race hatred intensified class hatred, for nonslaveholders preferred to have neither autocrats nor blacks around. A relatively slaveless situation, while most prevalent in the Border South, also predominated in western Virginia, in eastern Tennessee, and in piney woods and semimountainous areas of the Lower South. Here the Border South predicament came closer to home to worried Lower and Middle South slavocrats. Could upper-class ideology command lower-class loyalties in areas where no racial tensions united the whites?

2

Struggles for ideological command often take a dialectical form of charge and response. In the United States, intensified versions of white republicanism and antiblack racism generated a dialectic about slavery different than that in Latin America. At the heart of the difference lay two fears foreign to Latin America. First, slavery and the slavery issue might destroy an advanced white men's republic. Second, emancipation might also devastate a white republic unless freed blacks were removed.

The North American dialogue about emancipation began with the foundation of U.S. republicanism, the Declaration of Independence. When the Founding Fathers asserted that *all* men are created equal, they immediately confronted a moral dilemma: their long unquestioned institution of slavery had become an anomaly in the republic they sought. Thomas Jefferson of Virginia, author of the Declaration and a large slaveholder, believed that all men would and should rise up against so antirepublican a horror as slavery. He thus feared that slave insurrection would disrupt white republics unless white republicans freed blacks. He also worried that southern republican leaders would become irresponsible tyrants if youths learned to exercise power by lashing dissolute blacks. Thus did the U.S. slavery controversy early take its special tack: Whites would always worry not only about whether blacks ought to be freed but about how white republicanism could be preserved.

Yet if Jefferson called slavery antithetical to republicanism, he considered racism compatible with the Declaration of Independence. Whites and blacks, thought Jefferson, were innately different. Whites allegedly possessed a keener abstract intelligence; blacks, a keener sexual ardency. Ex-slaves, he further worried, would be eager for revenge and ex-masters determined to repress the avengers. If slaves were freed and remained in the United States, "deep-rooted prejudices entertained by the whites" and "ten thousand recollections by the blacks, of the injuries they have sustained" would "produce convulsions, which will probably never end but in the extermination of one or the other race."[8]

Thus to preserve white republics, freed blacks had to be deported. The dangerous alternative was to keep blacks enslaved. Jefferson's conviction that emancipation must be conditional on removing blacks, the first thrust in the U.S. dialectic on abolition, was rare in Latin America.[9] An insistence on race removal would have ill-suited Latin American nations, where individual bargains between masters and slaves slowly led to a third class of semifree blacks and a fourth class of free blacks. The supposed necessity that U.S. slaveholders must choose between enslaving or removing blacks also misfit the situation in Delaware and Maryland, where black freedmen formed an orderly working class. But because U.S. slaveholders saw the world through the lens of a rigid non-Latin-American-style racism, the successful manumissions in Maryland and Delaware went unacknowledged, even unseen, as if the phenomenon of orderly free blacks *could* not happen and therefore *had* not happened. Instead, that more common Upper South phenomenon, the removal of slaves by sales to the Lower South, became the model for further action in the selling region. Proposals for stepping up the removal of blacks from the Upper South included expulsion to Africa, deportation to the Caribbean, and legislatively induced accelerated sales to the Lower South through the passage of post-nati laws.

By sometimes campaigning for Latin American–style post-nati proposals, with the non-Latin American purpose of forcing the removal of blacks, Upper South emancipators demonstrated again the U.S. slave regime's oddity in hemispheric perspective. In Latin America, free-womb laws were *nationally* enacted. Thus slaveholders in one part of the nation could not subvert emancipation by selling the bondsman before his emancipating birthday to another part of the nation. But in the United States, where only states passed post-nati laws, a slaveholder could sell his soon-to-be-freed slaves into permanent thralldom by transporting them to a state that lacked the law. Thus could one state remove its blacks, with slave purchasers in another state paying to "whiten" the selling state's population.

Some northern masters first discovered this singular black removal process. After their states passed post-nati laws, nineteenth-century New York and New Jersey slaveholders often sold their slaves down South before an emancipating birthday. Few northern legislators cheered such a cynical evasion of abolition. Most northern masters also deplored the loophole, but New York slaveholders still used it perhaps two-thirds of the time, thus permanently enslaving thousands of blacks whose future freedom had been decreed.[10]

This process, unintended by northern legislatures, became the deliberate intention of southern not-so-antislavery legislators when they appropriated the post-nati proposal. Southern propositions for the ploy began in the Virginia antislavery debate of 1831–32, an episode that ironically has been mistaken for the end of southern consideration of abolition.[11] In the wake of Nat Turner's slave revolt, the most successful (although still abortive) slave uprising in the United States, Thomas Jefferson Randolph, Jefferson's favorite grandson, proposed to the Virginia legislature that slaves born after 1840 be freed on their eighteenth (women) and twenty-first (men) birthdays. Thus far Randolph's proposal was standard Latin American–style free-womb emancipation. But Randolph's bill added the condition, alien to Latin America, that the state must remove the freedmen to Africa. Randolph's speech for the historic proposal also featured the cynical prediction, more alien still south of the U.S. border, that many Virginia masters would sell slaves to the Lower South before emancipating birthdays. Thus, Randolph cheered, masters would profitably remove slaves from Virginia at no cost to state coffers.

Randolph's proposal led to a famous state crisis, for Virginia's largely nonslaveholding areas rallied behind Jefferson's grandson in defiance of slaveholding areas. Never before in the history of the Slave South, and never again until western Virginia seceded from Virginia during the Civil War, was the potentially dangerous antagonism between slaveless and slaveholding geographic zones more obvious, for here western Virginian nonslaveholders sought to impose emancipation on eastern Virginia planters. Earlier, eastern squires had built a bulwark against the nonslaveholder threat. They had insisted that slaveholders have more seats in the Virginia House of Delegates (lower house) than eastern Virginia's white numbers justified. The underrepresented western Virginians responded, like later Northerners, that the Slavepower thus enslaved *them*. These nonslaveholders preferred that all blacks depart the commonwealth. Then true white democracy would replace Slavepower dominion in Virginia. So western Virginians cheered Thomas Jefferson Randolph's black removal proposal.

After two weeks of debate, the Virginia House of Delegates rejected a variation of Randolph's proposal by a vote of 73–58. The margin against antislavery would have shriveled to one vote if the slaveholders had not held those extra legislative seats. The shaky anti-Randolph majority warned that even after masters had sold off some blacks, state-financed removal of other slaves would bankrupt the government. Nor should the government bully masters into selling bondsmen by placing post-nati deadlines over capitalists' heads. But Randolph's none-too-proslavery opponents, also desiring an altogether white Virginia, predicted that masters' capitalistic decisions would dispatch Virginia slaves southward without the threat of post-nati laws. Thomas R. Dew, then Virginia's most famous advocate of slavery, was pleased that all Middle South slaves would eventually be sold to the Lower South, for Virginia was "too far north" for slavery.[12]

Dew's proposed remedy, removing slaves by altogether-voluntary private sales, could keep slavery and blacks too far north for a long time. Thomas Jefferson had proposed a swifter way to deport blacks: a federal constitutional amendment that would authorize compulsory emancipation and colonization to be financed by federal land sales, a richer source of funds than state taxation. Throughout the nation, antislavery moderates perpetuated this scheme for liberating slaves while also whitening the republic. The persistent admirers of Jefferson's black removal plan included the Border South's favorite statesman, Henry Clay; the Republicans' favorite politician, Abraham Lincoln; and the North's favorite novelist, Harriet Beecher Stowe. A national volunteer organization, the American Colonization Society, used private donations to establish a rather unstable African colony, Liberia, to receive American blacks. In those unusual days of a federal budgetary surplus, the national government had excess funds to help with the financing. But South Carolina threatened secession if Congress even discussed the possibility. So the debate stopped before much was said.[13]

3

In post-Jefferson America, as in post–Nat Turner Virginia, that first thrust of the U.S. dialectic on slavery, the abolition-conditional-on-removal argument, was yielding little black removal, save the slave drain southward, which was not antislavery at all. Thus did the conditional antislavery polemic, unusual in Latin America, generate its opposite, also uncommon in Latin America: northern extremists' exasperated attack on black removal and on all conditions that must be observed before slavery could be immediately abolished. William Lloyd Garrison's *Liberator* articulated this assault on procrastination, beginning in 1831. Black deportation, Garrison wrote angrily, was as outrageous as black slavery, for blacks were created equal. Furthermore, democracy must abolish slavery or slavery would abolish democracy, for masters with sinful absolute power and a republic with salutary limited power were deadly foes.

The black-removal idea lay forever discredited among northern antislavery extremists after Garrison's savage assault. But here as everywhere, posterity should never confuse the northern extremists with the northern mainstream. The argument that antislavery must be conditional on removing black freedmen retained thousands of northern supporters for every Garrisonian and hundreds of thousands of Upper South supporters with scarcely a southern Garrisonian to be found. The debate between Garrison's unconditional immediatism and Jefferson's conditional gradualism would persist until deep into the Civil War. Then blacks' wartime utility helped the Garrisonians rout the long-more-powerful Jeffersonian black-removal tradition.

Jefferson's and Garrison's positions, while clashing on black removal, agreed that black slavery poisoned white democracy. That concurrence did not augur well for the slaveholding minority. White racist nonslaveholders, the majority of citizens in the South and in the nation, had to be deterred from believing that black slavery endangered white democracy and/or that blacks could safely be removed. Thus conditional and unconditional antislavery together generated, in the next phase of the United States' unique dialogue on slavery, the predictable proslavery response: Without slavery, both blacks and democracy would expire.

Although proslavery Latin Americans also sometimes dwelled on blacks' alleged inferiority, the racial argument for *black* slavery was more necessary in a white men's republic, and race-based arguments were more central in U.S. proslavery polemics. South of the United States, proslavery articulations emphasized more strongly the color-blind message that abolition portended *social* upheaval. Proslavery polemicists in the United States characteristically added that emancipation portended specifically *racial* upheaval. The Lower South slavocracy compared blacks to orangutans and gorillas. Such barbarians, went the ugly argument, would revert to African cannibalism if freed.[14]

But though this argument for *black* slavery was almost always front and center, a few proslavery theorists wrought the final uniquely U.S. rationale: Not "mere Negro" slavery but slavery per se was especially right in a republic, regardless of its special rightness for blacks.[15] This color-blind aspect of the U.S. proslavery argument reaffirmed the Latin American emphasis on social upheaval and added an emphasis on political upheaval. Abolition would unhinge not just the society but also the republic, according to the peculiarly U.S. version of color-blind proslavery.

This nonracial proslavery argument reversed Jefferson's racist antislavery thesis. Early experience in despotism over blacks, Jefferson had argued, would corrupt republican leaders of whites. Defenders of color-blind paternalism countered that the plantation system trained the best men to command lesser blacks and thus to command lesser whites. Inferiors of any age or sex, class or color, needed patriarchal direction, lest children revolt from parents, wives leave husbands, lower classes assault upper classes, and especially lest patriarchal republics degenerate into depraved mobocracies.

These, then, were the prime ideological contestants on the issue of slavery in the mid-nineteenth-century United States: antislavery moderates, who would abolish slavery only if free blacks were deported; antislavery extremists, who denounced the black-removal condition; advocates for race-based slavery, who denounced freedom for blacks; and advocates for slavery per se, who would extend paternal authority beyond blacks to whites of lesser status, partly to salvage patriarchal republicanism. This ideological pattern, when laid over the geographical pattern of slaveholding locations in the United States, indicates how majoritarian democracy could menace the Lower South minority. The color-blind argument that slaveholders must rule nonslaveholders outraged the southern (and northern) nonslaveholding majority, as western Virginians had shown in 1832. The far more politic (and thus far more frequent) color-based argument that slaveholders must control blacks played into the rigid racism that everywhere differentiated the U.S. slavery controversy from other New World varieties.

But racist ideology remained a fragile basis for universal proslavery opinion. American whites in areas with few or no slaves preferred to live among no blacks at all. The race-based argument that blacks must be enslaved would thus become academic to Middle and Border South moderates if they thought their region's blacks could be removed somewhere else, including to the Lower South. Proslavery persuasion, in short, could not permanently consolidate the South's quasi-consolidated northern extremities. How, then, could Lower South zealots banish antislavery opinion from those vulnerable hinterlands?

4

The more republican U.S. slavocracy ironically outdid their less republican Latin American counterparts in eradicating antislavery opinion. Inside Spanish-owned Cuba, the Old World metropolitan authority, not the New World provincial slaveholders, usually dictated which opinion was to be silenced. Inside quasi-republican Brazil, where slaveholders constantly argued antislavery with one another, the ruling class could hardly silence its own debate. Discussion thus raged uncontested in Rio de Janeiro, the heart of the Coffee Kingdom. In U.S. areas with heavy slave populations, in contrast, local lynch mobs violently repressed supposedly incendiary discussion. American republicanism, in the black-belt South, meant that all ideas could compete in the open—except antislavery.

Local closure of antislavery discussion, however, could not transcend its local basis of legitimacy. Democratic agitation most menaced the Border South with fewer slaves, not the Lower South with more; and according to southern dogma, each neighborhood could police only itself. No slaveholders' mob could lynch a man inside a nonslaveholders' community, and no Lower South mob could violate Border South white dissenters.[16]

Nor could Border South whites altogether deter their most threatening black dissenters—fugitive slaves. Group insurrectionists in the United States, though momentarily more terrifying than individual runaways, were less numerous. They were also less threatening, for whites knew that slave conspirators had few guns and some potential turncoats. In contrast, individual slaves, when they escaped without telling another black, could not initially be betrayed and could liberate themselves before the master could react. A solitary slave could most easily reach the North from the Border South, as Maryland's Frederick Douglass, the most famous fugitive slave, demonstrated. Although less than 1 percent of Border South slaves annually escaped to the North, their loss cost their masters over $100,000; and if more Frederick Douglasses freed themselves, more Border South slaveholders might cash in their investments at Lower South slave auctions before still more blacks could flee. Then Border South white moderates, whom Lower South extremists could neither convince nor lynch, might agitate harder for further removal of blacks.

Thus fugitives achieved more than their own freedom in the

seemingly apolitical act of running away from masters (and from millions of enslaved brethren). The runaways advanced the political process that led to war and emancipation. Particularly Border South fugitives illuminated the slavocracy's geographic area of weakness—an illumination that provoked border masters into initiating Union-shattering political controversies. The slaveholders' political answer to border fugitives lay in the national forum, for only national laws could consolidate the line between South and North, as well as the barrier between slavery and free democratic discourse.[17]

The electoral numbers might seem to have forbidden slaveholders from wielding national governmental power to deter border fugitives or otherwise consolidate their outposts. During pre–Civil War controversies, around 70 percent of U.S. whites lived outside the Slave South, and around 70 percent of southern white families did not own slaves. In those overwhelming numbers lay the slaveholders' potential peril. But the democratic system, as ever both threatening and empowering for a besieged minority, long enabled the master class to protect its borderlands and dominate Yankee majorities.

The federal Constitution provided the minority's most obvious defensive weapon. Abolitionists often conceded that the Constitution protected slavery, not least because it authorized Congress to pass fugitive slave laws. The Constitution also contained many restrictions on majority antislavery action, including the ultimate one: a forbidding amendment process. Three-fourths of the states have to agree on a constitutional amendment before it becomes operative. If all fifteen slaveholding states had voted against any future emancipation amendment, the free-labor states would have had to swell from sixteen to forty-five and the Union from thirty-one to sixty states before abolitionists could have triumphed by this route. Moreover, if Texas had split itself into five slave states, as Congress authorized it to do any time after its admission to the Union in 1845, the resulting nineteen slave states could not have been outvoted on a constitutional amendment until a seventy-six-state union had been achieved. Armed with these numbers, the Slavepower minority apparently could stand forever behind unamendable constitutional bulwarks.

Proslavery forces accordingly appealed constantly to constitutional prohibition of majoritarian impositions. John C. Calhoun's doctrine of the concurrent majority took this dogma of "majorities-shall-not" to its logical extreme. Calhoun asserted that every minority must unanimously concur before a numerical majority could pass constitutional law. In 1832, Calhoun's state, South Carolina, transformed this logic into action. In the so-called Nullification Controversy, South Carolina declared the national numerical majority's protective tariff null and void in that state. Only the Compromise Tariff of 1833 stopped President Andrew Jackson from militarily imposing the countervailing postulate: When majorities decide, minorities must obey.[18]

By the 1840s, Calhoun had come to see proslavery utility in Jackson's majoritarian postulate, for the nullification dogma of majorities-shall-not provided an arguably useless constitutional protection. Unless a congressional majority, for example, provided coercive mechanisms to enforce fugitive slave laws, Yankee rescuers of slaves could raid the Border South and flout the Constitution's fugitive slave clause. Then slaveholders in the four Border South states might sell their slaves to the Lower South. Were the fifteen slave states to shrink to eleven, an antislavery constitutional amendment could be enacted against slave states' wishes in a not-so-far-off forty-four-state Union, instead of in an incredibly distant sixty-state or impossibly distant seventy-six-state Union.

This potential Border South problem illustrated the slaveholders' provokingly small margin for error. Totally to control 11/15 of slaveholders' territory and largely to control the other 4/15 of their world would have been a miracle in any other New World slaveholding regime. But U.S. slaveholders, unlike Latin American counterparts, were seeking to stonewall the Age of Emancipation; and the singular effort would fail if the slaveholders' large degree of control over their most vulnerable four states weakened. In part for that reason, southern extremists, including Calhoun, came to eschew the doctrine of federal hands off slavery and to urge that federal hands be heavily laid on, especially in the borderlands, to protect the slaveholders' interests there. National majorities must annex Texas on the Lower South's flank, admit Kansas on the Border South's edge, and ensure the return of fugitive slaves who escaped over any border.

Two more empowerments of the southern minority long enabled slaveholders to maneuver congressional majorities into fortifying southern outposts. First, the Constitution let the slaveholding states count three out of five slaves, in addition to all whites, when the number of southern congressmen and presidential electors was calculated. Thus in 1860 the Slave South, containing 30 percent of the nation's white citizens, had 36 percent of the nation's congressmen and presidential electors. That extra power (which had first prompted the coining of the word *Slavepower*) turned southern defeat into victory on key occasions, including the election of Virginia's Thomas Jefferson over Massachusetts's John Adams to the presidency in 1800, the Missouri Controversy, the Gag Rule Controversy, and the Kansas-Nebraska Controversy.

Second, national political parties gave a 30 percent popular minority with a 36 percent congressional minority the leverage to secure another 14 percent or more of congressional votes. Especially the dubiously titled Democratic Party became a bulwark of the slavocracy. The party could be entitled "democratic" only in the way the American Revolution could be called socially revolutionary: if white men alone counted as Americans. Just as the Founding Fathers' principal emancipation policy, antislavery conditional on black removal, commenced a nonrevolutionary crawl toward black freedom, so the Democratic Party's leading ideology, egalitarian democracy for white men only, consolidated undemocratic dominion over Native Americans, blacks, and women. Andrew Jackson's agenda included enslaving blacks, dominating females, removing Native Americans from land coveted by whites, and treating as equals only white male adults. Jackson's egalitarianism, for white males only, won him huge majorities in the Lower South but progressively smaller majorities at every step northward and few majorities in New England. That voting distribution gave the Democratic Party a majority control in the nation and Southerners a majority control in the party. Thus when slavery controversies emerged in national politics, Southern Democrats could use the leverage of the nation's usually dominant party to demand that Northern Democrats help consolidate the slavocracy's frontiers.

A powerful minority of southern reactionaries, gathered around Calhoun in South Carolina and eastern Virginia, usually remained aloof from the Democratic Party. They espoused the most extreme proslavery argument, that patriarchs should rule not only blacks but all poorer persons.[19] They scorned American electioneering with its, so they thought, party demagogues appealing to the passions of white plebeians. These eighteenth-century-style aristocratic republicans feared even the southern-dominated Democratic Party. They doubted that southern spoilsmen would insist that northern spoilsmen support extreme proslavery legislation. They prophesied instead that demagogical Northern Democrats would persuade demagogical Southern Democrats to dilute proslavery legislation. Then all Democrats would secure national electoral triumphs and patronage feasts.

Calhoun suspected the Whig Party even more. He knew that while Democrats won in the South more often than in the North, Whigs won in the North more often than in the South. Thus though Southerners held the balance of power inside the Democracy, Northerners held the balance of power inside Whiggery. Worse, the Border South's most popular politician, Henry Clay, favored Jefferson-style antislavery, conditional on deporting black freedmen. According to Clay's utopian scenario, Border South moderates would edge away from Lower South extremists, fuse with northern antislavery moderates in the Whig Party, and secure national funding for removal of blacks.

If national politics were to reverse Clay's preferred course, Southern Democrats had to insist that Northern Democrats support the fullest proslavery protection. Southern Whigs also had to repel the Northern Whigs' slightest conditional antislavery overture. To goad southern waverers toward maintaining the neccessary intransigence, proslavery warriors possessed yet another empowering gift from a democratic political system. When a besieged democratic society fears attack from outside and softness within, crusaders demand that trimmers prove their loyalty. The nineteenth-century cry that Southerners must not be soft on slavery, like the twentieth-century cry that Americans must not be soft on communism, aimed at shaming private doubters into public displays of solidarity. Then a unanimous South might force the national parties to back proslavery laws.

Southern politics periodically became a three-ring loyalty circus. Southern Democrats accused Southern Whigs of treasonous alliances with antislavery Yankees. The accusers had a point. Northern Whigs, unlike Northern Democrats, composed the majority in their party, and they would never compromise on slavery-related matters. Southern Whigs, in retaliation, accused Southern Democrats of disloyally compromising on proslavery laws. These accusers also had a point. To secure Northern Democrats' proslavery votes, Southern Democrats often had to compromise a little. Calhounite aristocratic republicans meanwhile damned Southerners in both egalitarian republican parties for disloyally compromising the South.

Ironically, northern extremists were southern extremists' best ally in these loyalty contests. Garrison's righteous denunciations, aimed at all who opposed unconditional emancipation, damned all Southerners, whether they hoped to remove or to retain slaves. Southern moderates, enraged at being called sinners, passionately joined proslavery extremists in resenting the slur on their honor. On the subject of Yankee holier-than-thouism, Henry Clay sounded like John C. Calhoun.[20]

Southern loyalty contests worked such "democratic" magic most effectively in Washington, D.C. Back home, Lower South extremists and Border South compromisers lived hundreds of miles apart. But in Washington, they crowded into the same boarding-houses. Here Yankees called Southerners sinners to their faces, and any Southerner who cherished his self-esteem and honor, went the tribal cry, must show the colors. In such an atmosphere, when Lower South militants demanded the Border South's support for slavery's expansion, the less militant Southerners usually felt compelled to go along. When border slaveholders demanded federal protection, the Lower South always went along. When a united South demanded proslavery legislation, Northern Democrats usually acquiesced, lest their party, their nation, and their national political aspirations be damaged. But Northern Democrats' appeasement of minority demands instead put the National Democratic Party, the Union, majoritarian republicanism, and the appeasers' northern reelection prospects at ever-greater risk.

5

The Gag Rule Controversy, the first national slavery crisis after Garrison's emergence, introduced the deadly process.[21] In 1835, antislavery zealots petitioned Congress to abolish slavery in Washington, D.C. The petitions inadvertently demonstrated that abolitionists constituted a fringe group outside the northern mainstream. Only a tiny fraction of Northerners signed the appeals, and a large number of signers were women, barred from the electorate.

Nevertheless, the petitioners reshaped national mainstream slavery politics. Their Garrisonian tone, insulting to Southerners, would have been counterproductive in Latin American countries, where slaveholders and abolitionists often negotiated gradual manumissions and free-womb laws. But in a U.S. world where Lower South extremists rejected any form of gradualism, the Garrisonian holier-than-thou polemics evoked a violent southern response. That provocative response shook northern complacency about the slavery issue more than any abolitionist could.

The slaveholders' provocative demand was that petitions for congressional action against slavery must be barred from congressional deliberations. Antislavery must not be discussed in secret committees, much less publicly. To justify this repression of democratic debate, Southerners emphasized that congressional discussions might swell northern antislavery sentiment, increase the Upper South's distaste for the institution, incite slave insurrection and flight, and rob Southerners of that self-esteem and pride necessary to defend themselves. By attempting to gag congressional debate, Southerners tried to impose on the nation their regional version of republicanism: all ideas, *except* antislavery, were open to discussion.

Northerners responded that republicanism would lie in ruins unless *all* ideas could be debated. Representative republicanism especially would become a mockery, said Northerners, unless citizens could request that their representatives discuss whether slavery, an arguably antirepublican institution, should exist in the republic's capital city. The southern gag rule tactic, an irrelevant strategy in largely undemocratic Latin America, thus immediately produced the key non–Latin American question: Were slavery for blacks and democratic procedures for whites compatible? From that question, an otherwise rather isolated abolitionist movement would spread in the North, and the U.S. slavery controversy would assume its irrepressible—and non–Latin American—form.

In the Gag Rule Controversy as ever afterward, Southern Whigs, Southern Democrats, and Calhounites competed to secure the most thoroughgoing protection of slavery, whatever the North's understanding of democratic niceties. That southern competition escalated the pressure on Southerners' northern party allies. In 1836, Northern Democrats, exhorted by the southern majority in their party, agreed to enact a gag rule after they had watered it down. Northern Whigs, in the majority in their party, denounced any gag rule, watered down or not. Southern Whigs, unable to secure proslavery legislation, scoffed that the Democracy's watered-down gag rule was ineffective. Calhounites, opposing all national parties, condemned all southern compromisers as disloyal. Southern Democrats, now besieged from all southern sides as soft on the issue, subsequently demanded tighter gag rules. Northern Democrats succumbed, but with ever-increasing resentments, in ever-smaller numbers, and at ever-greater risk of losing northern support.

The most airtight of the Democratic Party's gag rules, passed in 1840, forbade the House of Representatives from receiving, much less considering, antislavery petitions. To the embarrassment of Southern Whigs, the Northern Whigs, led by Massachusetts's ex-President John Quincy Adams, refused to be gagged. Adams relentlessly attacked Northern Democrats as the Slavepower's slaves. The issue, he said, was not black slavery but white republicanism. The minority South must not rule the majority North. The slaveholding minority must not gag republican citizens. Northern Democrats must represent the majority North, sustain white men's democracy, and repeal the minority South's antidemocratic gag rule.

In December 1844, Northern Democrats finally acted to protect their home base. By voting down all gag rules, after eight years of caving in to ever-tighter gags, they signaled that the southern minority could push Northerners only so far. This denouement of the Gag Rule Controversy also signaled that northern and southern antiparty extremists had unintentionally collaborated to weaken their mutual foe: national party moderates. Just as the Garrisonians' antisouthern insults had helped southern extremists rally moderate Southern Democrats, so proslavery diehards' antirepublican procedure had helped northern extremists rally moderate Northern Democrats.

Without inadvertent aid from Southrons and when agitating about just black men's rights, Garrisonian polemicists had converted only a tiny minority of the very conservative, highly racist antebellum Northerners to crusade against slaves' antirepublican plight. But with the aid of provoked Southerners and when agitating about white men's rights too, abolitionists had raised northern consciousness about slavery's inherently antirepublican nature. By demanding a gag on the discussion of that one issue, slaveholders had confirmed one aspect of the abolitionists' case: The preservation of southern-style black slavery meant the annihilation of northern-style white republicanism. These dynamics of northern consciousness raising ultimately forced those key northern appeasers, Northern Democrats, to join Northern Whigs and northern extremists in opposing all gags, just as the dynamics of southern consciousness raising forced southern moderates to join southern extremists in seeking ever-tighter gags. Then neither centrist national party could find a middle position between the two sections' different versions of republicanism. And in any democracy, the erosion of the vital center can be the first step toward civil war.

6

In 1844, an ominous second step was taken. Southern Democrats surrendered on the gag rules, partly to press Northern Democrats to support the annexation of the then-independent Republic of Texas.[22] Slaveholders' fight to save slavery in Washington, D.C., could and would successfully continue, whether Congress debated abolitionists' petitions or not. Meanwhile, Southern Democrats thought that they must immediately annex Texas, of whose population only 20 percent was enslaved in the early 1840s. That was a Border South percentage of slaves. But this time, the borderland with a low proportion of slaves abutted the slaveholders' southwestern flank, thick with slaves. A Texas republic with relatively few slaves, Southerners worried, might submit to English antislavery blandishments in exchange for diplomatic protection. Then an emancipated Texas, under English control, would beckon fugitive slaves from the Lower South. In contrast, an annexed Texas, under U.S. control, would consolidate the Lower South frontier. In early 1844, Secretary of State Abel P. Upshur, a Virginia Whig, started negotiations toward an annexation treaty. In April, after Upshur's death, John C. Calhoun completed the negotiations and President John Tyler, another Virginia Whig, asked the Senate to ratify the treaty. In June, when the administration could not secure the necessary two-thirds majority for ratification, Tyler and Calhoun urged Congress to admit the proposed slave state by a simple majority of each house.

A Southern Whig administration had proposed a border safeguard. But as usual, only the National Democratic Party could pass prosouthern legislation. Northern Whigs, as usual, denounced the southern proposal. Southern Democrats, however, induced reluctant Northern Democrats to replace the lukewarm annexationist New Yorker, Martin Van Buren, with the strongly annexationist Tennessean, James K. Polk, as the party's presidential candidate in 1844. After Polk won the election, Southern Democrats, now pressured by Southern Whigs to do still more for the South, successfully insisted that reluctant Northern Democrats not only admit Texas to the Union but also allow the annexed state, any time in the future, to divide itself into five slave states. Four years later, a resentful Van Buren bolted the Democratic Party, arguing that white men's majoritarian democracy must be protected from minority dictation. Van Buren ran for president on the Free-Soil ticket, hoping to stop slavery from spreading into federal territories.

At midcentury, while Van Buren sought to contain the Slavepower in the South, Southerners sought to stop the flight of slaves to the North. In 1850, border Southerners proposed a new fugitive slave law, especially designed to protect the South's northernmost hinterlands from northern slave raiders.[23] The proposed law contained notorious antirepublican features, as the North (but not the South) defined republicanism. Black fugitives were denied a jury trial, as they were in the South (but not in the North). Any non-slaveholder could be compelled to join a slave-chasing posse in the manner of a southern patrol—an outrageous requirement in the North.

In the face of the southern minority's latest attempt to impose on the nation southern-style republicanism, Northern Whigs again balked. But again Northern Democrats reluctantly acquiesced, and again the minority South, using the National Democratic Party as a congressional fulcrum, had gained protection of vulnerable frontiers. When Southerners subsequently attempted to extradite captured fugitives from the North, the new procedures returned the alleged slaves 90 percent of the time. But in the remaining cases, northern mobs blocked the return of the escapees. The well-publicized stories of rare fugitive slave rescues dramatized Garrison's most telling lesson: Southern-style power over blacks damaged northern-style republics for whites.

The Kansas-Nebraska Act of 1854 drove the lesson home.[24] Once again a vulnerable slaveholders' hinterland, this time the Border South's Missouri, with only 10 percent of its population enslaved, demanded protection of its frontier. Proslavery Missourians urged that slaveholders be allowed to enter the uninhabited territory to their west, Kansas, if Congress opened the area for settlement. Missouri's senator David R. Atchison claimed that if free laborers controlled Kansas, Missouri slaves would flee to Kansas sanctuaries, the number of Missouri's still-scarce antislavery politicians would increase, and worried Missouri slaveholders would sell their slaves southward. The erosion of Missouri slavery would then spread east to Kentucky, Maryland, and Delaware, toppling slavery in the South's northern outposts.

Before any citizen could come to the federal area west of Missouri, Congress would have to authorize migration. Before slaveholding citizens could come, Congress would have to repeal the Missouri Compromise of 1820, which had prohibited slavery in all

Louisiana Purchase territories north of the 36° 30' line. That man-made geographic boundary continued westward from the latitude of Missouri's southern border, thus barring slaveholders from living west of Missouri, once Congress allowed settlement there. Stephen A. Douglas, the Northern Democrats' leader in the post–Van Buren era, warned Southerners that repeal of the Missouri Compromise would raise "a hell of a storm." But most Border South Democrats adamantly demanded repeal, the Lower South rallied to the cause, and another borderite, Southern Whig Senator Archibald Dixon of Kentucky, insisted that Southern Democrats go all the way for slavery.

Douglas, although a Northern Democrat, could not withstand this latest competition within the South to be most southern. Above all, he wished to open the Kansas-Nebraska area for white settlers, an objective that would achieve his own goals: a revital-ized Democratic Party, its presidential nomination, and a West open to white entrepreneurs' economic development, especially railroads (including one in which Douglas owned shares). But not enough southern congressmen would vote for a Kansas-Nebraska bill, inviting settlers to come, unless the bill honored *their* anti–Missouri Compromise proposal that slaveholding and non-slaveholding settlers alike be permitted. Their stance, they pointed out to Douglas, sustained *his* Popular Sovereignty principle. Ac-cording to Douglas's dogma, local populations, not distant con-gressmen, should have sovereignty over local institutions. Then Washington congressmen of 1820 should not have dictated Kan-sans' labor arrangements in 1854; and this misguided bar to settler sovereignty and to slaveholding settlers must be repealed.

So Douglas, pressed to repeal a Missouri Compromise measure that violated his principles, agreed to sponsor a Kansas-Nebraska bill that sustained Popular Sovereignty. No pre–Civil War moment was more revealing. Douglas was as convinced as any Southerner that supposedly superior whites should evict supposedly inferior Native Americans from the West and that the enslavement of sup-posedly inferior blacks was no Northerner's moral business. Yet Southern Democrats had to pressure Douglas to be Douglas, for their shared program bore the taint of Slavepower domination. And this astute majoritarian politician did not want to be labeled a tool of the minority.

Nevertheless, he had to risk the noxious designation. What be-came known as *his* Kansas-Nebraska Act, passed by a Douglas-rallied National Democratic Party plus a majority of Southern

Whigs, repealed the Missouri Compromise ban on slavery in Kansas Territory, located due west of Missouri, and in Nebraska Territory, located due north of Kansas. Any settler with any form of property could come to these two territories, declared the law, and the majority of settlers in each territory would decide which institutions should thereafter prevail. This most important of all mid-nineteenth-century American laws authorized slaveholding migrants to move to Kansas, seek to make it a slave state, and thus protect the Border South's western flank, just as Texas Annexation had fortified the Lower South's western frontier and the Fugitive Slave Law guarded the Border South's northern extremities. Douglas's law also invited the Democrats' northern opponents to claim that the Slavepower minority, in its anxiety to quarantine border slavery from neighboring democratic currents, had again bullied a congressional majority in the manner of an imperious dictator.

In 1854, in the perspective of the Slavepower's influence on Douglas and on the Kansas-Nebraska Act, the uncertainty of the Border South's long-run commitment to slavery hardly seemed disastrous. Although Border South vulnerabilities existed, Southerners worked to overcome them. The resulting national legal antidotes seemed promising. The Kansas borderlands were open to slaveholders. Border South conditional antislavery advocates rarely campaigned and almost never collaborated with Northerners. A few spectacular rescues aside, nine times out of ten northern communities returned captured slave fugitives to the South in compliance with the Fugitive Slave Law. While neither proslavery polemics nor vigilante mobs had totally consolidated the South, national laws had apparently secured tolerably safe Border South outposts, to say nothing of an ultra-safe Texas hinterland. Majoritarian democracy and the National Democratic Party guarded an enslaving minority's frontiers.

7

In the next six years the northern majority would revoke the minority's domination of the republic, making problems inside the southern outposts more threatening. A similar phenomenon would happen during the Civil War. Halfway through that war, as halfway down the road to disunion, the slaveholders' internal world would seem well enough consolidated and their external attackers well enough contained. But in the antebellum years after 1854, as in the wartime years after 1863, disagreements inside the slavocracy would seem more lethal as northern assaults became more alarming.

In post-1854 politics, the South's most vulnerable instrument was the national party. Long useful in passing the slaveholders' favorite legislation, it had lately buckled under the weight of the minority's attempts to seek ever-more domination over the majority. Northern Democrats' resentment of the minority's demands had led to the 1844 defeat of the gag rule and to Van Buren's 1848 revolt. Despite Van Buren's defection, most Northern Democrats remained in the fold, and the National Democracy remained largely intact.

In the early 1850s, however, the National Whig Party collapsed. Until the middle of the century, Lower South Whigs had hoped that Northern Whigs would relent on slavery-related matters. But after Northern Whigs said no to the Fugitive Slave Law, no to the Kansas-Nebraska Act, and, all too often, yes to the rescue of fugitive slaves, the Southern Democrats' charge rang all too true: Southerners who cooperated with Yankee Whigs might be secretly soft on slavery. After the Kansas-Nebraska Act, Whiggery lost all credibility in the Lower South.

Whiggery simultaneously lost some northern credibility. Old Whig rhetoric did not sufficiently convey many Yankees' twin indignations in 1854: hostility toward new immigrants and loathing for the Kansas-Nebraska Act. The anti-immigrant nativist impulse had been eroding northern Whiggery even before the Kansas-Nebraska Act finished off Lower South Whiggery.[25] Since the early 1840s, an unprecedented wave of European migrants had begun arriving in the North—some 300,000 annually. The North's predominantly Protestant natives, usually English in origin and often Whiggish in politics, considered the newcomers too Irish or German, too Catholic, and too enraptured with the southern-dominated Democratic Party. A fusion of northern immigrants and southern slaveholders, many native Yankees thought, bid fair to destroy American republicanism, using as the agent of destruction the deplorably named *Democratic* Party.

A countervailing fusion swiftly transpired. Northern campaigns against immigrants and the Kansas-Nebraska Act, originally separate matters, partly funneled into one deliberately named *Republican* Party in time for the presidential election of 1856.[26] The Republicans' first presidential campaign almost swept enough northern votes to win the White House, despite the lack of southern votes. Some Northerners especially welcomed most Republicans' secondary mission: to serve free laborers' economic interests. Republicans often saw southern and immigrant economic threats as similar. Impoverished immigrants could displace Yankee wage earners by accepting low wages, just as affluent slaveholders could displace Yankee farmers by making Kansas a slave territory.

But most Republicans considered free-republican government more endangered than free labor capitalism.[27] Here again, they saw immigrants and Southerners as related perils. Immigrants, not educated in American schools, supposedly voted as the pope or Democratic city bosses instructed, just as Northern Democrats, swollen in power by immigrant support, supposedly voted as the Slavepower instructed. In confronting these intertwined political dangers, Republicans emphasized containment more than abolition. Nativists in the 1850s did not usually urge abolition of immigration in order to save American jobs. Rather, they sought to contain foreigners from voting for many years in order to save the American republic. So too, Republican campaigners did not usually emphasize abolition of slavery, with or without expulsion of free blacks. Instead they usually stressed that the spread of slavery to the new territories must be contained, lest the slaveholding minority further control the national majority.

The events of the mid-1850s enhanced the long-standing northern suspicions that slaveholders menaced American white majoritarianism. In 1856, South Carolina's congressman Preston Brooks, by beating Massachusetts's senator Charles Sumner unconscious on the Senate floor, recalled southern attempts to gag congressional debate. Simultaneously, southern vigilantes, by marauding in Bleeding Kansas neighborhoods, reminded Yankees of lynch mobs in southern neighborhoods. In 1857–58 Southerners, by attempting to impose Kansas as a slave state on the northern congressional majority, rekindled memories of the imposition of Texas annexation. Then also Southern Democrats had handed aspiring Northern Democrats such as Martin Van Buren an infuriating ultimatum: Give us our slave state or forfeit your national political ambitions.

Republicans' drive to contain the imperious masters' alleged travesties against white men's republicanism shrewdly seized on Garrison's popular denunciations of sinning despots, while just as shrewdly shedding his unpopular demand for immediate abolition. Republicans often called absolute power over blacks a sin against Christianity, against free-labor ideology, and against the Declaration of Independence. But their anti-Slavepower rhetoric made minority domination of white republics the intolerable crime. Republicans would confine slaveholders to the now-existing slave states, like rats in a cage. Then the Slavepower's undemocratic domination would poison neither the free-labor economy nor republican deliberations in the nation and its territories.

Occasionally, Republicans such as Abraham Lincoln talked of probing inside the poisonous cage to secure the ultimate extinction of slavery. But this sporadic Republican rhetoric remained vague on *how* party leaders meant to achieve abolition. On the few occasions when they dropped hints about how the confinement of slavery to the South would escalate into emancipation, the Lincolns speculated about voluntary southern collaboration. They would impose nothing on the sinning region. Rather, they would help Southerners remove blacks, probably first from the Border South and with federal funding for deportation.

This Republican rhetoric showed how much (and how little) William Lloyd Garrison had triumphed. Lincoln's mainstream rhetoric appropriated Garrison's extremist vocabulary about southern sinfulness, his conception that free-labor and slave-labor economies were antithetical, his demand for inclusion of blacks in the Declaration of Independence, his hopes for slavery's extinction, and his detestation of slaveholders' imperiousness. Still, Republicans' condemnation of the Slavepower's tyrannizing over whites, not Garrison's condemnation of slaveholders' tyrannizing over blacks, had been most responsible for spreading moral outrage about slaveholders from the northern extreme to the northern mainstream. The average Northerner rejected Slavepower imposition on *him*. But most Northerners were as fearful as ever that federally imposed abolition would break up the Union, jeopardize national commerce, and lead northern blacks to demand *their* egalitarian rights.

The Republicans' resulting caution outraged Garrison. He loathed Lincoln's political formula: Always emphasize containment of the Slavepower and occasionally add a vague hope of slavery's ultimate extinction. Garrison equally detested Lincoln's emphasis on the slow transformation of public opinion North and South, even if abolition was delayed a hundred years. Moreover, Lincoln's program for achieving the delayed extinction of slavery was exactly the one Garrison had furiously denounced in 1831. Lincoln, like Henry Clay and Harriet Beecher Stowe, was back with Thomas Jefferson, advocating the removal of slavery *and* freed blacks from the republic with federal funds—and seeking southern consent before doing either.

This strategy, if anathema to Garrison, was exactly the highly conditional form of antislavery gradualism that southern extremists most feared. The Border South deplored immediate emancipation without removal of blacks. But the offer of a northern hand to help consenting whites transport blacks gradually out of the South—that could be seductive among black-hating Border South nonslaveholders. In the face of the Republicans' clarity about containing southern sinners like lepers and their hints about helping southern softhearts cure a black plague, the Lower South response escalated. At the southern extreme, particularly in South Carolina, secessionists wanted out of this hateful Union, not territorial expansion within it. But the far more numerous southern moderates preferred to stay in the Union if they could expand their territory, particularly the territory bordering on their vulnerable outposts.

The Southern Democratic majority on the U.S. Supreme Court provided the clearest protection for slaveholders' right to expand into the nation's territories. In its notorious Dred Scott decision (1857), the Court pronounced the Republican Party's containment program unconstitutional. Congress could not bar slavery from national territory, ruled the Court, for slaves were property and seizure of property violated the due process clause of the Constitution. Alarmed Republicans replied (and apparently believed) that a second Dred Scott decision would follow. Since citizens of one state had the rights and immunities of citizens of another state, the Court allegedly would next empower slaveholders to take (human) property into northern states![28]

If Republicans needed post–Dred Scott evidence that Southerners meant to extend slavery into northern latitudes, southern insistence on admitting Kansas as a slave state in 1857–58 seemed to provide it. The Kansas-Nebraska Act had allowed both Southerners and Northerners to come to the area, with the majority of settlers to decide on an eventual state's constitution and its labor arrangements. Three years later, when Kansans applied for admission to the Union as a state, northern settlers predominated. But the minority of southern settlers demanded admission as a slave state anyway, despite the majority of Kansans' frenzied objections. This time, Stephen A. Douglas defied the Southerners, for they were asking him to abjure his Popular Sovereignty principle that the majority of settlers should determine their own institutions. Despite Douglas's protests, the U.S. Senate voted 33–25 to admit Kansas as a slave state, with most Northern Democrats casting their usual prosouthern vote. The House then rejected a proslavery Kansas, 120–112.[29]

Southerners, enraged at their first congressional loss on a major slavery issue since gag rule times, principally blamed the 40 percent of House Northern Democrats, admirers of Douglas, who had voted against them. Two years later, at the first of two 1860 Democratic National Conventions, Lower South Democrats insisted that the party platform contain anti-popular-sovereignty language on slaveholders' rights in the territories. Douglas and his supporters balked, just as Martin Van Buren had balked at southern control of the party during the Texas episode. But this time, when the key Northern Democrat said no to Slavepower rule, Lower South convention delegates walked out. At the subsequent Democratic convention, Northern Democrats barred those who had left from returning as accredited delegates.

With the split of the National Democratic Party, the minority South lost its long-standing leverage to secure majority laws protective of its hinterlands. The need never seemed greater. When the House of Representatives rejected a proslavery Kansas, six Upper South ex-Whigs voted with the North. Had they voted with the South, the slaveholders' 120–112 defeat would have been a 118–114 triumph. The episode again illuminated one reason for southern defensive maneuverers' frantic quality: Even a small amount of southern internal disunity could destroy slaveholders' national dominion. To control all but six of ninety-one Slave South congressmen would have been a degree of dominance unthinkable in any other New World slavocracy. But the minority's control of 93 percent of its regime was not enough to impose Kansas on the majority. Only a little erosion at the fringes could undercut the slaveholders' chance, not found elsewhere in the New World, to bring an antislavery century to a standstill.

At the time the six deserters helped defeat a proslavery Kansas, other departures from proslavery solidarity arose. For many U.S. slaveholders, the most profitable expansion seemed to lie southward toward Latin America. Yet when southern adventurers sought to annex Nicaragua and Cuba, many South Carolina and Upper South slaveholders decried such Caribbean expansion as folly, indeed as piracy. More revealingly still, antebellum Southerners intemperately clashed over the fastest rising Lower South political movement of the 1850s, the crusade to reopen the African slave trade. Proponents of moving Africans to America wished to reverse southern thinking about population movement. Border Southerners should not advocate removal of African Americans from the civilized United States. Africans should instead be removed from the barbarism of the Dark Continent. So too, the Border South should not sell its too few slaves to the Lower South. Lower South slaveholders should instead buy slaves from Africa so that slaves could be kept up North.[30]

Every southern region a permanent slavocracy! Every border Southerner a devotee of perpetual slavery! Reopening the African slave trade seemed to offer the most hopeful remedy yet for uncertain southern commitment. But hope swiftly gave way to a sinking realization: that instead of permanently fortifying a slightly shaky Border South, the proposed panacea drove the more northern and the more southern South further apart. Border South masters denied that slavery would be bolstered in their region if Lower South masters could buy cheap Africans. Instead, the more northern South would find its slaves devalued and its slave sales ended; and then its rationale for complicity in slavery would evaporate.

More ominous still for Lower South slaveholders who wished to import Africans in the 1850s, the Border South preference for exporting African Americans grew stronger. From the perspective of those who wanted an all-white, all-free-labor South, slave sales had removed blacks from the Upper South too slowly. Thomas Jefferson, and after him Henry Clay, had suggested a faster solution: federally financed colonization to the Caribbean or Africa. Although these emancipation-and-removal schemes still inspired Upper South support, the post-nati Upper South heresy, popularized by Thomas Jefferson Randolph in the Virginia debate of 1832, grew in importance in the 1850s. Cassius Clay in Kentucky and Frank Blair, Jr., in Missouri, the two most politically powerful Border South heretics, campaigned in their respective states for a legislative decree of freedom for future-born slaves when these blacks reached a distant birthday. Like Randolph earlier, Blair and Clay cynically hoped that slaves would be sold southward before emancipating birthdays. Let Lower South masters pay to remove the Upper South's blacks!

Despite that enticement, Kentucky voters trounced Cassius Clay's bid for governor in 1851. St. Louis voters, however, sent Blair to Congress in the mid-1850s. Simultaneously, Maryland voters overwhelmed a slaveholders' counteroffensive designed to reenslave free blacks. And in North Carolina, Hinton R. Helper's *Impending Crisis in the South: How to Meet It* was published in 1857. Helper urged the southern nonslaveholder majority to serve both its own economic interests and America's racial interests by deporting slaveholders' blacks. With this publication, the 1850s, not the 1830s, had become the Upper South's great age of dispute over removing slaves.

More important, in the 1850s for the first time, northern leaders threatened to make southern black-removal programs national in scope. Northern Republicans printed hundreds of thousands of copies of Helper's emancipation-by-removal scheme. Did Republicans, many Southerners wondered, thereby hope to provoke a southern white lower-class revolt against the slaveholding class? Meanwhile, many Northern Republicans, including Lincoln, endorsed the Thomas Jefferson–Henry Clay colonization proposal. Did the Lincolns thereby seek a national collaboration between conditional antislavery moderates in the North and in the Upper South? Lincoln's hero, the Border South's Henry Clay, had dreamed of exactly that fusion in the now-expired Clay-Lincoln Whig Party.

Such a post–Whig Party collaboration across sectional lines could have a new partisan foundation. Although in the Lower South most ex-Whigs joined the Democrats, in the Upper South ex-Whigs formed a powerful Opposition Party that defeated the Democracy in a number of elections. These Upper South Oppositionists, never happy about being de-Whigged, wished again to form a southern wing of a national party. They approached Northern Republicans. If Lincoln's party would cease its insulting condemnation of slavery, they would accept a fusion with Republicans on some black-removal platform. And that politically powerful advocate of black removal, St. Louis congressman Frank Blair, Jr., became a Republican; he helped secure 17,028 Missouri votes, 10 percent of the state's total, for Lincoln in 1860. In addition, 24 percent of Delaware voters cast their ballots for Lincoln.

Lincoln, who also disliked being de-Whigged, would have liked to build a national Whiggish party on this promising Border South foundation—a preference he later signaled by placing a couple of Border Southerners in his cabinet. But with no southern votes needed to gain the presidency, the biggest northern issue in the 1860 election remained the southern minority's domination of the white man's majoritarian republic. Upset over the recent southern triumph in the Dred Scott case and near-triumph on the Kansas issue, the majoritarian section now meant to rule like a majority. That determination could be seen in the Northern Democrats' rejection of the Lower South's demand for a proslavery platform at the party's conventions and in the northern electorate's sweeping affirmation of Lincoln's leading message: that the *Republican* Party must keep the South from destroying *republicanism*. Yet the question remained, after Lincoln's election in November 1860 would the southern minority now truly destroy the republic by withdrawing its consent to be ruled by the victorious majority?

8

Before southern secessionists could escape the northern majority they had to win over their own majority.[31] If some Southwide Gallup poll had inquired whether Southerners wished to secede immediately after Lincoln's election, the secessionists' vote likely would have been down in the 25 percent range. In the Border South where secessionists lost even after civil war began, 37 percent o all southern whites resided. Another 31 percent lived in the Middle South, where secessionists lost until civil war began. Even in the Lower South, a slim majority might have voted against secession had a Southwide referendum occurred immediately after Lincoln's election. In late November 1860, only Mississippi and Florida probably would have affirmed the expediency of secession, and only South Carolina assuredly would have done so.

The Southwide majority against disunion in November 1860 fed on conservatives' dread of revolution, on Southerners' patriotism as Americans, and on moderates' doubts that Lincoln could or would threaten slavery. Southern Unionists denounced the President-elect for declaring slavery immoral, for calling its spread to new territory unacceptable, and for terming its ultimate extinction desirable. But Lincoln conceded, Unionists pointed out, that the Constitution barred federal intervention in the South to force slavery's extinction. To reemphasize this federal powerlessness Lincoln in his inaugural address supported an unamendable constitutional amendment, already passed by Congress, that would have forever banned federal antislavery coercion in the South. But no constitutional amendment was needed, Unionists added. Lincoln' party did not have a majority in the Senate or in the House or on the Supreme Court. If Lincoln nevertheless managed to act against slavery, the South could *then* secede. Why secede now over an uncertain northern menace, thereby subjecting slavery to certain menace in a civil war?

Secessionists retorted that a stealthy northern majority would initially let Southerners do the menacing. Southern politician would form a wing of the Black Republican Party, dedicated to agi tating against slavery, especially in the Border South. South Carolina patricians, the most avid secessionists, considered all agitating parties dangerous. These aristocratic republicans had long taken the proslavery rationale beyond a vision of whites directing blacks. Theirs was a more universal paternalistic conception: The best men should direct lesser humans of all races. To them all national parties portended mobocratic republicanism. Patronage-hungry demagogues would stir up the masses and thus overwhelm disinterested paternalists.

In contrast, Lower South mainstream politicians beyond crusty South Carolina, having long happily participated in national parties, feared not democratic parties in general but a prospective Southern Republican Party in particular. They uneasily recalled Frank Blair's delivery of 10 percent of Missourians to Lincoln in the election of 1860, Delaware's 24 percent vote for Lincoln, the more northern South's Opposition Party's recent overtures to the Republicans, and Northern Republicans' publication of Helper's call for nonslaveholder war against slaveholders. They knew that Lincoln had patronage jobs at his disposal and that Border South leaders wanted them. They understood that Lincoln, like the Border South's hero, Henry Clay, carried on Thomas Jefferson's vision of emancipation with freedmen's removal financed by the federal government. Lincoln, in short, need not force abolition on the most northern South. He could instead encourage and bribe Border Southerners to agitate for their misty hope of, and his nebulous plan for, removing blacks from a whitened republic.

Nor, warned the secessionists, would Republican efforts for black removal be restricted to rallying a Border South *white* majority. Republicans would encourage slaves to flee the Border South. With white support melting away and black slaves running away, border slaveholders would dispatch their human property to Lower South slave markets. Then nothing could deter a Border South Republican Party. The Slave South, shrunk to eleven states or less and prevented from expanding into new territories, could only watch while northern free-labor states swelled from sixteen to thirty-three. In that forty-four-state Union, concluded secessionists, Republican emancipators would have the three-fourths majority to abolish slavery in eleven states by constitutional amendment.

Southern extremists meant to cancel that democratic drama before the staging began. They would not let northern-style republicanism, with all issues open for discussion, replace southern-style republicanism, in which debate about slavery was impermissible. They would not sit back and watch while a new president used patronage to forge a new centrist position on the forbidden subject. They would not allow Lincoln's method of antislavery, the slow transformation of public opinion, to operate within the South. They had long especially feared democratic agitation in the Border South, that nontropical vestige of seventeenth-century slaveholders' effort to defy tropical geography. Many of the Slavepower's aggressive defenses, including the Fugitive Slave Law and the Kansas-Nebraska Act, had sought to keep Border South whites and Border South blacks separated from contamination by freedom.

Now Lincoln's and the Border South's favorite national solution to slavery—compensated emancipation conditional on federally financed black removal—might establish the most contaminating and indestructible vital center yet. Since gag rule times, southern and northern extremists had unintentionally collaborated to destroy centrist ideological positions and centrist national parties. After twenty years of slavery crises, the Democratic Party could no longer find a middle position between that of southern moderates, enraged by Yankee insults, and that of northern moderates, enraged by proslavery ultimatums. But no extremist tactic in the Union might deter a new centrist program, institutionalized in a newly national Republican Party. Cries of "traitor" would not deter Border South Republicans, for the region's numerous advocates of black removal thought an all-white Border South exceedingly patriotic. Fear of losing southern elections would not deter conditional antislavery moderates, for Henry Clay Whiggery had done well in the Border South, and Lincoln's party figured to be a rebuilt Whiggish coalition. Furthermore, Border South demagogues could now feast on Lincoln's national patronage. After well-fed politicians started agitating, wouldn't Border South inhabitants agree to remove blacks at federal expense, or Border South masters sell out at Lower South purchasers' expense, especially if more and more of the region's slaves ran away?

For the first time, many Lower South slaveholders felt powerless to answer such questions. Their feeling of impotence rivaled that of Latin American colonists when European metropolitan centers abolished slavery and that of Brazilian coffee planters when sugar planters assaulted the institution. But if Lincoln's election seemed to revoke a democracy's unique invitation for slaveholders to control their fate, the U.S. republican system offered a final invitation for minority self-protection, unavailable in less democratic

Latin America. The people of a single colony, the American Revolutionaries had declared, had a right to withdraw their consent to be governed. It was as if the Brazilian coffee provinces had a *right* to secede, which the sugar provinces might feel an obligation to defend.

A *right* of secession, held by a single one of the South's fifteen states! That right did empower a secessionist minority to force the southern majority's hand on the expediency of secession. But to force-feed secession to the antisecessionist majority, secessionists had to abort the southern Unionists' favorite idea: a regionwide southern convention, where a Southwide majority would veto immediate secession. Secessionists instead wanted the most secessionist state to call a convention to consider disunion. If the most secessionist state seceded, other southern state conventions would have to decide not whether secession was *expedient* but whether a seceded state could be denied its *right* of secession. Furthermore, other slave states might discern less expediency in remaining in the Union after several states with large slave populations had departed to form a proslavery confederacy.

The single-state secession strategy neatly countered Lincoln's supposed fusion strategy. Instead of the Union's president building a Republican Party in southern buffer zones and drawing the Upper South away from slavery's Lower South base, secessionists would build a southern nation in the Lower South and drag the Upper South beyond Lincoln's patronage bribes. Or to use the modern metaphor, instead of slavery falling like the top row of a pile of dominoes, with the Border South and then the Middle South collapsing onto the Lower South, the Union would fall by secessionists' pulling out the lower row, with the Lower South and then the Middle South leaving the Border South no foundation for staying in the Union.

That was the secessionists' master plan, devised in private correspondence and carried out in public lockstep. On December 20, 1860, the secessionists' stronghold, South Carolina, withdrew its consent to Union. South Carolina's neighbor, Georgia, was wary of secession. But with its neighbor out, could Georgia stay in? After a brilliant internal debate, Georgia decided, narrowly, to join South Carolina. And so it went, neighbor following neighbor, throughout the Cotton South. By the time Lincoln was inaugurated on March 4, 1861, the seven Lower South states had left the Union. But the eight Upper South states, containing the majority of southern whites, still opposed secession.

The balance of power changed in mid-April after the Civil War started. Now the more northern South had to decide not on secession per se but on whether to join a northern or a southern army. In making that decision, the Middle South affirmed that each state had the American right to withdraw its consent to be governed. These southern men in the middle also reaffirmed that Yankee extremists were more hateful than secessionist extremists. The Garrisonian insult, encompassing all Southerners who would not unconditionally and immediately emancipate, had long infuriated most Southerners. The Republican insult, encompassing all Southerners who sought to dominate or depart the Union, was equally enraging. To protect their self-respect and honor, Southerners usually felt compelled to unite against taunting Yankees. That duty had so often drawn together a region otherwise partially disunited. In April 1861, when Lincoln sent reinforcements to federal troops in Charleston's harbor, the old tribal fury swept the Middle South. By May 1861, eleven angry southern states had departed the Union. In that fury, parallel to Republican rage over an allegedly antirepublican Slavepower, lies the solution to the largest apparent puzzle about secession: why 260,000 men, whatever their initial preference for Union, died for the Confederacy.

9

Thus did the secessionist minority of the no-longer-ruling southern minority escape the at-last-ruling northern majority. Thus did southern extremists move to abort the expected Republican attempt to rally a new Border South–northern national majority, with Lincoln's patronage supplying the organizational basis, with race removal providing the ideological basis, and with an ultimate constitutional amendment auguring the worst danger. But by moving outside a majoritarian Union's sway, the secessionist minority of the southern minority moved toward a more perilous rendezvous with majoritarianism's own requirement: the need to win men's minds and hearts. Considering the free-labor states' somewhat greater predominance of military power and considering northern determination to save majoritarian government from the southern minority, secession, to be effective, would have to sweep farther than the Middle South. Border Southerners would have to make common cause with secessionists rather than with Republicans.

Or to put the Confederacy's problem in the most revealing way, the secessionists, having secured a southern numerical majority, now had to rally a Calhoun-style concurrent majority: a concurrence of everyone. Now more than ever, the margin of error was thin for the only slaveholders in the New World who defied worldwide antislavery currents. The U.S. slavocracy, to prevail in its extraordinary Civil War gamble, had to control all Southerners, black and white. Several southern minorities could nullify the white majority in the eleven Confederate states, for the North was passionately united in its sixteen free-labor states. Let the four Border South states refuse to secede from the Union; let western Virginia nonslaveholders secede from Virginia; let eastern Tennessee nonslaveholders desert Tennessee; let the slaves depart from the slaveholders and . . . .

The sequels would fill in the rest. Slave runaways, having initiated the fugitive slave controversies that helped lead to civil war, would join northern armies and help secure an emancipating triumph. So too Border Southerners, whose possible fusion with Yankees had helped fuel disunion, would unite with Black Republicans on the battlefields.[32] But though much is fittingly democratic about fugitive slaves doing in slaveholders and about the conditional antislavery Border South doing in the unconditional proslavery Lower South, democrats can hardly cheer the spectacle. The coming of the American Civil War is a case study in democracy's limitations.

Only an especially convulsive internal issue could expose those limits. As the American antebellum experience shows, a democratic system can survive a very large degree of divisiveness. Such national issues as nativism, temperance, national banks, protective tariffs, women's rights, and religious freedom were settled peaceably. Nor did some singular aspects of U.S. culture, peculiar among the world's republics to these North Americans, destroy this democracy. The unusually constant stream of U.S. localistic elections, for example, did not lead to more electioneering agitation than a stable governing system could handle. Those localistic elections usually focused on resolvable local issues. In contrast, national presidential campaigns, occurring only every four years, focused increasingly on the only unresolvable issue, slavery. Nor did America's unusually strong encouragement of individualistic eccentricity destroy nationalizing institutions. The national political parties found a peaceable common ground on every issue involving white individuals' opportunities except slavery—and for a long while on that issue too.

The point is that agitation over slavery ultimately superseded all other agitations and alone could expose a democratic system's most deep-seated, most universal limits. Despite its cult of majority rule, democracy is very susceptible to minority control. A minority that knows what it wants and knows how to manipulate the system will defeat a less determined majority every time. The impasse comes when a majority grows equally determined and the minority can not accept defeat. The problem is particularly explosive when the minority is a powerful ruling class and the dogma of government by consent permits imperious rulers to withdraw from the republic. In the United States, only the slavery issue called forth this sort of inflexible minority, determined to use every available power to rule supposedly barbaric blacks, assuredly infuriating outsiders, and uncertainly softhearted insiders. And in the New World, only the U.S. republican system swelled intransigent slaveholders with the illusion that they could command their own fate, whether by dominating or by departing a republic.

Lower South slaveholders exhausted all means of dominating before they departed. They tried ideological persuasion. That partly failing, they tried lynchings. That partly failing, they tried shaming dissenters into loyalty. Fearing verbal coercion would fail, they tried protective laws that might consolidate vulnerable outposts. When the northern majority finally found minority governance intolerable, the southern minority (or rather, initially, the secessionist minority of the southern minority) withdrew its consent to be ruled.

Two democratic imperatives clashed here: the majority's right to govern, Lincoln's favorite wartime slogan, and the minority's right to withdraw consent to be governed, Jefferson Davis's favorite patriotic emblem. The ideological clash would blur in the second half of the Civil War, after Lincoln's Union came to fight for slaves' right to withdraw their consent to be ruled by slaveholders. But in the first half of the Civil War, when Lincoln rejected black troops and repudiated his generals' emancipation initiatives, the issue was stark. Lincoln's Union initially fought to contain a minority that had controlled and now would revoke majority rule. The slaveholders fought to establish a Confederacy that would save a minority's consent to be governed and prevent the minority's property from becoming a discussable issue. Latin American slavery controversies never carried the added burden of these showdowns over republicanism. And so in all the Americas after the Haitian slave revolt, only in the United States did the final fate of slavery hang on the verdict supposedly reserved for undemocratic governments: Whose regime can rally the largest and most sustained commitment on the battlefields?

10 / The Divided South, the Causes of Confederate Defeat, and the Reintegration of Narrative History

To gain perspective on the southern secession crisis, I have usually studied increasingly extended time periods before 1861. Perspectives after 1861, however, also illuminate disunion. The Confederate States of America lost the Civil War for many of the same reasons that secessionists risked war in the first place. Or to put it another way, southern internal divisions, having made President-elect Lincoln seem a menace to slavery in the short run, helped President Lincoln's armies destroy the institution in the long run.

In order to reintegrate the analysis of the prewar and war periods, as well as the analysis of a vulnerable southern social structure and an unshakable northern armed siege, the narrator must transcend the Civil War narrative's conventional form. That literary strategy usually features an almost uninterrupted account of battlefield excitement. The challenge, for the historian as storyteller, is to interrupt the military lore, to interweave military and nonmilitary causes of battlefield triumph, yet still retain the emotional impact of an epic drama.

I tried out the following new exploration of that literary challenge at seminars at the University of California, San Diego, at the University of Western Ontario, at the State University of New York, Buffalo, and at the West Point Academy. I am indebted to Stephanie McCurry, Steve Hahn, Craig Simpson, and Judy Luckett for arranging these enlightening sessions, to several dozen seminar participants on these occasions, and to Jonathan Bryant, Herman Hattaway, Greg Edwards, Peter Wallenstein, and Joel Silbey for constructive suggestions. Thanks to this collaboration—a treasure of the academic community—this nonmilitary specialist saw far

more clearly how to reintegrate the critical subject of military his-
tory with the social history of slavery and the political history
of disunion.

Old-fashioned epic narratives usually feature great men (and a few
great women) acting out extraordinary public events. Nonacademics have always enjoyed these epics. Academic historians, however,
have increasingly considered such narratives superficial. Famous
statesmen's and generals' actions, they tend to think, were usually
but the effects of the society's underlying tensions. And public
events, most now agree, seldom changed commoners' intimate
lives to any large extent.

In today's historical academy, the highest praise usually goes
not to narrators of epics about the face of public spectacle but to
analysts of the foundations of private life. Conceptual power usually wins the honors, especially politically correct theories about
race, class, gender, the family, and the environment. As for literary
style, analytical clarity is the only universally accepted value. But
with nonacademic readers still eager for portraits of public events,
journalists are happy to fill the vacuum. With nonprofessionals
writing ever more of our popular histories, academics tend to find
narrative epics ever more superficial, and the reading public tends
to find academic writing ever more forbidding.

Among narrators of public events, only military historians still
generally serve both the professors and the public. Descriptions of
Civil War battles remain particularly valued, not least because
these public events did transform the slaves' private lives. Most
chroniclers of Civil War battles urge that the event was decided in
the trenches, that reconstructions of battle must predominate, that
tales of charge and retreat convey not superficial epics but the very
reason that the Union triumphed and the slaves were freed. As military narrators defend this perspective, military outcomes shaped
social outcomes, not vice versa, and military outcomes might easily have been reversed. To the objection that southern social conflicts made northern military advances irresistible, chroniclers of
military contingency respond that northern social conflicts were
just as serious. They conclude that since northern and southern
nonbattlefield conflicts neutralized each other, and since at the
crucial turning points, the losers might easily have won in the
trenches, historians must reject nonbattlefield explanations of battlefield victory, which imply military inevitabilities, and concen-

trate on the reversible contingencies that made each battle so exciting.[1]

This conception of battlefield contingency legitimates a suspense-filled literary genre, with the slaves' and the nation's fate hanging on (supposedly reversible) charges and retreats. Here at last some academic writers and many nonacademic readers meet, with no mutual suspicions. But the congenial meeting ground illustrates why most professors consider narrative history analytically thin. A suspicion of superficiality hangs over the theory that the Civil War was decided solely on the battleground, and the theory that southern social conflict was no worse than northern social conflict, and the theory that the South almost won the Civil War on several occasions. Beneath the battlefield surface was the nature of the contending societies; and the slave society was, after several years, no match for the free-labor society. I will here contend that Union armies became an irresistible force—and a force that the Confederacy became devoid of the will to resist—because Union soldiers exploited weaknesses on the southern home front.[2] The fatal southern social flaws during the Civil War were precisely the feared defects that slaveholders had tried to shore up throughout the pre–Civil War period—precisely the social divisions that secessionists had left the Union to protect.

An analysis of how northern military relentlessness eventually exposed southern societal flaws, of how the slaveholders' prewar social control could not forever withstand a lengthy war of attrition, may be conceptually richer than epics of battlefield contingency. But can artistic swings from prewar to war, from military to social, replace battlefield suspense as a plot for a dramatic epic? On the answers to such questions hangs the future of a sophisticated narrative history.

1

A sheerly military narrative of the Civil War faces literary problems of its own, for the focus must shift between the trans-Mississippi battlegrounds, the combat on the waters, and the two major theaters of war, all demanding different images. In the most famous and most photographed Civil War locale, the eastern theater, narratives tend to stress the great generals' strategic virtuosity or blunders. But while Robert E. Lee's, George B. McClellan's, and Ulysses S. Grant's lightning maneuvers must be portrayed, the truer image, as the English prime minister Lord Henry John Palmerston pointed out, was of heavy-footed brawlers barely moving as they traded heavy-handed punches.[3] This center-of-the-ring slug-fest usually transpired within a few miles of Richmond. The Union's McClellan invaded the Virginia Peninsula, unsuccessfully. The Confederacy's Lee invaded Maryland and Pennsylvania, unsuccessfully. On the famous eastern battlefields of 1861–63—Bull Run, Antietam, Gettysburg—neither lumbering behemoth could exhaust the other.

But out West, in the second major theater of war, the carnage was spread over thousands of miles, and Union soldiers advanced relentlessly. True, seemingly interminable stalemates and horrifying brutality also occurred on western battlefields. Still, the more accurate image is of quick-footed Union generals, who constantly turned the Confederate flank and spun ahead out of harm's way. These supple western movements carried out the so-called Anaconda Plan of Lincoln's first chief general, the aging Winfield Scott. Scott envisioned a blockade of the Confederacy's Atlantic Ocean ports, a combined army-navy conquest of the Mississippi River, then an armed march across the Lower South, and then a sweep up toward the Virginia battlefields. The Anaconda Plan deployed the Union's two initial physical superiorities: its larger pool of fighting men (and thus its greater capacity to man a second major military front) and its more advanced industrial technology (and thus its greater capacity to float the most technically sophisticated weapon of war, the fighting ship). The plan also exploited the Slave South's greatest cultural weakness—its vulnerable network of social cohesion—if invaders hammered at the brittle spots in the slaveholders' home front control.

The Anaconda Plan triumphed, albeit years after Winfield Scott had been cast aside. Out West, Ulysses S. Grant's brutal victory at Shiloh in 1862 and his limber maneuvers at Vicksburg in 1863 set the stage for William Tecumseh Sherman's shattering march to the Atlantic in 1864. By the time Sherman turned toward Virginia, the encircling strategy had debilitated Lee's troops, leaving them too short of willpower to withstand Grant's final butchery. Thus the problem, for historians who claim that some battlefield contingency almost saved the Confederacy, is to demonstrate something almost happening in the trenches that almost stymied the strangling anaconda.

2

Such historians always envision a two-stage scenario. Some reversed outcome on the battlefield, which allegedly came close to occurring, would have triggered a reversed outcome off the battle-field, which again allegedly came close to happening. After this double contingency occurred, the anaconda, it is claimed, could no longer have choked the Confederacy. The second stage of this imagined twin contingency, however, itself forbids a sheer concentration on the military, for the nonmilitary occurrence must also be shown to have almost happened. Military chroniclers have usually devoted a few paragraphs to that nonmilitary assignment. But such minimal proofs cannot demonstrate a near Confederate victory. For example, no brief nonmilitary aside can make plausible the two most frequently claimed putative occurrences, that England almost rescued the Confederacy in 1862 and that the North almost gave up in 1864.

According to the theory of an English near-rescue of the Confederacy, had the Union lost the Battle of Antietam in September 1862, England would have intervened on the Confederate side. But as the historian Howard Jones has recently shown, the English considered only the preliminary step of mediation between the two sides, not the final step of intervention on the Confederate side. The results at Antietam had little impact on that continuing consideration. Lord Palmerston, the critical figure in the British decision, consistently looked upon possible British mediation as if he were a boxing referee committed to stepping between the brawlers only when one side was ready to throw in the towel. As Palmerston explained to his foreign minister Lord John Russell, "they who in quarrels interpose, will often get a bloody nose."[4] Or as the prime minister told Parliament in the crucial debate on the subject, England must do nothing unless the South "firmly and permanently" established its independence. Any earlier "direct active interference" would lead to "greater evils, greater sufferings, and greater privations."[5]

Palmerston feared greater privations than a bloody nose if England interposed before one of the antagonists sank to its knees. He worried that the Union would seize Canada if England offered mediation prematurely. He also shied away from pouring English wealth and men into that bottomless pit, New World warfare, as had happened in the American Revolutionary War and the War of 1812. He knew that an English offer to mediate impartially between the two sides need not necessarily lead to war with the Union. Failed mediation, however, could lead to English recognition of the Confederacy. Recognition, the Lincoln administration persistently warned Palmerston, could mean war.

So the cautious Palmerston would not risk the first step of mediation until a series of battlefield disasters had brought the North to the verge of surrender. He could always abort any steps beyond mediation, toward recognition and on toward intervention, unless more battlefield disasters kept the North on its knees. Given the primitive state of transatlantic communication, those subsequent steps would have taken months. Palmerston determined not to take the first step until the winter of 1862–63 had passed. He would not offer mediation until the ice melted in the North, permitting defense of Canada. Nor would he suggest mediation without Russia, and Russia favored the Union. No way, then, could some battlefield contingency at Antietam have brought England to the Confederacy's rescue in September 1862.

3

The other supposed stream of contingencies is that if Sherman had lost the Battle of Atlanta in September 1864, the war-weary North would have "thrown in the towel," to use the historian James McPherson's stylistically appropriate extension of Lord Palmerston's boxing metaphor.[6] As this throw-in-the-towel scenario is envisioned, if Union voters had received bad news from Atlanta, they would have voted for the Democrats' George McClellan instead of Abraham Lincoln for president in 1864. After being inaugurated in March 1865, President McClellan allegedly would have peacefully accepted a permanently independent Confederacy.

This version of contingency correctly focuses on the only way the Confederacy could have escaped the anaconda: if northern determination had faltered before the noose was tightened. The interpretation also correctly recognizes that Sherman's March to the Sea was choking the Confederacy and that the Battle of Atlanta was the Confederacy's last best hope to escape strangulation. Sherman's seizure of Atlanta annihilated the Confederacy's most extensive railroad hub, devastated its important Georgia munitions industry, and denied critical Georgia foodstuffs to Lee's army. The contingency interpretation is moreover right that Sherman's victory on September 1–2, 1864, dissolved any uncertainty about whether Lincoln would be reelected.

But for military historians to be declared right that Sherman's victory alone could have saved Lincoln's victory, or that Lincoln's victory alone could have saved Union victory, political historians must be proved dead wrong about antebellum politics in general and the Democratic Party in particular. As the New Political History has demonstrated, 90 percent of mid-nineteenth-century voters, unlike more independent-minded twentieth-century voters, remained virtuously loyal to their party.[7] Modern readers have trouble crediting that nineteenth-century version of virtuous balloting, for the very definition of the virtuous voter has changed. Today, a citizen earns a reputation for good civil character by weighing each candidate and each party at each election separately, even if past judgments must be repudiated. In antebellum times, in contrast, a voter who shifted between parties earned a reputation as flighty, superficial. A moral man with ethically steady opinion was expected to cast the same straight party vote in election after election, whatever ephemeral event transpired. Northern Republicans were particularly consistent nineteenth-century partisans. Lincoln's followers marched to war, as they had marched to the polls in 1856 and 1860, determined never to surrender white men's republicanism, as encased in the Union, to the Slavepower or to the southern-dominated Democratic Party.

The only massive defection from mid-nineteenth-century partisanship forms one of those exceptions that prove the rule. In the early 1850s, the National Whig Party fell apart, leaving Whig partisans no national party candidate to vote for. But only in the slavery-obsessed Lower South did ex-Whigs defect to their ancient enemy, the increasingly proslavery Democratic Party. In the Middle and Border South, ex-Whigs usually voted for the so-called Opposition Party—so called because it opposed the hated Democracy. In the North, ex-Whigs' route away from the Democracy went through the short-lived Know-Nothing Party to the Republican Party. In 1864, these lifelong anti-Democrats would not likely have deserted to the despised Democrats, not at least merely because one general could not win one city in time for one election.

Moreover, Republicans would surely not have caved in to the partisan enemy in order to betray their nonpartisan shrine, Union. Nor would Northern Democrats have deserted that nonpartisan shrine, the Republican Party's partisan propaganda to the contrary. According to the Republicans' campaign charges, most Northern Democrats were Peace Democrats, and most Peace Democrats favored Confederate independence, even to the point of treasonously sabotaging the Union war efforts. But that Republican slur had the ratio of traitors to patriots in the Democratic Party exactly wrong, as another mountain of dispassionate scholarship has demonstrated.[8] Most Democrats were War Democrats, few Peace Democrats favored peace with an independent Confederacy, and fewer still conceived of blowing up troop trains or factories. In 1864, the central issue between the War and Peace Democrats involved not acceptance of peace with an independent Confederacy but acceptance of a thirty-day truce to attempt to negotiate the South back into the Union. The Confederate government, however, called reunion nonnegotiable; and General McClellan, the War Democrat who won the party's nomination in 1864, deplored even a thirty-day armistice unless the Confederacy would negotiate on reunion. Three weeks *before* Sherman captured Atlanta, McClellan exploded at a Peace Democrat's plea "that I should write a letter suggesting an armistice!!!! If these fools will ruin the country, I won't help them."[9]

This general was famous—infamous—for his horror of sending his men to their death. In his earlier role as commander of the Union's main army, McClellan had balked at ordering Union soldiers to charge into Robert E. Lee's fortified positions. In his later role as candidate for president, he honestly (and wrongly) believed that if the Union surrendered emancipation as a war aim, the Confederacy would surrender disunion without another life lost.

But General McClellan, for all his determination to spare life, scorned breaking faith with his dead troops. "I could not look in the face of my gallant comrades," McClellan wrote in his letter accepting the Democratic Party presidential nomination, "who have survived so many bloody battles, and tell them that their labors and the sacrifice of many of our slain and wounded brethren had been in vain, that we had abandoned that Union for which we have so often periled our lives."[10] McClellan accordingly sought the presidency not to accept disunion but to secure Union more swiftly and with less bloodshed. He would repudiate emancipation as a war aim, renounce military arrests of civilians, and thereby give the Confederate states an inviting Union to rejoin. His was a crusade for keeping black men's affairs from extending white men's war. Only that racist campaign for Union, McClellan understood, stood a chance of wrenching barely enough Republicans from their cherished party.

To make *this* George McClellan a potential winner of the White House on a platform of "throwing in the towel," devotees of military contingency would have to prolong their battlefield saga for a very long time to refute the massive countervailing evidence. The chroniclers do not usually commit that sin against narrative flow. They instead usually argue, in several paragraphs, that the

Democratic Party's platform looked toward peace with disunion; that preliminary drafts of McClellan's acceptance speech endorsed that surrender; and that certain Republicans, especially Lincoln, feared that McClellan would be elected.

These arguments cannot sustain the throw-in-the-towel contingency. Lincoln's fear that he might lose reelection hardly constitutes evidence that McClellan would have won. If every worried candidate is headed for defeat, almost every winning politician in American history would have lost. Nor does the Democratic Party platform of 1864, written to appease the losing Peace Democrat wing of the party, establish what the War Democrats' candidate would have done in office. Moreover, the platform hardly endorsed peace with disunion; to the contrary, it prayed that "peace may be restored on the basis of Federal Union." Nor do rejected drafts of a candidate's acceptance letter demonstrate his ultimate intention. Moreover, none of McClellan's six drafts remotely hints that he would accept either a temporary truce or a permanent peace without assurances that Confederates would accept reunion.[11]

If McClellan had secured the presidency, he likely would have tested out his pet theory: that if the Union offered to surrender emancipation, the Confederacy would surrender disunion. But after the Confederates had turned him down on reunion, would the Union's new commander in chief have "looked in the face of my gallant comrades" and told them to surrender Union, "for which we have so often periled our lives"? Nothing in McClellan's or his party's past record indicates that any such politically suicidal unconditional surrender of the Union would have been possible, any more than anything about Jefferson Davis's or his government's past record indicates that a voluntary surrender of the Confederacy would have been conceivable. Nor does the likely new military situation of March 1865 indicate that McClellan could have newly conceived of surrender. The critical document on the likely military situation, President Lincoln's famous "blind memo" of August 1864, pledged a more ferocious war for Union if McClellan won in November 1864. A victorious War Democrat would have had to await inauguration until March 4, 1865. Given Lincoln's presidential determination, could Sherman's victory and the imminent collapse of the Confederacy have been stalled long enough for McClellan to surrender in March?

It is hard to see how, unless Sherman had stopped being Sherman, for this Union general consistently conserved his military superiority, exploited the Confederacy's nonmilitary inferiority, and left opposing Confederate generals with no viable options. Sherman commanded around 100,000 Union soldiers in the Atlanta theater, compared to the Confederates' 70,000. Despite his almost three-to-two predominance, Sherman was no squanderer. He understood that operating in Georgia, hundreds of miles from northern terrain, he must guard his supply lines and conserve his soldiers. He also understood that in Civil War campaigns, the defense, if dug in behind earthworks, had the advantage. A headlong charge into rebel fortifications, by killing too many of his troops, might have made southern terrain too dangerous. Sherman preferred to advance as far as possible while fighting as little as possible—and to force outmanned Confederates to charge his fortifications if they wished to fight.

Sherman accordingly crept toward Atlanta not through but around the weaker Confederate armies. If the less numerous Confederate soldiers failed to fall back after one of his flanking operations, they risked stretching their lines too thin. Meanwhile, every time Sherman exercised another successful end run, he kept a large portion of his troops in a fortified place, inviting Confederates to expend their men and resources attacking him.

The Confederates tried the extreme version of both their countervailing options. Gen. Joseph E. Johnston, a cautious defender, fell back judiciously whenever Sherman outflanked him. Johnston's careful retreats toward Atlanta gave Sherman wider control of the countryside, more food for his army, and heightened capacity to starve and demoralize Atlanta's twenty thousand citizens.

After Confederate President Jefferson Davis became fed up with Johnston's backpedaling and replaced him with Gen. John B. Hood, Sherman faced the other extreme: a reckless attacker. Three times in the July 20–28, 1864, period, Hood sent his men swarming at Sherman's fortifications. The result: Hood lost twelve thousand men, 20 percent of his inherited sixty-thousand-man army. Sherman lost six thousand men, only 6 percent of his troops. With one final flanking movement, Sherman then grasped the last railroad supplying Atlanta. The cautious Yankee general could now sit safely around the isolated city, awaiting surrender. Hood proceeded to flee the scene faster than Atlanta's near-mutinous citizens. The city, and the best chance of stopping Sherman's March to the Sea, fell with the dawning of September.

How could September have been a better month for the Confederacy? One can concoct an imaginary portrait of Sherman's ideal Confederate adversary, combining Joe Johnston's genius at retreat with John Hood's fury during assault. That phantom Confederate commander might have struck Sherman's supply lines at strategic moments during the summer of 1864, stalling the cautious Yankee's conquest by weeks or even a couple of months. But as to how Sherman could have been permanently routed as opposed to temporarily delayed, Johnston had the only plausible answer: "I know I should have beaten him had he made . . . assaults on me."[12] The one time Sherman deliberately tried a headlong assault on Johnston's fortified troops, in the Kennesaw Mountain area, he proved Johnston to be right. Sherman retreated, with three thousand casualties. Johnston won the battle and lost only seven hundred men. This single intentional Sherman charge at a massively fortified position, however, convinced Johnston anew that the outmanned Confederate army must fall back whenever Sherman turned its flank. Otherwise, the Union invader might order yet another charge, this time on some Confederate position rendered too vulnerable by lines stretched too widely over the countryside. The debacle at Kennesaw Mountain also affirmed Sherman's conviction that assaults must be rarely assayed, and only to make flanking operations invincible.

Sherman's cunning provided the climactic demonstration that no external contingency would rescue the Confederacy. This invader of Georgia never would have given the outmanned Confederacy a chance, for if anything Sherman was too careful about pressing his advantages. Nor would Yankee war-weariness have bailed out the war-devastated slavocracy, for Lincoln would have intensified military pressure until his first term was over, and that was long enough. Nor would Peace Democrats have salvaged the slavocracy, for bipartisan zeal for Union swept up most Democrats, all Republicans, and both Lincoln and McClellan. Nor would Great Britain have saved the Confederacy, for Englishmen had determined never again to waste their resources in New World warfare.

Since nothing external could compensate for the Confederacy's escalating internal weakness, the question of why the slaveholders lost the Civil War comes down to the reasons the anaconda strategy was ultimately so successful. That question, like the question of why northern and English politics precluded a rescue operation from outside the Confederacy, must be answered, in part, far from the supposedly contingent battlefields. As dangerous as Sherman's sharpshooters were to Confederate soldiers, his invasion more thoroughly devastated the Confederacy's nonmilitary social structure.

Why, then, was slaveholders' mobilization of nonmilitary folk so vulnerable to Sherman's sweep over the countryside?

4

Slaveholders had long had to mobilize other Southerners to defend their regime. In prewar politics, the nonslaveholders, around 70 percent of the southern voters, had to be rallied. In wartime, wives and slaves also had to stand with the slavocracy. The white male slaveholders, composing 5 percent of the total southern population, could never fight off the northern 61 percent of the American population unless the supposedly lesser sex and the allegedly lesser race and the assuredly poorer nonslaveholders would prefer death to the dishonor of collaborating with Yankees.

To secure allegiance, the slaveholders possessed enormous coercive power, especially over their slaves. Yet the slaveholder as democrat still sought even their slaves' consent to be coerced. During the war, as slaveholders' coercive power dissolved, slaves' consent to be enslaved became ever more important. So did wives' and nonslaveholders' consent to stand with the slavocracy.

Behind consent has to be ideology—a rationale for laying down one's life for a cause. To achieve a universal sacrificial spirit, the slaveholders urged that slavery alone preserved the perfect society. The bane of human community, these rulers argued, was human selfishness. Patriarchal slavery alone produced selflessness. The white male, commander of wife, children, and blacks in his family, had a self-interest in ruling dependents selflessly. If the patriarch commanded selfishly, he hurt his own and thereby damaged himself. If his kin and property defied his benevolent orders, they damaged their family and thereby themselves.

The creed invited slaves not to cower before the lash but to love their enslaver as a biblical patriarch. Slaveholder paternalism allegedly offered blacks a dependent's paradise: guaranteed lifetime care, training in Christ's Word, space and time to enjoy fellow slaves after the workday. So too, the patriarchal worldview invited white wives not to submit haplessly to their husbands but to cherish their provider as paternalistic hero. The patriarch allegedly gave his woman protection against so-called black barbarians, sustenance for her household, and respect for her maternal influence.

Slaveholders' patriarchal faith also invited nonslaveholders not to become rich men's dependents but to share the starring role of independent patriarch. No matter that poor whites owned no blacks. They might some day purchase servants to aid their wives; and in the interim, they commanded their white families in the manner of the largest planters. Lower-class white husbands were also as free of "nigger-like" dependency as were the wealthy, for no white told them what to do. Instead, they joined rich whites in telling dependent women what to do.

All classes of southern white men, so patriarchal theory proclaimed, must die rather than submit to America's antipatriarchal conquerors, those holier-than-thou Yankees. Puritanical Northerners supposedly wished to force whites to emancipate blacks in the name of the color-blind assertion that blacks and whites were equal. Northern would-be conquerors of southern white males also allegedly wished to force husbands to liberate wives in the name of the feminist apostasy that both sexes were equal. Fanatics furthermore supposedly wished to reduce all southern whites to moral dependency in the name of the condescending opinion that Southerners were too morally blind to perceive slavery's evil. To support slavery was to legitimate white men's independence from Yankee moral intrusion, independent whites' control over dependent blacks, and independent males' capacity to rule in the only selfless government, the family, sacrosanct with or without slaves.

This crusade for white male independence reached its apogee in the Civil War. Then the master sex of the master race fought for a new declaration of independence, dedicated to the proposition that Yankees must not reduce white males to dependence or raise blacks or females to independence. In fighting for the Confederacy's independence from the Union and slaveholders' independence from the abolitionists, white males of all classes also fought for their own independence—for their mission to protect dependent women, children, and blacks and for their right to choose their own government rather than submit to meddling Yankees' imposed order.

On nonslaveholders' commitment to fight for independence— and on the consent of blacks and women to remain dependents— rested the slaveholders' fate. Before the Civil War, the ideology had been most vulnerable neither to class divisions between planters and poor neighbors nor to sexist differences between husbands and wives nor to racist clashes between blacks and whites, but to demographic differences between slaveholding and slaveless southern areas. During the Civil War, the South's most lily-white areas were the first to decide that Confederate independence reduced nonslaveholders to insufferable dependence. Yeomen in largely white areas accused the black-belt South of treating *them* like slaves in seeking to drag them out of the Union.

Within six months of the firing on Fort Sumter, the most northern third of the slave states had decided, often after bitter debate and ugly violence, to side with the free-labor states. The Border South slave states of Missouri, Kentucky, Maryland, and Delaware refused to secede. The Middle South area of West Virginia, after seceding from Virginia, joined the Union.[13] These five states, by remaining loyal to Union, kept from the Confederacy 52 percent of the slave states' factory capacity, 37 percent of their corn, 20 percent of their livestock, and 28.5 percent of their peoples. Because of the five slave states' decision to remain in the Union, the Confederate states' percentage of American resources, compared to the fifteen slave states' percentage, plunged in population from 39 percent to 27 percent, in livestock from 43 percent to 34 percent, in corn from 52 percent to 33 percent, and in factory capacity from 15 percent to 7 percent.

Moreover, as soon as Union troops broke into eastern Tennessee mountainous areas, slaveless Unionists trooped into Lincoln's army, 30,000 strong. In all, over 100,000 white residents of Upper South Confederate areas joined the Union army,[14] as did almost 250,000 white residents of Delaware, Missouri, Kentucky, and Maryland. So 350,000 white Southerners fought in Union armies, or over a third of the number of white Southerners who fought in Confederate armies.

The Border South's decision tipped the balance of militarily controlled terrain as much as of factory-troop-food resources. Because most Marylanders preferred the Union, their neighbor, the District of Columbia, the nation's symbolically important capital, was spared invasion. Because the upper third of the slave states remained loyal, the Union invasion could commence in Virginia and points southward. As Lincoln is said to have summed it up, "I hope to have God on my side, but I *have* to have Kentucky." Or as Lincoln definitely did say, "to deprive" the Confederacy of the Border South "substantially ends the rebellion."[15]

Jefferson Davis had hoped to have the Border South on his side, for substantial pro-Confederacy sentiment existed in these slaveholder hinterlands.[16] Confederate supporters especially peopled relatively rare Border South black belts: southern Maryland, Blue Grass Kentucky, the Greenbriar River valley of West Virginia, and the Missouri River–Mississippi River area of Missouri. In important part because he feared the Border South's Confederate sympathizers, Lincoln resisted both emancipation and the enrollment of black troops during the stalemated (in the eastern theater) first half of the Civil War. Lincoln also allowed a rather wide imposition of martial law in western Missouri and permitted the arrest of twenty-six possibly secessionist Maryland legislators before a critical legislative session.[17] When the state of Kentucky declared its official neutrality at the beginning of the war, Lincoln judicially delayed before declaring the obvious: that citizens cannot be neutral about obeying or not obeying their government. Only after Confederate troops marched into southern Kentucky did Union troops march into northern Kentucky.

This maneuver showed off Lincoln's tactical genius. His combination of forbearance and ruthlessness helped kill Confederate hopes for the Border South. But the hope had always been dim; only an incredibly impolitic president could have made it realistic. If Lincoln stupidly had violated Kentucky's neutrality, or equally stupidly had failed to send in troops after the Confederacy did, or more stupidly still had declared Kentucky's slaves free before the Union secured the state, Kentuckians might have overcome their antipathy to disunion. But Lincoln never gave such counterproductive folly a thought.

His discretion allowed Kentuckians to sort out their conflicting priorities. At every showdown, Unionism routed secessionism. At the final moment of decision, after both Union and Confederate forces had violated Kentucky's neutrality, the state legislature, over the secessionist governor's veto, demanded the withdrawal of Confederate troops. The legislature then voted down a demand for withdrawal of Union troops. Similarly, in Maryland, months before any legislator was jailed, the legislature refused to call a secession convention. So too in Missouri, after the secessionist-controlled state legislature had called a popularly elected state convention, the convenors rejected secession 70–23.

That margin approximated Unionists' predominance over secessionists throughout the Border South. The huge margin explains why Confederate marches through the Kentucky countryside, in hopes of achieving a secessionist groundswell, produced little, whereas Unionist marches through Maryland, in hopes of destroying Confederate saboteurs, almost immediately pacified the countryside. Only in western Missouri, with its history of guerrilla warfare dating back a decade to the Bleeding Kansas episodes, was pacification excruciating and arbitrary arrest of citizens a constant practice.[18] Yet in Missouri, too, Unionist armies easily rolled over the antisecessionist, more populated eastern part of the state and soon controlled the western areas where more slaves lived. For every one Marylander or Missourian who fought for the Confederacy, three fought for the Union.

Here was yet another 75 percent majority for Union—appropriate in a southern hinterland where only 12.2 percent of white families owned slaves (compared to 32.6 percent in the Confederate states). Border South slaveholders, narrowly concentrated in a fraction of their states, faced daunting numbers statewide: only 587 slaveholders in Delaware; only 3,593 in West Virginia; almost as many free blacks as slaves in Maryland. Slavery had long been losing relative strength in this South on the edge of the North. In 1790 one in four Border South inhabitants had been enslaved, including 32 percent in Maryland and 15 percent in Delaware. In 1820, when Missouri entered the Union, 20 percent of its people were enslaved. By 1860, those percentages were down to 10 percent in Missouri, 13 percent in Maryland, and 1.6 percent in Delaware. Meanwhile, this Border South region had developed a passion for Union and a reverence for the most famous American Unionist, Henry Clay. The Border South stayed in the Union primarily for one reason: When secessionists forced them to sort out their conflicting allegiances, most borderites cared more about their citizenship in the United States than about whether their relatively few blacks were slaves or free.

In a broader perspective, the deeper South's influence on the entire borderlands, North and South, had long been ebbing. The more southern portions of Illinois, Indiana, Ohio, New Jersey, and Pennsylvania had all contained many southern white migrants and some slaves in the early nineteenth century. The showdown in Lincoln's Illinois over the institution had occurred as late as 1824, when 42 percent of Illinoisans had voted for slavery. Thereafter, the state, like the entire Border North region, had drifted toward free labor. But as late as 1856, much of the Border North had voted against the Republican Party, thus stopping a Republican presidential triumph that year. When these most geographically and culturally southern of northern states turned Republican in 1860, Lincoln was assured election. When the Border North remained resolute for the Union, despite being the prime spawning ground of those Peace Democrats, the northern hinterland consolidated Lincoln's dominance of the pivotal iffy ground between the intransigent South and the intransigent North.

Since the border area between North and South leaned strongly northward, how can Civil War historians perceive equal internal disunity, in both the North and the South? They do it, first of all, by counting the Border *South* as Union states and then calling that *slave* area's minority of Confederate sympathizers a defection from the free-labor *North!* That misses the point: that the Border South, despite its one-eighth slave population and its one-fourth fraction of Confederate sympathizers, went for the Union as did the Border North, despite its one-tenth fraction of Peace Democrats.

Historians who claim northern division canceled southern division argue, second, that Northern Democrats' opposition to Lincoln neutralized southern opposition to Jefferson Davis. That position conflates Davis's pro-Confederate southern critics, who thought the Confederate President was waging war incorrectly, with southern anti-Confederates, who went to war on the Union's side. Just as in the North, most Democrats opposed both peace with disunion and Lincoln's ways of waging war, so in the Confederacy, a powerful anti-Davis faction opposed both reunion with the North and some of the President's wartime policies. In both nations, the loyal opposition sought less nationalistic consolidation, more states' rights, an end to arbitrary arrests and to the coercive drafting of white citizens, and no use of black troops or emancipating of black slaves. Davis's and Lincoln's respective patriotic critics did indeed cancel each other out.

In contrast, the disloyal opposition in the North, those few pro-Confederate Peace Democrats, could not begin to cancel out the disloyal opposition in the South, that huge pro-Union majority in five nonseceding slaveholding states. Southern Illinoisans would never have seceded from Illinois, as West Virginia seceded from Virginia. Nor would southern Indianians have raced to join Jefferson Davis's armies, as eastern Tennesseans sped to join Abraham Lincoln's armies. Nor would the rather recently emancipated states of Pennsylvania, New York, and New Jersey have fought for the Confederacy, as the slowly less enslaved states of Missouri, Kentucky, and Maryland fought for the Union. Nor would the Border South have joined the Confederacy unless Lincoln had handled the situation with uncharacteristic political stupidity. Of the many epitaphs that could be written on the Confederacy's gravestone, few would be more appropriate than "Here Lie the Slaveholders, Buried First in the Borderlands."

5

But that epitaph expresses too narrowly the slaveholders' loss of social control. The Confederacy's waning control over blacks, only a little less than the slavocracy's waning control over the borderlands, made Union forces numerically overwhelming.[19] During the first eighteen months of the war, the Union army had not yet massively penetrated the southern countryside, and Lincoln had not yet accepted black troops. In this exclusively white men's warfare, the 3.5 million black slaves in the eleven seceded states usually sustained the slavocracy's extractions from the soil. Slaves also provided nonmilitary labor on the battlefields, adding many earthwork fortifications to 1862's bumper crop of cotton and corn.

Then in 1863–65, the Confederacy's control over this 40 percent of its population increasingly dissolved. Lincoln's Emancipation Proclamation of January 1, 1863, theoretically freed slaves in Confederate areas. His acceptance of black troops and his intensification of raiding operations deep into the southern countryside also made the Civil War a black man's no less than a white man's fight. Something like 600,000 slaves, or approximately 17 percent of the Confederacy's total, ran off to Union lines.[20] Of these ex-slaves, 146,000 joined the Union army. Together with the 34,000 enlisted northern free blacks, they supplied over 15 percent of Union troops—more troops than were still present for duty in Confederate armies late in the war. The 146,000 southern blacks in Union armies, when added to the 350,000 southern white Union soldiers, meant that almost 500,000 residents of slave states fought in Union armies—or over half of the number of Southerners who fought in Confederate armies!

The blacks' countervailing willpower, when added to the Border South's countervailing willpower, swelled Union power into a truly overwhelming war machine. Where the fifteen slave states had had 39 percent of the nation's population, and the Border South disaffection had cut the percentage to 27 percent, blacks' allegiance to the enemy cut the Confederacy's source of troops to 15.5 percent of the Union's potential. To make this huge disadvantage greater, the Union suffered few civilian casualties and the Confederacy endured 50,000. The Union did suffer more troops killed than the Confederacy, 360,000 to 260,000, and more troops wounded, 278,000 to 198,000.

But the Union, with seventeen fighting men potentially available for every three available to the Confederacy, could afford much greater comparative losses than these. To put such butchery crudely, the Union could almost congratulate itself on losing three men for every two Confederates, for at that rate a temporarily stalemated (in the eastern theater) war of attrition was incrementally annihilating the Confederacy. About 50 percent of the 900,000 Confederate soldiers were killed or wounded, leaving a potential 450,000 to fight on. About 30 percent of the 2.1 million Union soldiers were killed or wounded, leaving a potential 1.5 million to fight on.

Worse than this three-to-one advantage in unwounded veterans of battle was the mammoth Union advantage in men who never wore a soldier's uniform. As the war drew to a close, the Union had some 2 million white men of fighting age who had never served in the army, to say nothing of a huge potential pool of black soldiers. The Confederacy had just about no white nonsoldiers left to be cajoled or forced to fight. By 1864, the Union had approximately 1 million troops on the rolls. The Confederates, in dismal contrast, had under 200,000 troops on the battlefields.

In the last month of the war, a desperate Confederate Congress tried to offset the Union's now-tremendous advantage by agreeing to enroll and free black troops, with the "consent of the owners and of the states" where slave soldiers resided.[21] This carefully-hedged measure came far too late to counter the Border South's and the blacks' massive swelling of the enemy. The law, a step toward giving up slavery to continue to pursue disunion, was also passed on almost the very day George McClellan had hoped to be inaugurated president and to offer to give up emancipation if the Confederacy would give up disunion.

In view of the massive black defections from the slavocracy, which changed the very nature of the war on both sides, how, once again, can military historians claim that northern defections canceled out southern defections? They usually do so by arguing that northern wage labor dissension canceled out southern slave labor dissension. The best example of northern lower-class upheaval, the New York City draft riots of 1863, indeed demonstrated significant northern anger over wages, over Irishmen who competed with native whites for jobs, and especially over the coercive draft of unwilling whites into northern armies. Lower-class draft-haters particularly resented the squires' legal right to duck conscription by purchasing a substitute.[22]

Northern whites' lower-class resentment, however, found its southern equivalent not in black slaves who deserted to the enemy but in white nonslaveholders who hated the Confederate draft. In the South as in the North, the wealthy could avoid military service. Any Southerner who owned over twenty slaves could win exemption from the draft for himself or an overseer in order to control the blacks. Yeoman detestation of the Twenty-Slave Law helped drive southern desertion rates from the army to around the same levels as those in the North, until southern desertion ran wild in the last months of the war.

But where poor whites' draft resistance, North and South, canceled each other out, no northern equivalent can be found for the hundreds of thousands of blacks who fled slavery. The difference lay at the heart of the two social orders. Northern lower-class laborers almost always consented to the free-labor system, even when they sought higher wages and better working conditions. In contrast, southern blacks showed with their feet that they had only acted a charade of consent to slavery before the Civil War. As northern military power weakened southern military power, coercive control of slaves—and therefore enslavement of blacks—dissolved. This profound rupture of social cohesion could never have affected the free-labor North. If Robert E. Lee could have marched an army through the North, hundreds of thousands of wage earners would never have fled so-called wage slavery.

Worse, the blacks who fled from a far more vulnerable southern system of social control massively eased the most threatening northern social dissension.[23] Since almost 200,000 blacks served in the Union army, the hated northern draft system could conscript 200,000 fewer whites. That number, in this context, was overwhelming. The Union army drafted 207,000 men in all—or one-half as many as would have been needed without blacks' enrollments!

Dissident blacks, having reduced northern conflict over conscription, also caused the worst southern conflict over conscription. Without black dissent from permanent dependency, no Twenty-Slave Law would have been necessary. Worse, southern soldiers, already outmatched by Sherman's troops, often had to aim their guns at potential black fugitives instead of at Yankee invaders. In early March 1865, for example, just when the manpower crisis drove the Confederate Congress to authorize slaves to serve as soldiers, the Georgia legislature authorized Governor Joseph E. Brown to organize a battalion of cavalry in Savannah "to prevent the escape of slaves to the enemy." Brown swiftly deployed three hundred mounted warriors. The soldiers, desperately needed to drive Yankees outside the Savannah environs, instead had to cage blacks inside the area.[24] With that depletion of their army in order to prevent a depletion of their countryside, Confederates implicitly conceded how impossible their internal problems were—and how thoroughly dissident blacks, like dissident Border Southerners earlier, were contributing to the Confederacy's desperate shortage of manpower.

6

Slaves' and Border Southerners' defections left the southern internal order not only underpopulated but also underfed. The most northern areas of the South had always produced more grain than southern areas. In the Lower South, plantations produced much of the food, especially after yeomen went off to war. When the border went for the Union and slaves fled the plantations, one of the worst famines ever to strike an American area spread over the Lower South countryside. Sherman's army, which had invited this agricultural havoc, seized much of the diminishing supply of food, thus intensifying the desperate situation behind the lines.

Food was scarcer still up in Virginia in Lee's trenches, especially after the Union's Philip Sheridan conquered the breadbasket of the Virginia front, the Shenandoah Valley. Troops ate poorly not only because slaves were running away from farms but also because railroads were no longer running toward the army. The railroad problem epitomized another deficiency of the southern social order compared to the northern: a much less advanced industrial economy. The slaveholders' more primitive manufacturing system served Confederate soldiers remarkably well in supplying them with rifles. But half of the southern industrial plant had been lost with the Border South, and much of the other half had to be mortgaged to small arms production. That left little factory capacity to correct the massive shortfall in the most sophisticated means of waging war. The huge northern lead in naval warfare was critical in that first stage of the Anaconda Plan, the conquering of the Mississippi River and the blockading of the Atlantic coast. Then the still larger initial northern advantage in railroads became lethal as Sherman tore up southern tracks.[25]

Even before Sherman twisted these Confederate lifelines into useless iron, southern railroads had been inadequate for national warfare. The tracks had been built not for national integration but for provincial markets. The gauges usually did not match from area to area; sometimes the lines ended miles apart; and always the tracks were too few for Lee's comfort. Although much was said then and repeated later about the Davis administration's failure to solve these problems and much about the government was short-sighted, the internal problems, here as elsewhere, would have baf-fled the greatest statesmen. To develop almost from scratch a so-phisticated military-industrial complex, in the midst of a debilitat-ing invasion, when most of the crude southern factories were crafting rifles instead of rolling railroad rails, would have been mi-raculous. Nor is it clear how such a putative war industry could have built railroads as fast as Sherman tore them up.

Imaginary solutions aside, the Anaconda Plan's results were all too grim. By mid-1863, the South could no longer move troops eas-ily along interior lines from theater to theater. The consequence: An undermanned army could not switch its resources when Yan-kees attacked on multiple fronts. Worse, by mid-1864, the South could no longer move food easily up to Lee's desperate troops. The consequence: Famished soldiers faced Grant's murderous charges.

As with the defections of the Border South and the blacks, no northern equivalent canceled out this southern internal weakness. At the beginning of the war, the much more developed North had over twice as many miles of railroad tracks as the underdeveloped South and under half as many sizes of gauges. During the war, the North added 20 percent more tracks and the South none. The war-time North also fit its gauges together or constructed rolling stock that could run over different gauges. The Confederacy could ac-complish little of that critical modernization. No southern inva-sion of the North could have ripped up the far more sophisticated northern infrastructure and left Yankees starving. Once again, Sherman's plan was brilliant military strategy precisely because it tore into the southern nonmilitary soft spots, leaving Lee's troops armed with little besides dearly purchased rifles.

7

Whoever was president of the Union on March 4, 1865, Lee's army would have been reduced to two options. The famished soldiers could go home, or the overwhelmed troops could take to the hills, like guerrillas. Any such determination would have been very un-usual after Sherman's home front devastation. The war instead ended the usual way. Confederate soldiers massively deserted or surrendered. Folks back home saluted their troops' submission.

Terror of death, whether by bullets or starvation, explains much—but not all—about the soldiers' collapse of determination. More outnumbered troops have sometimes refused to surrender, just as more famished home fronts have sometimes rejected capitulation and more decimated home fronts have been rebuilt after the Shermans have moved on. Such almost-inhuman courage has sometimes saved a seemingly doomed society.

Confederate morale, however, evaporated before any final fight to the death. Especially nonslaveholders' determination dissipated in 1864–65. During the war's last months, desertions from Lee's Virginia army approached 8 percent a *month*, compared to the previous rate of slightly over 8 percent a *year*.[26] Worse, Lee lamented, his remaining soldiers had lost their "moral condition." His men no longer fought with that "boldness and decision which formerly characterized them."[27]

His men had previously demonstrated historic boldness and decisiveness. The nonslaveholders, *when* they lived in black-belt areas, had been the backbone of the Confederacy's war for independence. But precisely that cult of independence ultimately sent too many yeoman soldiers homeward. The slaveholders' worldview had promised nonslaveholders the power to keep blacks and wives dependent and the power to provide for their flock like independent patriarchs. Until the Civil War, black-belt nonslaveholders had to sacrifice none of their autonomy in order to stand with slaveholders against the moralizing Yankees.

In 1863–65, nonslaveholding soldiers' wives, previously staunchly loyal Confederates, were the first to cry that the rich man's war was driving the poor man's family to dangerous dependency. In the wake of Sherman's incursion, white women were helpless against roaming black "family friends." Houses were scarred rubble. Children were starving. Cotton was unharvested, unsaleable. A silent scream went up in a wave of letters to the battlefront: Come home, my husband, and save us. "An army cannot be organized or supported," Lee said grimly in April 1865, in the face of the "communications received by the men from their homes, urging their return and the abandonment of the field."[28]

Nonslaveholding soldiers increasingly heeded their wives' communications instead of their commanders' orders. The Civil War had finally removed every advantage that rich men's version of independence supposedly showered on poor men. Slavery allegedly consecrated nonslaveholders as providers of their dependents; but now the yeomen's service on the slaveholders' battlefields was

tarving their loved ones. Slavery supposedly kept black "barbar-
ans" from rising up and raping; but now women faced frightening
lares from black runaways. Slavery supposedly legitimated the co-
rcion only of blacks; but now the Confederate Congress was entic-
ng blacks with emancipation promises to serve in the army, while
oercing whites with draft laws to fight for—for their family's de-
endence?! No wonder Lee's army was melting away. For slaveless
vhites, male and female, as for border Southerners and slaves (and
Middle South mountain folk who had deserted earlier), the war for
lavery had become only rich folks' fight for independence.

Even the rich folks came to wonder if this fight had God's ap-
roval. At the heart of the patriarchal code had always been a big
f: *if* slaveholders fulfilled biblical obligations, the Bible sanctioned
lavery. Many slaveholders had always defied Christian obligations
y breaking up slaves' families, by not permitting preachers to con-
ert blacks, and by not allowing blacks to read the Bible. The slave-
olders' preachers had long warned that God would take vengeance
n those who defied their biblical obligations. Then came Sherman
nd many preachers' insistence that the slavocracy must reform
r perish.

What a time to demand the easing of control over slaves, when
lacks were already increasingly out of control! To require slave
iteracy was to risk blacks reading pro-Union propaganda and anti-
lavery texts. To outlaw slave sales that broke up families was to
orfeit one deterrence to slave disobedience. The preachers' solu-
ion to saving slavery could drown the Confederacy in racial strife,
s could the Confederate Congress's desperate solution in March
865 of accepting slaves to fight in the army. But could the preach-
rs be ignored? [29]

For slaveholders as for nonslaveholders, the Confederacy's
light demonstrated that letters from home must be heeded. Rob-
rt E. Lee's vanishing army could not be confused with a guerrilla
rigade determined to fight to the death. The demoralized corps
vere instead full of dependents, rich and poor alike, eager to return
ome and resume their lives as independent patriarchs.

The army's melting away was symptomatic of a creed that had
een pushed too far. Whatever slavery gave to the slaveholders (and
t gave them an impossibly bad conscience only after God appar-
ntly lined up on the side of the strongest armies), it did not, could
ot, give everyone else everything dear. The system was too re-
note from the Border South and too coercive for the slaves. It was
ot the only way to control blacks. It was not the only way to

consecrate white husbands as patriarchs. It was not the only way to save poor folks from dependence. In the end, it gave nonslave holders only a ravaged independence and Americans everywhere a ravaged nation. And so a world died and few mourned it, until post war Southerners, now safely at home, began to write of a sacred Lost Cause.

8

This internal collapse during the second half of the Civil War played out the very sequence of events that the secessionists had left the Union to avoid. Or to put the social disintegration in it most ironic terms, the slaveholders, by seceding, brought upon themselves the home front nightmare that their thirty years of pre–Civil War endeavors had sought to avert.

After Lincoln won the presidency, secessionists declared th President-elect an immediate menace if slaveholders stayed in th Union. By honoring his campaign pledge to stop slavery from ex panding, so secessionists claimed, Lincoln would surround a froze number of slave states with a multiplying number of free-labo states. Then slavery would be encircled in a ring of fire. The flame would burn hottest where slavery was weakest, in the Borde South. Neighboring free-labor states would encourage border slave to flee. President Lincoln would use patronage to raise up a Blac Republican Party in southern borderlands. Southern Republican would urge racist nonslaveholders to expel blacks, slave or free from marginally enslaved areas. The President would offer federa funds to free and resettle blacks outside America.

Slavery in the borderland, continued the secessionists' argu ment, could not withstand these pressures. The institution woul be swiftly imprisoned in the eleven Middle and Lower South state The prison would be packed with blacks sold southward by par icky border masters. Trapped slaveholders would then perish lik rats in a cage. Or to use the slaveholders' other image, the encircle scorpion would sting itself to death. Better, in short, disunion an possible civil war than death by strangulation in a Lincol controlled Union.

Earlier versions of this viewpoint had initially inspired th South's prewar political provocations. Southern initiators of na tional controversy had especially feared the relatively thin commi ment to slavery at the edges of the South. They had demanded tha the United States annex Texas, lest English antislavery advocate help Texans emancipate the Lone Star Republic's sparse slave population; that Kansas become a slave state, lest the neighboring Border South state of Missouri with its relatively few slaves be menaced; and that a draconian fugitive slave law be enacted, lest Border South slaves escape to the Border North. When secessionists finally demanded that the South secede, lest Lincoln build a Republican Party in the Border South, they brought to a climax three decades of militant efforts to keep Yankees distanced from slavery's vulnerabilities.

The slaveholders thereby entered a truly withering ring of fire. The Civil War progressed according to the secessionists' most dreaded plot. Gen. Winfield Scott's Anaconda Plan, like an encircling scorpion, squeezed slavery's defenders between that ocean blockade, that invasion down the Mississippi River, Sherman's march from the Mississippi to the Atlantic, and Grant's attacks from the north. The South's northern frontier, just as slaveholding militants had feared, proved especially vulnerable to hostile encirclement. The Border South stayed in the Union, and Lincoln used patronage to build a powerful Republican Party in the region. He chose Montgomery Blair of Maryland and Edward Bates of Missouri for his cabinet. He selected Cassius Clay of Kentucky as his minister to Russia. He made Andrew Johnson of Tennessee his vice presidential running mate in 1864. Missouri, Maryland, and West Virginia gave him their electoral votes that year, and border Southerners gave him 54 percent of their popular votes.

Border South Republicans soon worked for emancipation in their states. The President encouraged such native-born southern efforts. He offered federal funds to pay for emancipating and deporting blacks. After Lincoln's offers, the big issue in Missouri became not whether but how to abolish slavery. West Virginia ended the institution before Lincoln's offers; Maryland declared it history in 1864.

This first act of the drama of disintegration, staged in the Border South, swiftly led to the second and third and fourth acts that secessionists had foreseen. Slaves indeed ran away when Yankees drew near. Nonslaveholders indeed deserted after their commitment to slavery was tested beyond endurance. Slaveholders indeed came to doubt their holy cause after Sherman's unholy vengeance suggested God's disapproval.

We cannot know whether all this would have happened as secessionists had feared if the South had peacefully submitted to Lincoln's inauguration, as most Southerners had initially desired. But we do know that the secessionist minority of Southerners, out of fear of contingencies in the Union, brought those contingencies to the fastest, bloodiest fruition. Better even than the epitaph "Here Lie the Slaveholders, Buried First in the Borderlands" is this inscription for Dixie's gravestone: "Here Lie the Secessionists, Who Subjected Slaveholder Ideology and Social Control to a Fatal Test."

9

This emphasis on southern *internal* flaws, some military historians will respond, ignores the larger reason for northern victory: northern *external* might. Critics of this analysis may tell the tale of George Pickett, the Confederate general who led the crucial failed charge on the crucial day of the Gettysburg battle. When asked why Pickett's Charge had failed, Pickett responded, "I've always thought the Yankees had something to do with it."[30]

The Yankees' military power had much—but not everything—to do with the Confederacy's dissolving resoluteness. External pressure had to precede internal disintegration, for prewar slaveholder domination of nonslaveholders, women, and slaves was unparalleled among New World slavocracies. But the U.S. slaveholders had provoked prewar controversies and ultimately the war itself in part because of concern about faultlines in the internal structure. Until Union armies appeared, the faultlines never became fissures. Yankee soldiers had to swarm over relatively slaveless areas before the Border South was totally safe for Union, before West Virginians seceded from Virginia, and before eastern Tennesseans contributed thirty thousand men to the Union army. The enemy had to savage the Lower South before wives, nonslaveholders, and finally even slaveholders saw that the patriarchal creed stretched too far to be credible. The northern military had to appear in the vicinity of plantations before hundreds of thousands of slaves would flee. The anaconda had to strangle economic production and transportation before starvation set in.

But to anoint northern military power as *the* cause of southern collapse is to inflate a necessary factor into a sufficient cause. Had the South's transportation infrastructure and industrial plant been as modern as the Yankees', Sherman's economic devastation would not have been so irreparable. Had the relatively slaveless areas' allegiances to slavery been as strong as their allegiances to Union, pacification of the Border South would have been as excruciating as it was in western Missouri.

Above all else, had the slaves been genuine in their pretended consent to slavery, they would not have fled in huge numbers. True, Union armies had to appear nearby before slave flight became epidemic. To make Union soldiers solely the cause and black fugitives solely the effect, however, is to make blacks, all over again, the passive puppets of white men's power. United States blacks in fact seized their freedom at their first opportunity. In Brazil, abolitionists actually entered slaves' huts, begging them to flee. In the United States, Union armies were often miles away and frequently considered the runaways a nuisance. Slaves had to *decide* to take their chances. Union armies created their opportunity to decide, not the decision itself, just as Yankee military pressure everywhere turned faultlines into fissures, rather than creating the faultlines or the anti-Confederate resentments that poured forth.

The nature of the faultlines indeed partly dictated the strategy of northern invaders. The Anaconda Plan, especially as wielded by Sherman in 1864, explored the internal southern soft spots. Grant's Virginia strategy in 1865, risking huge northern casualties in order to force enough southern casualties, seized advantage of the softnesses that Sherman's march had exposed.

So too, internal problems constantly molded Robert E. Lee's military strategies. Lee chose to invade the North in 1861–63 despite the risk of greater casualties when rushing at fortified positions and the fact that the South could not afford greater casualties. He rejected the alternate strategy, continual retreats deeper into the South. He thus never drew Yankees ever farther into hostile terrain or forced Union armies to attempt ever more debilitating charges at fortified defenses. He did not choose the strategy of incremental retreat, whatever its battlefield advantages, because of the nature of northern and southern nonbattlefield regimes. To win against a mightier foe, he had to prevent strong northern resolve. By invading the North, he hoped to convince the Yankees that southern resolve could not be broken.

He also knew that if his armies sank deeper into the South, he might decimate his home front. The slaveholder mentality, for thirty years before the Civil War, was to attack, not to shrink, to defend by aggressively demanding new proslavery laws. A retreat now would rob the Southerner of his self-identity. A retreat, furthermore, would risk losing the Middle South, an area less committed to the Confederacy than was the Lower South. A retreat would also invite Union soldiers into the black belts and inspire slave dissidence. The Confederate general *had* to stay northward and to invade farther North, whatever the military consequences, because of the nature of his internal world.

Southern and northern generals' strategic response to the non-military situation here contrasted with the nonbattlefield differences dictating battlefield tactics. Lee, who could not afford casualties equal to the North's, felt compelled to charge up those killing Gettysburg hills. George McClellan, who could afford far greater casualties than the South, did not feel forced to charge toward what he perceived would be slaughters around Richmond. McClellan could be the cautious Yankee preserver; Lee had to be the "squandering" southern defender. So internal imperatives cost the Confederacy even more military capacity.

Internal reasons also prevented the Confederacy from fighting a never-say-die guerrilla war after Lee's army was routed. In 1865, nonslaveholders and slaveholders alike were deserting; and a guerrilla war would have to be fought in the southern mountain terrain, the domain of the very nonslaveholders, such as the West Virginians and eastern Tennesseans, who loathed the slaveholders' war. To fight exclusively in the mountains, furthermore, meant surrendering nonmountainous areas where slavery was concentrated.

The story of the Civil War thus must include factors other than battlefield events, for home front dynamics determined battlefield strength, even battle tactics and locations. But then again the story of the home front must sometimes focus on the soldiers, for the battles tested home front allegiances and economic strength. Unless Civil War narrators swing back and forth between home front pressures and battlefield pressures, their narrative histories will remain shallow portraits. Yet how can such swings yield as riveting a saga as the straight-line tale of battlefield drama?

10

Most academics will answer, why try? Or as a superb academic historian once asked me, if you have a rich conceptual design, "why bother with all that other stuff?" By "other stuff," he meant history as the story of people, places, events—superficial stuff, so he thought, which only distracts the reader from sophisticated abstractions. He also meant that a rich conceptual design has as emotional and aesthetic an impact on a person of abstract intelligence as any novelistic tale can provide.

Academics, however, are not just high-powered abstractionists. Put an exciting idea in the form of a stirring tale and professors comprehend the abstraction more intuitively, more emphatically, more totally. Thus the theoretical conception of slaves dashing for freedom is intellectually inspiring. The story of Frederick Douglass fleeing, with capture and psychic annihilation looming in every stranger's glance, is conceptually unforgettable. So too, the proslavery polemicists' diatribe against slaveholders' antipaternalistic practices is abstractly fascinating. The story of the Reverend James Henry Thornwell, once himself an afflicted orphan, agonizing on the eve of disunion about protecting the afflicted slave encases an idea in a memorable image.

The academic historian must also remain a storyteller because history is too important to be written only for academics. A nonacademic audience for historians is out there; it is not as large as the audience for novelists but still includes tens of thousands of readers. These readers' sense of history matters. In fact, popular perception of our history matters so much that historians can become obsessed with spreading politically correct historical interpretations. Yet many academics write politically crucial texts in such an abstract form that common folk, the ultimate arbiters of the politically correct, will not read them. Informed citizens, however, welcome vivid narratives.

Few professors want to sacrifice intellectual depth for popular appeal. An intellectually satisfying colorful tale must explore analytical ideas *and* enclose the ideas in striking stories. That reintegrated narrative history must be conceptually driven. Its analytical ideas must be front and center. It must not shrink from abstract models of behavior. It must not avoid the parsing of critical documents. But the abstractions eventually must be illustrated in dramatically rich episodes.

In a narrative of the Civil War, for example, the story must be woven around an abstract inquiry: why and how Union troops, for three years locked in inconclusive battles on the eastern front, incrementally broke through on the western front and in the process helped shatter the southern social structure. This story must emphasize the Union armies' relentless pressure on all aspects of the eventually splintering slavocracy. To explain and illuminate northern relentlessness, the election of 1864 must be given as much space as Grant's charges at Lee. The narrator must constantly interrupt the narrative flow to explain: to stop and recount the New Political History's abstract model of partisan politics as holy shrine, to stop and report the full documentary evidence of McClellan's devotion to the shrine of Union. After such pauses for analysis, however, the narrator must speed ahead with that "other stuff," a memorable story. Perhaps no story will be so affecting—or make Northerners' persistent Unionism more unforgettable—than a biographical sketch of George McClellan. The tale must make vivid this most misunderstood of Civil War titans, the general and politician who would never surrender Union, but prayed he need not butcher a people to save it.

Just as narrators must replace some of their emphasis on battles with explorations of the McClellans' Unionism, so a reintegrated narrative history must continually turn away from the bloodshed to explicate the slow splintering of southern society. Each splinter—each breakdown of an element of the Confederate social order—must be described not only abstractly but with a vivid illustration. As much time must be spent colorfully describing Missouri's wartime debate on abolishing slavery as in recounting Pickett's Charge at Gettysburg. The fully told tale of one slave dashing toward Sherman must become as unforgettable as Sherman turning Joe Johnston's flank. Vivid sketches of domestic life, in both the planters' Big Houses and the nonslaveholders' cabins, must become as absorbing as Grant bearing down on the weakened Lee.

The form of the narrative must be not a straight line but a mosaic. The collage of images must include military and family history, private and public history, social and political history, minorities' histories and white male history, each bearing on all the others to yield total history. We will then see how this total war between two societies finally strangled the Confederacy in the manner of an anaconda.

That narrative must overcome an artistic disadvantage. The tale of an unstoppable anaconda must forfeit the suspense of military contingency, where surrender supposedly looms if one general charges the wrong way. A narrative that attends to the deeper cultural causes of victory, however, will gain two artistic advantages. First of all, while tales (and TV documentaries) about the Civil War's grotesque violence attract one audience, horrifying sagas repel another audience. In a curious way, the late attempt to democratize brutality—to show how mutilation brutalized common folk and itself stemmed from a deplorable defect in America's violence-prone society—has all the more legitimated the dwelling on Civil War ugliness.

Historians should never beautify a subject. If gore was most of the story, battlefield horror must be most of the narrative. But if half the cause of military victory lay off the battlefield, an excessive dwelling on brutalization underplays half the history. The uplifting story of blacks racing toward freedom, if told in the same detail as the dispiriting story of corpses lying mangled, will give the epic not only new analytical truth but also richer artistic resonance.

That artistry can also offer a more satisfying rendition of human contingency. Tales of battlefield contingency make a change in historical outcome too easy, too trivial, too random, too superficial to convey a human predicament that transcends battlefields. To be human, in or out of armies, is to strive for a destiny and to fight against an unhappier resolution. Triumph depends equally on power and perception. The successful striver must possess the force to attain the goal and the vision to see all the contingencies that block the path.

In the Civil War, nothing was inevitable about Union victory, unless and until northern leaders correctly perceived all the ways they could lose their huge plurality of nonmilitary and therefore military force. Lincoln could have lost all his Border South advantages if he had pushed through immediate emancipation. Sherman could have jettisoned all his Georgia advantages if he had continually charged Joe Johnston's earthworks. Secretary of State William H. Seward could have thrown away diplomatic advantages if he had failed to warn the skittish English to stay out of a New World brawl. Because Lincoln and his fellow shrewd Yankee pragmatists always saw clearly the potential for defeat, they could avoid the traps and continue to press their advantages.

Then in a long war of attrition, Confederate leaders could not forever overcome the slavocracy's disadvantages. Civil War buffs often playfully ask what would have happened if Lincoln had been President of the Confederacy and Jefferson Davis President of the Union? Well, Davis might have frittered away the Union's advantages. If he hadn't, Lincoln could not have overcome the Confederacy's shortcomings. What could any statesman have done to overcome the three-to-one popular sentiment for Union in the Border South or to keep enslaved the 600,000 blacks who bravely opted for freedom? Sometimes people think contingencies are available that are in fact unavailable. To seek the unavailable is often to be patriotic and courageous and honorable—and doomed.

The historians' advantage, in writing epics about human contingency, is their double perspective. They know what people at the time thought were the contingencies. They also know how mistaken or clairvoyant were the thoughts, for they know how actions on the thoughts came out. Here is the potential for sagas more stirring than fiction, of how people hasten or avoid their own nightmares.

Few tales in this vein are as chilling as the epic of the southern slaveholders. In the way they threw themselves against the fate they thought they saw, as in everything they did, these masters stretched for more mastery than they could sustain. They persistently demanded more consent from their slaves, more worship from their wives, more sacrifice from their neighbors, more laws from prewar Yankees, more surrender from northern Unionists, more bravery from southern armies, more diplomatic leverage from King Cotton, more economic advantage from an underdeveloped infrastructure, even more Christian patriarchy from themselves, than could be eternally delivered. The story of those overreaching men uncomfortably illuminates the limits and mortality of our species. That is the stuff of a haunting epic. It is the "other stuff" that high-powered abstractionists would do well to portray.

11 / Toward a Newer Political History—and a Reintegrated Multicultural History

Two years ago, when I began my tenure as the first Lockwood Professor of American History at the State University of New York, Buffalo, the chair of the history department asked me to deliver an inaugural lecture, in the style of professors at England's Oxford and Cambridge. I initially considered the idea pretentious. Then I remembered that Buffalo is the farthest thing from pretentiousness. I also realized that the occasion usefully called for an analysis of where my generation of American historians had been and where we should be heading. The resulting previously unpublished essay sums up my aspiration to write political history as creation and creator of a social world—and to base the reintegration of American history on narratives of all the American peoples.

When we have more perspective on American historical writing during my first thirty years in the profession, 1960–90, two conclusions will likely emerge. First of all, the field never broadened so much, in terms of past Americans studied. Second, the field never narrowed so much, in terms of segmentation into constricted specialties.

Thirty years ago, historians concentrated, with what now seems old-fashioned narrowness, on white males, particularly on white male politicians. Yet the most famous historians also produced, with what now seems old-fashioned breadth, syntheses of our history. When I entered the profession, a debate was flourishing between two synthetic positions. Some synthesizers claimed that American history must be organized around the eternal conflict between rich and poor. Others claimed that all Americans, whether rich or poor, have usually shared a consensus on capitalism, democracy, and Christianity.[1]

For a time, this clash between conflict and consensus as organizing themes seemed illuminating. Then the either/or choice seemed misguided, for both conflict and consensus clearly pervaded white male political struggles. Historians also began to notice that whether "all" Americans' conflict or consensus was emphasized, that "all" included only white males. Until the twentieth century, few other Americans visibly controlled politics, the only subject constantly dealt with in either conflict or consensus history. Throughout most of American history, women, African Americans, and Native Americans could not vote, much less sit in Congress. The disenfranchised constituted at least 80 percent of the pre–Civil War adult American population.

Since the late 1960s, wave after wave of New Social Historians have sought to make this American majority visible. These historians argue that narratives of white male politics usually turned politically excluded Americans into invisible men and women. True, the old politics-centered history did notice that governmental decrees affected the politically invisible majority. The history of those decrees, however, usually emphasized imposition. The willful in Washington imposed history on will-less subjects in the slums, over the stoves, in the slave quarters, within immigrants' ghettos, and on Indian reservations.

The New Social History brings those so-called victims back into American history as willful escapees from victimization. The spotlight turns from the politicians to the commoners. Headline political events, it is usually assumed, scarcely matter to the politically excluded, who care more about creating their own styles of labor, mating, child rearing, religion, literature, music. American historians' most important story now usually involves intimate interactions in families and neighborhoods, where the politically excluded supposedly make their own local world, immune from national political impositions. But national decrees *do* matter to the excluded, when politicians remake the very basis of local society. Emancipation, enfranchisement, and the granting of civil rights, for example, have transformed much of African-American history, just as enfranchisement and fair employment laws have transformed much of women's history.

"History from the bottom up," with national politics largely left out, has also fragmented American history. We have fine new histories of local villages, of different genders and races, of different worldviews of many ethnocultural underclasses—of everything except an integrated American history. A New Social History without a national political dimension is becoming a history of a nonnation, a disassociated chronicle of severed multicultural identities.

A New Political History has also emerged, but neither to emphasize that politics is relevant to, and affected by, the politically invisible nor to reintegrate a national story of multicultural groups. Instead, the New Political History, like the New Social History, tends to describe a localistic community, this time the community of white male politicians. We now better understand how the politicians' shrine of party operates, how roll calls turn out, how partisan imperatives shift and mostly stay the same. All this enriched fabric of politics, however, retains the look of white members of the political club, maneuvering only to attain advantage within the clubhouse. Little attention is paid to disenfranchised groups outside Congress. Less attempt is made to describe how politicians affect, or are affected by, multicultural minorities. If politics continues to be seen as irrelevant to the disadvantaged, and if the disenfranchised majority continues to be seen as powerless in white male politics, the New Political History, for all its technical sophistication, will be dismissed as an insufficient, unintegrated chronicle of the American peoples.

Signs now abound that the fragmentation of American history is coming to an end. The New Social Historians more often seek to integrate the state into a yet newer social history. The New Political Historians more frequently recognize that social tensions and social groups outside the white male political clubhouse influence everything within it.[2] I cherish these integrating trends. My own convictions are that political assumptions profoundly influence social institutions and vice versa, that the politically invis ible masses greatly influence the politically visible elite and vice versa, and that political historians, by incorporating the best of the New Social History, may reintegrate the national story of colliding localities, classes, ethnics, sexes, and races.

For these purposes, the institution and politics of slavery offer a seemingly counterproductive, and paradoxically therefore, wonderfully productive case study. In the vast literature on slavery as a social institution, politics is just about invisible. No decision in the white male political clubhouse apparently molded private relationships between slaveholders and slaves. So too, in the vast literature on the causes of the Civil War, black men's impact is invisible. No slave apparently influenced any pre–Civil War congressional decision about slavery. If, with these unlikely materials, politics can be shown to have shaped a social institution, and if the exploited can be shown to have shaped the exploiter's political decisions and therefore the political transformation of social exploitation, we might be on the road toward a newer political history—even toward a reintegrated American multicultural history.

1

During the past thirty years, while I concentrated on the Slave South's politics, most Old South scholars have concentrated on slavery as a social institution. The resulting literature is a jewel of the New Social History. In the manner of that school, studies of slavery have increasingly proceeded from the bottom up. Emphasis has increasingly focused on slaves who sought to escape dehumanization by fashioning their own worldview in the quarters. We have learned about slave tales, slave songs, slave religions, slave families. We have been told that although slaves did not, could not shatter their chains, their indigenous culture allowed them to endure as a proud community. What with all this emphasis on slaves' countervailing culture, slaveholders' impositions have faded into the background. My favorite subject, the slaveholders' politics, is not even in the background of other scholars' favorite tale: the story of slaves' partial escape from psychological and cultural subjection inside the supposedly inescapable quarters.

In the new slavery studies, slaveholders' governments seem irrelevant not only to slaves' means of psychological escape but also to whites' means of physical domination. In this Peculiar Institution, scholars rightly point out, private power, not public power, usually dominated within the plantation gates. Government power almost never either augmented or restrained the masters' sweeping prerogative to lash or brand or imprison or sell slaves. Only on the rare occasion when slaveholders' private authority totally failed to keep public order, as in a servile insurrection, did state punishment massively replace masters' punishments. So scholarly debates about the nature of slavery need pay no attention to politics.

Unfortunately for that conception of private power as unrelated to governmental power, public governance conditioned the slaveholders' very conception of private coercion. The South's Peculiar

Institution has been compared to every conceivable oppressive governing institution—prisons, Nazi concentration camps, Russian serfdom, Brazilian slavery—with scant emphasis on this defining governmental fact: Throughout the New World, only southern slave society deployed absolute power inside the world's most advanced democratic state, inside an egalitarian republic designed to check and balance absolute power.

Because only these New World slaveholders had to reconcile an antiabsolutist version of public democracy with an antidemocratic version of private absolutism, they had to separate black and white with unusual rigidity. Slavery only for blacks, democracy only for whites—the peculiarly democratic slaveholder needed that kind of racist dichotomy more than did nondemocratic Latin American slaveholders. Slaveholders in the United States were far more determined than the Latin Americans to prevent a semifree class of mulattoes from developing. So too, the U.S. slavocracy, alone in the New World, usually insisted that after any widespread emancipation, blacks would have to be deported from the country. Several aspects of American civilization helped generate this unusually severe racism. But the necessity to quarantine democracy from slavery made the white enslaver of blacks a racist with a vengeance. This partially political origin of American cultural racism illuminates why social and political history must be integrated. The political realm sometimes defines intimate social mores, just as the cultural realm sometimes defines impersonal political decisions.

Yet extreme racism did not assuage the democrat in the slaveholder quite enough. Slaveholders constantly demanded proof that blacks *consented* to be ruled from above. Consent to be governed was the first requirement of American republican legitimacy, and few American slaveholders could respect themselves if they altogether embodied the antithetical despotic creed: that the governed must be terrorized into subjection. These peculiar slaveholders wished that their black so-called family friends would voluntarily, even lovingly, accept their absolute command.

The slaveholders' words "family friends" reveal much; when seeking a model of absolute power above and consent below, the slaveholder found the answer in his familial parlor. The patriarch's disenfranchised, dependent white wife and children seemed to consent to his absolute rule over the household. The southern slaveholder aspired to make his rule over equally dependent, equally disenfranchised black "family friends" parallel his reign over white intimates in the Big House. He would be a leader of his consenting flock, just as politicians would be leaders of consenting citizens. To win consent, the domestic absolutist had to be a caring paternalist. In this political imperative lies one solution to the critical mystery that is not even posed in the apolitical literature on slavery as a social institution: why the U.S. slaveholder insisted peculiarly often, with peculiar vehemence, that his was a paternalistic institution and that his dependents consented to his benevolent rule.

The patriarchal insistence led to the patriarchal charade. Southern slaveholders constantly demanded that blacks stage a tableau of consent for their commander. Or to be more accurate, slaveholders demanded that the slave's act of consent become no act, that the slave's personality truly become that of grateful ward. Posterity calls the fawning slave Sambo; and slaves put on the demanded Sambo performance constantly—at celebrations of master's homecoming, at Christmas receptions, in the Big House when visitors came. That drama cherished by the slaveholder was seldom staged in nondemocratic Latin America.

This democratic charade of consent, however, required destruction of the classic democratic consenter: the questioning, thinking citizen. The slaveholders knew that without some heavy-handed psychological conditioning and physical terrorizing, slaves would never pretend to consent to enslavement, much less genuinely agree to be perpetually a slave. The slaveholders' need to destroy slaves' free will could turn this version of slavery into a suffocating absolutism. Slavery elsewhere was more physically cruel, but U.S. slavery was more psychologically invasive. By demanding not just obedience from their slaves but also abject consent to be mastered, owners reached inside their bondsmen's souls, sought to undermine their serviles' self-esteem, endeavored to hammer men into fawning "boys."

The slaves, in response to this not-so-democratic script for consent, demonstrated that human willpower cannot be altogether annihilated. True, blacks put on their masters' demanded Sambo charade. True, some charaders *became* their Sambo act. True, most slaves lost some self-esteem, as those forced to fawn inevitably do. But many slaves partially repelled their masters' psychological invasion. In the fields, black laborers resisted psychic annihilation by dissimulating, lying, setting fires, misunderstanding orders, feigning sickness—in short, by merely posing as consenting

Samboes. So too, back in the quarters, where no whites were omnipresent, non-Samboes' counterculture somewhat protected slaves from considering themselves as Samboish as the masters proclaimed.

Although some masters suspected that the culture in the quarters was no Sambo's worldview, the South's aspiring paternalists worried more about work-shirking non-Samboes in the fields. Mild punishment, if successful with a patriarch's own wife and children, did not suffice to turn disobedient slaves into hardworking toilers. The difference between "family friends," black and white, was too obvious, too vast. Some terrorizing, unthinkable to inflict on whites, was necessary to procure a decent day's labor from dissimulating blacks. Some lashing, branding, and worst of all, selling recalcitrant slaves downriver ensued. Day-to-day plantation life more often resembled low-grade guerrilla warfare than a compromise between caring patriarchs and consenting wards.

United States patriarchs still deployed more caring guidance of slaves than did slaveholders elsewhere, who had less aspiration toward paternalism. Upper-class deviations from paternalistic behavior, however, provoked the slaveholders' preachers to issue weekly warnings that the owners must meet biblical standards of patriarchy. The Christian patriarch, frequently battling a dissimulating Sambo and sometimes wincing at a neighboring angry lasher, ultimately found, in the paternalist-Sambo charade, a demonstration that much of life was a dubious act.

The southern slaveholder was among the most suspicious of Americans, and for that deep distrust of others, the deceitful slave deserves partial credit. Which is to say that just as the slaveholder partially molded the slave personality, so the slave partially molded the slaveholder personality. The vicious circle is a case study in the inseparability of impersonal politics and social intimacy, for slaves and slaveholders' interactions began with a political problem: that clash between slaveholders' despotic and democratic sensibilities. By demanding a charade of domestic consent, the slaveholder sought to wipe out the disparity in his regimes. By resisting and/or faking the Sambo role, slaves sought to avoid reduction to will-less puppets. By seeking to lash dissimulating Samboes into true-blue performances, the aspiring paternalist could become fearfully antipaternalistic. By skeptically observing whites' pretense to paternalism and slaves' pretense to Samboism, the slaveholder became mistrustful of everyone's performances.

This mistrustful attitude turned altogether antipaternalistic when the duplicitous slave ripped up the Sambo script. Although the state rarely intruded between master and slave, the government massively intervened to smash black rebellion. Not only local and state governments but also the national government stood poised to smother revolt, as when U.S. Marines, led by Robert E. Lee, marched into Virginia to destroy John Brown at Harpers Ferry. Slaves thus learned that the state's crushing power, although usually invisible, was always there at the ready. Slaves also learned that when the supposedly democratic state intervened, judicial trials for suspected rebels could be partially, fearfully undemocratic. The resulting state-sanctioned hangings of suspected blacks help explain why slaves tended to trick their owner rather than rise in revolution. Behind that tendency lay the nature of the state as well as the nature of the master.

2

Another form of slave resistance, individual flight, occurred much more often than group insurrection, not least because governmental deterrence was less automatic and less overwhelming. The southern patrol, the great communal police force for helping masters control slave runaways, consisted of government-sanctioned mounted militiamen, who *often* rode around their own *neighborhoods* at night. That word *often* is important. Equally often, no patrol was deployed, since each master was expected to police his own slaves. That word *neighborhood* is also important. No trans-neighborhood governmental bureaucracy directed the erratically appearing neighborhood patrols. If a runaway could escape from one neighborhood, the next neighborhood's patrol would probably not be alerted in time and might not itself be patrolling.

Assuming fugitives eluded enough unconnected patrols and ran through enough unpatrolled neighborhoods, they might reach the North. Then they would encounter another somewhat sievelike governmental deterrent. Some northern states passed so-called Personal Liberty Laws, passively refusing to help federal authorities track down fugitives. Furthermore, some Northerners, black and white, actively helped runaways. Some of the aid was quasi-organized—and more organized across neighborhood lines than was the southern patrol system. The northern so-called Liberty Line sometimes helped hidden fugitives move to the next neighborhood's hiding place.

Despite the loopholes in governmental deterrence, flight from masters required incredible courage. Most often desperate fugitives were on their own. Most often a southern patrolman or Yankee slave catcher blocked the way. Always runaways lost much if they escaped and risked more if they were captured. Successful flight meant escape from the quarters as well as from the master—escape from mates and children and companions as well as from the lasher. Failed flight meant a dreaded lashing at least and a sale downriver at worst.

Still, for those who dared take resistance beyond day-to-day sabotage and black counterculture, lonely flight was less forbidding than group insurrection. The slave escaping alone, unlike revolutionaries conspiring together, did not risk a turncoat's betrayal. The fugitive also did not risk charging with pikes against a ruling class with all the guns. Most important of all, the runaway, not the insurrectionist, could best explore white governmental weakness. True, crudely armed slave revolutionaries might seize sophisticated arsenals before sleepy or nonexistent patrols noticed. But even assuming the raid triumphed, rebels would still be right there in the neighborhood, facing the government-organized might of surrounding neighborhoods, the state militia, and even national troops. In contrast, a solitary fugitive might slip through southern patrols and receive some aid from northern citizens. Here again, the nature of public as well as private deterrence determined the nature of slaves' resistance to slaveholders. Only a few hundred antebellum rebels dared to rise up against the Man's public armies, while tens of thousands of fugitives fled their private masters through the cracks in the state's coerciveness.

The escapees remained a fraction of the 4 million slaves. Most blacks preferred the lesser risks of deceit in the fields and counterculture in the quarters. But that is the normal story of human resistance. Most of us make our partial accommodations, cherish our partial triumphs, and look with awe upon the comparatively few who dare go all the way in defiance of authority. The mystery is never why ordinary folk cannot muster superhuman audacity. The question is always whether the extreme courage of the few can decisively augment the circumspect protests of the many. Did the dissimulating slave, and especially his extremist cousin, the fugitive slave, decisively influence the political process that led to abolition?

3

The answer must be that just as the political order helped mold the nature of slaveholder imposition and of slave resistance, so the slaves' resistance to masters' social control helped mold the nature of the political emancipating process. Dissimulating slaves generated suspicious slaveholders; and slaveholder mistrusts carried over to nonslaveholding whites, whenever yeomen pretended to consent to slavery. Masters were a little wary about nonslaveholding neighbors, more distrustful of nonslaveholders who lived in relatively slaveless southern hinterlands, and most suspicious of allegedly friendly Yankees. Slaveholders constantly asked their professed northern and southern nonslaveholding friends to supply proof of friendship by passing increasingly provocative proslavery laws.

From nonslaveholders as from slaves, the ultrasuspicious slaveholder personality ultimately demanded more than humans can give. Just as slaveholders meant to extract from slaves not just a decent day's work but also consent to slavery, even love for the paternalist, so Southerners demanded of Northerners not just renunciation of abolition but also national bulwarks for slavery, even personal complicity in reenslaving black fugitives. Slaves begrudgingly put on Sambo acts; Northerners begrudgingly passed laws to protect slavery; and slaveholders, stung by and worried about the reluctance, ever demanded more surrender than the self-respecting could yield. The process, begun on the plantation and furthered in tense congressional confrontations and in tenser northern crises over individual fugitives, could yield only the slaveholder's conviction that no one beyond the slaveholding class loved slavery quite enough.

The laws demanded by slaveholders usually aimed, in important part, at deterring fugitive slaves from fleeing toward nearby areas hostile to slavery. Runaways such as Frederick Douglass sought to free themselves, not to make an impact on Congress. But black fugitives could not have altered congressional deliberations more decisively if they had fled into the House or Senate chambers. They created widespread slaveholder knowledge that slaves were on the alert for any fissures in the system. That realization—that ability of slaves to invade slaveholders' heads—fueled provocative slaveholder attempts to use national politics to close off openings to free-labor worlds. The following tritest sentence in this book is the truest and carries the thought most ignored in histories of the coming of the Civil War: Without (politically invisible) fugitives, there could have been no (highly politically visible) fugitive slave crises, and any road to disunion would have passed through entirely different terrain.

Flights from slavery were usually relatively few, since white controls usually contained only small cracks. When outside forces widened the cracks, pragmatic slaves seized their opportunity. Escapes from slavery first reached massive proportions during the American Revolutionary War, when the invading English army created the first huge gaps in whites' public and private power. Wherever the British soldiers invaded a slaveholding area, some 25 percent of slaves fled. Masters forcibly reenslaved most of the fugitives after English armies departed.

The problem of deterring fugitive slaves, however, remained serious wherever masters' power was waning in post-Revolutionary America. After northern legislatures, partly inspired by the Declaration of Independence, enacted gradual emancipation, and after Border South masters gradually manumitted some slaves, the pace of slave runaways quickened, as fugitives pressed to make emancipation/manumission less gradual. Fugitives most endangered slavery in cities like Philadelphia and Baltimore that contained some slaves but were largely free labor. Here the chances to hide in free black enclaves or to reach neighboring free-labor states attracted more risk takers. Here fugitives freed themselves more often than masters manumitted slaves. The runaways also led some masters to accept a compromised form of slavery. Masters in border areas often came to an informal agreement with individual slaves, whereby decent work for a few years would be rewarded with manumission at the end of the term. This partial evolution of permanent slavery toward temporary indentured servitude helped end slavery over many years in the North and helped dilute the institution in the Border South.

Politically invisible fugitives were not the only cause of slaveholders' political vulnerability in the Border South. Politically visible border nonslaveholders, outnumbering border slaveholders seven to one in 1860, usually preferred a South without slaves *if* blacks could be removed from their area. In the most likely scenario for widespread removal of blacks, Border South slaveholders might cash in their slaves at Lower South auctions. An increase of both white opposition and black runaways could lead Border South masters to sell their property out of the area especially quickly, leaving slavery in only eleven of the fifteen slave states.

Apprehensions about border fugitives helped produce the Fugitive Slave Law of 1850. Because of that law, more slaves invisible to the political process helped drive white men toward political controversy. When a fugitive arrived in the North and a master swore out an indictment, the new law required every Northerner to join a slave-capturing posse when asked. Most Northerners obeyed the law. A few, resenting the insistence that they be slave catchers, instead helped the slave escape, thereby infuriating Southerners. The names of these well-publicized cases resound like a drumbeat on the path to civil war: Jerry, Shadrack, Anthony Burns. But the most revealing incident involved the less-well-known Edward Gorsuch of Baltimore County. Gorsuch and some relatives went after four slave runaways in Christiana, Pennsylvania, in 1851. Slave rescuers killed Gorsuch and wounded his son. Gorsuch's slaves permanently escaped, and none of their rescuers was convicted.

The most curious part of the explosive incident might seem to be Gorsuch's motives. He had promised to free his blacks in some eight years, under one of those private pacts rather common in the border states. With so limited a time left to enjoy the fruits of his slaves' labor, wasn't Gorsuch's suicidal pursuit just a case of an impractical Southerner overinfected with a quixotic sense of honor?[3] No. Gorsuch's runaways threatened the very practicality of slavery as a compromised border institution. If fugitives could escape at will, this sometimes temporary form of slavery would collapse. Then the permanent enslavement of other border blacks would be further endangered. The slaying of Edward Gorsuch is a jewel-like example of fugitive slaves' power first to inspire a sometimes temporary form of Border South slavery, then to depart the enslavement prematurely, and then to create nation-shattering episodes involving individual Northerners' painfully personal decisions about whether to help shutter the slavocracy's openings.

Another politically invisible group furthered politically invisible black fugitives' political provocations. In the antebellum years, white women were for the first time "unsexing" themselves, as most males saw it, by lecturing to public audiences on public issues. Women such as Angelina Grimké joined blacks such as Frederick Douglass as brilliant speakers on antislavery podiums. Still, it was a housewife opposed to what were called "promiscuous" agitations who most publicized the cause. Harriet Beecher Stowe, who believed women's political work lay in the task of privately teaching men to be moral, wrote her *Uncle Tom's Cabin* at home.

The novel featured the slave Tom's home, his cabin, and the heroes were fugitive slaves who fled northward toward a better home. The thousands of disenfranchised Frederick Douglasses, having helped inspire the disenfranchised Stowe to influence millions of voters, also helped produce yet another slaveholder defensive tactic, even more politically disruptive than the Fugitive Slave Act: the demand that national territories permit slavery. Southern drives for territorial expansion grew out of many impulses: fear of racial claustrophobia if the black population swelled and southern territory did not; fear of political powerlessness if the North secured more states and the South did not; fear of lost honor and self-respect if Southerners were judged too depraved to expand their hegemony into other areas. But the South's most coveted territories all involved an additional fear: alarm about hostile neighbors abutting the South's borders, not least because nearby enemies might aid fugitive slaves. The most desired lands encircled the South: Florida, which in Seminole and Spanish hands was an invitation to South Carolina and Georgia fugitive slaves; Texas, which under English influence might beckon Louisiana and Arkansas fugitives; and Kansas, which under northern control might be an oasis for Missouri fugitives. Southerners' demands for these neighboring territories produced an intense antisouthern reaction in the North. Abraham Lincoln's Republican Party, feeding on the majority's rage at minority ultimatums, sought the containment of the ever-demanding Southerner.

When Lincoln triumphed on this containment platform in 1860 and Southerners seceded, fugitive slaves found new ways to influence white politics. As southern white males marched out to the battlefields and northern soldiers marched into the South, cracks in the masters' power opened wider than at any time since the American Revolution. Once again, blacks seized their opportunity. An estimated 600,000 of the Confederacy's 3.5 million slaves reached the Union armies or the North. Several hundred thousand more fugitives roamed the southern countryside. Eventually almost 150,000 of these runaways joined the Union army, comprising almost 10 percent of Lincoln's soldiers. Meanwhile black compatriots demoralized the southern home front. These runaways frightened whites, disrupted food production, and caused some southern soldiers, desperately needed to repel Yankee invaders, instead to turn their guns on "family friends."

A comparison with the notorious São Paulo situation in Brazil in 1887 is here apt, for supposedly nothing in the Slave South was comparable to the internal disintegration of that large coffee province in the year before emancipation. In São Paulo an aggressive abolitionist movement led by Antônio Bento, a conspiratorial leader spiritually akin to John Brown of Harpers Ferry fame, entered slaves' cabins, pleaded with them to flee, helped them escape, and even provided them with free-labor jobs. Tens of thousands of the 150,000 Paulista slaves fled, causing slavery to disintegrate and slaveholders to capitulate to abolitionists.[4]

During the year before U.S. emancipation, fugitives' impact on the countryside was similar, the myth of São Paulo exceptionalism to the contrary. True, southern escapees, unlike São Paulo fugitives, rarely used violence unless they joined the Union army. Still, although northern soldiers offered nothing like Bento's inducements and protections, fugitives in the areas of Union invasion also fled by the tens of thousands. The southern fugitives undermined the Confederate home front, convinced many Southerners that the Confederacy must surrender, and turned southern thoughts to controlling blacks without slavery.

Meanwhile northern blacks, although still invisible in the Washington power structure, again made themselves highly visible to white policymakers. Despite the Fugitive Slave Law, President Lincoln could not long order his army to return valuable (human) property to the enemy. Nor could he long refrain from conceding that fugitive blacks who had de facto liberated themselves had a right to freedom—and a right to fight for their brothers' freedom in the Union army. The ensuing Emancipation Proclamation and Thirteenth Amendment hardly represented whites' gift of freedom to hapless black victims. Black liberation, the greatest *social* revolution in American history, had been *politically* initiated partly by fugitive slaves long before the Civil War and was brought to climax partly by black fugitives in the Union army. And the political process had itself wrenched the social institution toward producing fugitive slaves, duplicitous Samboes, and that suspicious slaveholder, whose shrill demands for more proofs of friendship ultimately brought a liberating army all too close to his fleeing non-Samboes.

Just as fugitive slaves were only one element in prewar Border South political crises, so they were only one element in the wartime collapse of the Confederacy. Whites in the Union army were more important, and Border South whites' desertions of their slaveholding brethren were as important. Perhaps equally important were Confederate women's successful appeals to their soldier husbands to come home, in part to stop fugitives from marauding. Here again, as with Harriet Beecher Stowe's alliance with prewar fugitives, disenfranchised blacks and women collaborated, this time ironically, to help impose a social revolution on politically enfranchised white males.

4

Not a single part of this epic American story of slavery, sectional crisis, Civil War, and emancipation can be understood unless social and political history are reintegrated. To write the social history of slavery without politics, as has been customary in recent studies of the Peculiar Institution, is to omit the largest part of what the New Social History most aims for: an exploration of how ethnocultural minorities make their own destinies. To ignore blacks' (invisible) participation in white political decisions is to explore only the way blacks adjusted to slavery—with songs, religion, tales, and so on—and to miss the way blacks helped destroy the adjustments, obliterate the masters' power, shatter all pretense of compromise with would-be paternalists. Conceptions that slaves were Samboes, or that non-Samboes settled for cultural space under slavery, imply that slaves could do nothing politically to end their servitude. The fugitives' resistance seems too individualistic to be political. Political resistance usually means group resistance. Fugitives, furthermore, fled *from* their enslaved brothers. That seems a strange way to free those left enchained.

But though individual flight may have been a strange route toward group liberation, governmental deterrence made it the only viable path, and fugitives triumphed down the road. "We'll soon be free," ran a typical slave spiritual, "we'll soon be free, we'll soon be free, when da Lord will call us home." Without the fugitives, those lines can be read as an adjustment to slavery, a compromise on earth with the supposed paternalist's rule, a preservation of an autonomous soul, and a praying for freedom in the afterlife. But with the fugitive slave experience acknowledged, "soon be free" instead must be read as an only temporary acquiescence in slavery in the present and a search for ways to be free on earth as soon as possible. And the slaves did search. In the American Revolution, in northern states, in the Border South, and especially in the antebellum and Civil War periods, fugitive slaves found their openings. That political triumph must be in the forefront of any viable portrait of slavery as a social institution—and in any accurate portrait of slave personality.

So too, to write the political history of the coming of the Civil War without the social history of slavery, as has been customary in the New Political History, is to omit the way this social institution generated the conditions for its own political demise. The masters had a highly suspicious personality, generated by duplicitous slaves, and a problem in social control, generated by fugitive slaves. By seeking political solutions before the Civil War, masters conceded the fugitives' potential power to invalidate any paternalistic compromise. By seceding, Confederates empowered fugitives to be forerunners of São Paulo escapees. The politics of slavery, like the politics of any explosive social problem, could never be "just politics," not to the aspiring paternalist, seeking national protection of vulnerable hinterlands, and not to the slave, fleeing to destroy would-be paternalists.

5

One case study, even so wonderful an example as slavery and abolition, cannot by itself validate a sweeping generalization. But this method of political history can illuminate a wide range of American social phenomena. The effect of American political ideology on American social ideology, for example, still lies hidden to us, for historians have long considered social ideology the source of political ideology, never vice versa. The economic determinism of Charles Beard and the economic materialism of Karl Marx both presume that political ideas and impulses come from the social structure, that politics is but a weapon of the social classes. The causal stream does often run from embattled classes to political consciousness. Precisely for that reason, political endeavor, when a reflection of ruling-class domination or underclass resistance, cannot be dismissed as "mere politics."

But sometimes, the causal stream runs the other way: from the political order, which generates the ideology, to the social classes, which must adjust to political creeds. The American political system has its own powerful worldview, including egalitarian republicanism and consent of the governed. Both the home and the school convey that mentality to the young. Just as republican political conditioning helped turn the slaveholder into an aspirant for slaves' consent, so the democratic style of thought has crept into other privileged white males' worldviews, influencing the way they deploy their capitalistic power, establish their public schools, hesitantly concede space to their feminist wives, permissively bring up their demanding children, and reluctantly admit ethnocultural minorities into the seats of social power.

Just as the impact of republican ideology on masters' concept of consenting slavery has many multicultural parallels, so many slaves' refusal to consent to slaveholders' alleged paternalism was hardly a one-time oddity. All disenfranchised Americans, whether blacks or immigrants, women or Native Americans, have ultimately won partial emancipation, not least by indirectly influencing their dominators. To trace that process of invisible goading (and later on, highly visible agitation) is to read the dispossessed as active agents into a multicultural American political history.

To recapture the tale of partial multicultural inclusion in American political decisions is not, let us be very clear, to celebrate yet another American success story. Too much pain has been mixed with progress. Too many white male elites have preferred to keep minorities outside the establishment, even to send minorities outside the nation. Too many minorities, finding their inclusion in the mainstream process infuriatingly slow and incomplete, have continued to stress their separatist ideology. Exploitation has indeed been so stifling that almost all of America's afflicted multicultural groups have considered accepting the powerful establishment opinion that they should leave this so-called land of freedom. Just as the history of slavery shows that social and political analysis must be reintegrated, so the history of race relations shows that the hope of multicultural exodus, among both blacks and whites, must be as much a part of a reintegrated American multicultural history as the hope that the mainstream could include all Americans.

In this time of urgent quest for a new American history synthesis, two sides seem locked in distorting warfare. Both concur that a viable synthesis must be multicultural in nature. But some, distressed at worldwide late-twentieth-century trends toward national disintegration and ethnic separatism, insist that our history must tell of the coming together of America. Others, distressed that exploited groups may lose their protective cultures, insist that ours is a history of multicultural separation.

The historian's job is to report what happened, not what would be politically congenial to believe happened. What really happened in the past makes the present warfare irrelevant, for both multicultural diversification and national homogenization have always been present. The dialectic between the two strains, not the victory of either, is the main theme of American multicultural history. Here as everywhere in American national history, the slavery issue was pivotal in defining an American civilization—and from the beginning. Almost all the Founding Fathers thought that the Declaration of Independence required that *all* men be liberated. But few whites wished liberated blacks to be integrated into a homogenized political or social order. Many Founding Fathers instead conceived that emancipation should be conditional on colonizing the freedmen outside the nation. In the nineteenth century, moderate antislavery men such as Henry Clay and Abraham Lincoln carried on that hope for a monoracial United States. But radical abolitionists such as William Lloyd Garrison had a color-blind vision of black equality *in* America, and the battle for America's multicultural soul was joined.

Blacks, when deciding between fighting for inclusion in the American mainstream or fighting for separation from it, increasingly understood in the 1850s that the Garrisonian campaign for color-blind homogenization was a loser, at least for the foreseeable future. Most whites offered blacks not racial egalitarianism but slavery, segregation, disenfranchisement, or colonization. The colonization option seemed particularly viable among whites, for Northerners such as Harriet Beecher Stowe no less than Lincoln favored it. The resettlement option, moreover, had worked well (so most whites thought) for Native Americans, who had been forcibly moved along their Trail of Tears to trans-Mississippi reservations.

Some Native Americans, raising another option relevant for blacks, had voluntarily embraced separatism, even accepting its resettlement extreme. If a color-blind America was not available to join and white racists coerced minorities to leave, why not consent to depart? Voluntary exodus would avoid coercion and maximize the development of a saving separatist identity. That position led the Cherokees' Elias Boudinot to fight for voluntary departure against Chief John Ross, who preferred the Native American battle for color-blind inclusion. So too, the lure of voluntary black exodus from America attracted such important black leaders as Martin R. Delany, James Holly, and Henry Highland Garnet in the 1850s.

The Ross-Boudinot showdown over Cherokee departure, like blacks' showdowns over exodus from America (and Mormons' showdowns over migration to the West), was an extreme result of the multicultural confrontation between separatists and integrationists. Among the separatists, the more numerous, less extreme leaders sought not physical departure from America but cultural departure from the oppressor. The slaves' counterculture in the quarters was a typical minority strategy, also wielded by Native Americans inside their tribes and immigrants inside ghettos and women's rights activists inside their associations. By remaining geographically inside the oppressors' area of dominion but seeking cultural isolation from the dominators, oppressed groups endeavored to develop their own protective identity.

Yet this partially separatist strategy could doubly falter, for a shrinking inside could deflect energies from an all-out war against oppressors outside, and the oppressors' cultural view beyond the enclave could infect the viewpoint within. Thus the black culture in the quarters could not be purely Afro. The worldview bore its marks of white men's attempts to acculturate blacks as well as of the blacks' African cultural traditions, just as the white culture in the Big House bore its marks of the blacks' influence. To seek merely cultural separation was in part to remain culturally integrated; and the very cultural difficulty—and the horrendous difficulty of overcoming the oppressor beyond the imperfectly purified enclave—fed dreams of total and therefore geographic separation. But by failing to battle for color-blind integration into an America truly dedicated to equality of opportunity for all its people, the ethnic separatist, whether of the geographic or cultural variety, deserted the Garrisonian fight to achieve a mainstream fit for all Americans of every shape and color.

6

To visualize how political historians might synthesize American history around multicultural battles between and among separatists and integrationists, let us glance once again at America's most famous fugitive slave. Frederick Douglass had a white father and a black mother. The mulatto usually leaned toward integration into the white mainstream and away from blacks who would separate themselves from white culture. As a slave, Douglass considered the counterculture in the quarters too black, too African, too primitive, too much an accommodation to slavery. He cherished instead his masters' white ideals. He scrubbed his voice of all black dialect and accent. In consciousness-raising sessions with fellow bondsmen, this brilliant orator, wielding the white man's voice and principles, preached individualism, self-help, freedom. In his magnificent autobiography, this mulatto integrationist spread the tale of his flight from color-obsessed slaveholders and from the supposedly over-Africanized slave culture, toward a career as northern agitator for a color-blind nation. He thus brought to climax fugitives' ability to claim white republicanism as blacks' ideology and to force the issue of slavery onto the reluctant whites' political agenda.

Subsequently, as a northern abolitionist, Douglass again usually held black separatism at bay. He decried Martin R. Delany and other black nationalists, who achieved a small but growing black following in the 1850s. These black separatists hoped that slaves' flights would not stop in the North. Blacks should flee America for a land more racially tolerant, whether in Africa, in Canada, or in the Caribbean. Against this swelling dream of black departure from America, Douglass reasserted his vision of blacks needing to run only from the South. He would not surrender the fight to raise the North to color-blind egalitarianism. "I thank God," said Douglass, "for making me a man, but Delany thanks Him for making him a *black* man."[5]

Douglass's resistance to separate black consciousness reached a personal climax in his second marriage, to a white woman. But unlike his wife, most American whites would not let loose of *their* separatist consciousness. Despite Douglass's and other abolitionists' crusades in antebellum America, slaves remained enchained, free blacks remained noncitizens, the Lincolns remained hopeful that freedmen could be colonized, and Douglass remained even to the most enlightened whites a second-class companion.

In response, a resentful Frederick Douglass sporadically considered that alternate dream: separation from American whites. When in England seeking antislavery support, Douglass, significantly, stayed long after his work was finished. In England, whites did not as often make a black hero feel like a "nigger." So too, on the eve of the Civil War, a discouraged Douglass fleetingly considered the lure of black exodus to Haiti.[6]

When the Civil War began, Douglass refocused on his characteristic integrationist strategy. His agitation for black inclusion in the Union army and his recruitment of black troops to fight inside the South, like his earlier flight toward white liberators, ultimately helped achieve black liberation. After emancipation, however, white Americans still held blacks at arm's length. Douglass's ambition for a position inside white government during Reconstruction, like the inclusion of black freedmen inside white schools or white neighborhoods, was fulfilled only to a degree. Douglass became the historic first African-American U.S. minister to a foreign nation.

His mission, however, was to Haiti, the very place he had toyed with visiting during his 1860–61 moment of darkest despair. To achieve full entrance into the white establishment, Douglass had no place to go except to a black separatist destination. Whatever a color-blind nation would have thought about Martin R. Delany and Frederick Douglass, white Americans always cast them both partly outside, as unalterably *black* men.

The painful history of the partial coming together of this multicultural nation, whether of African Americans or Native Americans or immigrants or women, always bears echoes of Frederick Douglass's travail. American national history has featured a constant dialectic of minority influence and minority despair, of white male drives to deport or segregate others and majority drives to repudiate exclusion, of minority crusades for inclusion and minority embrace of separation, of multicultural entrance into the American white male ruling system and multicultural defiance of American homogenization. No one can trace this great theme of national integration versus multicultural separation better than the political historian, for the dialectic often led to great national political crises. But if political historians are to write a new American multicultural history, they must remember that all those supposedly invisible men and women, wonderfully visible in the New Social History, must be rendered equally visible, equally agents of their own partial triumphs, in the political dialectic that has slowly made America one nation—and that still leaves this pluralistic country with many cultures, partially and proudly apart.

7

Will such a reintegrated American history flourish in the next thirty years? Historians more skillfully analyze the past than predict the future. The standard prophecies about the profession in 1960 do not invite confidence about predictions in the mid-1990s. When I entered the field, historians would have been astounded to hear that their either/or choice between conflict and consensus would swiftly seem simplistic; that a new multicultural history would tend to make histories of white males seem archaically narrow; that a New Social History would tend to make political history seem quaintly old-fashioned; that a New Political History would tend to sever the politicians' world from the society's world; that a new either/or controversy would arise over whether America has been a land of ethnic separatism or of cultural homogeneity;

and that the aspiration to synthesize American history would almost vanish.

Despite remembrance of misguided past prophecies, I would still wager that thirty years from now, our successors will call our widening of American history, to include all Americans, a historiographic triumph. Our appraisers will add, I fear, that our pathbreaking advance had the defect of its virtues: that studies of all the trees lost sight of a forest; that the compartmentalization of social and political history obscured the essence of both; and that the clash between historians of ethnic separatism and historians of mainstream homogenization was as misleading an either/or controversy as was the earlier clash over white males' consensus or conflict.

I hope that future historians will also say that the fusion of the social history of slavery with the political history of disunion and with the military history of the Civil War became a case study in how to reintegrate the fragments. The Civil War, our worst national disintegration, especially forces its historians to study the whole culture. The slaveholders' social institutions flowed from their political assumptions and vice versa; the slaves' personalities and politics flowed from the slaveholders' and vice versa; the slaveholders' military successes and failures flowed from their partially defective, partially triumphant social control; the American impulse toward ethnic separation, particularly of blacks, flowed against impulses toward national unity, particularly in a biracial Union army; and the whole socio/political/military history flowed in one piece from 1776 to 1865. To dam up any part of the flow is to miss the meaning not only of the whole but of the parts. To spread this synthetic spirit over all of American history is my next assignment. I doubt that I will labor alone.

Notes

1. The Editorial Revolution, Virginia, and the Coming of the Civil War: A Review Essay

1. William W. Freehling, "The Editorial Revolution, Virginia, and the Coming of the Civil War: A Review Essay," *Civil War History*, 16 (1970): 64–72.

2. *The Papers of John C. Calhoun*, ed. Robert L. Meriwether, W. Edwin Hemphill, and Clyde N. Wilson, 20 vols. published to date (Columbia, S.C., 1959–91); *Freedom: A Documentary History of Emancipation, 1861–1867*, ed. Ira Berlin et al., 3 vols. published to date (New York, 1983–91). Wilson and Berlin have also published important secondary accounts: Clyde N. Wilson, *Carolina Cavalier: The Life and Mind of James Johnston Pettigrew* (Athens, Ga., 1990); Ira Berlin, *Slaves without Masters: The Free Negro in the Antebellum South* (New York, 1974).

3. *Secession Debated: Georgia's Showdown in 1860*, ed. William W. Freehling and Craig M. Simpson (New York, 1992).

4. *The Papers of Thomas Jefferson*, ed. Julian P. Boyd et al., 25 vols. published to date (Princeton, N.J., 1950–92), *Pamphlets of the American Revolution, 1750–1776*, ed. Bernard Bailyn, 1 vol. published to date (Cambridge, Mass., 1965); *The Transcendentalists: An Anthology*, ed. Perry Miller (Cambridge, Mass., 1950).

5. *Proceedings of the Virginia State Convention of 1861*, ed. George H. Reese, 4 vols. (Richmond, Va., 1965).

6. Ibid., 4:144.

7. Ibid., 2:99.

8. Ibid., 1:134.

9. Ibid., 2:69.

10. Ibid., 3:106.

11. Ibid., 1:44.

12. Ibid., 1:257.
13. Ibid., 1:738.
14. Ibid., 1:757–58.
15. Ibid., 2:82.
16. Ibid., 1:62, 65–66. For Benning's similar remarks in Georgia, see *Secession Debated*, ed. Freehling and Simpson, 116–20.

2. The Founding Fathers, Conditional Antislavery, and the Nonradicalism of the American Revolution

1. William W. Freehling, "The Founding Fathers and Slavery," *American Historical Review*, 77 (1972): 81–93.

2. See, for example, Robert McColley, *Slavery and Jeffersonian Virginia* (Urbana, Ill., 1964); Donald L. Robinson, *Slavery in the Structure of American Politics, 1765–1820* (New York, 1971); William Cohen, "Thomas Jefferson and the Problem of Slavery," *Journal of American History*, 56(1969): 503–26.

3. Later writers have also extended the blame for failure to emancipate to encompass Northerners as well as Southerners. See, for example, Larry E. Tise, *Proslavery: A History of the Defense of Slavery in America, 1701–1840* (Athens, Ga., 1987), and Gary B. Nash, *Race and Revolution* (Madison, Wisc., 1990).

4. David Brion Davis, *The Problem of Slavery in the Age of Revolution, 1770–1823* (Ithaca, N.Y., 1975), 168.

5. Most recently and notably in Gordon S. Wood, *The Radicalism of the American Revolution* (New York, 1992), 186–87, 401 n. 43. For an estimate of this matter very close to my own, see Drew R. McCoy in *Journal of American History*, 79 (1993): 1563–64.

6. David Brion Davis, *The Problem of Slavery in Western Culture* (Ithaca, N.Y., 1966), and Davis, *The Problem of Slavery in the Age of Revolution*.

7. Quoted in ibid., 292.

8. A phenomenon splendidly illustrated in Winthrop D. Jordan, *White over Black: American Attitudes toward the Negro, 1550–1812* (Chapel Hill, N.C., 1968).

9. For further discussion of Jefferson's conditional antislavery position, see William W. Freehling, *The Road to Disunion*, Vol. 1, *Secessionists at Bay, 1776–1854* (New York, 1990), 123–31. For further discussion of the black-removal condition, see below, ch. 7.

10. For an excellent discussion of this episode, see Drew R. McCoy, *The Last of the Fathers: James Madison and the Republican Legacy* (New York, 1989), 310–16.

11. All demographic statistics in this essay derive from *The Statistics of the Population of the United States*, comp. Francis A. Walker (Washington, D.C., 1872), 11–74, and U.S. Bureau of the Census, *A Century of Pop-*

ulation Growth; From the First Census of the United States to the Twelfth, 1790–1900 (Washington, D.C., 1909).

12. The classic study of emancipation in the North is Arthur Zilversmit, *The First Emancipation: The Abolition of Slavery in the North* (Chicago, 1967).

13. For an excellent discussion of the Pennsylvania episode, see Gary B. Nash and Jean R. Soderlund, *Freedom by Degrees: Emancipation and Its Aftermath in Pennsylvania* (New York, 1991).

14. For a fine recent study of the New York phase, see Shane White, *Somewhat More Independent: The End of Slavery in New York City, 1770–1810* (Athens, Ga., 1991).

15. Claudia Dale Golden, "The Economics of Emancipation," *Journal of Economic History*, 33 (1973): 70.

16. Torrey Stephen Whitman, "Slavery, Manumission, and Free Black Workers in Early National Baltimore," Ph.D. diss., Johns Hopkins University, 1993, expertly develops these themes. On the broader Maryland milieu, see Barbara J. Fields, *Slavery and Freedom on the Middle Ground: Maryland during the Nineteenth Century* (New Haven, Conn., 1985).

17. Joseph C. Burke, "The Pro-Slavery Argument in the First Congress," *Duquesne Review*, 16 (1969): 3–15; Howard Ohline, "Slavery, Economics, and Congressional Politics," *Journal of Southern History*, 46 (1980): 335–60; Richard Newman, "The First Gag Rule," forthcoming. I am grateful to Mr. Newman for allowing me to use his excellent essay before its publication.

18. Quoted in Merrill D. Peterson, *Thomas Jefferson and the New Nation: A Biography* (New York, 1970), 283.

19. William Grayson to James Monroe, August 8, 1787, in *Letters of Members of the Continental Congress*, ed. Edmund C. Burnett, 8 vols. (Washington, D.C., 1921–36), 8:631–33. The following account of the Northwest Ordinance and its Illinois aftermath has been much influenced by the salutary notes of cynicism in Peter Onuf's fine *Statehood and Union: A History of the Northwest Ordinance* (Indianapolis, Ind., 1987) and in Paul Finkelman's several illuminating essays, especially "Slavery and the Northwest Ordinance. A Study in Ambiguity," *Journal of the Early Republic*, 6 (1986): 343–70, and "Evading the Ordinance: The Persistence of Bondage in Indiana and Illinois," *Journal of the Early Republic*, 9 (1989): 21–51. But for a cautionary note, see David Brion Davis's judicious "The Significance of Excluding Slavery from the Old Northwest in 1787," *Indiana Magazine of History*, 84 (1988): 75–89.

20. Jefferson to John Holmes, April 22, 1820, in *The Writings of Thomas Jefferson*, ed. Paul Leicester Ford, 10 vols. (New York, 1892–99), 10:157–58.

21. Jefferson to Jared Sparks, February 24, 1824, ibid., 10:289–92.

22. Phillip J. Staudenraus, *The African Colonization Movement, 1816–1865* (New York, 1961).

23. The theme is discussed at length in William W. Freehling, *Prelude to Civil War: The Nullification Controversy in South Carolina, 1816–1836* (New York, 1966).

24. See, for example, Paul Finkelman's otherwise illuminating "Slavery and the Constitutional Convention: Making a Covenant with Death," in *Beyond Confederation: Origins of the Constitution and National Identity*, ed. Richard Beeman et al. (Chapel Hill, N.C., 1987), 188–225.

25. *A Compilation of the Messages and Papers of the Presidents*, comp. James D. Richardson, 10 vols. (Washington, D.C., 1900), 1:408.

26. See, for example, Nash, *Race and Revolution*.

27. David Eltis, *Economic Growth and the Ending of the Transatlantic Slave Trade* (New York, 1987).

28. John Jay to the English Anti-Slavery Society, [1788], in *The Correspondence and Public Papers of John Jay*, ed. Henry P. Johnston, 4 vols. (New York, 1890–93), 3:342.

29. See below, pp. 98–100.

30. Jack P. Greene, *Pursuits of Happiness: The Social Development of Early Modern British Colonies and the Formation of American Culture* (Chapel Hill, N.C., 1988).

31. Jefferson to John Holmes, April 22, 1820, in *Jefferson's Writings*, ed. Ford, 10:157–58.

3. Denmark Vesey's Antipaternalistic Reality

1. William W. Freehling, "Denmark Vesey's Peculiar Reality," in *New Perspectives on Race and Slavery in America: Essays in Honor of Kenneth M. Stampp*, ed. Robert H. Abzug and Stephen E. Maizlish (Lexington, Ky., 1986), 25–50.

2. For elaboration and documentation of this overall view of slavery, see my *The Road to Disunion, Vol. I, Secessionists at Bay, 1776–1860* (New York, 1990), chs. 4–5.

3. See below, pp. 97–8.

4. See below, ch. 4.

5. A point nicely made in Norrece T. Jones, Jr., *Born a Child of Freedom Yet a Slave: Mechanisms of Control and Strategies of Resistance in Antebellum South Carolina* (Hanover, Conn., 1990).

6. Unless otherwise noted, my narrative of the Vesey plot is drawn from Lionel H. Kennedy and Thomas Parker, *An Official Report of the Trials of Sundry Negroes, Charged with an Attempt to Raise an Insurrection . . .* (Charleston, S.C., 1822) and from *Denmark Vesey: The Slave Conspiracy of 1822*, ed. Robert S. Starobin (Englewood Cliffs, N.J., 1970). The best full-length book is John Lofton, *Insurrection in South Carolina: The Turbulent World of Denmark Vesey* (Yellow Springs, Ohio, 1964). The most discerning essay is Robert S. Starobin, "Denmark Vesey's Slave Conspiracy of 1822: A Study in Rebellion and Repression," in *American Slavery: The Question of Resistance*, ed. John H. Bracey et al. (Belmont, Calif.,

1971), 142–57. For the perspective of superb studies of parallel conspiracies, see James Sidbury, "Gabriel's World: Race Relations in Richmond, Virginia, 1750–1810," Ph.D. diss., Johns Hopkins University, 1991, and Winthrop D. Jordan, *Tumult and Silence at Second Creek: An Inquiry into a Civil War Slave Conspiracy* (Baton Rouge, La., 1993).

7. See, for example, C. B. Marryat, *Second Series of a Diary in America* (Philadelphia, 1840), 255.

8. Petition of Charleston citizens to the state legislature, 1822, in *Denmark Vesey*, ed. Starobin, 141–42.

9. A point well made in Eugene Genovese, *From Rebellion to Revolution: Afro-American Slaves in the Making of the New World* (Baton Rouge, La., 1979), 8–10.

10. Confession of Bacchus, the slave of Mr. [benjamin] Hammett, in William and Benjamin Hammett Papers, Duke University Library, printed in *Denmark Vesey*, ed. Starobin, 61–65, especially 61.

11. Kennedy and Parker, *Trial of Sundry Negroes*, 75.

12. John Potter to Langdon Cheves, June 29, 1822, Cheves Papers, South Carolina Historical Society, Charleston, printed in *Denmark Vesey*, ed. Starobin, 76.

13. Potter to Cheves, July 10, 16, 20, 1822, Cheves Papers, printed in ibid., 77–79.

14. As reported in Martha Proctor Richardson to My Dear James, August 7, 1822, Arnold-Screven Papers, Southern Historical Collection, University of North Carolina, Chapel Hill, printed in ibid., 83.

15. Richard C. Wade, "The Vesey Plot: A Reconsideration," *Journal of Southern History*, 30 (1964): 144–61. For a more detailed and technical disproof of Wade's methods than now seems to me necessary, see Freehling, "Vesey's Reality," in *New Perspectives*, ed. Abzug and Maizlish, 36–38.

16. For the two pretrial confessions, see *Denmark Vesey*, ed. Starobin, 61–66.

17. For the manuscript trial record, see Document B, copies 1 and 2, accompanying Governor Thomas Bennett's Ms. Message no. 2 to the Senate and House of Representatives, Legislative Papers, South Carolina Archives, Columbia.

18. Kennedy and Parker, *Trial of Sundry Negroes*, iii.

19. Ibid., 107.

20. Richard Wade's mode of phrasing implied that his favorite contemporaries *might* have concurred in his "loose talk" thesis. "The Governor *probably* believed in a plot of some kind," wrote Wade ("The Vesey Plot," 153; emphasis mine). But Bennett *did* believe in a "plot of some kind"; he was so convinced of certain conspirators' guilt that he refused to grant them executive clemency (see Ms. Message no. 2, pp. 8–10). Again, when summing up Bennett's niece's opinion, Wade wrote that "*if she believed a conspiracy existed at all*," she thought it exaggerated ("The Vesey Plot," 152; emphasis mine). But the lady *did* believe those hung

"were guilty most certainly" (Anna Hayes Johnson to Elizabeth E. W. Haywood, July 24, 1822, printed in *Denmark Vesey*, ed. Starobin, 74). Any balanced account of the Charlestonians' controversy over Vesey's conspiracy must concede that differences over its extent occurred within a unanimous concurrence that more than "loose talk" happened.

21. Kennedy and Parker, *Trials of Sundry Negroes*, 63.

22. Ibid., 66 *n*.

23. Axson's cross-examination, briefly summarized in the published court record, can be followed more fully in the manuscript trial transcript. See Document B, copy 2, accompanying Gov. Thomas Bennett's Ms. Message no. 2 to the Senate and House of Representatives, Legislative Papers, South Carolina Archives, June-July trials, pp. 10–11.

24. Kennedy and Parker, *Trial of Sundry Negroes*, 68.

25. Anna Hayes Johnson to Elizabeth E. W. Haywood, June 23, 1822, Ernest Haywood Papers, Southern Historical Collection, printed in *Denmark Vesey*, ed. Starobin, 72.

26. Bennett's Ms. Message no. 2, pp. 14, 17.

27. Just as Bennett's Ms. Message no. 2 is the best summary of his (minority) position, so the best summaries of the majority position are in Kennedy and Parker, *Trials of Sundry Negroes*, 17–60, and in James Hamilton, Jr., *An Account of the Late Intended Insurrection* (Charleston, S.C., 1822). Justice William Johnson of the United States Supreme Court, Bennett's brother-in-law, was the only prominent leader who publicly supported the governor. For an excellent account of Johnson's position and actions, see Donald G. Morgan, *Justice William Johnson, the First Dissenter* (Columbia, S.C., 1954), 126–40.

28. Kennedy and Parker, *Trial of Sundry Negroes*, 36, 55.

29. Bennett's Ms. Message no. 2, pp. 15–16.

30. Ibid., p. 14.

31. Kennedy and Parker, *Trial of Sundry Negroes*, 24–26.

32. Ibid., 25, 27.

33. Ibid., 31–34.

34. Bennett's Ms. Message no. 2, p. 14.

35. Kennedy and Parker, *Trial of Sundry Negroes*, 37–38.

36. For the relevant laws, see ibid., vii–xv.

37. Bennett's Ms. Message no. 2, p. 4.

38. Kennedy and Parker, *Trial of Sundry Negroes*, vii.

39. Ibid., 61–87.

40. Robert Y. Hayne to Bennett, July 1, 1822, filed with Bennett's Ms. Message no. 2; Bennett's Ms. Message no. 2, pp. 4–7.

41. Ibid., 5–8.

42. Bennett to Richard I. Manning, April 11, 1826, Williams-Chesnut-Manning Papers, on loan to the South Caroliniana Library, University of South Carolina, Columbia.

43. Kennedy and Parker, *Trial of Sundry Negroes*, vii.

44. Ibid., vi.
45. Ibid., 125, 163.
46. Bennett's Ms. Message no. 2, pp. 9–10.
47. Kennedy and Parker, *Trial of Sundry Negroes*, 56, 110, 174–75.
48. Document B, copy 1, pp. 42–43; Document B, copy 2, June-July trials, pp. 23–46, August trials, pp. 1–8, all accompanying Bennett's Ms. Message no. 2.
49. See n. 48 above.
50. Kennedy and Parker, *Trial of Sundry Negroes*, 183–88.
51. Ibid., 59; Bennett's Ms. Message no. 2, p. 11.
52. *Charleston City Gazette,* December 4, 1822; *Charleston Mercury,* December 11, 1822. The anti-Bennett feeling was more lopsided than even the 2:1 numbers indicate, because many of the thirty five voting against tabling wished an investigation to clear the court of Bennett's charges. *Charleston City Gazette,* December 14, 1822.
53. For Hayne's message and the legislature's response, see Howell M. Henry, *Police Control of the Slave in South Carolina* (Emory, Va., 1914), 59–64.
54. Document B accompanying Bennett's Ms. Message no. 2, copy 2, June-July trials, p. 21.
55. Hamilton, *Account of the Insurrection,* 4.

4. Defective Paternalism: James Henley Thornwell's Mysterious Antislavery Moment

1. William W. Freehling, "James Henley Thornwell's Mysterious Antislavery Moment," *Journal of Southern History,* 57 (1991): 383–406.
2. Although this question about Thornwell has never been fully addressed, the cleric is no longer the most neglected important mid-nineteenth-century southern intellectual. Studies by Elizabeth Fox-Genovese, Eugene D. Genovese, and Jack P. Maddex will appear soon, and informative monographs have been published recently. The fullest modern biography is James Oscar Farmer, Jr., *The Metaphysical Confederacy: James Henley Thornwell and the Synthesis of Southern Values* (Macon, Ga., 1986). Older but still useful, especially for its Thornwell letters, is Benjamin Morgan Palmer, *The Life and Letters of James Henley Thornwell* . . . (Richmond, Va., 1875). My favorite essay on Thornwell, nicely catching the clergyman's proslavery apprehensions from a different angle than mine, is Charles C. Bishop, "The Pro-slavery Argument Reconsidered: James Henley Thornwell, Millennial Abolitionist," *South Carolina Historical Magazine,* 73 (1972): 18–26. Useful material for my purposes is also in Marilyn J. Westerkamp's excellent "James Henley Thornwell, Pro-slavery Spokesman within a Calvinist Faith," ibid., 87 (1986): 49–64, and in H. Shelton Smith's relentless "The Church and the Social Order in the Old

South as Interpreted by James H. Thornwell," *Church History*, 7 (1938): 115–24.

3. While I differ with the Geneveses about aspects of this subject, I applaud some of their recent contentions, especially that the Old South had a subtle intellectual life, not merely a simplistic polemical life, and that Christian discourse, especially Thornwell's, was at the heart of the sophisticated mentality. See Eugene D. Genovese, *"Slavery Ordained of God": The Southern Slaveholders' View of Biblical History and Modern Politics* (Gettysburg, Pa., 1985); Eugene D. Genovese and Elizabeth Fox-Genovese, "The Religious Ideals of Southern Slave Society," *Georgia Historical Quarterly*, 70 (1986): 1–16; and Fox-Genovese and Genovese, "The Divine Sanction of Social Order: Religious Foundations of the Slaveholders' World View," *Journal of the American Academy of Religion*, 45 (1987): 211–33.

4. For excellent analyses of the broader evangelical proslavery movement, see Anne C. Loveland, *Southern Evangelicals and the Social Order, 1800–1860* (Baton Rouge, La., 1980); David T. Bailey, *Shadow on the Church: Southwestern Evangelical Religion and the Issue of Slavery, 1783–1860* (Ithaca, N.Y., 1985); H. Shelton Smith, *In His Image, But . . . Racism in Southern Religion, 1780–1910* (Durham, N.C., 1972); E. Brooks Holifield, *The Gentlemen Theologians: American Theology in Southern Culture, 1795–1860* (Durham, N.C., 1978); and Edward R. Crowther, "Holy Honor: Sacred and Secular in the Old South," *Journal of Southern History*, 68 (1992): 619–36.

5. Palmer, *Thornwell*, 4.

6. Thornwell to Robbins, June 30, 1829, ibid., 50.

7. Thornwell to Robbins, January 1829, ibid., 47–48.

8. Ibid., 48.

9. Thornwell to A. H. Peques, August 14, 1834, and Thornwell to his wife, June 16, 1841, ibid., 117–18, 167–70.

10. On Thornwell's personal appearance and characteristics, see ibid., 135, 566–69, and Farmer, *Metaphysical Confederacy*, 59–60.

11. Thornwell, "Report on Slavery," *Southern Presbyterian Review*, 5 (1852): 380–92.

12. Thornwell, "The Religious Instruction of the Black Population," ibid., 1 (1847): 89–120, especially 89. The Scriptural quote is from Colossians 4:1.

13. Thornwell, "Slavery and the Religious Instruction of the Coloured Population," *Southern Presbyterian Review*, 4 (1850): 105–41, especially 135. This sermon was Thornwell's greatest proslavery statement and among the two or three masterpieces of the genre. No student of the Old South should miss its resourceful, anguished polemics. It was also published as a pamphlet, *The Rights and the Duties of Masters . . .* (Charleston, S.C., 1850). For shrewd comments on its importance, see Craig M. Simpson, *A Good Southerner: The Life of Henry A. Wise of Virginia*

(Chapel Hill, N.C., 1985), 338–39. Mitchell Snay, "American Thought and Southern Distinctiveness: The Southern Clergy and the Sanctification of Slavery," *Civil War History,* 35 (1989): 311–28, especially 315–19, analyses the sermon's importance from another perspective. For a broader discussion of sanctification and amelioration, see Jack P. Maddex, Jr., "A Paradox of Christian Amelioration: Proslavery Ideology and Church Ministries to Slaves," in *The Southern Enigma: Essays on Race, Class, and Folk Culture,* ed. Walter J. Fraser and Winfred B. Moore, Jr. (Westport, Conn., 1983), 105–17.

14. Thornwell, "Slavery and the Religious Instruction," 114.

15. Thornwell, "Religious Instruction of the Black Population," 108.

16. Thornwell made these points in almost every essay but especially powerfully in "The Baptism of Servants," *Southern Presbyterian Review,* 1 (1847), 64–102. The slave marriage problem, including South Carolina's, is illuminated in Michael Tadman, *Speculators and Slaves: Masters, Traders, and Slaves in the Old South* (Madison, Wisc., 1989).

17. Thornwell, "Slavery and the Religious Instruction," 138. I am indebted to Professor Michael McCormick of Harvard University for the translation, placed here in brackets.

18. Ibid., 116, 120.

19. Ibid., 121.

20. The prevalence of the Paley definition is perhaps the most prominent of the unanalyzed complexities in the proslavery argument—unanalyzed because of the misconception that the polemic was boring and simplistic. Almost half a century ago, William Sumner Jenkins spotted the Paley phenomenon, but as often happened with Jenkins, the good idea lay hidden in a numbing catalog of arguments. See Jenkins, *Pro-Slavery Thought in the Old South* (Chapel Hill, N.C., 1935), 108. In more recent times only Kenneth S. Greenberg has emphasized the limited slavery argument, and as can happen with Greenberg, the superb emphasis is dulled by an analysis overly focused on republican conceptions. See Greenberg, *Masters and Statesmen: The Political Culture of American Slavery* (Baltimore, 1985), 92–96. Greenberg is right that absolute power collided with the republican mentality and that Paley-style limited slavery was more congenial to democrats. But the Paley definition was far more the property of evangelical than of secular proslavery writers, and the problem distressing clerics was religious, not political: the puppet rendered will-less by absolute power has no moral responsibility for his conduct or his salvation. Among the many proslavery writers who used the Paley definition were Edward B. Bryan, Thornton Stringfellow, Albert Taylor Bledsoe, William J. Grayson, and William A. Smith.

21. *Domestic Slavery Considered as a Scriptural Institution: In a Correspondence between the Reverend Richard Fuller . . . and the Reverend Francis Wayland . . .* (New York and Boston, 1845), especially 7–9, 23–24, 139, 152, 155, 234.

22. Thornwell, "Slavery and the Religious Instruction," 120–22.

23. Ibid., 122.

24. Thornwell, "Our National Sins . . . ," in *Fast Day Sermons: or the Pulpit on the State of the Country* (New York, 1861), 9–56, especially 46–49.

25. Thornwell, "Slavery and the Religious Instruction," 128. Fitzhugh's revealing rejection of slavery for U.S. whites is discussed below, pp. 98–100.

26. Thornwell, "Religious Instruction of the Black Population," 103, 108.

27. Thornwell, "Slavery and the Religious Instruction," 127–28.

28. For some choice examples, see William A. Smith, *Lectures on the Philosophy and Practice of Slavery* (Nashville, Tenn., 1856), 276–328; H. N. McTyeire, C. F. Sturgis, and A. T. Holmes, *Duties of Masters to Servants* . . . (Charleston, S.C., 1851).

29. Which is not to deny that secular ambitions influenced Drew Gilpin Faust's smaller, less influential circle of Virginia–South Carolina lay proslavery writers. See Faust, *A Sacred Circle: The Dilemma of the Intellectual in the Old South, 1840–1860* (Baltimore, 1977). Still, for understanding the wider proslavery argument, I prefer Faust's emphasis on Christian stewardship in her splendid "Evangelicalism and the Meaning of the Proslavery Argument: The Reverend Thornton Stringfellow of Virginia," *Virginia Magazine of History and Biography*, 85 (1977): 3–17.

30. Bertram Wyatt-Brown's "Modernizing Southern Slavery: The Proslavery Argument Reinterpreted," in *Region, Race and Reconstruction: Essays in Honor of C. Vann Woodward*, ed. J. Morgan Kousser and James M. McPherson (New York, 1982), 27–49, shrewdly describes proslavery as an attempt to improve no less than to defend slavery. My other favorite essay on the motives behind proslavery, Clarence L. Mohr's "Slaves and White Churches in Confederate Georgia," in *Masters and Slaves in the House of the Lord: Race and Religion in the American South, 1740–1870*, ed. John B. Boles (Lexington, Ky., 1988), 153–72, makes the same point for Georgia. David Donald's "The Proslavery Argument Reconsidered," *Journal of Southern History*, 37 (1971): 3–18, emphasizes that proslavery polemics contained antislavery criticisms and then puts the critique in an exclusively secular context. I think Donald underestimates the evangelical context, but his focus on lay writers and their concerns demonstrates that apprehensions about internal defects transcended the gloom-and-doom clerics.

31. A point made very well in Eugene D. Genovese, *Roll, Jordan, Roll: The World the Slaves Made* (New York, 1974).

32. This position, recently a boldly revisionist one, now assuming some hint of unexamined stereotype, is elaborated in Genovese, *Roll, Jordan, Roll*; Mechal Sobel, *Trabelin' On: The Slave Journey to an Afro-Baptist Faith* (Westport, Conn., 1979); Sobel, *The World They Made To-*

gether: Black and White Values in Eighteenth-Century Virginia (Princeton, N.J., 1987); Albert J. Raboteau, *Slave Religion: The "Invisible Institution" in the Antebellum South* (New York, 1978); and Sterling Stuckey, *Slave Culture: Nationalist Theory and the Foundations of Black America* (New York, 1987).

33. For a fine example, embedded in one of the best essays on proslavery Christianity, see Donald G. Mathews, "Charles Colcock Jones and the Southern Evangelical Crusade to Form a Biracial Community," *Journal of Southern History*, 41 (1975): 299–320, especially 318.

34. Thornwell to his wife, August 25, 1860, in Palmer, *Thornwell*, 459–61.

35. Behind the preceding paragraphs stands *Masters and Slaves in the House of the Lord*, edited by John B. Boles. All the essays, but especially Clarence L. Mohr's account of Frederick Douglass's conversion, Randy J. Spark's and Robert L. Hall's statistics on black memberships in white churches, and Blake Touchstone's many examples of white missions to slaves, show that some blacks *did* worship, in a somewhat meaningful way, in white houses of the Lord. Black churches probably provided more meaningful experiences for those slaves who enjoyed the opportunity to compare. Blacks certainly voted that way with their feet after 1863. But I see no way around accepting the prevalence of alternative religious experiences for blacks in slavery times, now that Boles and his colleagues have presented their extensive evidence.

36. Thornwell to R. J. Breckinridge, October 20, 1847, in Palmer, *Thornwell*, 301.

37. Thornwell, "Slavery and the Religious Instruction," 138–39.

38. Ibid., 137–38.

39. Ibid., 123.

40. Thornwell, "Religious Instruction of the Black Population," 110. For a broader discussion of Thornwell's subtle views on church and state, see yet another of Jack P. Maddex, Jr.'s, fine essays on Presbyterianism and proslavery: "From Theocracy to Spirituality: The Southern Presbyterian Reversal on Church and State," *Journal of Presbyterian History*, 54 (1976): 438–57.

41. Thornwell private journal, entry for May 14, 1836, in Palmer, *Thornwell*, 140.

42. Thornwell to Dr. Hooper, March 8, 1850, ibid., 477–78.

43. Thornwell to Dr. Hooper, March 8, 1850, and Thornwell to Mathew J. Williams, July 17, 1850, both in Palmer, *Thornwell*, 477–78.

44. Thornwell to his wife, August 15, 1860, ibid., 457. For an intriguing parallel view, also from an important South Carolina preacher who thought the South errant and the North more so, see James H. Elliott, "Are These His Doings," *Charleston Triweekly Courier*, November 24, 1860, p. 4. I am indebted to Craig M. Simpson for the reference.

45. Reported by Palmer in *Thornwell*, 482–83. For a similar interpre-

tation of this incident, see Eugene D. Genovese, *The Slaveholders' Dilemma: Freedom and Progress in Southern Conservative Thought, 1820–1860* (Columbia, S.C., 1992), 59–63.

46. James O. Farmer, Jr., to the author, September 8, 1989.

47. William Sumner Jenkins's again underrated *Pro-Slavery*, 217–18, illuminates slavery's defenders' internal debate over the institution's permanence, but his fine insight, as usual, gets lost in the thicket of his encyclopedic text. For some prime examples of key Upper South proslavery polemicists who suspected or believed that slavery was a *temporary* blessing, see William A. Smith, *Lectures on . . . Slavery*, 123, 156, 182–83, 216, 246–47, 256; Richard Fuller, *Domestic Slavery Considered as a Scriptural Institution*, 9; Fuller, *Our Duty to the African Race . . .* (Baltimore, 1851), 7, 9, 14; George D. Armstrong, *The Christian Doctrine of Slavery* (New York, 1857), 134–36; Thornton Stringfellow, "The Bible Argument . . . ," in *Cotton Is King, and Proslavery Arguments*, ed. E. N. Elliott (Augusta, Ga., 1860), 546; and Albert Taylor Bledsoe, *An Essay on Liberty and Slavery* (Philadelphia, 1856), 54–55, 139.

48. See Bishop, "Thornwell: Millennial Abolitionist," and Jack P. Maddex, Jr., "Proslavery Millennialism: Social Eschatology in Antebellum Southern Calvinism," *American Quarterly*, 31 (1979): 46–62.

49. Lawrence T. McDonnell, "Struggle against Suicide: James Henry Hammond and the Secession of South Carolina," *Southern Studies*, 22 (1983): 109–37.

50. Thornwell to James Gillespie, November 19, 1861, in Palmer, *Thornwell*, 497–98.

51. "Our National Sins," in *Fast Day Sermons*, 9–56. See also the sigh of relief in Thornwell to J. Leighton Wilson, January 7, 1861, in Palmer, *Thornwell*, 486–87.

52. The moment the slavocracy began to break apart throws much light on long-standing half-hidden attitudes of proslavery preachers no less than of slaves, and for the same reason: pressures to cheer planter paternalism were dissolving. Ministers' escalating frankness is analyzed in Bell I. Wiley, "The Movement to Humanize the Institution of Slavery during the Confederacy," *Emory University Quarterly*, 5 (1949): 207–20; and more recently in Drew Gilpin Faust, *The Creation of Confederate Nationalism: Ideology and Identity in the Civil War South* (Baton Rouge, La., 1988), 73–81. The great primary source is Calvin H. Wiley, *Scriptural Views of National Trials . . .* (Greensboro, N.C., 1863).

53. Quoted in Mohr, "Slaves in White Churches," 167.

54. I am indebted to Tulane professors Lawrence N. Powell, for warning me that this broader question could not be evaded, and Clarence L. Mohr, for suggesting some shrewd answers.

55. The historiography of "guiltomania," to use Eugene Genovese's disparaging term, has been surveyed in Gaines M. Foster, "Guilt over Slavery: A Historiographical Analysis," *Journal of Southern History*, 56 (1990): 665–94; and in Genovese, *The World the Slaveholders Made: Two Essays*

in *Interpretation* (New York, 1969), 144–50. Foster, on p. 673, discusses my own "guiltomaniac" position in *Prelude to Civil War*, ch. 3, but omits mention of my almost immediate second thoughts in the *New York Review of Books*, 17 (1971): 36. Twenty years later, I pray that a thesis of modest utility has not been destroyed by its early proponents' immodest claims. As I confess in my *The Road to Disunion*, Vol. 1, *Secessionists at Bay, 1776–1860* (New York, 1990), 597–98, my own former claim that low-country South Carolinians were especially guilty and, for that reason, especially fanatical about nullification now seems to me especially underwhelming. Other historians' thesis that "guilt" was the only or the main cause of the South's propulsion to secession, or eventual loss of will to fight on the battlefield also seems to me an exaggeration. But the peculiar way the religious proslavery argument was shaped and received, in this overwhelmingly Christian society, indicates a degree of unease, if not about slavery per se, then about certain slaveholder practices (to repeat slaveholders' sacred distinction, one that the more advanced clerics came to consider a distinction without a difference if the unholy practices continued). Those anti-Christian practices, especially devastated slave marriages, were exactly the ones Northerners, especially Harriet Beecher Stowe, harped on. The slaveholders' inflamed response in part stemmed, I think undeniably, from the human propensity to rage especially at the critics who one knows are a little right.

56. Palmer, *Thornwell*, 519–21.
57. Thornwell to his wife, July 6, 1862, ibid., 518–19.
58. Ibid., 523.

5. Beyond Racial Limits: Paternalism over Whites in the Thought of Calhoun and Fitzhugh

1. William W. Freehling, "Spoilsmen and Interests in the Thought and Career of John C. Calhoun," *Journal of American History*, 52 (1965): 25–42.
2. *The Works of John C. Calhoun*, ed. Richard K. Crallé, 6 vols. (New York, 1851–57): 1:3, 16, 31–34.
3. Ibid., 1:38–39, 65.
4. Ibid., 1:68–69.
5. Ibid., 1:49.
6. Ibid., 1:18.
7. Ibid., 1:40–44. See also 17–24, 37–39.
8. Ibid., 1:17.
9. Although Calhoun only hinted at this point in the *Disquisition*, he stressed it elsewhere. See, for example, Calhoun to Armisted Burt, December 24, 1838, *The Papers of John C. Calhoun*, ed. Robert L. Meriwether, W. Edwin Hemphill, and Clyde N. Wilson, 20 vols. published to date (Columbia, S.C., 1959–91), 14:98–99.

10. *Calhoun's Works*, ed. Crallé, 1:17–18.

11. Ibid., 1:49–50.

12. Ibid., 1:46.

13. For a splendid development of Jacksonian egalitarianism, for white men only, as the prime basis of the slaveholders' mainstream politics, see J. Mills Thornton, III, *Politics and Power in a Slave Society: Alabama, 1800–1860* (Baton Rouge, La., 1978). Thornton is right about *most* southern politicians, but his explanatory model leaves insufficient room for the few elitists who despised mainstream egalitarianism. I quarrel more with Lacy Ford's attempt to apply the Thornton thesis to South Carolina, because paternalistic elitism for white men, too, was more powerful in South Carolina than in Alabama. We see that South Carolina exceptionalism in the pivotal case of Calhoun's patriarchal opposition to Andrew Jackson's egalitarian version of slaveholder republicanism. See Ford's otherwise fine *Origins of Southern Radicalism: The South Carolina Upcountry, 1800–1860* (New York, 1988).

14. *The Federalist*, ed. Benjamin Fletcher Wright (Cambridge, Mass., 1961), 129–36.

15. *Ibid.*, 134. See also 111, 271–72, 441, 459, 487–88.

16. Quoted in Richard Hofstadter, *The American Political Tradition and the Men Who Made It* (New York, 1948), 13n.

17. *A Compilation of the Messages and Papers of the Presidents*, comp. James D. Richardson, 10 vols. (New York, 1900), 1:218–19. For an excellent discussion of Calhoun and the Founding Fathers, see J. William Harris, "Last of the Classical Republicans: An Interpretation of John C. Calhoun," *Civil War History*, 30 (1984): 255–67.

18. Calhoun to Charles Fischer, August 1, 1823, *Calhoun's Papers*, ed. Wilson, 8:203.

19. Calhoun to Micah Sterling, August 12, 1827, ibid., 10:298–99.

20. Calhoun to John McLean, September 22, 1829, ibid., 11:75–76.

21. Calhoun to a committee in Anderson District, South Carolina, September 5, 1836, *ibid.*, 13:284.

22. *Calhoun's Works*, ed. Crallé, 5:148–90, especially 163.

23. Calhoun to Armisted Burt, December 24, 1838, *Calhoun's Papers*, ed. Wilson, 14:498–99.

24. James Hamilton, Jr., to Stephen Miller, August 9, 1830, Chesnut-Manning-Miller Papers, South Carolina Historical Society, Charleston.

25. Quoted in John B. O'Neall, *Biographical Sketches of the Bench and Bar of South Carolina*, 2 vols. (Charleston, S.C., 1859), 1:181.

26. The Carolina statesmen did indulge in extensive public debates during moments of high excitement. They always used these political methods with revealing misgivings, however. During the Nullification Controversy, for example, the nullifiers created statewide political "associations." But they defended these political clubs only as an extraordinary response to an unusual crisis and disbanded them immediately after the

tariff was lowered. The more conservative Unionists feared the demagoguery and corruption of parties so deeply that they refused to form rival political clubs and thereby handed the nullifiers a decisive advantage. For extended discussion, see William W. Freehling, *Prelude to Civil War: The Nullification Controversy in South Carolina, 1816–1836* (New York, 1966), 235–54.

27. Calhoun to A. H. Pemberton, November 19, 1838, *Calhoun's Papers*, ed. Wilson, 14:472–75.

28. The fullest biography of Fitzhugh is Harvey Wish, *George Fitzhugh: Conservative of the Old South* (Charlottesville, 1938).

29. Quoted in C. Vann Woodward's helpful introduction to George Fitzhugh, *Cannibals All! or Slaves without Masters*, ed. Woodward (Cambridge, Mass., 1960), xii.

30. Ibid., 239.

31. Ibid., 246, 298; *De Bow's Review*, 22 (1857): 570; George Fitzhugh, *Sociology for the South, or the Failure of Free Labor Society* (Richmond, Va., 1854), 46, 246, 298.

32. *De Bow's Review*, 22 (1857): 422–23; George Fitzhugh to William Lloyd Garrison, December 10, 1856, Garrison Papers, Boston Public Library; Fitzhugh to A. Hogeboom, January 14, 1856, in Fitzhugh, *Cannibals All*, 104; Fitzhugh, *Sociology*, 94, 225.

33. Fitzhugh, *Cannibals All*, 40. For Fitzhugh's fullest development of the point, see ibid., 199–203.

34. *De Bow's Review*, 25 (1858): 655–61; 30(1861): 404; 23 (1857): 337–49.

35. Fitzhugh, *Sociology*, 45; Fitzhugh, *Cannibals All*, 199; *De Bow's Review*, 22 (1857): 633–44; 23 (1857): 337–49.

36. Fitzhugh, *Sociology*, 264, 84–88.

37. Fitzhugh, *Cannibals All*, 187, 199.

38. *Richmond Enquirer*, September 12, 1856.

39. *De Bow's Review*, 26 (1859): 121–35, especially 124–25.

40. Ibid., 26 (1859): 125; 27 (1859): 161–62.

41. Ibid., 27 (1859): 159–78.

42. Fitzhugh, *Sociology*, 95, 171.

43. Fitzhugh to Gerrit Smith, August 14, 1850, Smith Papers, Syracuse University, Syracuse, New York. The whole corpus of Fitzhugh's correspondence with Smith is an eye-opener, in this vein.

44. Fitzhugh to George Frederick Holmes, April 11, 1855, Holmes Papers, Duke University Library.

45. A critical proslavery theorist in this vein was Henry Hughes, author of *Treatise on Sociology: Theoretical and Practical* (Philadelphia, 1854). For shrewd comments on Hughes and on the underappreciated impulse toward state regulation of slaveholders which he shared with Thornwell, Fitzhugh, and many others, see Bertram Wyatt-Brown, "Modernizing Southern Slavery: The Proslavery Argument Reinterpreted," in

Region, Race and Reconstruction: Essays in Honor of C. Vann Woodward, ed. J. Morgan Kousser and James M. McPherson (New York, 1982), 27–49.

6. Unlimited Paternalism's Problems: The Transforming Moment on My Road Toward Understanding Disunion

1. Kenneth M. Stampp, *And the War Came: The North and the Secession Crisis, 1860–1861* (Baton Rouge, La., 1950), vii.

2. For some good examples, see Avery Craven, *The Coming of the Civil War* (Chicago, 1957); George Fort Milton, *The Eve of Conflict: Stephen A. Douglas and the Needless War* (Boston and New York, 1934); James G. Randall, "The Blundering Generation," *Mississippi Valley Historical Review*, 27 (1940): 3–28; Randall, *Lincoln the President*, 4 vols. (New York, 1945–55), especially vol. 1.

3. Pierre van den Berghe, *Race and Racism: A Comparative Perspective* (New York, 1967); George M. Fredrickson, *The Black Image in the White Mind: The Debate on Afro-American Character and Destiny, 1817–1914* (New York, 1971).

4. Stephanie McCurry, "The Politics of Yeoman Households in South Carolina," in *Divided Households: Gender and the Civil War*, ed. Catherine Clinton and Nina Silber (New York, 1992), 22–38.

5. See the good discussion of this episode in Lawrence T. McDonnell, "Struggle against Suicide: James Henry Hammond and the Secession of South Carolina," *Southern Studies*, 22 (1983): 109–37.

6. A. P. Aldrich to James Henry Hammond, November 25, 1860, Hammond Papers, Library of Congress.

7. Don E. Fehrenbacher, *The Dred Scott Case: Its Significance in American Law and Politics* (New York, 1978); David Brion Davis, *The Problem of Slavery in Western Culture* (Ithaca, N.Y., 1966); Davis, *The Problem of Slavery in the Age of Revolution* (Ithaca, N.Y., 1975).

8. Frederick Merk, *Manifest Destiny and Mission in American History: A Reinterpretation* (New York, 1963); Merk, *Fruits of Propaganda in the Tyler Administration* (Cambridge, Mass., 1971); Merk, *Slavery and the Annexation of Texas* (New York, N.Y., 1972).

9. Upshur to Tucker, March 13, 1843, Tucker-Coleman Papers, Swem Library, William and Mary College. I am indebted to Margaret Cook, the library's custodian of this magnificent collection, for permission to publish the letter.

10. See below, pp. 167–69.

11. Upshur to Calhoun, August 14, 1843, printed in *William and Mary Quarterly*, 16 (1936): 554–57.

7. "Absurd" Issues and the Causes of the Civil War: Colonization as a Test Case

1. See above, pp. 125–29.

2. See above, ch. 1, and Brooks Simpson, "Editors, Editing, and the

Historical Professor," *Organization of American Historians Newsletter*, May 1989, 8–9; John David Smith, "Ulrich Bonnell Phillips' *Plantation and Frontier:* The Historian as Documentary Editor," *Georgia Historical Quarterly*, 77 (1993): 123–43.

3. See above, ch. 6, *n.* 2.

4. Michael Holt, *The Political Crisis of the 1850s* (New York, 1978); Larry Gara, "Slavery and the Slave Power: A Crucial Distinction," *Civil War History*, 15 (1969): 5–18; William E. Gienapp, "The Republican Party and the Slave Power," in *New Perspectives on Race and Slavery in America: Essays in Honor of Kenneth M. Stampp*, ed. Robert H. Abzug and Stephen E. Maizlish (Lexington, Ky., 1986), 51–78.

5. For documentation and more extensive discussion, see below, ch. 9.

6. Excellent examples include J. Mills Thornton, III, *Politics and Power in a Slave Society: Alabama, 1800–1860* (Baton Rouge, La., 1978), and Charles G. Sellers, Jr., "The Travail of Slavery," in *The Southerner as American*, ed. Sellers (Chapel Hill, N.C., 1960), ch. 3.

7. I will discuss and document this secessionist viewpoint at length in *Road to Disunion*, vol. 2. For preliminary examples, see above, ch. 1.

8. The best discussion of these matters is in Alison Goodyear Freehling, *Drift toward Dissolution: The Virginia Slavery Debate of 1831–32* (Baton Rouge, La., 1982).

9. Sheldon H. Harris, *Paul Cuffe: Black American and the African Return* (New York, 1972).

10. David M. Dean, *Defender of the Race: James Theodore Holly, Black Nationalist Bishop* (Boston, 1978); Nell Irvin Painter, "Martin R. Delany: Elitism and Black Nationalism," in *Black Leaders of the Nineteenth Century*, ed. Leon Litwack and August Meier (Urbana, Ill., 1988), 149–71; Floyd John Miller, *The Search for a Black Nationality: Black Emigration and Colonization, 1787–1863* (Urbana, Ill., 1975).

11. Quoted in ibid., 239–40.

12. William E. Parrish, *Turbulent Partnership: Missouri and the Union, 1861–1865* (Columbia, Mo., 1963), ch. 7.

The subject of Lincoln and colonization has inspired a rich controversial literature, with great skill displayed on both sides. For an excellent statement of a position somewhat different from mine, see G. S. Boritt, "The Voyage to the Colony of Linconia: The Sixteenth President, Black Colonization, and the Defense Mechanism of Avoidance," *Historian*, 37 (1975): 619–32. For an equally excellent statement, this time of a position closer to mine, see George M. Fredrickson, "'A Man but Not a Brother': Abraham Lincoln and Racial Equality," *Journal of Southern History*, 41 (1975): 39–58.

13. William S. McFeely, *Grant: A Biography* (New York, 1981), ch. 21; Nell Irvin Painter, *Exodusters: Black Migration to Kansas after Reconstruction* (New York, 1976); Edwin S. Redkey, *Black Exodus: Black Nationalist and Back-to-Africa Movements, 1890–1910* (New Haven, Conn.,

1969); Judith Stein, *The World of Marcus Garvey: Race and Class in Modern Society* (Baton Rouge, La., 1986); Ernest Dunbar, ed., *The Black Expatriates: A Study of American Negroes in Exile* (New York, 1968).

14. P. J. Staudenraus, *The African Colonization Movement, 1816–1865* (New York, 1961); Robin W. Winks, *The Blacks in Canada: A History* (New Haven, Conn., 1971); Merton Dillon, *Benjamin Lundy and the Struggle for Negro Freedom* (Urbana, Ill., 1966).

15. Gerda Lerner, *The Grimké Sisters from South Carolina: Pioneers for Women's Rights and Abolition* (Boston, 1967); Katherine DuPre Lumpkin, *The Emancipation of Angelina Grimké* (Chapel Hill, N.C., 1974); Kathryn Kish Sklar, *Catharine Beecher: A Study in American Domesticity* (New Haven, Conn., 1973); Jeanne Boydston, Mary Kelley, and Anne Margolis, *The Limits of Sisterhood: The Beecher Sisters on Women's Rights and Women's Sphere* (Chapel Hill, N.C., 1988); Charles Capper, *Margaret Fuller: An American Romantic Life*, 1 vol. published to date (New York, 1992).

16. Peter D. McClelland and Richard J. Zeckhauser, *Demographic Dimensions of the New Republic* . . . (Cambridge, Mass., 1982); Malcolm J. Rohrbough, *The Trans-Appalachian Frontier: People, Society, and Institutions, 1775–1850* (New York, 1978); Marcus Lee Hansen, *The Atlantic Migration, 1607–1860* (Cambridge, Mass., 1940).

17. Ray Allen Billington, *The Protestant Crusade, 1800–1860: A Study of the Origins of American Nativism* (Chicago, 1938); Tyler Anbinder, *Nativism and Slavery: The Northern Know Nothings and the Politics of the 1850s* (New York, 1992); Daniel Walker Howe, *The Political Culture of the American Whigs* (Chicago, 1979).

18. Ronald N. Satz, *American Indian Policy in the Jacksonian Era* (Lincoln, Neb., 1975); Michael D. Green, *The Politics of Indian Removal: Creek Government and Society in Crisis* (Lincoln, Neb., 1982).

19. Sister Mary Gilbert Kelly, *Catholic Immigration Colonization Projects in the U.S., 1815–1860* (New York, 1939); James P. Shannon, *Catholic Colonization on the Western Frontier* (New Haven, Conn., 1957).

20. William McLoughlin, *Cherokee Renascence in the New Republic* (Princeton, N.J., 1986); McLoughlin, *Champions of the Cherokees: Evan and John B. Jones* (Princeton, N.J., 1990).

21. David Eltis, *Economic Growth and the Ending of the Transatlantic Slave Trade* (New York, 1987).

22. Ronald T. Takaki, *A Pro-Slavery Crusade: The Agitation to Reopen the African Slave Trade* (New York, 1971).

8. The Complex Career of Slaveholder Expansionism

1. This colonial non-Anglo-American area, soon to become the heart of the Anglo- American Cotton Kingdom, has inspired much recent historical work, which at its superb best is a prototype for a viable multicultural history of the United States. See, for example, Daniel H. Usner, Jr., *Indi-*

ans, Settlers, and Slaves in a Frontier Exchange Economy: The Lower Mississippi Valley before 1783 (Chapel Hill, N.C., 1992); Edward J. Cashin, *Lachlan McGillivray, Indian Trader: The Shaping of the Southern Colonial Frontier* (Athens, Ga., 1992); Gwendolyn Midlo Hall, *Africans in Colonial Louisiana: The Development of Afro-Creole Culture in the Eighteenth Century* (Baton Rouge, La., 1992).

2. A subject well developed in Rachel N. Klein, *Unification of a Slave State: The Rise of the Planter Class in the South Carolina Backcountry, 1760–1808* (Chapel Hill, N.C., 1990). The colonial low country's story is expertly related in Peter H. Wood, *Black Majority: Negroes in Colonial South Carolina from 1670 through the Stono Rebellion* (New York, 1974).

3. For further discussions, see above, ch. 2. The key document is Jefferson to John Holmes, April 22, 1820, *The Writings of Thomas Jefferson*, ed. Paul Leicester Ford, 10 vols. (New York, 1892–99), 10:157–58.

4. The best histories of American early national territorial expansionism are encased in biographies, especially Samuel Flagg Bemis, *John Quincy Adams and the Foundations of American Foreign Policy* (New York, 1977), and Robert Remini, *Andrew Jackson and the Course of American Empire, 1767–1821* (New York, 1977).

5. For elaboration and documentation of this argument, see Freehling, *The Road to Disunion*, Vol. 1, *Secessionists at Bay, 1776–1854* (New York, 1990), 353–452.

6. For a fine discussion of the antebellum importance of partisan allegiances in determining political positions, see Joel H. Silbey, *The Shrine of Party: Congressional Voting Behavior, 1841–1852* (Pittsburgh, 1967).

7. *Niles' Weekly Register*, 16 (1844): 316–19.

8. See Clay's Alabama letter of July 27, 1844, reprinted in *History of American Presidential Elections, 1789–1968*, ed. Arthur M. Schlesinger, Jr., and Fred J. Israel, 3 vols. (New York, 1971), 1:855–56.

9. The fullest discussion of southern expansionism in the 1850s is in Robert E. May, *The Southern Dream of Caribbean Empire, 1854–1861* (Baton Rouge, La., 1973).

10. The fullest discussion of the episode is in Ronald Takaki, *A Pro-Slavery Crusade: The Agitation to Reopen the African Slave Trade* (New York, 1971).

11. See Dale E. Swain, *The Structure and Profitability of the American Rice Industry, 1859* (New York, 1975), and more broadly Peter Coclanis, *The Shadow of a Dream: Economic Life and Death in the South Carolina Lowcountry, 1670–1920* (New York, 1988).

12. Sumter to James Chesnut, Jr., February 2, 1859, Chesnut-Manning-Miller Papers, South Carolina Historical Society, Charleston.

13. For a superb example, see Lewis M. Ayer, *Southern Rights and the Labour Question: An Address Delivered at Whippy Swamp on the 4th of July, 1855* (Charleston, S.C., 1855).

14. *Secret and Sacred: The Diaries of James Henry Hammond, a Southern Slaveholder*, ed. Carol Bleser (New York, 1988), entry for March 31, 1841.

15. The best study is C. Stanley Urban's unfortunately unpublished "The Idea of Progress and Southern Imperialism: New Orleans and the Caribbean, 1845–1861," Ph.D. diss., Northwestern University, 1943. Urban's best publication on the subject is "The Ideology of Southern Imperialism: New Orleans and the Caribbean, 1845–1860," *Louisiana Historical Quarterly*, 39 (1956): 48–73. See also Richard Tansey, "Southern Expansionism: Urban Interests in the Cuban Filibusters," *Plantation Society*, 1 (1979): 227–51.

16. The Charleston–New Orleans controversy became particularly bitter in early 1859. See the *New Orleans Delta*, February 18, March 16, March 30, 1859.

17. See particularly Eugene Genovese, *The Political Economy of Slavery: Studies in the Economy and Society of the Slave South* (New York, 1965).

18. C. Stanley Urban, "The Africanization of Cuba Scare, 1853–1855," *Hispanic American Historical Review*, 37 (1957): 29–45.

19. William Marcy to John Y. Mason, July 23, 1854, quoted in Ivor Debenham Spencer, *The Victor and the Spoils: A Life of William L. Marcy* (Providence, R.I., 1959), 324.

20. *Speeches, Messages, and Other Writings of the Hon. Albert G. Brown . . .*, ed. M. W. Cluskey (Philadelphia, 1859), 324–29.

9. The Divided South, Democracy's Limitations, and the Causes of the Peculiarly North American Civil War

1. My information on the Latin American side of emancipation is almost entirely gleaned from the (fortunately excellent) secondary literature. The best overall comparative treatments of emancipation in the Americas are David Brion Davis, *Slavery and Human Progress* (New York, 1984), and C. Duncan Rice, *The Rise and Fall of Black Slavery* (New York, 1975). Seymour Drescher, "Brazilian Abolition in Comparative Perspective," in *The Abolition of Slavery and the Aftermath of Emancipation in Brazil*, ed. Rebecca J. Scott et al. (Durham, N.C., 1988), is a particularly suggestive essay. Other useful accounts of Brazilian emancipation include Robert E. Conrad, *The Destruction of Brazilian Slavery, 1850–1888* (Berkeley, Calif., 1972), best on the early phase of free-womb emancipation; Robert Brent Toplin, *The Abolition of Slavery in Brazil* (New York, 1972), best on the later phase of immediatist emancipation; and Carl Degler, *Neither Black nor White: Slavery and Race Relations in Brazil and the United States* (Madison, Wisc., 1986), best on racial/sexual differences between the two countries but weaker on democratic/political differences. Fine localistic studies of Brazilian slavery and its collapse include Stuart B.

Schwartz, *Sugar Plantations in the Formation of Brazilian Society: Bahia, 1550–1835* (Cambridge, Eng., 1985); Mary C. Karasch, *Slave Life in Rio de Janeiro, 1808–1850* (Princeton, N.J., 1987); and Stanley Stein, *Vassouras: A Brazilian Coffee Country, 1850–1900: The Roles of Planter and Slaves in a Plantation Society* (Princeton, N.J., 1985).

For studies of emancipation in Cuba, second in importance only to Brazil for U.S. comparisons, the excellent literature includes Rebecca J. Scott, *Slave Emancipation in Cuba: The Transition to Free Labor, 1860–1899* (Princeton, N.J., 1985); Franklin W. Knight, *Slave Society in Cuba during the Nineteenth Century* (Madison, Wisc., 1970); Arthur F. Corwin, *Spain and the Abolition of Slavery in Cuba, 1817–1886* (Austin, Tex., 1967); and Robert L. Paquette, *Sugar Is Made with Blood: The Conspiracy of LaEscalera and the Conflict between Empires over Slavery in Cuba* (Middletown, Conn., 1988). Among the helpful books on other Latin American countries are Peter Blanchard, *Slavery and Abolition in Early Republican Peru* (Wilmington, Del., 1992); C. L. R. James, *The Black Jacobins: Toussaint L'Ouverture and the San Domingo Revolution* (New York, 1963); John V. Lombardi, *The Decline and Abolition of Negro Slavery in Venezuela, 1820–1854* (Westport, Conn., 1971); and Francisco A. Scarno, *Sugar and Slavery in Puerto Rico: The Plantation Economy of Ponce, 1800–1850* (Madison, Wisc., 1984).

2. A point forcefully made in Seymour Drescher, "The Long Goodby: Dutch Capitalism and Antislavery in Comparative Perspective," forthcoming. I am grateful to Professor Drescher for allowing me to read his unpublished paper.

3. All U.S. demographic statistics in this essay are drawn from *The Statistics of the Population of the United States*, comp. Francis A. Walker (Washington, D.C., 1872), 11–74, and U.S. Bureau of the Census, *A Century of Population Growth; From the First Census of the United States to the Twelfth, 1790–1900* (Washington, D.C., 1909).

4. For further discussion and documentation of my interpretation of slavery and the Founding Fathers, see above, ch. 2.

5. For the Brazilian-Cuban figures, see Conrad, *Destruction of Brazilian Slavery*, 283, and Scott, *Emancipation in Cuba*, 7.

6. Davis, *Slavery and Human Progress*, 291.

7. Conrad, *Destruction of Brazilian Slavery*, 301.

8. *The Writings of Thomas Jefferson*, ed. Alfred A. Lipscomb, 20 vols. (Washington, D.C., 1903), 2:192.

9. For the only very brief Latin American parallel I know of to this singular and crucial U.S. phenomenon, see Seymour Drescher, "Brazilian Slavery in Comparative Perspective," 49 n. 72.

10. Claudia Dale Golden, "The Economics of Emancipation," *Journal of Economic History*, 33 (1973): 70.

11. The latest and fullest account of this revealing episode is Alison Goodyear Freehling, *Drift toward Dissolution: The Virginia Slavery Debate of 1831–32* (Baton Rouge, La., 1982).

12. See Dew's "Review of the Debate in the Virginia Legislature," in *The Pro-slavery Argument* . . . (Philadelphia, 1853), especially 482–84.

13. For further discussion of the critical colonization idea, see above, ch. 7.

14. Racial proslavery thought is brilliantly illuminated in William Stanton, *The Leopard Spots: Scientific Attitudes toward Race in America, 1815–59* (Chicago, 1960).

15. Of Eugene D. Genovese's illuminating books on nonracial proslavery thought, the latest and best is *The Slaveholders' Dilemma: Freedom and Progress in Southern Conservative Thought, 1820–1860* (Columbia, S.C., 1992).

16. For further discussion and documentation, see my *The Road to Disunion*, Vol. 1, *Secessionists at Bay, 1776–1854* (New York, 1990), 98–118.

17. For further discussion and documentation, see below, ch. 11.

18. The Nullification Crisis is discussed in William W. Freehling, *Prelude to Civil War: The Nullification Controversy in South Carolina, 1816–1836* (New York, 1966), and in Richard E. Ellis, *The Union at Risk: Jacksonian Democracy, States' Rights, and the Nullification Crisis* (New York, 1987).

19. For further discussion and documentation of the Calhoun position, see above, ch. 5.

20. William J. Cooper, *The South and the Politics of Slavery, 1828–1856* (Baton Rouge, La., 1978), expertly underlines the importance of southern loyalty politics. Bertram Wyatt-Brown, *Southern Honor: Ethics and Behavior in the Old South* (New York, 1982), illuminates honor as one source of loyalty politics.

21. For further discussion and documentation of this interpretation of the Gag Rule Controversy, see Freehling, *Road to Disunion*, 1:287–352. The importance of such concerns about *white men's* civil liberties is brilliantly illuminated in Russel B. Nye, *Fettered Freedom: Civil Liberties and the Slavery Controversy, 1830–1860* (East Lansing, Mich., 1963).

22. For further discussion and documentation of this interpretation of Texas Annexation, see above, pp. 121–32, and Freehling, *Road to Disunion*, 1:353–452.

23. On the fugitive slave law and its impact, see ibid., 1:489, 500–05, 536–37; Stanley W. Campbell, *The Slave Catchers: Enforcement of the Fugitive Slave Law, 1850–1860* (Chapel Hill, N.C., 1968).

24. On the Kansas-Nebraska Act, see Freehling, *Road to Disunion*, 1:536–65; Robert W. Johannsen, *Stephen A. Douglas* (New York, 1973); and Roy F. Nichols, "The Kansas-Nebraska Act: A Century of Historiography," *Mississippi Valley Historical Review*, 43 (1956): 187–212.

25. Except for its conflation of northern nativists' anti-Slavepower sentiments (which they abundantly possessed) and their antislavery determinations (which they far less often possessed), the best monograph on

the movement is Tyler Anbinder, *Nativism and Slavery: The Northern Know Nothings and the Politics of the 1850s* (New York, 1992).

26. The best study of the phenomenon is William E. Gienapp, *The Origins of the Republican Party, 1852–1856* (New York, 1987).

27. Some fellow specialists will think I overemphasize Republicans' fear for white men's republicanism. They would instead emphasize that a moral outrage about black slavery or an economic lust for free laborers' capitalistic opportunity lay more at the heart of the Republican persuasion. But after reading the massive collection of Republican newspapers and pamphlets in the American Antiquarian Society, I am convinced that those other themes were emphasized less often—and the abolition theme in a very vague way. This is not to deny, however, that economic drives and, less often, humanitarian concern for blacks lent further zeal to a Republican persuasion that needed all the passion it could muster in order to secure victory in 1860.

The difference between my reading of this evidence and some other scholars' view of these Republican sources, I am convinced, has nothing to do with the amount of time, skill, or care spent reading the documents or with the amount of space devoted to anti-Slavepower rhetoric in the sources. Instead, the differing perceptual lenses of the researching historians yield different readings of the evidence. My assumptions about the historical process are perhaps too catholic, for I do not believe that any one factor necessarily causes historical events. I am therefore impressed when one factor, in this case the Slavepower's impact on the republican political process, is emphasized in the Republican sources more often than any other. But were I to believe that economic fears, hopes, or ideologies govern the historical process, I would more emphasize the Republicans' free-labor ideology. Similarly, were I to think that the Declaration of Independence relentlessly drove white men toward color-blind egalitarianism, I would more emphasize Republican rhetoric on the moral disaster of enslaving blacks and on the need to secure slavery's ultimate extinction. But since I am convinced that defense of a cherished political system can be as important to the human species as defense of a cherished economic system and since I consistently find that the acceptance of other multicultural minorities into the white male political system, in keeping with an indisputable implication of the Declaration, was a weaker impulse to antebellum white males than their pursuit of white republican Union, both in Lincoln's era and in Jefferson's, I believe the sources when they emphasize the Slavepower's threat to the white male political system more than slaveholders' threats to blacks or to white male economic opportunity.

For a further discussion of my conviction that defense of white men's political values and institutions can be as important as either defense of economic values or aspiration toward color-blind moral values, see above, ch. 11. Fellow specialists will see the parallel in my way of reading the proslavery literature. The U.S. slaveholders defended *racial* slavery, for blacks only, more often than color-blind slavery, for all lower classes. If I believed that economics always lies at the foundation of a worldview, I would more emphasize the theme less emphasized in the sources: the defense of slavery per se, regardless of race. But since I conceive that peoples' worldviews can be founded on racial identities no less than on class identities, I again am influenced by the predominant theme in the sources when choosing what to emphasize.

Given my reading of the Republican sources, I agree most often with the historians of the North who never lose sight of antebellum Northerners' distinction between white men's freedom from the Slavepower and black men's freedom from slavery. Pride of place belongs to Michael Holt, *The Political Crisis of the 1850s* (New York, 1978); Larry Gara, "Slavery and the Slave Power: A Crucial Distinction," *Civil War History*, 15 (1969): 5–18; and William E. Gienapp, "The Republican Party and the Slave Power," in *New Perspectives on Race and Slavery in America: Essays in Honor of Kenneth M. Stampp*, ed. Robert H. Abzug and Stephen E. Maizlish (Lexington, Ky., 1986), 51–78. For countervailing emphases on antislavery and on economics, see Richard H. Sewell, *Ballots for Freedom: Antislavery Politics in the United States, 1837–1860* (New York, 1976), and Robert W. Fogel, *Without Consent or Contract: The Rise and Fall of American Slavery* (New York, 1989). My favorite synthesis of the Republicans' worldview, even though I think it stresses a little heavily the economic side of the mentality, is Eric Foner, *Free Soil, Free Labor, Free Men: The Ideology of the Republican Party before the Civil War* (New York, 1970). The best synthesis of the whole period, North and South, remains David M. Potter, *The Impending Crisis, 1848–1861* (New York, 1976).

28. Don E. Fehrenbacher, *The Dred Scott Case: Its Significance in American Law and Politics* (New York, 1978), is a model monograph.

29. The latest account of the Kansas aftermath is in Kenneth M. Stampp, *America in 1857: A Nation on the Brink* (New York, 1990).

30. Ronald T. Takaki, *A Pro-Slavery Crusade: The Agitation to Reopen the African Slave Trade* (New York, 1971), and Robert E. May, *The Southern Dream of Caribbean Empire, 1854–1862* (Baton Rouge, La., 1973), are best on their respective subjects.

31. I will document and demonstrate the following assertions in *Road to Disunion*, vol. 2. Since at the moment we lack a modern synthesis, the subject must be pursued in a series of (fortunately excellent) local or state studies. Among the best are J. William Harris, *Plain Folk and Gentry in a Slave Society: White Labor and Black Slavery in Augusta's Hinterlands* (Middletown, Conn., 1986); J. Mills Thornton, III, *Politics and Power in a Slave Society: Alabama, 1800–1860* (Baton Rouge, La., 1978); Paul D. Escott, *Many Excellent People: Power and Privilege in North Carolina, 1850–1900* (Chapel Hill, N.C., 1985); Lacy K. Ford, Jr., *Origins of Southern Radicalism: The South Carolina Upcountry, 1800–1860* (New York, 1988); Michael P. Johnson, *Toward a Patriarchal Republic: The Secession*

of Georgia (Baton Rouge, La., 1977); William L. Barney, *The Secessionist Impulse: Alabama and Mississippi in 1860* (Princeton, N.J., 1974); and Daniel W. Crofts, *Reluctant Confederates: Upper South Unionists in the Secession Crisis* (Chapel Hill, N.C., 1989).

32. For further discussion and documentation, see below, ch. 10.

10. The Divided South, the Causes of Confederate Defeat, and the Reintegration of Narrative History

1. This position, standard fare in Civil War military books, has been most recently and most fully defended in James M. McPherson, *Battle Cry of Freedom: The Civil War Era* (New York, 1988), and in McPherson, "American Victory, American Defeat," in *Why the Confederacy Lost*, ed. Gabor S. Boritt (New York, 1992), 17–42. Ironically, McPherson has been one of the leaders in the attempt to push Civil War historiography beyond military history, to encompass the concerns of social history. See his excellent foreword to *Divided Houses: Gender and the Civil War*, ed. Catherine Clinton and Nina Silber (New York, 1992), xiii–xvii. But McPherson's integrations run only one way: the events on the battlefield cause the changes in society, never vice versa. Until we see Civil War history as a two-way street, with social changes causing military events and military events causing social changes, Confederate defeat will remain as mysterious as it is to McPherson himself. See *Why the Confederacy Lost*, ed. Boritt, 18.

2. This general slant is hardly my creation. As the following notes will attest, a social interpretation of the causes of Confederate defeat is coming to the fore; and in the perspective of that wave of scholarship, the renewed military-causes emphasis in the Boritt volume seems likely to become the counterattack that fell short. Indeed, several of the essays in Boritt's very useful collection, particularly Joseph T. Glatthaar's and Reid Mitchell's, sustain the opposite of Boritt's and McPherson's military emphasis. For some overviews of the new, more socially oriented explanations of Confederate military defeat, see Joseph T. Glatthaar, "The 'New' Civil War History: An Overview," *Pennsylvania Magazine of History and Biography*, 115 (1991): 339–69; David Usher and Peter Wallenstein, "Why the Confederacy Lost: An Essay Review," *Maryland Historical Magazine*, 88 (1993): 95–108; and *Toward a Social History of the American Civil War: Exploratory Essays*, ed. Maris A. Vinovskis (Cambridge, Eng., 1990).

3. See, for example, Palmerston to Lord John Russell, October 8, 23, 24, 1862; quoted in Howard Jones, *Union in Peril: The Crisis over British Intervention in the Civil War* (Chapel Hill, N.C., 1992), 186, 193.

4. Quoted in ibid., 50.

5. Palmerston's speech to Parliament, July 19, 1862, quoted in ibid., 135.

6. McPherson in *Why the Confederacy Lost*, ed. Boritt, 32.

7. The latest and best summary of this position is in Joel H. Silbey, *The American Political Nation, 1838–1893* (Stanford, Calif., 1991). The persistent power of the Democratic Party persuasion is nicely explained in Jean H. Baker, *Affairs of Party: The Political Culture of Northern Democrats in the Mid-Nineteenth Century* (Ithaca, N.Y., 1983).

8. The pivotal book on this subject—and the most important neglected book in the whole corpus of Civil War volumes—is Joel H. Silbey, *A Respectable Minority: The Democratic Party in the Civil War Era, 1860–1868* (New York, 1977). That military historians should continue to misinterpret the politics of 1864, without paying any attention to Silbey's (I think) indisputable findings, itself indicates the gulf between these historical specialists.

9. McClellan to W. C. Prime, August 10, 1862, quoted in Charles R. Wilson, "McClellan's Changing Views on the Peace Plank of 1864," *American Historical Review*, 38 (1933): 499.

10. *The Civil War Papers of George McClellan: Selected Correspondence, 1860–1865*, ed. Stephen W. Sears (New York, 1989), 595–97.

11. A point well made in Stephen W. Sears, "McClellan and the Peace Plank of 1864: A Reappraisal," *Civil War History*, 36 (1990): 57–64. Some historians, while conceding Sears's point that candidate McClellan never endorsed the temporary-truce-without-reunion-guarantees strategy, still believe that the Democratic Party would have forced a President McClellan to give the strategy a try. After a temporary truce, continues the speculation, McClellan could never have restarted the war. But even *if* (a mammoth if) McClellan had turned tail and surrendered to the temporary-truce strategy, he would have had no choice but to resume the war after the failed negotiations, for almost no Northerner, in or out of his party, wanted peace with disunion, just as the Davis administration would not accept voluntary reunion. Wars are restarted all the time—and with greater determination on both sides—when each side discovers, during a pause for negotiation, that the basic issue is nonnegotiable. After some imaginary temporary truce had ended, a President McClellan would have delightedly discovered that candidate (and General) McClellan's typical-soldiery forebodings about a temporary military lull had been erroneous. A brief pause from battle could not have rescued the Confederacy from its terrible attrition. Instead, the luckless negotiations could have only united the previously disputatious North behind the now indisputable logic that only a victorious war could save the Union. Indeed, once McClellan found, to his uncomprehending shock, that the Confederacy meant to arm its blacks, even if they must be freed, he could hardly have gone ahead with dismissing blacks from *his* army. Thus northern disputes between Republicans and Democrats would have eased the more.

For a succinct recent statement of the countervailing position, see Albert Castel, *Decision in the West: The Atlanta Campaign of 1864* (Lawrence, Kans., 1992), 572. While I disagree with Mr. Castel on this political history point, I have drawn heavily on his magnificent account of the battlefield history.

12. Quoted in Charles Royster, *The Destructive War: William Tecumseh Sherman, Stonewall Jackson, and the Americans* (New York, 1991), 327.

13. Very helpful studies of this tier of states include William J. Evitts, *A Matter of Allegiances: Maryland from 1850 to 1861* (Baltimore, 1974); Jean H. Baker, *The Politics of Continuity: Maryland Political Parties from 1858 to 1870* (Baltimore, 1973); Harry A. Volz, III, "Party, State, and Nation: Kentucky and the Coming of the American Civil War," Ph.D. diss., University of Virginia, 1982; Richard O. Curry, *A House Divided: Statehood Politics and the Copperhead Movement in West Virginia* (Pittsburgh, 1964); William E. Parrish, *Turbulent Partnership: Missouri and the Union, 1861–1865* (Columbia, Mo., 1963); and Harold Hancock, "Civil War Comes to Delaware," *Civil War History*, 2 (1956): 29–56.

14. On the critical topic of division in the Middle South, three fine books, none of them celebrated sufficiently when they were published, seem destined to become classics: Craig M. Simpson, *A Good Southerner: The Life of Henry A. Wise of Virginia* (Chapel Hill, N.C., 1985); Richard Nelson Current, *Lincoln's Loyalists: Union Soldiers from the Confederacy* (Boston, 1992); and Daniel W. Crofts, *Reluctant Confederates: Upper South Unionists in the Secession Crisis* (Chapel Hill, N.C., 1989). Also very helpful are Peter Wallenstein, "Which Side Are You On? The Social Origins of White Troops from Civil War Tennessee," *Journal of East Tennessee History*, 63 (1991): 72–103; Stephen V. Ash, *Middle Tennessee Society Transformed, 1860–1870: War and Peace in the Upper South* (Baton Rouge, La., 1988); Fred A. Bailey, *Class and Tennessee's Confederate Generation* (Chapel Hill, N.C., 1987); Wayne K. Durrill, *War of Another Kind: A Southern Community in the Great Rebellion* (New York, 1990); and John Cimprich, *Slavery's End in Tennessee, 1861–1865* (University, Ala., 1985).

15. *The Collected Works of Abraham Lincoln*, ed. Roy P. Basler et al., 8 vols. (New Brunswick, N.J., 1953), 5:145.

16. The best recent analysis of proslavery sentiment in the heart of the Unionist South—and another useful corrective to the proposition that the South was *anywhere* united—is John C. Inscoe, *Mountain Masters, Slavery, and the Sectional Crisis in Western North Carolina* (Knoxville, Tenn., 1989).

17. A subject expertly handled in Mark E. Neely, Jr., *The Fate of Liberty: Abraham Lincoln and Civil Liberties* (New York, 1991).

18. See Michael Fellman's intriguing *Inside War: The Guerrilla Conflict inside Missouri during the American Civil War* (New York, 1989).

19. This critical point is the most important emphasis in the new social history of the causes of emancipation and of Confederate defeat. For some of the richest contributions to the insight, see Ira Berlin et al., *Slaves*

No More: Three Essays on Emancipation and the Civil War (Cambridge, Eng., 1992); Armistead Robinson, *Bitter Fruits of Bondage: Slavery's Demise and the Collapse of the Confederacy* (forthcoming); Dudley Taylor Cornish, *The Sable Arm: Negro Troops in the Union Army, 1861–1865* (1956; reprint, Lawrence, Kans., 1987); and Joseph T. Glatthaar, *Forged in Battle: The Civil War Alliance of Black Soldiers and White Officers* (New York, 1990). Glatthaar succinctly sums up his position in "Black Glory: The African-American Role in Union Victory," in *Why the Confederacy Lost,* ed. Boritt, 133–62.

20. As the phrasing indicates, the number here is a guess; the sources do not allow precision. I have taken the middle of the 500,000-to-700,000 estimate of Joe Glatthaar, the best student of the subject, in ibid., 142. But if the number is imprecise, it is even larger than it looks. Lest anyone say that even if 17 percent of slaves entered Union lines or territories, 83 percent did not, let it be remembered that Union armies passed through only a part of the black belt South, that a huge percentage of the blacks who reached Union lines were the able-bodied male adults, and that many Civil War fugitives successfully escaped without taking sanctuary in Union-held positions. We are talking about a massive disintegration of the lower-class adult male working force whenever Union invaders passed through, which is a critical reason the plantation economy could not be pulled back together after Union armies moved on.

21. Emory M. Thomas expertly describes this incident and plausibly puts it in the context of the Civil War as an ironically revolutionizing experience for reactionary slaveholders. See Thomas, *The Confederate Nation, 1861–1865* (New York, 1979), 290 ff. See also Robert M. Durden's excellent *The Gray and the Black: The Confederate Debate on Emancipation* (Baton Rouge, La., 1972).

22. Excellent analyses of the faultlines in northern free-labor society, which were certainly *there* although *much* less lethal than the faultlines in southern slave-labor society, include Iver Bernstein, *The New York City Draft Riots: Their Significance for American Society and Politics in the Age of the Civil War* (New York, 1990); Grace Palladino, *Another Civil War: Labor, Capital, and the State in the Anthracite Regions of Pennsylvania, 1840–1868* (Urbana, Ill., 1990); and Phillip Shaw Paludan, *"A People's Contest": The Union and Civil War, 1861–1865* (New York, 1988).

23. I am indebted to Michael Johnson for first suggesting that I pursue this line of analysis.

24. *Augusta Chronicle and Sentinel,* March 17, 22, 1865. I am indebted to Jonathan M. Bryant for the reference.

25. Thomas George Ziek, Jr., "The Effects of Southern Railroads on Interior Lines during the Civil War," M.A. thesis, Texas A&M, 1992; Robert C. Black, III, *The Railroads of the Confederacy* (Chapel Hill, N.C., 1972). For the best succinct statement of the economic causes of Confederate defeat, see Richard N. Current, "God and the Strongest Battalions," in

Why the South Lost the Civil War, ed. David Donald (Baton Rouge, La., 1960), 15–32. In one spectacular example of northern technical superiority, Sherman's railroad repairmen rebuilt Sherman's supply lines far faster than Georgia workers could rebuild the tracks the Confederacy needed, even though the Yankees had to haul along repair equipment and supplies. So too, though the Confederacy matched the Union in small arms, the Union had far superior large cannons, another tremendous advantage of Sherman's in his conquest of Atlanta: the pivotal spot where the Yankees' better technology *plus* more fighting men at last overwhelmed the Confederates.

26. McPherson, *Battle Cry of Freedom*, 821.

27. Quoted in Reid Mitchell's excellent essay on this subject in *Why the Confederacy Lost*, ed. Boritt, 123.

28. Quoted in ibid., 123. The study of southern women's contributions to Confederate fortunes is at last coming into its own. See particularly Drew Gilpin Faust's superb "Altars of Sacrifice: Confederate Women and the Narratives of War" as well as the other fine essays in *Divided Houses: Gender and the Civil War*, ed. Clinton and Silber; Victoria E. Bynum, *Unruly Women: The Politics of Social and Sexual Control in the Old South* (Chapel Hill, N.C., 1992); George C. Rable, *Civil Wars: Women and the Crisis of Southern Nationalism* (Urbana, Ill., 1989).

29. This point has become controversial because too many historians have blurred the critical distinction between many slaveholders' concern about slaveholders' behavior and fewer slaveholders' guilt about slavery per se, whatever the behavior. In fact, the escalating sense that slaveholders' treatment of slaves was sometimes un-Christian (as opposed to a sense that slavery per se was un-Christian) is rampant in the sources and energized the growing Civil War movement to regulate slaveholders' absolute power (as opposed to abolishing slaveholders' power altogether). That growing movement to ameliorate (rather than end) slavery befit a Christian people who had to explain to themselves why God was turning against his slaveholders, after he sanctioned slavery per se in the Bible.

The slaveholders' growing qualms have also unfortunately been inflated into *the* cause of Confederate loss of willpower. In fact, slaves', nonslaveholders', and women's escalating fears that the fight for the Confederacy's independence undercut *their* independence were more important. But the slaveholders' increasing doubts that God judged them fit for independence help explain why demoralization spread to upper-class males too.

Those who have made this point, or a version of it, include Kenneth M. Stampp, "The Southern Road to Appomattox," in Stampp's *The Imperiled Union: Essays on the Background of the Civil War* (New York, 1980), 246–69; Richard E. Beringer et al., *Why the South Lost the Civil War* (Athens, Ga., 1986); Bell Irvin Wiley, "The Movement to Humanize the Institution of Slavery during the Confederacy," *Emory University Quarterly*, 5

(1949): 207–20; Drew Gilpin Faust, *The Creation of Confederate Nationalism: Ideology and Identity in the Civil War South* (Baton Rouge, La.,
1988); and Clarence L. Mohr, *On the Threshold of Freedom: Masters and
Slaves in Civil War Georgia* (Athens, Ga., 1986).
30. Quoted in *Why the Confederacy Lost*, ed. Boritt, 19.

**11. Toward a Newer Political History—and a Reintegrated
Multicultural History**

1. For an example of conflict versus consensus history, see the contro-
versy over Arthur M. Schlesinger, Jr.'s, emphasis on class conflict in *The
Age of Jackson* (New York, 1945). Among the consensus critics were Bray
Hammond, *Banks and Politics from the Revolution to the Civil War*
(Princeton, N.J., 1957), and Richard Hofstadter, *The American Political
Tradition and the Men Who Made It* (New York, 1948), ch. 3. Among
those who sought to show that conflict indeed existed, but over ethnocultural rather than economic issues, the pioneer was Lee Benson, *The Concept of Jacksonian Democracy: New York as a Test Case* (Princeton, N.J.,
1961). Of those who thought the nature of conflict over Jacksonian issues
must be widened still further to include Native Americans and blacks, the
pioneering works were Michael Paul Rogin, *Fathers and Children: Andrew Jackson and the Subjugation of the American Indian* (New York,
1975), and Richard H. Brown, "The Missouri Crisis, Slavery, and the Politics of Jacksonianism," *South Atlantic Quarterly*, 65 (1966): 55–72. Of the
original "conflict" partisans who still cannot see that the defining conflicts did not necessarily involve white men's economic issues, the most
persistent has been Robert Remini, especially in *The Legacy of Andrew
Jackson: Essays on Democracy, Indian Removal, and Slavery* (Baton
Rouge, La., 1988).

The overall conflict versus consensus controversy is well summarized
in John Higham (with Leonard Krieger and Felix Gilbert), *History* (Englewood Cliffs, N.J., 1965), 212–32. The most enduring piece in the now-
fading debate is Higham's "Beyond Consensus: The Historian as Moral
Critic," *American Historical Review*, 67 (1962): 609–26. I am grateful to
Mr. Higham for a discerning critique of this essay.

2. Of the many works that call for or produce elements of a newly
synthetic American history, some of my favorites include *Bringing the
State Back In*, ed. Peter Evans et al. (Cambridge, Eng., 1985); Theda Skoc-
pol, "Social History and Historical Sociology: Contrasts and Complemen-
tarities," *Social Science History*, 11 (1987): 17–30; Thomas Bender,
"Wholes and Parts: The Need for Synthesis in American History," *Journal
of American History*, 73 (1986): 120–36; William E. Leuchtenburg, "The
Persistence of Political History," *Journal of American History*, 73 (1986):
585–600; Amy Bridges, *A City in the Republic: Antebellum New York
and the Origins of Machine Politics* (New York, 1984); David A. Gerber,

The Making of an American Pluralism: Buffalo, New York, 1825–60 (Urbana, Ill., 1989); Iver Bernstein, *The New York City Draft Riots: Their Significance for American Society and Politics in the Age of the Civil War* (New York, 1990); and Ronald P. Formisano, "The New Political History and the Election of 1840," *Journal of Interdisciplinary History*, 23 (1993): 661–82, especially 680–81.

3. A question asked, and answered in my judgment incorrectly, in Thomas Slaughter's generally admirable *Bloody Dawn: The Christiana Riot and Racial Violence in the Antebellum North* (New York, 1991), 14–15.

4. The Bento story is succinctly told in David B. Davis, *Slavery and Human Progress* (New York, 1984), 295.

5. Quoted in David W. Blight, "Martin R. Delany," in *The Reader's Companion to American History*, ed. Eric Foner and John A. Garraty (Boston, 1991), 274. My account of Douglass is drawn from his autobiography, of which the latest and best edition is *Narrative of the Life of Frederick Douglass, an American Slave, Written by Himself*, ed. David W. Blight (New York, 1993), and from William McFeely's excellent *Frederick Douglass* (New York, 1991).

6. Floyd John Miller, *The Search for a Black Nationality: Black Emigration and Colonization, 1787–1863* (Urbana, Ill., 1975), 239–40.

Index

Abolitionism: and causes of the Civil War, 139–40, 176, 190–92, 194, 197–98, 200, 206, 207; and Christian paternalism, 66–67; as color blind, 270; and secession, 8–9, 11
Adams, John Quincy, 92, 200
African Americans, 185, 188; attitudes toward colonization of, 146–48, 154; as disenfranchised, 254; as free laborers, 67–68; geographical distribution of, 186–87; supposed inferiority of, 35–36, 37, 82, 83, 99–100, 187, 191, 192, 203; influence on slaveholders of, 259–60; and religion, 66, 67, 69, 70–72, 74, 75, 77, 79, 149–50, 243; as slaveholders, 83; as soldiers, 32, 217, 218, 234, 237, 238, 239, 265, 266, 272; violence against, 259. *See also* Colonization; Demographic issues; Free blacks; Fugitive slaves; Slave insurrections
Alabama, 21, 22, 30, 163
American Antiquarian Society, 60
American Colonization Society, 24–26, 145, 146, 147, 148, 153, 190
American Revolution, x, 4–5, 13, 14, 15, 32–33, 179–80, 263
Anaconda Plan, 223, 224, 230, 240, 241, 245, 247
Antietam, battle of, 224, 225
Antislavery movement, 9, 181–82. *See also* Abolitionism; Emancipation; *specific person*
Apportionment. *See* Congress: election of members to
Arizona, 166
Arkansas, 30, 163, 166, 172
Atchison, David R., 119, 202

Atlanta, battle of, 225, 227, 228–29
Axson, Jacob, 48

Bailyn, Bernard, viii, 4–5, 11, 111
Bates, Edward, 245
Beard, Charles, 268
Beecher, Catharine, 151, 153, 154
Bennett, Ned, 42, 43, 47
Bennett, Rolla, 42, 47–49, 58
Bennett, Thomas, 42, 43, 46, 47–55, 56, 57
Benning, Henry L., 10
Benson, Lee, viii, 118, 122
Bento, Antônio, 266
Berlin, Ira, 3
Bible, 20, 41, 64–65, 68, 70, 75, 149–50, 243
Biography, 59, 118–19
Black removal plans. *See* Colonization; Slave sales; Slave trade: closing of the
Blacks. *See* African Americans; Free blacks
Blair family, 146
Blair, Frank, Jr., 144, 210, 211, 213
Blair, Montgomery, 245
Boles, John, 60
Border States: black population in the, 28, 144; and causes of the Civil War, 142–45, 156; and colonization, 197, 208, 209–10; and conditional antislavery, 14, 28, 31–32; crops of the, 180; and the defeat of the Confederacy, 226, 233, 234–36, 240, 245, 246, 266–67; definition of, 235; and the expansion of slavery, 114–15, 129, 159–60, 165, 169, 170–71, 174, 203, 204; and fugitive slaves, 170,